Consolidating Conquest

Consolidating Conquest

Ireland 1603–1727

Pádraig Lenihan

PEARSON

Longman

Harlow, England • London • New York • Boston • San Francisco • Toronto
Sydney • Tokyo • Singapore • Hong Kong • Seoul • Taipei • New Delhi
Cape Town • Madrid • Mexico City • Amsterdam • Munich • Paris • Milan

Pearson Education Limited
Edinburgh Gate
Harlow
Essex CM20 2JE
England

and Associated Companies throughout the world

Visit us on the World Wide Web at:
www.pearsoned.co.uk

First published 2008

ISBN: 978-0-582-77217-5

British Library Cataloguing-in-Publication Data
A catalogue record for this book is available from the British Library

10 9 8 7 6 5 4 3 2 1
11 10 09 08 07

Typeset in 10/13.5pt Sabon by 35

Printed and bound in Malaysia (CTP-KHL)

The publisher's policy is to use paper manufactured from sustainable forests.

Contents

List of maps

To Caitriona

Introduction

This survey of the long Irish seventeenth century is, I hope, readable and accessible. To this end it is presented in chronological narrative chapters linked by a coherent unifying theme. This theme should become apparent before it is made explicit in the conclusion. The narrative runs from 1603 to 1727, with the first and last chapters anchored in what came before and after this historical period.

The notion of such periods implies not just internal continuity but a clean break at its beginning and end. The box of time begins with the accession of James VI of Scotland to the throne of England. The same year marks the final conquest of Ireland, all of the island, by the English crown. The appropriate terminal date for a coherent and unified century is less obvious. Cromwell's conquest and settlement was such a traumatic rupture that it seems like an 'obvious and unquestionable' point to break off.[1] Yet the Irish Catholic community did not accept Cromwell's land grab as final. Those who would turn the clock back, and those who would not, wrestled to the last acre and this struggle underlay much of the politics and war of the next half century. One could break off a Stuart century with the Hanoverian succession of 1714, but that would leave too much hanging in the air. A terminal date some time around the accession of George II in 1727 works better. Politics bedded down in the years just following and there would be no general election until his long reign ended in 1761. Swift wrote nothing more of substance after his *Modest Proposal* of 1729. Archbishop King, Lord Midleton and the first 'undertaker' Speaker Conolly, dominating figures in Irish parliamentary politics for three decades, all died between 1728 and 1729. By then the Irish parliament had established itself as an institution to be reckoned with. Its enhanced role was captured in stone in the splendid parliament house built on College Green between 1729 and 1731. The last important penal laws were added to the statute books between 1729 and 1733 when Catholics were explicitly debarred from voting in parliamentary elections and from working even in the lower branches of the law as attorneys and solicitors.

Those years saw the dawn, albeit a false dawn, of an age of 'improvement' with the setting up of the Dublin Society in 1731 and the start to the cutting of an eighteen-mile canal between Lough Neagh and Newry. The aspirations of the improvers would be mocked by the horrific famine of 1740–41.

Tudor Ireland can be seen as a marcher zone comparable to, for example, the North of England and as a colonial laboratory in which the ideologies and techniques of the emergent Atlantic Empire were tested. It is helpful to set Ireland in both contexts.

Stuart Ireland belongs within the frame of archipelagic or 'British' history. To know why Tyrone fled the country in 1607 one must see, as he clearly saw, that Sir Robert Cecil, Earl of Salisbury, the minister who dominated the English Privy Council, was his enemy. A viceroy's supremacy usually depended not on Irish alliances but on the power of his factional allies at Whitehall.[2] Any claim that the Irish rose in self-defence in 1641 is incomprehensible unless the reader hears the far-off rumble of Covenanter rhetoric. The playing out of the three kingdom crisis or crises, war or wars, of 1637–52 in Ireland is not explicable unless the reader is reminded that the protagonists drew, or tried to draw, on the human and financial resources of Scotland and Ireland throughout the first and second 'English' civil wars.[3] The dizzying ups and downs of Irish Catholics during Charles II's reign seem random without a clear awareness of court faction, shifts of relative power between monarch and English parliament, and the putative 'grand design' of Charles II and his brother James for a Catholic England and a French alliance.

Yet this is still 'a tale of two islands': an archipelagic perspective sharpens the sense that Ireland was the odd one out, a colony, in fact if not in name, ripe for exploitation by the inhabitants of the other two kingdoms of what James I envisaged as 'Great Britain'.[4] So one need not, and should not, ignore or downplay the trauma and the 'catastrophic dimension' of the Irish experience.[5] At the same time a recital of wars, massacres, dispossession and cultural repression ought not to smooth over complexity and ignore episodes of co-existence and cooperation.

History, for most Irish people, begins with the Great Famine. To all intents, anything earlier is not taught at second level. Most university history departments do not do enough to remedy this ignorance. This book is written to help, in some small way, by supplying an accessible, uncluttered narrative that the reader might find relevant. In thus choosing what to put in or leave out, what is historically significant, one is aware of the danger of teleology or preoccupation with an historical process endowed with long-term, indeed present-day, relevance.[6] Jacobitism was, literally, inconsequential in terms of today's political reality. But to ignore it would be to deny the losers a hearing. Popular Jacobitism is important in its own right and in its own time and does not need to be justified as a precursor to Whiteboys, Defenders or United Irishmen. Take another example: to condemn poor Niall *garbh* O'Donnell as a bad Irishman because he switched sides from Tyrone to Dowcra would be to anachronistically project contemporary expectations onto someone who was too blinkered to see further than north-west Ulster.

Indeed, moral judgement of individuals is usually impertinent. Sir Arthur Chichester, the architect of the Ulster plantation, can be seen (from later unionist or nationalist perspectives) as either '. . . one of the greatest men that Ireland had seen' or '. . . malignant, cruel, devoid of sympathy, and solely intent on his own aggrandizement'.[7] Yet Chichester was but an example of a type, the reckless and unscrupulous adventurer, attracted to colonial frontiers. Had he been killed, someone very much like him would have stepped into his shoes. That there would be such a frontier was always likely given the juxtaposition of a centralising modern state and a fissiparous and archaic society unable to defend itself effectively until the eleventh hour. Moral judgement is best confined to those few actors who enjoy some agency, a James Stuart, Thomas Wentworth or Oliver Cromwell.

In referring to the respective religions in Ireland, 'Catholic' has been used to refer to what are often termed 'Roman Catholics', punctuated with the occasional rhetorical use of 'Papist', on the grounds that it is respectful to refer to communities where possible by the terms they preferred and prefer themselves. 'Protestant' or 'Anglican' usually denotes adherents of the Church of Ireland, while 'protestant' is used to refer to members of all protestant churches and Presbyterian, 'dissenter' or 'non-conformist' to non-Anglican protestants. Present-day forms of place names are usually preferred: Lisburn rather than 'Lisnagarvey', Castleblayney rather than 'Balle Lurgan', Bandon rather than 'Bandonbridge', Mallow rather than 'Moyallo', Laois and Offaly rather than 'Queen's County' and 'King's County'. The western province is Connacht, the most common modern form, but the provincial presidency is that of 'Connaught'. As to the contested names 'Derry' and 'Londonderry', the diocese should be Derry and the plantation company Londonderry. The city is called 'Derry' because that has been and is the common usage in Ireland, while the county is usually named 'Londonderry' because it was created by plantation and had no previous existence as a territory named 'Derry'.

Personal names present a greater challenge and the usage here is not altogether consistent. For example, the Ulster general of the 1640s is not called Owen roe O'Neale, though that is closest to the form that he most often used when writing in English; nor is he Eoghan *Rua* Ó Néill, to give him his proper spelling in modern Irish. Here I choose a compromise that contains the anglicised form of his surname and the Irish spelling of his Christian name and nickname: Eoghan *Rua* O'Neill. Such nicknames are given in their correct Irish spelling, *garbh* rather than 'garve'. They sometimes derive from the subject's lifetime experience or his character but usually refer to personal appearance: *mór, óg, bán, dubh, rua, bacach, ballach, garbh, dall, caoch* [great or older, younger, fair, black, red, lame, freckled, rough, blind] and so on.[8] In general I have opted for the modern and familiar form of Gaelic surnames in English except that I usually retain the 'O' or 'Mac' that was often discarded subsequently: Fionn O'Daly, Malachy O'Queally, Rory O'More (instead of Roger Moore) and so on. However, the proper form in Gaelic is given where otherwise something of importance could be lost: To call the poet Fearghal Óg Mac an Bhaird by the modern anglicisation of 'Ward' would be to miss the reminder in the surname that he came from an hereditary bardic family.

Kinsale was fought on 24 December 1601 by the Old Style calendar used by the English, and on 3 January 1602 by the new-fangled Gregorian calendar, used by the Spanish. Where exact dates are given (and I generally avoid them), they are Old Style.

I owe a great deal to colleagues who read individual chapters: Ciara Breathnach, Nicholas Canny, John Cronin, Steven Ellis, Alan Ford, Kevin Forkan, Liam Irwin, David Hayton, John Logan, Micheál MacCraith, James McGuire, Seosamh MacMuirí, Mary O'Dowd, Ciarán Ó Murchadha and Micheál Ó Siochrú. I also owe thanks to many others: these include Ken Bergin, Jean Turner, Carmel Ryan and Anne Butler, Glucksman Library, University of Limerick, Mari Boran and Margaret Hughes, Hardiman Library, National University of Ireland, Galway, Donnchar Lenihan, Sean Collins, David Fleming and Patrick John Rafferty. I must also thank the reader who helpfully pointed out gaps in my reading, ambiguities in my writing and some potentially embarrassing errors. *Go raibh maith agaibh.*

Endnotes

1   Brady and Ohlmeyer 2005, pp. 3–4.

2   Rutledge 1989, p. 235.

3 Ohlmeyer 1999, p. 450.

4 Morrill 1996, p. 89; Ohlmeyer 1999, p. 450.

5 Bradshaw 1994, p. 204.

6 Bradshaw 1994, p. 196.

7 Hamilton 1920, p. 65; Meehan 1886, p. 35.

8 Tait 2006, p. 329.

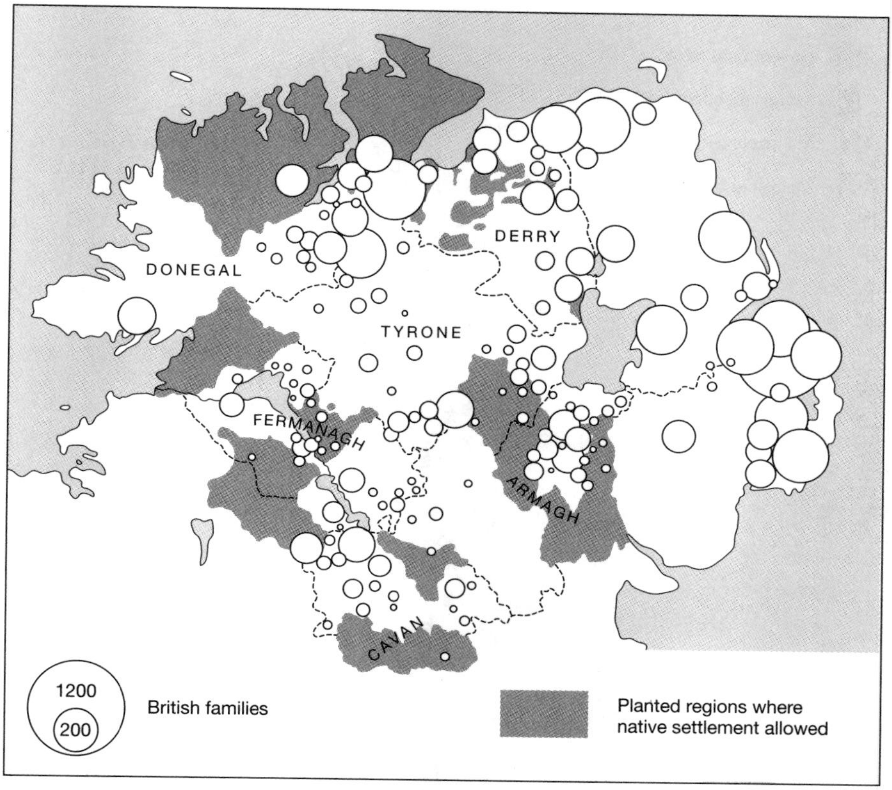

DONEGAL
DERRY
TYRONE
FERMANAGH
ARMAGH
CAVAN
1200
200
British families
Planted regions where native settlement allowed

MAP 1 ***British settlement in Ulster c. 1630 (planted counties named)***

Sources: Robinson *Plantation of Ulster*; Moody and Hunter *New history of Ireland iii*

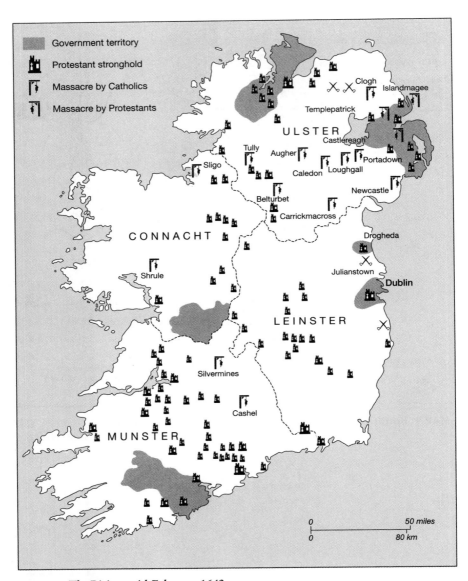

Legend:
- Government territory
- Protestant stronghold
- Massacre by Catholics
- Massacre by Protestants

Place labels:

ULSTER

Clogh
Islandmagee
Templepatrick
Castlereagh
Tully
Augher
Portadown
Sligo
Caledon
Loughgall
Newcastle
Belturbet
Carrickmacross

CONNACHT

Drogheda
Shrule
Julianstown
Dublin

LEINSTER

Silvermines

Cashel

MUNSTER

0   50 miles
0   80 km

MAP 2 *The Rising: mid-February 1642*

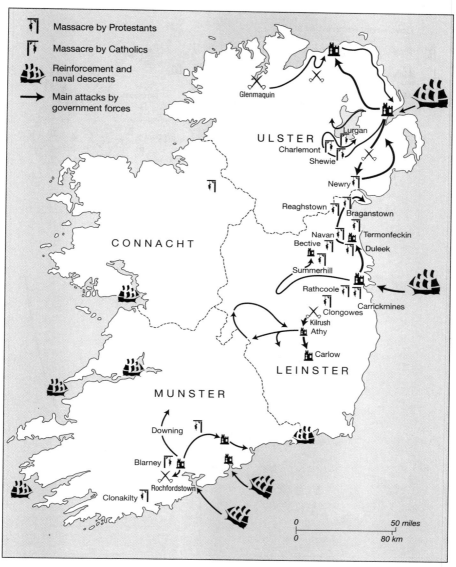

MAP 3 *The Rising: March–June 1642*

Massacre by Protestants

Massacre by Catholics

Reinforcement and naval descents

Main attacks by government forces

ULSTER

Glenmaquin

Lurgan

Charlemont

Shewie

Newry

Reaghstown

Braganstown

CONNACHT

Navan

Bective

Termonfeckin

Duleek

Summerhill

Rathcoole

Carrickmines

Clongowes

Kilrush

Athy

Carlow

LEINSTER

MUNSTER

Downing

Blarney

Rochfordstown

Clonakilty

0   50 miles

0   80 km

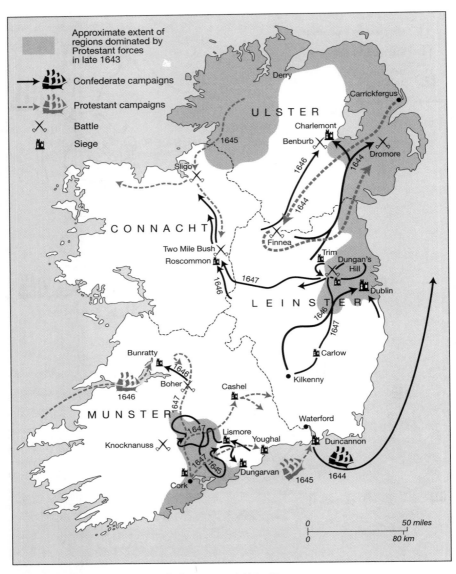

Approximate extent of regions dominated by Protestant forces in late 1643

Confederate campaigns

Protestant campaigns

Battle

Siege

Derry

Carrickfergus

ULSTER

Charlemont

Benburb

Dromore

1645

Sligo

1646

1644

CONNACHT

1644

Finnea

Two Mile Bush

Roscommon

Trim

Dungan's Hill

1647

Dublin

1646

LEINSTER

1646

1647

Carlow

Bunratty

Kilkenny

1646

Boher

Cashel

1646

1647

Waterford

MUNSTER

Lismore

Youghal

Duncannon

Knocknanuss

1647

1647

1645

Dungarvan

1644

Cork

1645

0   50 miles

0   80 km

MAP 4 *The Confederate Catholics at war 1644–47*

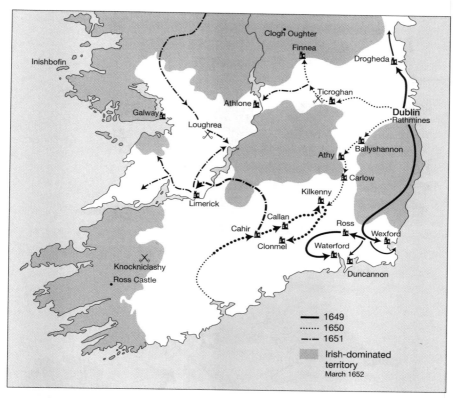

MAP 5 *Cromwellian conquest*

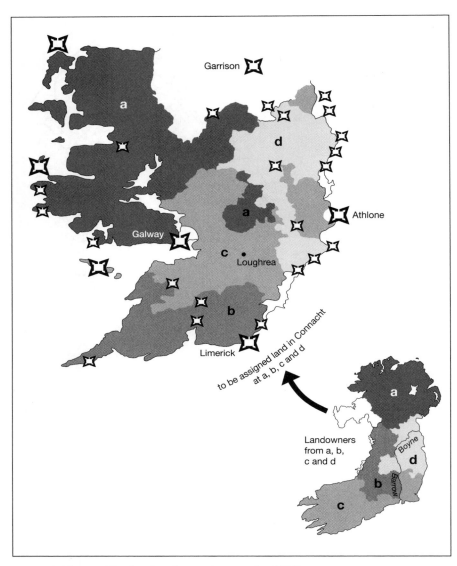

Garrison

a

d

a

Athlone

Galway

c

Loughrea

b

Limerick

to be assigned land in Connacht
at a, b, c and d

a

Boyne

Landowners
from a, b,
c and d

d

b

Barrow

c

MAP 6 *Cromwellian land settlement (proposed c. 1656)*

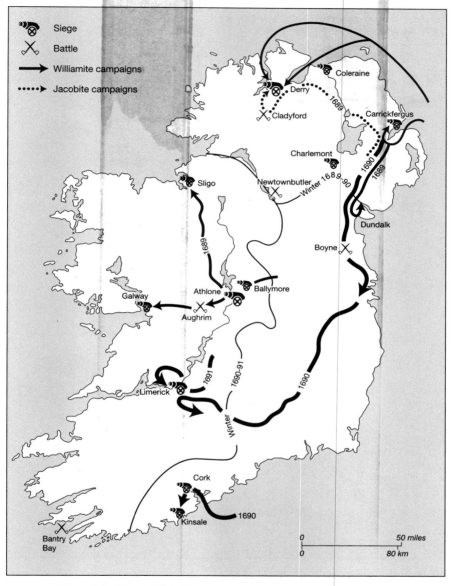

MAP 7 *'War of the Kings' 1689–91*

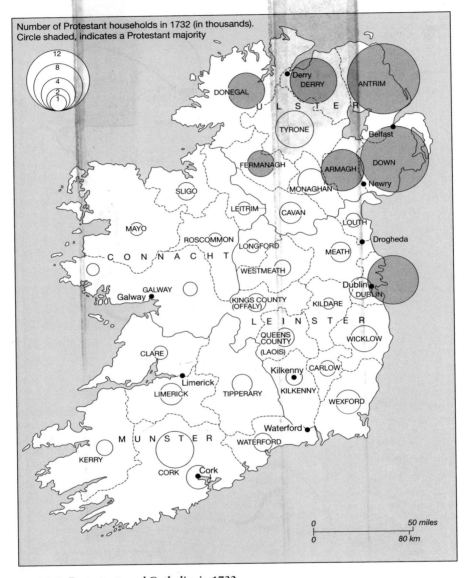

Number of Protestant households in 1732 (in thousands). Circle shaded, indicates a Protestant majority

MAP 8 *Protestants and Catholics in 1732*

Source: Adapted from D. Bindon *An Abstract of Protestant and Popish Families (Dublin 1736)*

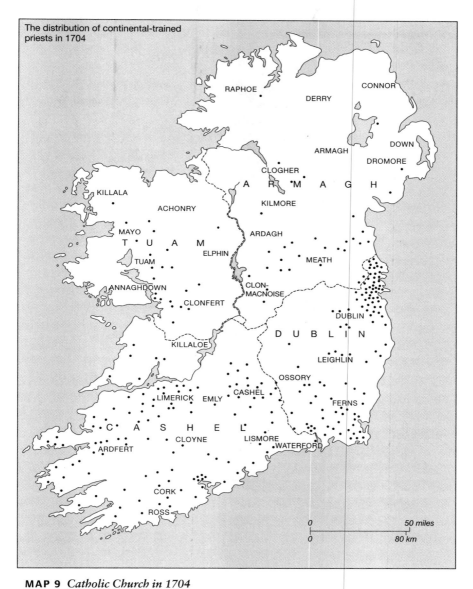

The distribution of continental-trained priests in 1704

RAPHOE

CONNOR

DERRY

ARMAGH

DOWN

DROMORE

CLOGHER

A R M A G H

KILLALA

KILMORE

ACHONRY

MAYO

ARDAGH

T   U   A   M

ELPHIN

MEATH

TUAM

ANNAGHDOWN

CLON-
MACNOISE

CLONFERT

DUBLIN

D   U   B   L   I   N

KILLALOE

LEIGHLIN

OSSORY

CASHEL

LIMERICK   EMLY

FERNS

C   A   S   H   E   L

CLOYNE

LISMORE

ARDFERT

WATERFORD

CORK

ROSS

0   50 miles
0   80 km

MAP 9 *Catholic Church in 1704*

Source: Adapted from K. Whelan *The Regional Impact of Irish Catholicism*

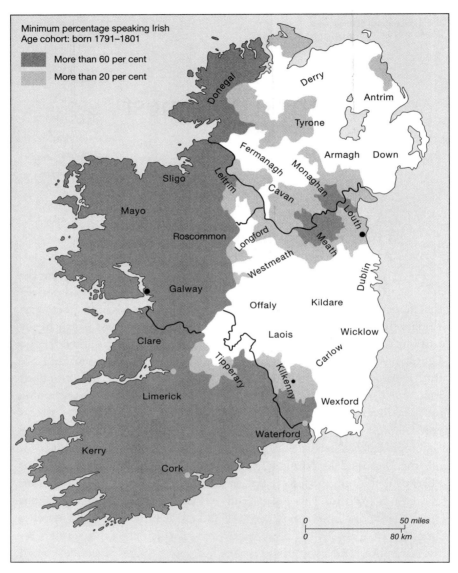

MAP 10 *Geographical distribution of Irish speakers*

CHAPTER 1

Reform to conquest 1534–1603

The English lordship

The core of the late medieval English lordship in Ireland was the fertile plain or 'maghery' of the English Pale which comprised the modern counties Dublin, Louth, south-east Meath and north-east Kildare. To this may be added outliers such as Bargy and Forth in the extreme south-east and the maritime towns.[1] Beyond the Pale, literally and figuratively, the Fitzgerald lordships of Kildare and Desmond and the Butler lordship of Ormond formed an extensive and discontinuous militarised buffer insulating the lordship from Gaelic territories spanning most of Ireland and western Scotland. The Kildare lordship was almost coterminous with the present-day county of the same name, Ormond encompassed counties Kilkenny and south Tipperary, while the largest of all, the Desmond lordship, sprawled across most of Limerick, adjacent parts of Cork and north Kerry, with detached blocks in Cork, Tipperary and east Waterford. This borderland was comparable (at least to Tudor monarchs) to the far north of England and to the principality and marcher lordships of Wales. All of these were areas in which laws and administrative structures and institutions (shires, assizes, Justices of the Peace and parliaments) devised for the English lowlands worked uncertainly and intermittently.[2] Local conditions demanded devolution of power to locally powerful feudal notables, but the perennial fear of over-mighty subjects suggested intensified centralisation, especially after Henry VIII's break with Rome forced him into a more interventionist strategy.

Late in 1534 the king abandoned the practice of delegating his authority to a prominent local magnate and dismissed Gerald óg Fitzgerald, 9th earl of Kildare, as deputy. It was not the first time he had done so. The revolt of Lord Offaly, better known as Silken Thomas, was an attempt to show his father's indispensability. Royal guns battered the walls of Maynooth Castle, which fell after just ten days. Here, as elsewhere in western Europe, the royal monopoly of siege guns tamed feudal nobles.[3]

In autumn 1535 Thomas Cromwell, Henry's chief minister, queried 'whether it shall be expedient to begin a conquest or a reformation' in Ireland.[4] The balkanised Gaelic and Gaelicised world was 'feeble to be conquered', urged a Palesman, Patrick Fingas, baron of the exchequer.[5] At any one time there were about ninety chieftains who obeyed only 'such persons as may subdue him with the sword'.[6] Individually most of their armies were quite small and presented no danger to the Pale so long as they did not coalesce. The MacMurrough Kavanaghs of south Leinster, to take an example of a smaller lordship, could put no more than 200 horsemen into the field, alongside 300 kern and a smaller 'battle' of gallowglass. The Gaelic horseman, riding without stirrups on an animal too small to be a charger, could not 'abide the shock' of a cavalry charge.[7] The 'naked' [unarmoured] kern, who comprised nearly three quarters of any Gaelic army, could harass a column marching through broken ground and defile, burn, forage and take prey but were useless in a stand-up fight in open country. The 'gallowglass' [*Gallóglaigh* or 'foreign soldier'] in metal helm and mail coat were the nearest the Gael came to professional soldiers. Originally recruited from the west of Scotland, the Mac Sheehys, Mac Sweeneys, Mac Donnells and the rest were 'grim of countenance, tall of stature, big of limb' and held in awe by English commentators. Yet their fearsome six-foot battleaxe was obsolescent, as was their way of fighting.

When the Tudor monarch's thoughts had turned earlier towards conquest in 1506 and 1521, he was advised it would take an army of 6,000 men and a large siege train to conquer these lordships.[8] This had seemed altogether too heavy a drain on English finances then. It would hardly be less now. The earl's destruction removed the network of Gaelic clientage and marriage alliances that had secured the marches of the Pale from encroachment. The alignment of O'Neill (Kildare's traditional ally) and O'Donnell, O'Connor Sligo, O'Brien of Thomond and O'Connor Faly in the Geraldine League amounted to a Gaelic confederation across all four provinces.[9] Indeed, an unprecedented invasion of the Pale itself by O'Neill and O'Donnell in 1539 underlined the lordship's military weakness. For security the crown would, at the very least, have to maintain an outside governor and a strong permanent garrison, but lands confiscated from Kildare and from the church yielded less than these escalating costs. The crown remained generally unwilling to accept a large drain on English finances as the cost of greater centralisation and conquest. This explains the general neglect of Ireland by the Tudors, interspersed with bursts of activity and sudden reversals of policy.[10] The fall of the king's chief minister, Thomas Cromwell, prompted the first of many such reversals.

Tudor reform

With hindsight the beginnings of a divergence of interests can be detected between longer established settlers and English-born newcomers. The former, who are often called Anglo-Irish for want of a better term, stood to benefit most from a peaceful assimilation of Gaelic Ireland, whereas coercion would require more troops and English officials and so lessen the government's dependence on local support. New English officials, meanwhile, tended to be hungrier for Gaelic land and were predisposed to conquest.[11] After Cromwell's fall there followed what local reform lobbyists had long wanted: a programme of gradualist political reform. Anthony St Leger, who served as governor on and off from 1540 to 1556, had as his local right-hand man Thomas Cusack, the Commons' speaker in the 1541–43 parliament, who rose to be Lord Chancellor in 1550.

Surrender and regrant

St Leger and Cusack's 'surrender and regrant' arrangements saw Gaelic chieftains agree to renounce their traditional Gaelic title in return for an English feudal title, to recognise the king as their liege lord and to apply for a crown grant of their lands and peerage. They further agreed to reject papal jurisdiction, accept and assist the machinery of royal government throughout their lordship, perform military service and pay rent as specified, adopt English customs and language and generally structure their territory in an English fashion. Forced by the defection of many of his *uirríthe* or under lords, Conn *bacach* O'Neill surrendered in 1541 and the following year he was created earl of Tyrone in a ceremony at Greenwich carefully staged to create the greatest stir.[12] The next such visit saw O'Brien and Burke created earls of Thomond and Clanricard respectively.

The second chief manifestation of the new policy was the parliament which met at Dublin in 1541 and continued in eight sessions until 1543 and saw the unprecedented participation of Gaelic lords. To affirm the king's new relationship with the Gaelic lords, parliament persuaded a reluctant Henry to take on the title of king, not lord, of Ireland. The Gaelic Irishman was now a royal subject, with accompanying legal status, and not an 'enemy' or alien. The English lordship in Ireland was now a separate constitutional entity, with a parliament, legal system and administrative structure of its own.[13] Unlike the councils established to govern Wales and the north of England, the governor in Dublin superintended a complete council and executive in miniature and enjoyed civil and military powers little short of those of the King in England.

Though suspended towards the end of 1543, surrender and regrant worked to the extent that it brought two prominent families, the O'Briens and Clanricard Burkes, permanently onto the side of crown government. There was reason to expect gradualist reform and assimilation would work over the next thirty years. A comparable local strategy was being successfully applied in Wales and the north of England: eliminate or emasculate the top magnates, transfer their wealth to crown dependants, set up regional councils with special powers, replace local institutions with English common law, shire the territories into recognisable territorial units and impose religious uniformity.

Gaelic and Gaelicised lords were more powerful and autonomous than magnates in the other Tudor borderlands and it became apparent in the governorships (1556–62) of Thomas Radcliffe, Earl of Sussex, that surrender and regrant would not lead to peaceful and gradual reform.[14] For one thing, he 'drastically' changed surrender and regrant to offer the O'More and O'Connor clansmen of Laois and Offaly just one third of their territory following surrender, with the rest to be assigned to frontier garrisons and to deserving 'Englishmen born in England or Ireland'.[15] It was a beginning, however faltering, to plantation. Expropriation by violence was the antithesis of gradualist reform.

Another reason for the failure of surrender and regrant has to do with the fissiparous nature of each little or large Gaelic 'country'. Any man whose great-grandfather had been chief could put himself forward for selection as chief of the sept or clan that dominated the fluctuating boundaries of their *oireacht*.[16] With most lordships at least 150 years old at this point, this was a dangerously large group indeed. 'Tanistry', to dignify this free-for-all with a name, referred to a practice whereby 'the worthiest of the blood' was elected heir-apparent or *tánaiste*. Indeed, where a chief outlived the more formidable of his younger brothers he might hope to pass on the chieftainship in an orderly way, but more often there would be a protracted succession dispute. Tudor governors naturally used resentful groups or individuals who felt cheated of the succession to drive wedges deeper into clans. To that extent tanistry was a boon to Tudor governance in Ireland. But the incautious governor could find himself

sucked into succession disputes and allow his prestige to hang on the outcome. Thomas Radcliffe, Earl of Sussex, who governed on and off between
1556 and 1562, was drawn into an avoidable dispute in order, as he saw
it, to defend the succession and regrant arrangements agreed with Conn
bacach O'Neill.[17]

Conn *bacach* O'Neill had nominated an illegitimate son, one Matthew
Kelly or Feardorcha O'Neill, as his heir and secured the succession on him
by his surrender and regrant indenture. Conn's eldest son, Seán or 'Shane'
(as it was pronounced in Ulster), established himself as O'Neill, killed off
his rival and imposed his power on lesser lords in pursuance of the traditional O'Neill claim of overlordship of Ulster. Shane claimed that his
father had not made a full submission and, in any case, that he was no bas-
tard but the rightful and undisputed leader of the O'Neills.[18] Sussex would
have done well to recognise the accomplished fact and with careful handling Shane could have been induced to accept the same agreement as his
father. Instead Sussex saw defeating Shane as the key to success: 'if Shane
is over thrown all is settled.' He proved unable to defeat Shane, while the
Palesmen suffered cattle raids, onerous war taxes and payment in debased
coinage.[19] Their leaders, Cusack and Gerald, the 11th earl of Kildare, succeeded in having Sussex recalled and an agreement made with Shane by
which the crown effectively capitulated, acknowledging him as O'Neill.

Protestant Reformation

The Protestant Reformation drive was renewed under Sussex's governorship and after the accession of Elizabeth I. Protestantism was not primarily
a critique of abuses in the late medieval church but a 'different religion'
launching a frontal attack on magic, both popular and sacramental.[20]
Reformers declaimed that the priest did not perform transubstantiation,
the magical transformation of bread and wine into the body and blood of
Christ. 'Works' or ritual observances were irrelevant, if not downright
idolatrous, and 'justification' or salvation was through faith alone. In this
respect Calvinistic theology, in particular, seemed unremittingly bleak:
God chose certain persons as an elect predestined to salvation, regardless
of their merits, and consigned the rest to eternal damnation.[21] The new
faith was individualistic, even lonely, whereas the key moments of Catholic
ritual, such as the consecration, were collective. The Church of England
was less shockingly new than most reformed churches. It kept the old
structure of ecclesiastical government intact, retained large chunks of the
Roman liturgy and form of service in direct translation, and took an

ambiguous position on the key question of transubstantiation.[22] But even Anglicanism represented a rupture with popular religious sensibility and ritual.[23] To take the most obvious difference, the physical setting of worship in a sixteenth-and early seventeenth-century Anglican church was a forbiddingly spartan, barn-like building with white-washed walls, dominated by a pulpit and a wooden table for communion. The Irish were repulsed by this change because, claimed John Roche, Catholic bishop of Ferns (1626–36), they were a 'simple' people who were 'averse to innovations'.[24] Such cultural conservatism can be equated with remoteness. Cities and towns are first to be exposed to novel fashions and ideas, in religion as in much else. The word 'pagan' derives from the disdainful response of town-dwelling Christians to the country dweller or *paganus* who still worshipped the old gods. Like Christianity, the Protestant Reformation began as 'an urban event'.[25] Remoteness in this context also meant distance from an increasingly powerful government in London which was driving the pace of Protestant change. Thus by 1603 one finds in England and Wales a general gradient of Catholic survival and travel time from London.[26]

The fact that most of Ireland was, as yet, beyond the writ of London explains only the tempo of religious change, not the ultimate outcome. Norway provides an interesting point of comparison and contrast to sixteenth-century Ireland. In 1536 Christian III of Denmark imposed a Lutheran settlement on recently acquired Norway and centralised power after a period of civil war. The Protestant Reformation had begun the same year in Ireland when the Irish parliament declared Henry VIII 'the only supreme head on earth of the whole church of Ireland', just two years later than his proclamation in England.[27] No printing press existed in Norway, no bible would be printed in Norwegian and the Danish language was used as the medium for all worship and religious instruction.[28] Poor, backward and remote Norse fisherfolk and farmers were unenthusiastic. Thus far the analogy with Tudor Ireland seems compelling. Yet in time Norwegians took to the new faith. Traditionalism, nostalgia and passive distaste for religious innovation might slow the march of Protestant Reform for a generation or two. It could not change the outcome.

Indeed, against the traditional view that the Protestant Reformation was doomed to fail, it is now clear that the reformers made headway until the early years of Elizabeth I's reign (1558–1603). Only the lower clergy, whose representatives then sat in the Irish parliament of 1536, offered any resistance to the Protestant programme. The dissolution of the monasteries in 1539–40 destroyed almost all the foundations in the lordship without any sign of remorse that could not be assuaged by grants of monastic land.

Converts were won among the wealthier burgesses of Dublin who had constant social and political dealings with English officials and would have had difficulty in eluding the social and legal pressures to win their compliance. Most inhabitants of the towns and the Pale conformed outwardly to the state church while manipulating services to suit their tastes.[29]

When parliament met in 1560 there was limited opposition to restoring royal supremacy of the church after the reign of the Catholic Queen Mary and to enacting Elizabeth's religious settlement. Parliament also decided to reaffirm the Henrician 'Act for the English order, Habite, and Language' (1537), which stipulated that the ministry should be English-speaking.[30] The Act later assumed great symbolic and practical importance as the definitive statement of the axiomatic link between anglicisation and the Anglican Church.[31] The 1560 Act of Uniformity demanded that Church of Ireland ministers use the Book of Common Prayer for services and, if they could not, Latin versions of the service were sanctioned.[32] Irish was not to be used.

An Erasmian strategy of religious persuasion reflected a basically optimistic view that people, no matter how benighted, retained the intellectual capacity to discern the good if reached through evangelisation, education and the provision of a liturgy in the vernacular language. This was of a piece with a gradualist strategy of political reform and so it is not surprising that Anglo–Irish conformists to the established church urged the government to trust in the word rather than the sword.[33] The Act of Uniformity pleaded the technical difficulty of cutting an Irish typeface and the 'few in the whole realm' who could read Irish as reasons for not supplying printed material in that language.[34] With this linguistic and cultural squeamishness the reformers, having already discarded ceremony, drama and icons, now constrained their preaching and the dissemination of the printed word: protestantism, after all, was 'the child of the printed book'.[35]

It must be remembered that Gaelic was spoken across the entire island in the closing decades of the sixteenth century and had conquered the hybridised Hiberno-English cultural zone of the Pale and the little urban oases of civility beyond it whose inhabitants 'commonly speak Irish among themselves'.[36] The only places where English was the dominant spoken language were the city of Dublin, 'Fingal' or north County Dublin, and Bargy and Forth in the south-eastern nook of County Wexford where a 'mingle mangle' of Irish and archaic English was spoken.[37] To judge from surname evidence, most of the peasantry of south County Kilkenny, east County Waterford (Gaultier and Middle Third baronies) and the eastern fringe of County Tipperary (Slievardagh barony) were of English descent but they were no longer English-speaking and were still Gaelic-speaking (**map 10**) well into the nineteenth century.[38]

The first printed work in Irish was Bishop Carswell's translation of John Knox's Book of Common Order, which appeared in Edinburgh in 1567. Carswell rendered the translation into classical common Gaelic readable by the educated Gael of Ireland as well as Scotland and his prefatory poem expressed the hope that his work would spread 'to Irish shores' [*go crích Eireand*] and 'to such of them as desire to receive the faithful words of God in their hearts and minds'.[39] With these words, Carswell announced the reorientation from ritual and observance to cognitive understanding. Fearful of a Scottish reformation in the Irish language and backed by the powerful Earl of Argyll, Elizabeth was provoked into sponsoring the *Aibidil Gaoidheilge et Caiticiosma* in 1571.[40] John Kearney or Seaán Ó Cearnaigh, an office holder in St Patrick's Cathedral, Dublin, wrote this Irish-language primer and evangelical catechism and just two hundred copies were printed. The failure this to reprint in later years suggests that the state church was lukewarm about catechising in Irish.[41]

Conquest
Sidney's governorships

One can argue that Sussex was a programmatic reformer like St Leger, driven against his better judgement into a war against the most powerful Gaelic lordship. His successor and one-time protégé Sir Henry Sidney, however, 'departed consciously and decisively' from his predecessors between 1565 and his final recall in 1579.[42]

His most striking innovations were provincial presidents set up over Munster and Connacht to supervise the introduction of English legal process, curb 'lewd Irish customs', purge their provinces of popery and find lands ripe for English settlement.[43] The new President of Connaught clumsily set up rivals to Clanricard and Thomond (the latter territory was initially considered part of the presidency of Connaught) as sheriffs with powers of martial law. Meanwhile other sheriffs, seneschals and provost-marshals (usually soldiers) were installed in tracts of Gaelic Leinster. They applied martial law with indiscriminate brutality, extorted, pocketed fees and pursued vendettas against their enemies.[44] This was entirely predictable. Officials, be they soldiers or quill pushers, had a vested interest in provoking rebellion, followed by attainder of the rebel, confiscation of his lands and their grant to the monarch's hard-working servants on the spot.

Potentially more far-reaching was Sidney's encouragement of dormant land claims. The medieval English lordship encompassed at its widest extent most of Munster and Leinster and parts of Connacht. Most of the occupiers abandoned their Irish holdings and fled to England during the late medieval Gaelic revival. As Sidney saw it, the original title belonged to the descendants of these settlers (or, in default, to the crown) and he backed opportunistic and doubtful claims such as those of Peter Carew, a Devonshire ne'er-do-well, to ancestral lands in the Pale, County Carlow and the heart of the Desmond lands in Munster.[45]

Such policies provoked revolts between 1569 and 1572 in the Thomond, Clanricard and Desmond earldoms and even drove the traditionally loyal Butlers out in rebellion. These revolts were more destructive of property than lives and the leaders and were orchestrated to impress on Queen Elizabeth the danger and expense of driving them from their natural English allegiance. Symbolic manifestations of disaffection, such as donning Gaelic dress, drove home the point. Some of the revolts were Irish manifestations of the court intrigues and fears that sparked the Northern Rising of 1569–70.

Like his predecessor, Sidney beguiled the Queen with absurdly optimistic promises into waging war in Ireland but had no more success in curbing Shane O'Neill and was fortunate that O'Neill was hacked to death by the MacDonnells during a parley. Sidney's characteristically grandiose response to this unwonted good fortune was to plan to break up the O'Neill lordship, install a provincial president and plant English settlers in east Ulster as a wedge between Irish and Scottish Gaeldom. None of this came to pass. Unprecedented and often pointless violence often marked this and Sidney's other failed enterprises. The best known such atrocity was the slaughter of O'More clansmen summoned to muster for military service at Mullaghmast in 1578 by Captain Francis Cosby, sheriff of County Kildare.[46] The ideological wellsprings of this new ruthlessness might have lain in New World discoveries awakening latent colonialist responses in England and prompting a reevaluation of Ireland not as a borderland but as an 'old colony gone wrong'.[47] A less often acknowledged source may have been Machiavelli's *Discourses on Livy*, which advocated colonies, coercion and a standing army as methods to revive a decayed polity and offered the justification of a higher political morality for violence.[48]

Sidney was discredited not by the violence of his forward policy but by its cost. 'Cess', used loosely, meant military exactions of provisions at an arbitrarily low price.[49] High cess rates at a time of poor harvests and a plague epidemic were already arousing resentment when Sidney went further and proposed to commute this to an annual 'composition' rent to be charged against every ploughland in the Pale.[50] The outraged Palesmen agitated against this tax, which was illegal in their eyes since it was not sanctioned by the Irish parliament. Their collective political action included petitions, strikes and sending agents directly to the court. This struggle determined their future political identity. Though professedly English and loyal, they nonetheless began to withdraw politically and culturally from *arriviste* English administrators and soldiers. The monarch unwittingly encouraged this withdrawal by abetting their resistance to unpopular officials, in this case by removing Sidney.[51]

Elizabeth seriously considered returning to the pre-1534 position of indirect rule. In the end she adopted the characteristically self-defeating half-measure of leaving Sidney's appointees in place and ineffectually urging restraint on them.[52]

Munster: war and plantation

The revolts of 1569–72 were tinctured with the rhetoric of continental religious war and so threatened to become a 'general matter' rather than a series of disparate dynastic risings and 'private quarrels'.[53] This threat materialised a decade later in the Desmond and Baltinglass risings (1579–83) in which the catalyst of counter-reformation Catholicism transformed resentment and alienation into violent opposition.[54] 'This war is undertaken for the defence of the Catholic religion against the heretics': James Fitzmaurice Fitzgerald issued this ringing battle cry of the counter-reformation and brought a nuncio and 600 papal troops to *Dún an Óir* on the Dingle Peninsula in 1579.[55] Papal invasion was a logical outcome of Pope Pius V's *Regnans in Excelsis* of 1570 which had excommunicated Queen Elizabeth and absolved her subjects from allegiance to a heretical monarch.[56] Lord Deputy Grey cut off the Golden Fort by land and sea, forced their surrender and slaughtered the lot. Another zealot, James Eustace, rose on the southern marches of the Pale in 1580. His O'Byrne and O'Toole supporters were motivated less by religion than by the local seneschal's campaign to anglicise and demilitarise their recently shired territory and they defeated a government army that blundered into the wooded defile of Glenmalure in the Wicklow Mountains.[57] Meanwhile the Munster rebels, relatives and clients of *Gearóid Iarla*, earl of Desmond, and later the reluctant earl himself generally avoided fighting royal troops in the open field and the war degenerated into a bitter counter-insurgency campaign spanning five counties and lasting four years.[58] There would be no pardon for Desmond. A hunted and lonely fugitive, he stayed out on his keeping until he was tracked down and killed in 1583.[59]

Desmond's attainder opened up a vast tract of Munster for confiscation by the crown, to be followed by plantation. Undertakers got a 'seignory' amounting to around 12,000 English acres of profitable land, or decreasing proportions of 8,000, 6,000 and 4,000. The grantees, mostly landowners from the western counties of England and Wales, undertook not to lease to the 'mere [pure] Irish, not descended of an English name'. Further, they promised to bring over ninety families comprising the full social pyramid of freeholders, farmers, copyholders and cottagers within seven years.[60] Additionally they and their freeholders and copyholders had to keep a specified number of horsemen and footmen in readiness. Achievement fell far short of aspiration. The grants were too big for any one man to supervise, especially when some undertakers got even more, like Sir Walter Raleigh who got 42,000 acres around Youghal. Many planters were assigned scattered parcels of property rather than the sort of self-contained compact units needed for model settlements. Local juries charged with giving effect to Desmond's attainder by finding title to his lands for the crown were disinclined to do so when it became apparent that the lands would go to interlopers.[61] A 1588 commission designed to be the final arbiter of Munster land suits found against undertakers in most cases.[62] Such long-running legal challenges deterred some undertakers and supplied a ready-made excuse for others to drop out.

The 'eternal contradiction' of such plantation schemes was that the most desirable would-be settlers, the skilled artisan and prosperous yeoman, had no need to uproot. All the while the surviving Irish tenantry drifted back to many of the estates which had been emptied after the war. They were willing to pay higher rents for their holdings than an Englishman and so were often left as subtenants to English farmers who formed the social layer below the undertaker. As labourers, too, they were essential.[63] There were some success stories. By 1589 there were 300–400 settlers on the Raleigh estates and 145 on the Grenville and St Leger seignories in west County Waterford. Estimates of the total settler population range from 3,000 to as high as 15,000, with most historians plumping for the lower band of estimates.[64]

The Munster plantation was 'carefully planned, if less successfully executed' and a good example of sixteenth-century governmental ambitions outstripping capacity.[65]

The composition of Connacht

Munster seems to exemplify a strategy of conquest, Connacht one of reform. From 1585 the president of Connaught raised an annual land charge through 'composition' in Thomond, Clanricard and elsewhere in the south of the province.[66] Transferring the military obligations and perquisites to the president weakened the lordship and later compositions in the north of the province struck more forcefully at the territorial integrity of the lordship. Perrot, Lord Deputy from 1584 to 1589, planned to divide the Lower Mac William *oireacht* (most of modern County Mayo) between no fewer than six contenders and also create a multitude of landowners or 'freeholders' to wean the common people from following the great chief lords and substitute a direct link to the monarch as subjects. By the late 1580s and early 1590s composition, and the associated process of shiring, was being extended to south Ulster. Shiring the lordships was more than just a paper exercise, a change of name from O'Reilly's east Breifne, Mac Mahon's Oriel, Maguire's lordship to Counties Cavan, Monaghan and Fermanagh, respectively. The dominant lord was undermined even where, as in east Breifne, he was left with four out of seven baronies as his own. Under the procedure customary duties had been abolished, though in reality Gaelic lords continued to exact them by violence. Deputy Fitzwilliam seized on this pretext to execute Hugh *Rua* MacMahon in 1589. This more predatory phase of surrender and regrant was inimical to the survival of Gaelic lordships. Reform was now conquest by another name.

The rise of Hugh O'Neill

If it were to be conquest, that would be a lot more difficult by the closing years of the century because of the eleventh-hour coalescing of Gaelic Ulster under the rule of the house of Tyrone.[67] This was owing to the breakdown of tried and trusted methods:

> . . . *it would be a wrong metaphor to say that they [English officialdom] put O'Neill in the saddle as earl of Tyrone; they put him on a rocking stone and from time to time they shook the stone a little to remind him of his position, and occasionally steadied it to remind his neighbours of theirs.*

Hugh *Rua* O'Neill, son of the hapless Feardorcha, was 'raised from nothing' by the crown, as he admitted, and created 3rd earl of Tyrone.[68] Tyrone killed off his main rivals, including many of Shane O'Neill's sons by various women, or made marriage alliances with them. Successively, he married a sister of Red Hugh O'Donnell, earl of Tyrconnell, a daughter of Turlough *Luineach* O'Neill, the reigning chief, and, least happily, a sister of Sir Henry Bagenal, marshal of Ulster. Moreover, O'Donnell and Hugh Maguire, chieftain of Fermanagh, were his sons-in-law. The web of marriage alliances represented a potentially formidable confederation. Tyrone used his political savvy and his contacts at court to outsmart governor Perrot (1584–88) and so was let slip off the rocking stone and win undisputed control of his lordship.[69] Perrot's successor, Fitzwilliam (1588–94), was probably in Tyrone's pocket and likely connived at O'Donnell's second and successful escape from custody in Dublin Castle in 1591.

The traditional picture of Tyrone has been that of a devious opportunist who cooperated with the Queen against other Gaelic lords in the expectation that he would be chosen to govern Ulster for the English monarchy. Disappointed in this, for a time he was, or pretended to be, the unrewarded loyalist whose followers would not obey him. Eventually, a reluctant and vacillating rebel to the last, he was pushed from below into assuming open leadership of a Gaelic confederacy in 1595.[70]

It is more likely, however, that he used kinsmen and allies as proxies to wage war on the state right from the beginning.[71] Tyrone surely knew and approved when his ally O'Donnell sent the Archbishop of Tuam to the court of Philip II with a plea for support and an offer of the crown of Ireland. It may be that Tyrone had already grasped the fundamental clash between his hegemony in Ulster and conquest by reform as it applied in north Connacht and south Ulster.

The Nine Years War

A sheriff backed by a company of soldiers settled in the heart of Fermanagh and Tyrone covertly helped Maguire besiege the sheriff in Enniskillen while ostentatiously serving alongside Bagenal. The 'Nine Years War' can be said to have begun in 1594 when Maguire ambushed an English column south of Enniskillen and Tyrone came out in open support. For the first few years O'Neill fought a limited defensive war, content to hinder enemy columns marching into his lordship. He was a capable logistician and subtle politician who strung out peace talks and could gauge just how far to provoke Elizabeth before she would overcome her reluctance to spend money.[72]

Stung by an English raid on Cádiz, Philip II of Spain sent letters by three separate envoys to the Ulster confederates in the spring of 1596, promising that he would send an armada if they broke off peace talks. In response, Tyrone repudiated the latest treaty with the crown and pledged himself to an alliance with Spain. The Spanish despaired of invading England but saw Ireland as a theatre where they might retaliate for Elizabeth's support for Dutch rebels.[73] The fleet sailed from Lisbon in October but was broken up by storms and wrecked off the coast of Galicia.[74] Tyrone was on his own.

That he survived was remarkable. The opening government gambit was to ring Ulster with forts and then tighten the noose. However, if placed patchily and supported half-heartedly, such garrisons were worse than useless. Henry Bagenal marched with 4,000 foot soldiers and 300 horsemen to relieve one such isolated garrison at a ford on the Blackwater in August 1598. Gaps opened in the straggling column and the marginally bigger combined hosts of O'Neill, O'Donnell and Maguire overwhelmed the vanguard and main body.

The English defeat at the battle of the Yellow Ford, so called after the crossing point of a stream where one of Bagenal's field guns became bogged down, was partly owing to the size of the Irish army. An English estimate suggested that all the Ulster confederates, squeezing their territories more efficiently, could put over 8,000 men in the field.[75] More shocking was the fact that Irish armies were better, as well as bigger. The kern or light infantrymen now hefted calivers rather than spears and could shoot straight: Bagenal was fatally shot in the face when he raised the visor of his helm to see about him.[76] Afterwards a clearly shaken Irish council warned: 'This rebellion is now thoroughly sorted to an Irish war . . . to shake off all English government.'

So it was. War now quickly spread across the country. Raids into County Limerick in October 1598 triggered a rising that 'broke out like a lightning' across Munster, with English settlers 'murdered, or stripped and banished', where they did not run for their lives to the nearest port.[77] The port towns and a handful of plantation castles – Kilmallock, Mallow Castle, Mogeely Castle and Lisfinny – held out amid the general destruction. Meanwhile Red Hugh O'Donnell set up a puppet MacWilliam Burke in Mayo and raided as far south as Thomond while 'the rebels of Leinster swarmed in the English Pale'.[78]

Tyrone's appeals for countrywide support invoked a common faith and fatherland, deploying terms such as Ireland and Irishmen with increasing frequency and deliberately unifying intent. Tyrone fought, in the words of Archbishop Peter Lombard, for 'the glory of God, the liberty of their country and their own security'. If such appeals struck a chord they threatened to transform regional disaffection into a coherent national movement.[79] The religious rhetoric was especially inflammatory. As discussed in the next chapter, the leaders of the Pale and the Munster towns had by now passed beyond sentimental and unreflecting loyalty to traditional Catholic rituals and consciously rejected Protestantism as 'the Devil's worship' and would not be browbeaten into swearing the oath acknowledging royal ecclesiastical supremacy which was a condition of taking up public office.[80] In the wake of the Yellow Ford some Anglo-Irish Catholics did support Tyrone, notably the Butler lords Mountgarret and Cahir. Yet most townsmen, Palesmen and Anglo-Irish lords remained aloof. Richard Nugent, baron Delvin, for instance, scathingly dismissed Tyrone's religious language as hypocritical posturing.[81] Tyrone had neither the spiritual weapons to compel support from the towns (Pope Clement VIII would not condemn Catholics who stood aloof) nor the siege guns to batter their walls.

His hope remained help from Spain. Philip III was constrained by near bankruptcy and the Duke of Lerma's lack of enthusiasm for Irish adventures, but helping his father's protégés appealed to the piety and sense of honour of the young king.[82] Moreover, the end of the war with France in 1598 made an Irish expedition a realistic proposition.[83] Buoyed up by Spanish gunrunning and promises of more help, Tyrone agreed with Spanish envoys to hold until July 1601.[84]

Elizabeth saw the gravity of the threat and sent what was, for the time and place, an enormous army of 17,300 men under her favourite, Robert Devereux, earl of Essex, in 1599. Notoriously, Essex squandered 'an army and a summer' when he turned south in what is usually written off as a futile march through Munster with half his army.[85] Essex was, in fact, a seasoned and professional commander and the march through Munster was by no means a futile exercise in coat trailing because it helped secure the province against a Spanish landing and reduced Lords Mountgarret and Cahir to obedience. The time was not quite ripe for his longer-term plan of a three-pronged attack on Ulster through Armagh, north Connacht and Lough Foyle.[86]

It would be left to Essex's successor, the bookish Charles Blount, Lord Mountjoy, who arrived in February 1600, to ship a 4,000-strong force to Lough Foyle under Sir Henry Dowcra. This proved the single most decisive move in reducing Ulster.[87] The disease-ridden soldiers were at first penned into a little fort at Derry, but they hung on until October 1600.[88] Then a dynastic rival of Tyrconnell's, Niall *Garbh* O'Donnell, switched sides and with his help the English expanded their foothold.[89] From Derry upriver to Dunalong and Lifford, the Foyle forts served as lightning rods for other malcontents besides Niall *Garbh*, constricted O'Neill, cut him off from O'Donnell and helped interdict supplies from Scotland. By the late summer of 1601 Red Hugh had been virtually driven out of Tyrconnell and Niall *Garbh* sat ensconced in Donegal Abbey, holding on against repeated Irish attacks. Meanwhile, Mountjoy had re-established the old Blackwater Fort, this time with other garrisons situated close enough for mutual support.[90]

Kinsale and after

After the collapse of the rising in Munster, the Ulster Lords sent a warning not to land there.[91] Too late: Águila, the Spanish commander, with a smallish army of 3,400 troops, made landfall at Kinsale, County Cork in September 1601.[92] Such a force landing in Donegal Bay (as had been Águila's original plan) would have turned the tables on Niall *Garbh* and Dowcra. Alternatively, a big army landing in the south would likely have encouraged or forced the Munster towns to revolt.[93] The Kinsale descent was too small and too far away.

Mountjoy reacted promptly, stripped his garrisons and had enough men near Kinsale by mid October to cut off the Spanish from the adjacent countryside.[94] For Tyrone and Tyrconnell to march south would be to leave Sir Arthur Chichester in Carrickfergus, Dowcra on the Foyle and Niall *Garbh* in Donegal Abbey.[95] They turned a deaf ear to Águila's pleas for help as long as they could but eventually relented:

> O'er many a river bridged with ice,
> Through many a vale with snowdrifts dumb,
> Past quaking fen and precipice,
> the Princes of the North have come.

The bitterly cold winter helped O'Donnell's army sidestep a blocking army and march over the frost-hardened Slieve Phelim mountains to join Tyrone near Kinsale.

Águila pressed the Irish to make a night march and occupy a ridge near the English siege lines surrounding the town. This would force Mountjoy to divide his army, whereupon Águila could attack from the direction of the town. The Irish march took an unaccountably long time and as dawn broke on Christmas Eve the vanguard and main battle had not quite reached the ridge while the rearguard lagged further behind.[96] Once

O'Neill saw enemy horsemen riding towards him he chose to move away from Kinsale and the chance for concerted action with Águila.[97] The Irish horsemen galloped off and 'broke fast through their own bodies of Foot'.[98] Each such body, or *tercio*, comprised around 2,000 soldiers in an unwieldy, rectangular block bristling with eighteen-foot pikes. Standing fast before charging horsemen demanded more steadiness and discipline than the Irish could maintain. A few hundred of Mountjoy's troopers scattered O'Neill's *tercio* and hacked at the fleeing soldiers and cut down around 1,000 of them.[99] No more than two or three Englishmen fell on the day.[100]

The wildy disproportionate outcome sounded 'the great death-gong of Irish history, echoing back and back into the hollow halls of the Celtic world'.[101] If O'Faolain's portentous assertion were true then Kinsale would not have been a tragedy at all but the inevitable extinction of a rigidly unchanging Gaelic way of life. On the contrary, it was a tragedy of 'arrested development' as a society belatedly developed the wherewithal to survive; namely, a degree of cohesiveness and common purpose, more ruthless and efficient extraction of resources, bigger armies and modern weapons.[102] The tragedy is all the more poignant because it could so easily have gone the other way. 'English power in that kingdom', confessed Mountjoy's secretary, Fynes Moryson, was saved 'by the providence of God'.

With the benefit of hindsight, Tyrone and Tyrconnell should have ignored the pleas of Águila's messengers and held off another few days. Cold and wet, Mountjoy's men, huddled together in their entrenched camps, were fast sickening of camp fevers: 6,000 of them died before the end of the siege. Mountjoy's horses had eaten all the forage and would have been sent away a few days after Christmas. The Irish could then have edged towards Kinsale free from the threat of cavalry.[103] This likely would have forced Mountjoy to raise the siege. Most Gaelic lords, tacking between loyalty and rebellion, would have promptly fallen in behind them. So, too, would the Munster townsmen. But tenuous communications by sea (the landing at Kinsale was their third attempt) and imperial over-stretch would have made it hard for the Spanish to hold on to Ireland when the English saw its loss as a mortal threat. It may be after all that 'an Irish victory at Kinsale would not have ended the war; it would have prolonged it'.[104] One cannot peer further through the mist of counter-factual speculation.

Kinsale confirmed that it was futile to fight on without assurance of sustained and dependable Spanish help.[105] Hugh O'Donnell took ship for Spain on 5 January to solicit further aid and four days later Águila capitulated. Philip III wanted to send a second and larger expedition of 14,000 men 'for the cause of religion and for the sake of my reputation' but in the meantime ignored O'Donnell's pleas to land a smaller expedition in Donegal Bay right away.[106]

After Kinsale, Dowcra won over Donal *ballach* O'Cahan, O'Neill's *uirrí* and son-in-law. Meanwhile, Dowcra's push from the Foyle Valley, Chichester's raids across Lough Neagh and Mountjoy's march via Blackwater Fort converged on the heart of Tyrone's lordship: 'The axe was nowe at the roote of the tree.'[107] Tyrone fled Dungannon and took to the woods for a further fourteen months with only a few hundred men. Chichester raided repeatedly across Lough Neagh in the depths of the winter of 1602–03, scouring the leafless woods of Glenconcoyne for O'Neill and destroying his followers with fire and sword. After one such raid, on the O'Quinns near Dungannon, Chichester exulted to his patron, Sir Robert Cecil, that '. . . we killed man, woman, child, horse, beast and whatever we found'.[108] 'It grieveth me,' confessed Thomas Phillips, another of Mountjoy's captains, that 'we kill so many churls'.[109]

Mountjoy wanted to kill Tyrone and end the war quickly, but 'never Traitor knew better how to keep his own head than this' he admitted in 1603.[110] He fretted about a succession crisis after the death of the aged and infirm Elizabeth, another Spanish landing, looming famine, a revolt in the towns provoked by currency debasement and religious disaffection, and above all financial exhaustion. With revenues eroded by the rampant inflation of her reign, Elizabeth was waging war in Ireland with not much more than one third of the income enjoyed by Henry VII in the mid 1540s. In 1600 spending on the Irish war swallowed over 85 per cent of her annual revenues.[111] She could not have borne the expense if Tyrone escaped to Spain and spurred Philip III to send another expedition. With just over a month to live, the dying queen authorised Mountjoy to offer Tyrone 'life, liberty and pardon'.[112]

Conclusion

The Tudor conquest, consummated days after the last of the Tudors passed away, was a major achievement. Elizabeth handed to her successor a kingdom united and secure from major internal threats. There was no inherent reason why a slower, less erratic and more consensual approach to government would not have worked just as well and at a lower human and financial cost. The natural beneficiaries and advocates of such gradualist reform would have been the 'well affected English-Irish', as Mountjoy described them.[113] Instead they were pushed out of the governorship, council, bench (the last surviving Catholic judge, Sir John Everard, would be dismissed in 1607) and later, municipal government. The local support base of the Dublin administration, then, was attenuated. This was the most dangerous, and most predictable, consequence of conquest.

Endnotes

1 Ellis 1998, p. 19.

2 Ellis 1995, p. 44.

3 Ellis 1998, p. 133; Lennon 2005, pp. 106–15.

4 Ellis 1998, p. 145.

5 'A Breviat of the Getting of Ireland . . .' in Walter Harris 1770, p. 89.

6 Nicholls 1972, p. 21; Ellis 1998, p. 248.

7 Kew 1998, p. 68; Falls 1950, p. 69.

8 Brady 1995, pp. 72–5; Ellis 1998, p. 112.

9 Ellis 1998, p. 149.

10 Ellis 1995, pp. 53–4.

11 Ellis 1998, p. 157.

12 O'Sullivan 2005, pp. 55–6; Nicholls 1999, p. 171.

13 Brady 1995, p. 75.

14 Ellis 1995, pp. 42, 71, 75, 258; Brady 1995, pp. 73–6.

15 Ellis 1995, p. 272.

16 Nicholls 1972, p. 27; Langford 1997, p. 511.

17 Nicholls 1999, pp. 172–3.

18 Brady 1996, pp. 38–9.

19 Ellis 1998, pp. 273, 275.

20 Russell 1996, pp. 263, 268–9.

21 Tawney 1922, p. 109.

22 Kenyon 1978, pp. 24–6.

23 Duffy 1992, pp. 95–6, 393, 458, 466.

24 Meigs 1997, p. 141.

25 Dickens 1974, p. 182.

26 Mullett 1998, pp. 19, 30: Such exceptions included, for instance, the concentration of seventeenth-century Welsh Catholicism in the counties adjacent to England.

27 Ford 1986, p. 50.

28 Derry 1970, pp. 88, 90.

29 Canny 1979, p. 433.

30 Ó Fiach 1969, p. 102; Ó Cuiv 1976, p. 509.

31 Ford 1997, p. 132; Ó Cuív 1976, p. 509.

32 Palmer 2001, p. 127.

33 Canny 1979, p. 438.

34 Dickens 1967, pp. 50–1.

35 Eisenstein 1983, pp. 153–4.

36 Falkiner 1904, p. 262; Carey 1999b, pp. 48, 50.

37 Lombard 1632, p. 7; Maley 1997, pp. 35–7.

38 Aalen 1997, p. 23; Ellis 1995, p. 33.

39 Ellis 1999, p. 465; Hazlett 2003, p. 98.

40 MacCraith 1996, p. 54; Barnard 2004, p. 205.

41 Hazlett 2003, p. 100.

42 Canny 1987, pp. 73, 75, 80; Brady 1994, p. 269.

43 Ellis 1998, p. 298; Lennon 2005, p. 215.

44 Edwards 1999, pp. 132–42; Ohlmeyer 1998b, pp. 124–47.

45 Ellis 1998, p. 293; Berleth 1978, pp. 42–7.

46 Carey 1999a, p. 321; Maxwell 1923, p. 236.

47 Ellis 1998, p. 285.

48 Brady 1994, p. 297.

49 Crawford 1993, pp. 369, 373–4.

50 Brady 1994, pp. 164, 166; Ellis 1998, p. 273.

51 Brady 1994, p. 242.

52 Ellis 1998, p. 355.

53 Bradshaw 1978a, pp. 64, 67.

54 Maginn 2003, pp. 230–1.

55 Morton 1971, p. 126.

56 Lennon 2005, p. 318; Mullet 1998, pp. 13–14.

57 Maginn 2003, p. 206.

58 McCormack 2005, pp. 150–1.

59 Hayes-McCoy 1976, pp. 108–9.

60 Canny 2001, pp. 129, 157; Loeber 1991, p. 49.

61 Ellis 1998, p. 327.

62 Sheehan 1982a, pp. 304, 306, 311–12.

63 Quinn 1966b, p. 28.

64 Sheehan 1982b, p. 115; McCarthy-Morrogh 1986, pp. 115–16; Quinn 1966b, p. 30.

65 Quinn 1966b, p. 24; Hayes-McCoy 1976, p. 113; Foster 1988, p. 67.

66 Cunningham 1984, pp. 1–14.

67 Hayes-McCoy 1976, pp. 115–16; Ellis 1998, p. 355.

68 O'Faolain 1942, p. 93.

69 Morgan 1993, pp. 33, 51.

70 Ellis 1998, p. 335; Morgan 1993, p. 139.

71 Morgan 1993, pp. 166, 274.

72 Morgan 1993, p. 219; Hayes-McCoy 1976, p. 122.

73 Parker 2002, p. 28.

74 Silke 1970, p. 5; Morgan 2004, p. 75; Garcia Hernán 2004, p. 56.

75 Falls 1950, p. 71.

76 Kew 1998, p. 68.

77 Maxwell 1923, p. 249; Quinn 1966b, p. 33.

78 Kew 1998, p. 112.

79 Lenman 2001, p. 127; O'Connor 2004, p. 60.

80 Bradshaw 1978a, pp. 50, 53.

81 O'Connor 2004, p. 25.

82 Recio Morales 2004, p. 94; Silke 1970, pp. 41, 50; Garcia Hernán 2004, p. 45.

83 Kerney Walsh 1986, p. 11; McGurk 1997, p. 263.

84 Hayes-McCoy 1976, p. 132.

85 Silke 1970, p. 57; Stewart 1991, p. 19; Hammer 2003, pp. 213–14.

86 MacCaffrey 1992, pp. 522–3.

87 Hayes-McCoy 1941, p. 269; McGurk 2004, p. 96.

88 McCavitt 1998, p. 45.

89 Stewart 1991, p. 29; Morgan 2004, pp. 85, 99.

90 McGurk 2004, p. 99.

91 Morgan 2004, pp. 82, 132.

92 Ellis 1998, p. 349.

93 Silke 1970, p. 7; Morgan 2004, p. 83; Fitzpatrick 1988, p. 7.

94 McGurk 2004, p. 151.

95 Hayes-McCoy 1969, pp. 154–6; Kelly 2003, pp. 60–1.

96 Morgan 2004, pp. 122, 125, 127–9.

97 Ellis 1998, p. 310; Hayes-McCoy 1969, p. 165.

98 Mc Donnell 2004, p. 273; Kew 1998, p. 69.

99 Morgan 2004, p. 122.

100 Hayes-McCoy 1969, pp. 162–8.

101 O Faolain 1947, pp. 84, 87.

102 Hayes-McCoy 1937, pp. 304–5.

103 Morgan 2004, pp. 3, 140.

104 MacCurtain 1972, p. 87; Morgan 2004, p. 4.

105 Edwards 2004, p. 292.

106 Kerney Walsh 1986, pp. 1, 22.

107 Bardon 1996, p. 64.

108 PRO.SP.63/208/ii, f. 68 Sir Arthur Chichester to Sir Robert Cecil. My thanks to John McGurk for this reference.

109 Carey 2004, p. 211; McGurk 1997, p. 261.

110 Cited in Nicholls 1990, p. 2336.

111 Hale 1985, p. 233; Kerney Walsh 1986, p. 27; Hammer 2003, p. 240.

112 Lee 2003, p. 314.

113 Lee 2003, p. 316.

CHAPTER 2

Consolidating conquest

The flight

When Tyrone submitted at Mellifont on the northern marches of the Pale in March 1603, he did not know that Elizabeth had died. Mountjoy was anxious to settle before he found out lest O'Neill claim, quite plausibly, that he had never been in rebellion against her successor, James VI of Scotland. His offer of due allegiance would have rendered submission unnecessary. Consequently, Mountjoy made two important concessions at Mellifont: he recognised Tyrone as the absolute owner of his lordship and accepted the earl's authority over O'Cahan, his chief *uirrí*.[1] Tyrone 'could not contain himself from shedding tears . . .' when Mountjoy revealed that the Queen was dead. On the face of it, Tyrone had little cause to weep.[2] He had lost the war but won the peace.

In April and May 1603, after hearing of Elizabeth's death, almost all the towns in Munster declared their independence of the provincial government. It would be anachronistic to see that episode as a belated response to Tyrone's appeal for religious and national unity. The townsmen complained of wartime disruption of trade, the settling of government debts in debased coinage and President Carew's unrelenting encroachment on traditional urban liberties. Religious disaffection was an undoubtedly important factor too.[3] In Munster, initial outward conformity tempered by vague religious conservatism had begun to harden into a 'knot of obdurate custom', as one Church of Ireland clergyman put it.[4] This more active form of religious identification was 'recusancy', so called from the explicit refusal to attend services of the state church.[5] The outward rejection of the state church was quite sudden. Between 1593 and 1595, for example, the size of congregations attending Cork cathedral fell from over 1,000 to a half-dozen, with a concurrent drying up of Protestant christenings, marriages and burial services.[6] This decade also saw the founding of Irish seminaries abroad at Salamanca (founded 1592), Lisbon (1593) and Douai (1594). It is probably not a coincidence that self-conscious recusancy emerged at a time when English government in Ireland was increasingly distracted by war and could not afford to crack down on the loyal inhabitants of the lordship.

The revolt was spontaneous and popular, arising from the supposition that James VI/I, son of the Catholic martyr Mary Queen of Scots, was sympathetic to Catholics. The many religious manifestations of revolt retrospectively illustrate the danger of the towns making common cause with Tyrone and the timeliness of the Mellifont agreement which left Mountjoy free to firmly quash revolt in each town. When the citizens of Waterford flourished a charter of King John to back their claim to close the city gates in front of Mountjoy's army, he threatened he would 'cut King John's Charter in pieces with King James's sword'.[7] Mountjoy asked them: 'What are you?' A priest in the delegation replied that he was 'a firm Catholic' but, like his fellow citizens, also 'a most loyal subject'.[8] By declining to recognize the king as head of the church but insisting they could still owe due temporal allegiance to him without compromising any religious principles, the citizens of Waterford were thus among the first to articulate a core belief of what would become known as the Old English community.[9]

James VI and I

Secret contacts between Elizabeth's Secretary of State Robert Cecil and James VI paved the way for a remarkably smooth accession whereby the two kingdoms of Ireland and England, united by their common ruler, now became three.[10] The accession of James VI of Scotland to the English throne in 1603 produced a union of crowns, but no union of kingdoms, a situation 'rich in unsettling ambiguity'.[11] James recognised that such ambiguity threatened the longer-term Stuart hold over either kingdom. That, and a characteristic impulse of grandiloquent vanity, underlay his enthusiasm for a constitutional and institutional union between England and Scotland. He dropped the project in the face of determined opposition (proposals for parliamentary union disappeared as early as 1604), but tried to promote the closest possible fusion based on consent, blur Anglo–Scottish distinctions and nurture a 'British' identity.[12] The multiple kingdoms were more contrasted than their relatively limited geographical range would suggest and in the longer term the greatest source of

instability would be religious diversity.[13] Each kingdom had its own majority religion: Catholic in Ireland, Episcopalian in England and Presbyterian
in Scotland. James was more concerned with outward obedience than with
the small print of religious conformity and a wide spectrum of theological
opinions was represented on the Jacobean bench of Anglican bishops. At
one end were Calvinistic 'Puritans', who favoured a Presbyterian form of
church government, and at the other were those who thirty years later
would be abused as 'Arminian', who bemoaned the neglect of ceremony
and stressed Episcopal authority. Not only did James's conciliatory policies
preserve the façade of a broad national church but he also took cautious
steps, culminating in the Articles of Perth (1618), to blur the distinctions
of organisation between the Scottish Kirk and the Church of England. It
could be argued that the differences lay 'only in the form of government of
the church and some ceremonies' while they were united by a common
written language and protestant culture based on the Geneva Bible.[14] Such
unity would be especially marked in Ireland where the Church of Ireland
absorbed Scots sufficiently well to remain intact.[15] Before the mid-1630s
the Church of Ireland demanded minimal conformity, merely that a minister read a token excerpt from the Common Prayer Book, while the church
articles of 1615 reflected the rigid Calvinism of the Lambeth Articles of
1596 which Elizabeth had refused to make official in England. The key
to Anglo–Scottish fusion was overriding protestant unity in the face of
the common papist threat. A successful fusion would not bode well for
Catholics in Ireland. This was especially so considering James's attitude
towards Gaeldom.

The Gaelic intelligentsia in Ireland hailed and legitimised their new
ruler as *ardrí* [high king]. The best-known example was Fearghal óg Mac
an Bhaird's *Trí coróna I gcairt Shéamais*, which valorised James as Éire's
husband and threw in a dollop of more commonplace flattery of this
'learned man' [*a fhir eóil na healadhna*].[16] The admiration was unrequited.
James's *Basilicon Doron*, penned as a guide to his son and heir, abused
all his Gaelic-speaking subjects in Scotland as 'barbarous'. The 'inland'
Gaelic-speaking highlanders made 'some show of civility', but those on the
western and northern islands were 'utterly barbarous'.[17] James's penchant
for planting colonies in the Gaelic western fringes of his realm is discussed
in the next chapter. For the present it is sufficient to note that James's
plantations did not take root and he did not persist with them after 1609.
His interventions elsewhere merely brought about shifts in the Gaelic
balance of power, notably the expansion of the Campbells at the expense
of the Mac Donalds of Islay and Kintyre, in which they did not, by and

large, oust Mac Donald tenants or lairds.[18] James's default policy was reformist and the Statutes of Iona (1609), co-opted nine clan chieftains into a decentralised system of government. It awarded them status and land in return for being answerable for their followers, embracing the protestant kirk and sending their sons off to be educated at lowland schools.[19] Would James's policy in newly conquered Ulster be based on plantation or reform?

The New English

Mellifont was a brittle settlement, the favourable terms a mismatch with the completeness of Tyrone's defeat. Most army officers and officials fumed that Mountjoy had betrayed them to 'that man who smileth in peace at those who did hazard their lives to destroy him'.[20] They dismissed Catholic protestations of loyalty as hollow and insisted that conformity in religion was an indispensable proof of loyalty. Mountjoy was recalled in 1605 and died the following year. Sir Arthur Chichester, a protégé of Cecil and one of the critics of Mellifont, took office as lord deputy in February 1605 and was in turn succeeded in 1614 by Oliver St John, who, like Chichester, had been an army captain. The servitor's uninterrupted occupation of the governorship from 1605 to 1622 was not greatly disturbed by the governorship of Henry Cary, Viscount Falkland (1626–29), a one-time confidant of Chichester. A New English class or group emerged at this point as a coherent group that would enjoy control of the governorship of Ireland, except for Falkland's period in office, until the arrival of Lord Deputy Wentworth in 1633.[21]

'No nation in Christendom they hate as they hate us New English, as they call us.' The complaint about the Irish by Vincent Gookin, a settler in west Cork, in 1633 serves as a reminder of the defensiveness that characterised Gookin's community and the fact that the name most commonly used to denote that community is not one the members would have chosen for themselves.[22] For present purposes 'New English' is a useful badge for a relatively small but rich and powerful grouping of Protestant stock as opposed to the settler population as a whole which, by 1640, may have amounted to as much as one tenth of the population.

The strength of the New English position rested on the possession of office and land, in that sequence. Even for Richard Boyle, Earl of Cork (d. 1643), who would become reputedly the wealthiest man in all the Stuart kingdoms, the first rung of the ladder was his appointment as a deputy escheator in 1590. Handling properties forfeit to the crown enabled him to discover flaws in land titles and profit on his own account.[23] It was a group that had a vested interest in pursuing a punitive policy against the former rebels and, indeed, Irish Catholic landowners in general.

The New English official in Ireland was often a younger son with little to support him but his pretensions and sometimes a violent misfit in the stable society of his birth. On the frontier, wielding the sword or quill, such men might do spectacularly well. Chichester and Sir John Davies, Irish Solicitor-General and later Attorney-General, are ideal examples of the type. Chichester fled to Ireland in his youth to escape arrest for robbing one of the Queen's purveyors. Pardoned, he served as a volunteer in the Cádiz expedition and was later sent to Ireland in command of a regiment. He was appointed governor of Carrickfergus in 1599, replacing his brother who had been killed by the neighbouring MacDonnells. Tyrone dismissed the corpulent Sir John Davies as 'more fit to be a stage player than a counsel', but this clown was violent and vindictive. He had been disbarred in 1597 for a coolly planned murderous attack on a fellow lawyer, complete with get-away boat and two swordsmen.[24]

Davies and Tyrone

It was for James and his Privy Council in London to determine policy and for the Dublin administration to implement it. In practice, the men on the spot enjoyed significant latitude. New English control of government was soon reflected in a change of policy embodied in a proclamation of March 1605 drafted by Davies. It declared that all subjects in Ireland were 'free, natural and immediate subjects of his majesty'.[25] On one reading, this represented the culmination of the long-standing efforts to extend English law. Ireland was now shired and the public peace thus proclaimed would be enforced by regular circuits of the judges on assize. More ominously, the proclamation was strengthened by legal rulings which denied any standing to customary Gaelic systems of tenure. With any parliament likely to be dominated by recusants, the government packed the Irish bench with English protestant lawyers. Davies was active among them in procuring judge-made law rather than parliamentary statutes to underpin government policies and in organising the assize circuits for Ireland.[26] The 1606 commission for remedying defective titles provided an opportunity for native landowners to secure clear title to their estates if they divided their holdings into clearly designated freeholds and tenancies. The commission, following on the March 1605 proclamation (and the October 1605 proclamation on religious conformity discussed below), gave officials the pretext to meddle in Ulster and harass the earls of Tyrone and Tyrconnell. The reading of the proclamations in O'Neill's own home at Dungannon must surely have driven the reality of defeat home to him.[27]

Davies revived the reorganisation of lordships that had been imposed in the 1590s in Counties Monaghan, Cavan and Fermanagh and had served as the proximate cause of the Nine Years War.[28] In the latter, for instance, the contending Maguire claimants were left with only the core or demesne lands of the lordship. It was Davies's intention to follow this precedent and break up Tyrone's lordship, in particular, and divest him of the ownership of the territories of subordinate septs. Tyrone anticipated this and divided his lordship into freeholds which he allocated to close relatives and loyal supporters, though Davies refused to accept Tyrone's nominees.[29] Rory O'Donnell was less adaptable and resilient: he lost his lands around Lifford, his 'only jewel', to Niall *Garbh* and skulked outside the lordship, 'very meanly followed'. Davies also called on the new Church of Ireland bishop of Derry, Clogher and Raphoe, George Montgomery, to identify the church lands belonging to the bishopric of Derry. Tyrone fumed that Montgomery 'seeketh not only to have from me unto him a great part of my lands' but incited others 'to call into question that which never heretofore was doubted to be mine and my ancestors'.[30] The 'other' lands in question were those of Donal *Ballach* O'Cahan, Tyrone's estranged son-in-law and *uirrí*. Montgomery persuaded O'Cahan to petition to hold his lands directly from the crown and Davies encouraged the claim as a way of prising a huge wedge of land away from Tyrone's lordship. In reality, Davies was pursuing a far more ambitious claim that ownership of O'Cahan's country was vested in the crown by virtue of Shane O'Neill's attainder in 1569–70. This was a test case that could be applied so that the crown could claim the freehold of all Tyrone's earldom. The council in Dublin found that O'Cahan's country was vested in the crown, but Tyrone won a major victory in having the final adjudication switched to London. Davies and Tyrone spent the year 1607 preparing their pleas for this crucial test case.

Davies also pressed a proposal to create a presidency of Ulster. This could have been the greatest weapon against residual Gaelic power. While county sheriffs, justices of assize, commissioners and their ilk were fleeting nuisances, a provincial president personified a much more serious threat of constant prying and interference.[31] In desperation, O'Neill wrote directly to the King in July 1606, importuning him not to appoint a president.[32] Tyrone also won this round. James responded by assuring him in September 1606 that he had no plans to create a presidency of Ulster.

Moreover the English Privy Council firmly warned Chichester not to harass Tyrone any further so long as he 'shall remain obedient to the state'.[33]

The 'Flight of the Earls'

The 'Flight of the Earls', as popularised by eighteenth-century Catholic historians, meant flight from charges of complicity in what they claimed was a trumped-up plot. Chichester's crackdown on recusants, discussed below, began in late 1605 and formed the backdrop to this sham plot, if such it was. In 1606 a Palesman, Christopher St Lawrence, 9th baron of Howth, allegedly called together Tyrone, Tyrconnell and Richard Nugent, Baron Delvin (the same man who had so contemptuously spurned Tyrone's overtures after the Yellow Ford), and they agreed 'to take up arms because of the imminent threat of destruction of religion'. St Lawrence's regiment had unmercifully pursued Tyrone's retreating soldiers through Munster, but the Palesman subsequently served under Henry O'Neill (Tyrone's son) in Flanders.[34] An alternative version is that they prudently turned down Howth's invitation, whereupon he unmasked himself as an agent provocateur and accused them of treasonable conspiracy.[35] Historians are unlikely to get to the bottom of the business. Rather than poison or the assassin's knife, catching an opponent in the tentacles of a treason plot was Cecil's (or Salisbury's as we should now call him) preferred way to eliminate opponents and its discovery through anonymous letters and an agent provocateur is suspiciously reminiscent of his *modus operandi*.[36]

In July 1607 James summoned O'Neill to London for his adjudication on the O'Cahan dispute. Until now the wily Tyrone had been able to counter the moves of his enemies in Dublin and enjoyed the apparent continued support of the King.[37] While riding to Dublin, Tyrone was overtaken by an invitation to join Maguire and Tyrconnell and their households, who were embarking in Lough Swilly for Spain: storms forced them to divert to Normandy. Tyrone made the fateful snap decision to turn back and embark with his erstwhile allies. At the time, he offered as an explanation the plea that the government would assume that he had been left behind by the fleeing lords to raise a rebellion when Tyrconnell returned with Spanish troops and supplies.[38] With Tyrone already under a cloud of suspicion because of what he later called Chichester's 'forged treason', it is likely that James would have suspected him of complicity in the flight of Maguire and Tyrconnell and (rightly) of treasonable correspondence with Spain.

What if he had gone on to London? He would probably have been arrested and lodged in the Tower of London. That was not as ominous as it might seem. Noblemen were not infrequently warded there and released, none the worse, if it proved politic to do so. However, the Spanish ambassador was well briefed by a spy in the Privy Council and reported to Madrid that 'they wish to kill him'.[39] One of the privy councillors, possibly Henry Howard, Earl of Northampton, may have tipped off O'Neill that the call to court was just a pretext to clap him in the Tower and 'not to let him linger there long'.[40]

Perhaps the enigmatic Tyrone planned to flee sooner or later and never believed that his enemies would ever rest after Mellifont. He had contemplated retreat before. In December 1602, just before Mellifont, he begged Philip III to send a warship to bring him and his followers 'safe from the fury of our enemies'.[41] Afterwards the earls and their confederates told the Spanish ambassador, in utmost secrecy, that they would wait for two years after the Spanish and English signed a peace treaty in 1604 to see whether it would last before asking for a ship to take them abroad to safety.[42] The two years were up. It is doubtful whether O'Neill could have hung on for another five years until Salisbury, his most powerful and implacable enemy, died.[43] Tyrone's flight, then, may have been a 'planned tactical retreat' to solicit Spanish aid in person. While the Spanish were no longer at war with James I, diplomatic relations remained strained as the latter continued to help the Dutch rebels covertly until April 1609.

The 'Flight of the Earls' was the defining catastrophe of early modern Ireland: 'Woe to the heart that mediated, woe to the mind that conceived, woe to the council that decided on the project of their setting out on this voyage' lamented the compilers of the Four Masters some thirty years later.[44] By sailing from Lough Swilly in 1607, Tyrone, Tyrconnell and Maguire exposed Ulster to a radical experiment in social engineering: plantation. An exiled Tyrone 'is far better', confided Chichester to Salisbury, 'than if he were in the Tower of London'.

Chichester and recusancy

Recusancy is the key to understanding why the 'Anglo–Irish' of the 1580s were, less than a generation later, 'Old English'. During that time most of them moved from outward conformity or 'church papistry' to this more emphatic identification.[45] Emphatic and substantially new: the pre-Reformation church in Ireland was just as much in need of reform as anywhere else.[46] That said, some healthy parts bridged the gap between conservatism and recusancy and Observant Franciscans, in particular, maintained and regained high standards and were 'almost adored, not only by the peasants but by the lords', claimed the Spanish ambassador in London.[47] An emphatic and positive religious commitment was far harder to obliterate than traditionalism. Harder, but not impossible: two ways existed, though not as mutually exclusive alternatives: 'the sword alone without the word is not sufficient', admitted Adam Loftus, Archbishop of Dublin (1567–1605).

The word

An Irish Dominican comforted himself for the discomfort and danger of his mission to western Scotland in the 1620s with the reflection that his flock 'detest Protestantism as a new religion'.[48] Here he put his finger on the key weakness of the reformers. To be new was to lack the legitimacy of time-honoured practice. The challenge for the Protestant reformer was to convince his audience that what he preached was not an upstart and alien heresy but the pure doctrine and practice of the 'primitive' or early church. Richard Davies in his 1567 'letter to the Welsh Nation' claimed that Joseph of Arimathea, no less, had planted the faith in all its gospel purity in Britain and it was the English who later dragged the Welsh into the mire of Roman idolatry.[49] James Ussher tried to fabricate a comparable Irish origin myth in his *Discourse of the Religion Anciently Professed by the Irish and Scottish* of 1622 and was adamant that a reformed Church of Ireland was a native growth from an originally pure Celtic church.[50] Conversely, Irish Catholic writers insisted on the continuity of their church in Ireland from the time of Saint Patrick.[51] A tract on the sacrament of penance by Hugh MacCaughwell or Aodh Mac Aingil (the third book in Irish produced by Catholic clergy, it was published at Louvain in 1618) reassured readers: 'This is not new learning I bring you but the same tune of penance which Patrick played' [*Ní nuailéighionn do-bheirim dhuit, acht an seanphort aithridhe do dhéinn Pádraig*].

The 1603 publication of a translation of the New Testament from Erasmus's Greek text into Irish was a promising start to evangelical activity. The project had taken a quarter of a century and was completed by William O'Donnell, Archbishop of Tuam (1609–28).[52] This was an impressive achievement when one considers that it preceded the definitive King James version of the English-language Bible and it preceded by eight years the first Catholic publication in Irish, Bonaventure O'Hussey's *Teagasg Críosdaidhe*. O'Donnell followed up in 1608 with an Irish version of the

Book of Common Prayer. Yet fewer and fewer Protestant clergymen had the linguistic skills to use these aids to reach out to an overwhelmingly Irish-speaking population at a time when, as James observed, the 'simple' Gaelic Irish might well be more malleable than the 'unconformable English' of the towns and the Pale.[53] He may well have been right. Contempt for the 'Lutheran leprosy' took root first in the towns and swept Gaelic Ireland only afterwards.[54]

For all Ussher's rhetorical assertions of Irishness, potential converts in Jacobean Ireland would encounter Anglicanism through an alien clergy and language. Native clergy supplied the backbone of the Church of Ireland ministry into the early seventeenth century. Their New English bishops often dismissed them as ignorant time-servers: 'fitter to keep hogs than serve in the church', was how one of them dismissed native clergy on a visitation of Cashel and Emly (**map 9**) in 1607.[55] Bishops usually recruited English and Scottish clergy to replace native clergy who increasingly comprised a lower stratum of older 'reading' ministers regarded as unfit to preach and usually assigned poorer livings. To take three examples from a 1615 episcopal visitation: the forty-two parishes in County Carlow were manned by nineteen resident clergymen, of whom seven were Irish, while Killaloe had only nine Irish clergymen (to guess from surnames) among the twenty-six resident clergy, a figure that fell to six by 1634, and the joint dioceses of Killala and Achonry had five reading ministers and one preacher, all natives before two successive Scots bishops packed the see with their countrymen.[56]

The fledgling Trinity College Dublin had not yet begun to turn out local graduates in big numbers, so there were relatively few preaching ministers countrywide, with over half of them located in Ulster.[57] The increasing proportion of English and Scots clergy among them usually could not speak and would not learn Irish. The gaelicisation of the Reformation suffered from 'paralysing ambivalence' as the link between anglicisation and the Anglican Church came to seem axiomatic.[58] This link may have been strengthened by predestination thinking which claimed the elect were few and the reprobates many.[59] It was all too comforting for clergymen to identify this godly minority with the Protestant community in Ireland and assume that few or no Irish were elected since they 'shut their ears'. They tacitly agreed, claims Bradshaw, to let them 'go to hell their own way'.[60]

The sword: mandates

The Church of Ireland articles of 1615 explicitly identified the Pope with Antichrist. This was not a scriptural metaphor but a settled conviction that the Pope was 'that man of sin foretold in the holy scriptures'.[61] When George Downham, Bishop of Derry (1617–34), equated 'Antichristians' and 'recusant papists' and thundered that they should not be 'spared', he was expressing what his colleagues implicitly believed.[62] Most of them were convinced the root of the recusancy problem lay in wilfulness rather than ignorance. The fateful legacy of St Augustine to the western Christian tradition was that obdurate heretics should be forced into the 'outward obedience' of attending church. This would not be an act of conversion, a product wholly of God's grace, but it did at least expose them to the grace of God.[63]

James professed that while he would rejoice if Irish Catholics conformed, he would not force them by 'violent compulsion', believing that persecution was the mark of a false church.[64] The sentiments echoed those of his predecessor, but James had a reputation for papist sympathies to live down.[65] Nor did he accept that allegiance was divisible between pope and monarch. The oath of allegiance, passed by the English parliament after the Gunpowder Plot, when maverick English Catholics tried to blow up the Houses of Parliament, was his main weapon against English recusants and required those taking the oath to deny that the Pope could, as of right, depose monarchs or dispense subjects from allegiance to him. The proposition was explicitly condemned by the Pope and was not one which a conscientious Catholic could accept.[66]

It was probably English pressures that led him to disavow any intention of granting religious toleration in Ireland and to back Chichester's persecution plans. Other than the shilling fine for not attending services imposed by the Act of Uniformity of 1560, there were no laws in Ireland to, as Chichester put it, 'reclaim' Papists.[67] A firmly Protestant parliament in England had reinforced Elizabethan legislation. A 1606 law tightened up on occasional conformists and stipulated that those who refused to come to services of the established church had to pay the enormous fine of £20 a month.[68] In Ireland, where parliament was not yet Protestant, the next important anti-recusancy law would not be added until 1653.[69]

Chichester, Davies, Loftus, Lord Chancellor, and Thomas Jones, Bishop of Meath, drew up a concerted plan to sidestep statute law and use the royal prerogative instead. At the end of September 1605 Lord Deputy Chichester issued a proclamation banishing Catholic priests and next sent a royal 'mandate' to sixteen wealthy Catholic aldermen of Dublin ordering them to attend Protestant services. The policy was to be exemplary and Chichester settled on the capital as 'the lantern of this whole kingdom' and picked on the wealthy as 'those by whose example the rest of the people are most led'.[70] A shilling a week would not cripple a wealthy and determined recusant but after three refusals he could find himself before the Court of Castle Chamber which could impose cripplingly heavy fines, confiscate property or imprison him for however long it chose, as the first sixteen victims duly found out.[71] Sir Patrick Barnewall, a friend and kinsman of Tyrone's, led a delegation of Palesmen to London to argue that the mandates were unlawful. Their mission coincided with the panic that followed the discovery of the Gunpowder Plot. James turned a deaf ear to their protests and on their return Chichester imprisoned the chief petitioners.[72]

In January 1606 the English Privy Council tried to rein in Chichester with Salisbury cautioning him to calm the 'strong discontent of the towns'.[73] Meanwhile, Sir Henry Brouncker, Lord President of Munster, enthusiastically issued mandates and demanded the Oath of Supremacy from municipal officials, deposing those who refused, including five successive mayors of Waterford, and levying heavy fines.[74] This success inspired Chichester and his administration to ignore warnings from London and reactivate persecution towards the end of 1606, with a number of Catholics fined in the Court of Castle Chamber for skipping Church of Ireland services. As word of this reached London the English Privy Council, worried about whispers of the supposed conspiracy by the Earl of Tyrone to raise the Pale in revolt with the backing of Spanish troops, sharply rebuked Chichester.[75] The mandates campaign and complicity in the plot, sham or real, certainly played a part in convincing Tyrone to flee Ireland.[76] The death of Henry Brouncker in May 1607 effectively brought this first spasm of persecution to an end; Catholics were pleased to spread tales Brouncker 'died raving and eating his flesh from his arms, lamenting his rigour against recusants'.[77] The lull lasted for three years while government's attention was distracted by the Flight of the Earls and the opportunities that event opened up.[78] After that lull, Chichester, having covered his back by getting explicit orders from London, set about renewing multifaceted persecution.[79]

The shilling fine for non-attendance was more widely imposed on the lower classes and no fewer than 2,000 Catholics may have been fined in County Meath alone in 1616, while fines from nine Dublin parishes during a nine-month period in 1617–18 amounted to over £2,500.[80] Before they were suspended in 1621, recusancy fines degenerated into an extortion racket rather than an instrument of religious change when ministers or their bailiffs let parishioners pay them off to avoid being presented for recusancy.[81] It was especially tempting to squeeze such revenues when, outside Ulster, so many livings were 'impropriate' or in the hands of laymen who owned the tithes and who, if they were Catholic, were not likely to pay tithe income to a Protestant pastor.[82] In addition to recusancy fines, tithes and church courts also bore down heavily on the native population. Tithes were often quite substantial, especially when farmed to extortionate bailiffs, while the scope for prosecutions by church courts was very wide because Catholics resorted to their own clergy for christenings, marriages and funerals.[83]

Chichester targeted priests as well as people. Catholicism 'simply cannot subsist' without priests.[84] The example of the western Highlands and Islands of Scotland showed what could happen without them, with extensive areas drifting from formal religious practice until this was reorganised by Presbyterians. The surviving pockets of Catholicism today, such as the Hebridean islands of Barra and South Uist, lay in the footsteps of the handful of intrepid early seventeenth-century missionaries. Banishing priests became almost a conditioned reflex, the very repetition of such decrees suggesting they were ineffectual. Chichester would have liked to give teeth to his 1605 banishment decree by making non-compliance punishable as treason, though his most prominent victim, the Franciscan Bishop Conor O'Devany of Down and Connor, was arraigned for facilitating Tyrone's flight four years earlier. The spectacle of his public execution outside Dublin was to be exemplary. So it was, but hardly in the way Chichester had hoped. The hagiographical accounts have the eighty-year-old O'Devany showing an edifying steadiness as he disputed in Latin with the attending Protestant ministers before switching to Irish to exhort the throng that 'the only crime they found in him was the exercise of his functions among the faithful'.[85] The clouds parted to unveil a blood-red sun:

They cut short his speech, and he was thrown off [the scaffold] and while yet half alive, his head was cut off and he was quartered. The faithful collected with great daring his blood and garments, and did not leave a single hair on his head or face, without the heretics being able to prevent them.[86]

If the mob venerates O'Devany as a martyr, growled Chichester, 'I will soon give them plenty more'. But he did not repeat this impolitic display.

In all, James's government put to death only five clerics, all of them members of religious orders. Chichester did not explicitly admit the distinction between regular and secular clergy, but later governors would and they bore down harder on the members of monastic orders like the

Franciscans, Dominicans or counter-Reformation orders like the Jesuits. Their international organisation and resources left them less amenable to government control and they were well placed and usually willing to act as agents and spies for Spain and, later, other foreign powers. Domestically, they were a more formidable foe. The prestige of regulars, and Franciscans in particular, remained high among the Irish during the seventeenth century. Regulars, by and large, were better educated than the secular clergy and the foundation of colleges at Louvain (1606), Rome (1625) and Prague (1630) provided secure bases where young friars could be trained. They benefited from Rome's predominant view of Ireland as a mission field falling under the ambit of *Propaganda Fide* where it was thought best to confer freedom of action on the religious orders, 'Catholicism's commandos'.[87] They enjoyed unusually wide faculties covering matrimonial dispensations, plenary indulgences, dispensation of penitents from offences, permission to celebrate mass outdoors and to administer the sacraments. Yet the friars also were responsive to traditional Irish forms of piety, especially the interment rituals; no lay person would wish to be buried without being clothed in a religious habit and buried in the grounds of an old monastic foundation.

A contemporaneous estimate counted close to 1,000 Catholic priests in Ireland in 1609, over fourth fifths of them secular clergy.[88] This total was small compared with the numbers after Chichester's deputyship when his successors, for various reasons, generally avoided persecuting Catholic clergymen. Chichester's policy of exemplary terror worked.

Conclusion

The New English emerge in Chichester's governorship as a class or group with a clear sense of purpose and identity. They, and especially the servitor or military element among them, condemned Mellifont as a betrayal. Davies devised an ingenious legal strategy to harass Tyrone and his confederates and break their residual power. More ambitiously, they simultaneously orchestrated a determined and well-orchestrated attack on recusancy using judge-made law and prerogative royal power rather than parliamentary statute. James and the English Privy Council remained fearful of renewed revolt and Spanish intervention in Ireland and, in pursuing both projects, the aggressiveness of the Dublin administration tested the limits of its authority. The wider project of stamping out recusancy failed, but the harassment of the Ulster confederates succeeded beyond expectations. The consequences of both success and failure would be fateful.

Endnotes

1 Canny 1987, p. 150; McCavitt 2002, p. 3.

2 Canny 1970, pp. 252, 256; McCavitt 2002, p. 50.

3 Gillespie 2006, p. 39.

4 Ford 2006, p. 101.

5 Bottigheimer 1985, p. 197.

6 Ford 1986, p. 58.

7 Sheehan 1983, pp. 11–12.

8 Ford 2001, p. 1.

9 Canny 1987, p. 155.

10 Miller 2004, p. 26.

11 Morrill 1996, p. 74.

12 Galloway 1986, p. 165.

13 Smith 1998, p. 5.

14 Kenyon 1978, pp. 24–6; Dawson 1995, pp. 102–3; Trevor Roper 1987, p. 58.

15 McCafferty 2002, pp. 199–203.

16 Ó Buachalla 1992, pp. 164–5; O'Riordan 1997, pp. 69–70.

17 Croft 2003, p. 138; Rhodes 2003, p. 222.

18 Lenman 2001, pp. 153–6; Wormwald 1981, pp. 164–5.

19 Croft 2003, pp. 139, 147; Schama 2001, p. 32.

20 Robinson 2000, p. 38; Hayes-McCoy 1976, p. 137.

21 Canny 1987, p. 157.

22 *CSPI* (1901), p. 182.

23 Canny 1982b, pp. 5–6.

24 McCavitt 2002, p. 56; Litton Falkiner 1909, p. 37; Kerney Walsh 1986, p. 38.

25 Morton 1971, p. 123.

26 Canny 1987, pp. 158–9.

27 Falls 1936, p. 91.

28 Canny 1971, pp. 383, 385.

29 Canny 1987, pp. 161–2.

30 Kerney Walsh 1986, pp. 38, 44.

31 Canny 1971, p. 389.

32 Lenman 2001, pp. 156–8.

33 McCavitt 1998, p. 136.

34 McGowan-Doyle 2004, p. 189.

35 Lynch 1667, p. 186; Reilly 1742, p. 9.

36 Edwards 2005, pp. 215, 295–6.

37 Canny 1971, pp. 262, 399.

38 Lenman 2001, p. 158.

39 Kerney Walsh 1996, pp. 51–2.

40 Kerney Walsh 1986, pp. 30–1, 40, 46.

41 Smith 1996, p. 20.

42 Kerney Walsh 1986, pp. 33–6.

43 Kerney Walsh 1996, pp. 54, 59, 111–16.

44 Nicholls 1990, p. 2359.

45 Bottigheimer 1985, p. 197; MacCurtain 1972, p. 125.

46 Hazlett 2003, pp. 90–1.

47 Ó Clabaigh 2002, p. 157; Mullett 1998, pp. 4–10.

48 Mullett 1998, p. 53.

49 Williams 1999, p. 245.

50 Ford 1998, p. 205; Gillespie 2006, pp. 86–7.

51 Cunningham and Gillespie 1995, p. 86.

52 Hazlett 2003, pp. 100–3.

53 Ford 1986, pp. 59, 62.

54 Corish 1981, p. 31; Bradshaw 1975, p. 47.

55 Ford 1986, p. 54.

56 Ryan 1833, pp. 144–5; O'Dowd 1991, p. 108.

57 Gillespie 2006, p. 67.

58 Ford 1997, p. 132; Ó Cuív 1976, p. 509.

59 Ford 1986, p. 69.

60 Bradshaw 1978a, pp. 480–1, 489, 502.

61 Trevor Roper 1987, p. 132; McCafferty 2002, p. 195.

62 Ford 1986, p. 67.

63 Ford 2006, pp. 100–5; Greaves 1997, p. 15.

64 Miller 2004, p. 60.

65 Clarke and Edwards 1976, pp. 190–1; Somerset 1997, p. 763.

66 Ford 2001, pp. 3–9.

67 Meehan 1872, p. 142.

68 Gillespie 2006, p. 41.

69 Ford 2006, p. 96.

70 McCavitt 1998, p. 116.

71 Corish 1981, p. 30.

72 Ford 2006, p. 126; Falls 1936, p. 97.

73 Kerney Walsh 1986, pp. 41, 50.

74 Gillespie 2006, p. 41.

75 McCavitt 1998, pp. 118, 124; McCavitt 2002, p. 87.

76 McCavitt, 1998, p. 132.

77 Ford 2006, p. 97; Hogan 1881, pp. 175–6; *CSPI* 1874a, p. 188; 1874b, pp. 33–5, 101–4.

78 McCavitt 1998, pp. 172, 174; McCavitt 2002, p. 178.

79 McCavitt 2002, p. 178.

80 Ford 2006, p. 120; Moran 1884b, p. 217; McCavitt 2002, p. 179.

81 Ford 1995, p. 86; Gillespie 2006, p. 68.

82 Gillespie 2006, p. 67.

83 Ford 1995, p. 87.

84 Mullett 1998, p. 9.

85 Moran 1884b, cvi–cviii, cxx.

86 Moran 1874, pp. 25, 126.

87 Mullett 1998, p. 65.

88 Flynn 1993, p. 138.

CHAPTER 3

Plantation 1608–22

Theory

The early Tudor strategy of state formation gradually assimilated outlying territories through the imposition of English administrative structures and common law, by building towns and promoting 'civility'. Initially Ireland was seen as a backward borderland with most of its inhabitants, the native Irishman, held back by environmental influences like the pastoralism that supposedly encouraged footloose idleness and thieving.[1] This relatively benign image gave way to perceptions of the Gael as inherently barbarous rather than circumstantially backward. A facile characterisation of civil and barbarous drew on classical models of barbarism, on Atlanticist or colonial analogues and, above all, on the wonder stories of the *Topographia Hiberniae* and *Expugnatio Hibernica* written by the twelfth-century cleric Giraldus Cambrensis.[2] 'Plantation' epitomised the requisite violent and radical response to irreformability. The first plantations in this sense date from 1570–73 and include Sir Thomas Smith's plantation in the Ards peninsula and the Earl of Essex's effort around Carrickfergus.

Better known to modern readers than Giraldus is the poet Edmund Spenser. The dialogue of two Englishmen in his 1596 *View of the Present State of Ireland* presents a complete ideology of conquest in which the crown is to be a conscious promoter of radical change.[3] The interlocutors companionably agree that the gradualist programme of using law as an instrument of reform was founded on a false premise that the Gael was ready for the common law. Rather, '. . . laws ought to be fashioned unto the manner & conditions of the people to whom they are meant'. The contempt of Spenser and others like Fynes Moryson is unrelenting and runs from clothing and farming practices to sexual behaviour: the Irish 'abhor from all things that agree with English civility'.[4] Much of this abuse was based on misunderstanding. For example, that much execrated practice of ploughing by the tail of the draught animal was used only to winnow out stones from land already opened.[5]

So, 'it is in vain to speak of planting laws', insists Irenius, 'for all those evils must first be cut away with a strong hand before any good can be planted'.[6] What Spenser means is scorched earth and famine of the kind that Lord Deputy Grey inflicted on Munster during the Desmond rising:

Out of every corner of the woods and glens they came creeping forth, upon their hands for their legs would not bear them; they looked like anatomies of death; they spoke like ghosts crying out of their graves, they did eat of the dead carrion, happy were they that could find them.

The often quoted passage is not evidence of Spenser's soft-heartedness. Rather, he emphasises that this was a necessary shock for native society and implicitly criticises the Queen for flinching from pursuing this further.[7] The next stage is to plant military colonies, dissolve existing clan groups and resettle the native among the English on the new estates or in towns where he can be bound up to an 'honest trade', 'quite forget his Irish nation' and embrace Protestantism.

At the time it was published in 1612, Davies's *Discoverie* was more influential than Spenser's *View*, which was not published until 1633 and then in fragmentary form. The *Discoverie* explains why the conquest took so many centuries, illustrating the barbarity of the Irish along the way. While Davies drew heavily on Spenser, he ostensibly differs in that he disclaimed any notion that the Irish were inherently incorrigible.[8] The mask slips when he abuses them as 'very beasts' or 'little better than cannibals'.[9] 'So,' concludes Davies, 'a barbarous countrie must be first broken by a warre.'

For the husbandman must first breake the Land, before it bee made capable of good seed: and when it is thoroughly broken and manured, if he do not forthwith cast good seed into it, it will grow wilde againe and beare nothing but weeds.[10]

The farming metaphor makes explicit the fragility of plantation. The unwanted seeds could spring up and choke the crop. The degeneracy of the medieval English settlers offered a compelling warning. Accounts of Gaelic life by Moryson or Davies ooze such contempt that they are hard put to explain why such a repugnant life could be so dangerously seductive and cause 'degeneracy' or backsliding by English colonists from the higher state of civility characteristic of their 'genus' or people.[11]

Degeneracy could be avoided and English speech and customs preserved by social separation. 'The way to perform that,' said Chichester, 'is to separate the Irish by themselves . . .'[12] Social segregation would be achieved by physical separation on the ground. Chichester was writing in the context of planning the Ulster plantation and he advocated that land blocks allotted to natives should be intermixed with those awarded to planters so the Irish 'may be environed with seas, strongholds and powerful men to overstay them'. The next stage was to 'utterly destroy the customs and practices of the natives' with the ultimate aim that the next generation of Irish would 'in tongue and heart and every way else become English'.[13]

Other rationalisations were grafted on to persuade a reluctant government. Plantation would unlock the productive potential of the Gaelic landscape, opening natural resources like woodland and fisheries for exploitation, and Ireland 'will hereafter bee as fruitfull as the land of *Canaan*'. Plantation would create the conditions for Protestant clergymen to preach rather than use 'terror and sharp penalties' which made Protestantism 'hated before it be understood'. A planted Ireland could absorb the 'idle poor' with whom England was considered to be over-populated.[14]

The most influential plantation theorist of all was James VI himself. His proposals to plant the Gaelic Western Isles in his *Basilicon Doron* neatly resolve the apparent contradiction between acculturation and separation. He advocated:

. . . planting colonies among them of answerable In-Land subjects, that within short time may reform and civilize the best inclined among them; rooting out or transporting the barbarous and stubborn sort.[15]

By 'inland' James meant English-speaking lowlanders and some Gaelic-speaking highlanders living well away from the utterly barbarous islands and west coast. They would found burghs, pay long-withheld rents, stimulate the economy and serve as a model for the natives, or at any rate those natives left to emulate them. Those natives who could not be won over by such examples of civility would be forced out. Ominously, James was given to anti-Gaelic 'genocidal fantasies', especially about Clan Mac Donald, Clan MacLeod and the Mac Iains of Ardnamurchan. In 1597, for instance, he offered the Marquess of Huntly, chief of Clan Gordon, the 'North Isles' (those north of Ardnamurchan, other than Skye and Lewis) on condition that he wipe out their entire populations.[16] The plan came to nothing. Repeated attempts by merchant adventurers from Fife to establish a plantation on Lewis between 1598 and 1609, foundered on the hostility of the local MacLeods. James was a grandiloquent but 'timorous' visionary who 'alters course with every breeze' and could be deflected by difficulties or determined opposition.[17] Such opposition no longer existed in Ulster after the Flight.

Practice

The attainder of O'Neill, O'Donnell and Maguire after the Flight presented the crown with a sizeable land bank.[18] It would grow even bigger. The loyalist Sir Cahir O'Doherty of Inishowen fell under suspicion of plotting to revolt with help from Spain and laid complaints before Chichester in November 1607 of harassment by Sir George Paulet, the abrasive governor of Derry. His arrival in Dublin came just days after Baron Delvin (imprisoned on suspicion of involvement in the Howth plot) clambered down a rope and escaped from Dublin Castle.[19] Chichester professed to suspect O'Doherty of collusion and threw him into prison. Released on a heavy bail, O'Doherty simmered but continued to cooperate with the English, chairing the jury that indicted Tyrone of treason in January 1608. Four months later he overran the new town of Derry and Culmore Fort and slaughtered Paulet's garrison. Niall *Garbh* O'Donnell may have promised to rise in support of O'Doherty but in the end did not do so.[20] Denounced for treason by his mother-in-law (none other than Fionnuala *Iníon Dubh*, mother of Red Hugh), Niall *Garbh* was arrested along with Donal *Ballach* O'Cahan. The latter was implicated on the thin pretext that he was in league with Tyrone. Both were packed off to the Tower of London where they languished until they died.[21] Together, O'Doherty and O'Donnell would have raised a dangerous revolt, the blame for goading them would have fallen on Chichester and he would likely have been recalled. As it was, all was forgiven when Chichester stamped out the revolt and O'Doherty was killed by one of his own men for the price on his head.[22] The last act was played out at a little fort on Tory Island held by a dozen men. To secure his own pardon the constable of the fort killed three of his men, but was cut down by a fourth who was then stabbed to death by a fifth. The English pardoned the survivors. It was a fitting epilogue to the disunity and duplicity of Gaelic Ireland.

Throughout 1608 the technicalities of planting Ulster were put in place. The wedge with which Davies originally hoped to pry Tyrone's lordship apart was the claim that he and other Gaelic lords owned only their demesne and mensal estates but not the lands of their 'freeholders' in cadet branches or subordinate septs. Now his crocodile tears for freeholders dried up and he assumed the Gaelic lords owned their entire lordships after all. Hence, 'the treason of the few justified the expropriation of all'.[23] This sleight of hand opened up 4 million acres of land in Counties Donegal, Fermanagh, Tyrone, Armagh, Cavan and Coleraine. The latter was re-named County Londonderry and was set aside for the London Merchant Companies. The six escheated counties were initially surveyed by inquisition and the survey was sent to London in mid-1608 to inform the detailed plans being devised there. The following year the escheated lands were resurveyed, mapped and divided into precincts. Meanwhile, the King and his Privy Council in London deliberated about the structures of the new society they would create.[24] They did not want for English advice that the purpose of any plantation should, variously, be to absorb the poor, earn profits and secure against rebellion. However, the Privy Council mainly drew on the advice of New English administrators, especially Chichester and Davies.

Chichester initially used the late sixteenth-century freeholding of County Monaghan as revived in 1606 as a precedent for a plantation that would remove Irish landowners from the control of greater lords. He expressed only lukewarm support for the radical alternative of driving all the natives 'as near as we may' out of Counties Tyrone, Donegal and Fermanagh (before O'Doherty's rising only three counties were to be planted) across the Bann, Blackwater and Erne.[25] While loyal natives would be rewarded with most of the planted land, 'servitors' or soldiers would get the lion's share of the choice land. Late in 1608 a committee was appointed in London, with Davies and Bishop Montgomery among its members, to draw up a detailed scheme of plantation. Davies succeeded in adding a stronger element of social engineering by introducing enough new settlers to outnumber the natives.[26] The original 'projecte for the devision and plantacon of the Escheated Landes . . .' drawn up in London in January 1609, as slightly revised and clarified by the printed book of conditions published in April 1610, set out three categories of grantee.[27]

First came chief 'undertakers' handpicked by James, who got the largest portions of 2,000–3,000 acres. English chief 'undertakers' would be joined by an equal number of Scottish chief undertakers of 'rank and quality'.[28] James was dazzled by the prospect of a joint English and Scottish civilising enterprise in Gaelic Ulster that could serve as the crucible of Britishness and the inclusion of the Scottish undertakers reflects his personal influence. Some of his key officials charged with civilising the western seaboard of Scotland were now to be involved in Ulster. Andrew

Stewart Lord Ochiltree was an undertaker in the precinct of Mountjoy in east County Tyrone, Andrew Knox, Bishop of the Isles, was given (in addition!) the diocese of Raphoe (**map 9**). Ludovic Stewart, Duke of Lennox, played a leading part in the plantation of Lewis in 1598 and received a great portion in the precinct of Portlough in County Donegal. The newly coined term 'British' had some official currency to encompass both English and Scottish interests in Ireland and this inclusive term would be most commonly deployed at times of crisis such as the 1640s and after 1688 to promote Protestant solidarity and blur distinctions between the English and the Scots.[29] These chief undertakers then chose other undertakers for their precincts who received relatively small (compared with Munster plantation grants) blocks of 1,000–2,000 acres, not including bogs and mountains, and bound themselves to build entirely British communities within nucleated and defensible settlements. They were explicitly barred from keeping Irish tenants. The 120 or so undertakers were expected to be on their land by September 1610. On every 1,000 acres they promised to settle 24 able-bodied Scots or English families; two of the families were to be freeholders, three leaseholders and the rest cottiers. Undertakers had to muster their tenants twice a year, arm them and build fortifications inside three and a half years. The size depended on the scale of the grant: undertakers of 2,000 acres, for example, had to build a small castle of stone or brick, with a stone wall surrounding it. Every proportion should have a parish church with glebe lands and tithes reserved for the incumbent clergyman. If the undertaker did not comply with the conditions, he was to lose his grant.

The sixty servitors, most of them English army officers, might take Irish tenants but they would then have to pay higher crown rents.[30] The third category of grantee were up to 300 'meritorious' natives. Consistent supporters of the government were rewarded. These included men such as Turlough Mac Henry O'Neill of the Fews, who got 9,900 acres – the largest grant to any Gaelic lord – and the heirs of Sir Henry Óg O'Neill, who was killed fighting O'Doherty. Of the formerly dominant septs, the O'Reillys of Cavan fared best and the O'Donnells probably worst. The sole O'Donnell grantee got only a small proportion around Ramelton, dwarfed by the great proportions awarded to the O'Boyles and Mac Sweeneys.[31] Most grants to natives were small 'with such equality in their partition that the contentment of the greater number may outweigh the displeasures and dissatisfaction of the smaller number of better blood'.[32] Their crown rents were double those of the undertakers, 'to keep them in subjection'. Such grants were sometimes well away from their homes.

For example, members of the O'Neill *Sliocht Airt* of north-west Tyrone received lands in the south-east of the county, near the Blackwater fort.[33]

O'Cahan's country was marked out for special treatment. Together with Derry and the north-eastern corner of County Tyrone, the wooded *Coill Íochtrach* or 'Killetra', it was formed in 1613 into County London-derry. All the temporal land in this county, except an area of 4 per cent awarded to servitors and 10 per cent to natives, would be managed by guilds of the City of London through a joint-stock company named the Irish Society which, like the Virginia Company established to settle part of North America, was a way of attracting mercantile capital. The territory was considered especially hard to settle but promised a cornucopia of unlocked wealth in woodland and inland fisheries.[34] Other exceptional areas included the Trinity College lands in Counties Armagh, Donegal and Fermanagh and Inishowen, which was granted to Chichester. The latter implemented the Ulster plantation with a 'clear heart and clean fingers', by the undemanding ethical standards of the time.[35] The stress James laid on the protestantising mission of plantation is reflected in the 'vast territories' set aside for the church from Termon and Erenagh lands which in Gaelic tenure yielded (in many cases nominally) dues to the church.[36] Much of this land was put in the hands of bishops whose dignity and status he took pains to boost.[37] Extensive lands were also set aside for Trinity College and Protestant free schools. The final distribution, as computed by Robinson, was as follows:[38]

Grantee	*Plantation acres %*
Undertakers	36
Natives	20
Church	16
Servitors	12
London companies and the Irish Society	10
Trinity College	3
Schools, towns and fortresses	3

Natives and settlers

The key feature of the Ulster plantation was that the corporate towns and land allotted to undertakers and to the London companies was to be entirely cleared of Irish. This roughly corresponds to the unshaded areas on **map 1**, though fragmented church lands, where natives could be kept as tenants, were scattered throughout the area.

As noted, this sweeping clearance reflected the views of Davies rather than those of Chichester, who seems to have assumed that natives would be left on most of the land.[39] The Elizabethan plantation of Munster had tried to replicate a microcosm of English society in Ireland whereby isolated model settlements would exert political and economic dominance over the Irish population and bring them to civility through imitation.[40] This was superseded by a scheme for more complete segregation in Ulster.[41] Writing to Salisbury in November 1610, Davies posed the rhetorical question as to whether it was right to 'remove the ancient tenants and bring in strangers among them'. Yes: 'without removal and transplantation of some of the natives,' he insinuated, 'civility cannot possibly be planted among them.' He concluded there was room enough for natives and newcomers because the latter would multiply the productivity of the land ten times over.[42] Implicit in 'plantation', then, was 'extirpation', or uprooting.

It is an emotional over-simplification to see the plantation in terms of ruthless Protestants seizing the best stretches of land and chasing the Catholics into the bogs and hills . . . the hills and bogs, providing as they did abundant rough grazing and fuel, were the preferred environment for the traditional pattern of rural life.[43]

In fact, pre-plantation natives did not exhibit a perverse preference for 'hills and bogs' but clustered where soil was best. The size of 'balliboes' [*baile bó*], units of more or less equal economic potential, illustrates that land potential as perceived by the native Irish broadly agreed with the land quality as assessed by the 1860s' Griffith land valuation.[44] Population density on such land was reasonably high. A list of the followers of Turlough Mac Henry O'Neill of the Fews in South Armagh suggests a minimum density of two to three households per balliboe, in this case about 100 acres. The supposedly ubiquitous dense woods of Elizabethan Ireland were open and fragmented, though large tracts of forest, Glenconkeyne, Killetra and Killultagh, girded Lough Neagh, while the Erne valley and Sperrin glens, too, were well wooded.

Directions that natives could and must move on before the undertakers came proved unworkable. Few undertakers had the resources to finance the colonisation of large estates without rental income from lands that would otherwise lie empty. The agent of the Ironmonger's estate in County Londonderry, for instance, craved a reprieve of two or three years, 'for it cannot all be suddenly planted with English'. Carew's survey of 1611 found the London company agents were not trying hard enough to replace

Irish tenants. The two servitor grantees in the county who could have kept Irish tenants, Thomas Phillips around Limavady and Edward Doddington around Dungiven, were having more success in replacing them.[45] Land value in a commercialising economy depended as much on nearness to ports and navigable waterways as on the quality of the soil. Consequently, it was especially difficult to abruptly and completely remove natives from the more remote estates until British tenants could be found to replace them.

Moreover, apart from the economic arguments, it was not easy to remove the natives *en masse*. Sir Toby Caulfield reported to Chichester in June 1610 that the Irish considered this to be 'the greatest cruelty that was ever inflicted on any people'.[46] In Laois it took all of four years to round up just 289 families (O'Mores, O'Kellys, O'Lawlors and others) and transport them to far-off Tarbert in County Kerry. The local captain had to resort to terror in summer 1610, hanging 'every one he could catch'.[47] It is not surprising, then, that a proclamation that all natives had to be gone from the undertakers' and London company's estates by Mayday 1615 was widely ignored. After 1621 a native could become 'British' for plantation purposes by religious conformity. Only a tiny number did so. Evidence from Lord Grandison's proportion suggests only thirteen Irish households conformed as compared with 200 'not coming to church'.[48]

So a native problem remained. Nicholas Pynnar fretted that 'the co-habitation of the Irish is dangerous' but his surveys of 1619 and 1622 recorded their continuing presence. Some 1,199 Irish families on the Tyrone undertaker's lands outnumbered the 866 British families.[49] The hilly precinct of Omagh granted to an English Catholic, George Audley (father-in-law of Davies, who doubtless wangled this grant), was worst of all.[50] His successor James Audley, executed for sensational sex crimes in 1616, let much of this in large blocks to Irish tenants-in-chief. Only Davies planted a significant number of British families, sixteen in all, on his 2,000-acre small portion around Castlederg. To sum up, the unshaded areas on **map 1** should have been Irish-free but weren't. The population distribution based on 1659 'census' or poll tax returns and hearth tax returns shows natives still predominating over most of the five (Cavan is not included) planted counties.[51]

Segregation

A comparison of British and Irish settlement in County Fermanagh in 1659 confirms that settlement did not match the original scheme of plantation.

The two precincts straddling the middle of the county on which the native Irish were to be allowed to stay do not display a greater density of Irish settlement than the five from which they were notionally excluded. However, there was an unmistakable clustering of Irish settlement on poorer land – towards the 500-foot contours of Slieve Beagh, for example, and along the lowlands fringing Upper Lough Erne.[52] The pattern of British/Irish segregation that emerged in a section of the adjacent Clogher Valley after mid-century also shows the Irish generally occupied uphill townlands close to the 500-foot contour line.[53] There was little enough overlap: 1659 poll tax returns for part of County Armagh show 361 townlands occupied exclusively by British or Irish families and only 112 mixed townlands. Legislation passed in 1628 allowing undertakers to take native tenants on a reserved quarter, invariably the poorest and most isolated section, of their estates merely recognised informal segregation.

Settlers

Regardless of the specific plans of plantation, settlers tended to gather on better land and near sea ports and by 1660 90 per cent of all British settlers in Ulster lived no more than five miles from a market centre.[54] Clusters of English and Scottish settlement stand out on **map 1** based on muster rolls taken about 1630. These clumps include the Laggan and the adjacent city of Derry, Coleraine and the adjacent Bann river valley, mid-County Cavan, Augher, and north County Armagh. The Laggan may be defined as the lowlands comprising the north-eastern half of County Donegal, with the exception of the Inishowen and Fanad peninsulas. Here the settler population was exceptionally heavy and compact. The 1659 'census' suggests that over half the inhabitants of the Laggan could boast settler origins and this was probably also the case two decades earlier.[55] The larger settlements in County Donegal, already comprising forty to fifty cabins and houses in the 1620s – Lifford, St Johnstown, Newtowncunningham, Letterkenny, Ramelton and Rathmullan – all clustered fairly tightly in the Laggan.[56]

British settlement poured into unplanted east Ulster where it trickled elsewhere in Ulster. North Clandeboy [*Clann Aodh Buí*] or most of modern-day south Antrim, South Clandeboy or Ards and the adjacent MacCartan's Country in north-east Down were thinly inhabited and settlers simply 'exploited areas previously sparsely settled'.[57] To take a specific example: in all the shoulder of the Ards peninsula, a box ten miles long and wide bound by Donaghadee, Newtownards, Grey Abbey and Comber, Scots settlers could not count 'thirty cabins' in the spring of

1606;[58] yet the Great Ards was described in 1588 as a 'champion and fertile land' and this observation is corroborated by the relatively large numbers of horses and soldiers O'Neill of Clandeboy could levy there, a number equivalent to the forces raised in North Clandeboy.[59]

The Ards and elsewhere in Clandeboy was not so much empty as emptied. Chichester's scorched earth raids from Carrickfergus must have driven out or killed the peasantry.[60] Clandeboy was opened up when Con O'Neill fell victim to legal chicanery, economic pressures and shortage of tenants. In return for most of the estate, Hugh Montgomery of Ayrshire secured a pardon and release from house arrest for O'Neill. Another Ayrshire man, James Hamilton, got in on the act and secured another third. O'Neill kept the north-west third of his lordship, around Castlereagh, while Montgomery and Hamilton secured the coast with directions to 'inhabit the said territories and lands with English and Scotch men'. This they did. A survey of 1611 noted eighty houses newly built by settlers at Bangor and Newtownards.[61] O'Neill was a drunkard and sold his lands bit by bit to his two acquisitive neighbours until in 1616 he lost his ancestral home of Castlereagh to an army officer named Hill, who renamed it Hillsborough.[62]

The pattern in south County Antrim, too, was one of initial coastal settlement, though later migrants pushed inland more quickly into the valley of the Six Mile Water and finally settled around Ballymena from the mid-1620s, an area that was until then 'a receptacle of rebels', in planter speak, Irish inhabited.[63] The wave of migrants left some pockets of Irish behind for the moment: for instance, a list of tenants on Sir Henry Upton's lands at Templepatrick in 1626 shows twenty-seven out of thirty-nine were natives.[64]

Security

Little enough violence was offered to the settlers. Only as settlers spread out and the native population picked up after the demographic catastrophe of the Nine Years War did competition for land intensify. Moreover, many potential native troublemakers were disarmed and exiled. Towards the end of his viceroyalty Chichester boasted that he had shipped some 6,000 men to fight for Charles IX, king of Sweden; in 1609 alone he embarked some 1,300 'idle swordsmen'.[65] Most were press-ganged, though some were 'volunteers' despite the urgings of their priests who railed against serving a heretical monarch or prophesied that the recruits would be cast overboard once they put to sea.[66] Complaints recur about native outlaws or 'wood kern' lurking in the woods and attacking settlers, sometimes fatally. But such reports accepted that the vast majority of the natives were cowed.[67] Well they might be. Military garrisons were sprinkled liberally across what had been Gaelic Ireland and, despite some scaling down, there was still quite a number of wards scattered across Ulster on the eve of the 1641 rising.[68]

Walls and nucleated settlements represented another response to the security threat. The London companies built the most impressive physical remains of plantation and left their mark in the names of some of the towns they founded, such as Salterstown and Draperstown and, above all, Derry. O'Doherty's soldiers had burned Derry in 1608, convincing the government to build what Pynnar would describe in 1618 as 'exceedingly stout and well-built' walls and bastions faced with stone that made the town 'one of the principal fortresses in Ireland'.[69] It was by far the largest town in the province. It was intended to have 500 houses and had 215 stone houses by 1616 and 265, excluding suburbs, by 1628. Well behind was Coleraine, with 116 stone houses (of an intended 300) by 1616.[70] The contemporaneous little triangular fort with three round bulwarks at Jamestown in Virginia could have fitted into Coleraine's walled area forty-eight times over.[71] Coleraine, Derry and Carrickfergus were endowed with modern projecting bastions designed to cut down attackers with flanking fire; unlike the walls of the maiden city, Coleraine's ramparts were faced with 'scraws' and stabilised with quickset hedges and so have not survived.[72] Most plantation settlements were far more modest and comprised a huddle of houses about a triangular or irregularly squared green (called 'diamonds' in Ulster), often in the shadow of a castle or fort that protected the more isolated farming population which fanned out into the surrounding countryside.[73] The Merchant Taylor's village of Macosquin, County Londonderry, in or around 1615 is a good example of the smaller plantation settlement. The dozen dwellings, 'good houses of stone and lime well slated', made this slightly larger than the average plantation village and formed a single straight, wide street with a 'fair large church', all overlooked by a battlemented castle 'built very strong'.[74]

The period from 1600 to 1660 marks a transition from the medieval tower house with its living accommodation stacked vertically for reasons of security to the undefended and more horizontal 'big house'. Most plantation castles, like most castles, were tower houses, but many were of an intermediate type, the fortified house comprising a rectangular central block with square or angle-bastion shaped towers at the corners. Plantation examples include Raphoe and Manorhamilton and they are broadly comparable to fortified houses built by native proprietors elsewhere, such as Portumna in County Galway. The most apparent difference between such fortified houses and older tower houses is that the mullioned window replacing the narrow loop strikes a different balance between comfort and defensive strength. Another intermediate type is represented by the three-storey mansion of Donegal Castle built on to an older tower house. The only distinctive planter castles are to be found in the Scottish-influenced castles of Fermanagh. For example, Monea, built by Malcolm Hamilton in 1622, has two circular towers at one end which are corbelled so as to change to a square shape at a higher level. The effect is reminiscent of Claypotts on Tayside, built in 1569.[75]

Arming settlers was an explicit injunction of plantation. Taking *Dúiche Úi Néill* (east County Tyrone and adjacent south-west County Londonderry) as an example: one fifth of the settlers reporting for the annual springtime musters carried firearms. This was a low proportion of firearms by contemporary military standards but it still gave the settlers a potentially decisive edge over any restless natives. Furthermore, the settlers had access to ready-made bases in the five government forts scattered across the region – Mountjoy, Draperstown, Desertmartin, Charlemont and Castlecaulfield – manned by skeleton garrisons of veteran regular soldiers. Yet the settlers here were quickly overwhelmed in 1641–42. Man for man, the most successful military settlement was in County Fermanagh. The three most numerous Protestant names in modern Fermanagh, Johnston, Armstrong and Elliot, all derived from Liddesdale and the 'Debatable Land' in the western and middle marches of England and Scotland. This rough border area was the home of a society based on reiving or 'riding', large, close-knit family groups and fierce feuds against outsiders.[76] In the 1640s and in 1689–91, Enniskillen horsemen would raid widely and usually beat even bigger Irish armies, notably at Clones (1642) and Newtownbutler (1689).

Time would prove that seeking security through settlement was self-defeating. The Ulster rising of 1641 was a long-term consequence of plantation and provided a major link in the chain of events that convulsed three kingdoms. The plantation's assumption of identity of interest between settler and government would prove unfounded.[77] In the subsequent war the Ulster settlers took sides against Charles I: 'the Plantation of Ulster cost the son of James I his head'.[78]

Ulster and Munster compared

Today one tends to overstate the importance of the Ulster plantation because this province bears the enduring mark of partition. Ulster plantation surveys are not reliable for demographic purposes because only adult males were counted and an unquantifiable number were counted twice at musters on different estates. Cavan had the second biggest settler population of all six planted counties in Ulster and my own estimate from the size of the refugee convoys in the early months of the 1641 rising suggest that there were hardly more than 5,000–6,000 British settlers in the whole county.[79] Estimates of an 80,000-strong British population in Ulster by 1641, dwarfing the 22,000 of Munster, may be wildly inflated.[80] A more realistic estimate may be that English, Scots and Welsh newcomers accounted for between 80,000 and 125,000 people by 1641, or about one tenth of the population of Ireland.[81] If one plumps for an estimate of up to 100,000 settlers, as many as 70,000 of them were in Munster and Leinster, including Dublin, and most of the balance were in Ulster.[82] Dublin experienced a fourfold increase in population to around 20,000 between 1600 and 1641, dwarfing its nearest competitor, Cork with 5,500.[83] As late as 1641 'the far greater number' of Dublin's population was Catholic.[84] The denominational balance in Cork city was 6:1 in favour of Catholics until many were driven out in 1644.[85]

A rough estimate of a 100,000-strong British settler community across Ireland by 1641 gives a base from which to measure the scale of the Irish plantations, compared with European settlement in the Americas. The English population in all of north America amounted to just 2,700 by the end of the 1620s; there were at least double that number of English in Bandon alone. The only point of comparison is with Spanish settlement; at least 100,000 people crossed the Atlantic to the Spanish possessions in America during the sixteenth century. The British plantations in Ireland, then, 'are amongst the largest population movements of their time'.[86]

Demographically, Ulster does not yet stand out. Plantation still left a majority native population over most of the province. We need to look forward another half century to explain east Ulster's religious and cultural distinctiveness today.

The re-plantation of the Desmond lands scattered across Limerick, Kerry, Cork and west Waterford brought an even greater concentration of ownership in fewer hands. Between them Richard Boyle (Earl of Cork from 1622), who assembled the vast Ralegh estates, and George Courtney owned roughly one third of the whole plantation. Boyle built on Ralegh's work and developed English-inhabited urban societies across his vast estates to meet the civilising and security mission that underpinned plantation.[87] His boroughs of Tallow and Bandon were the largest inland plantation towns in Munster.[88] Bandon's circuit of walls and round towers was almost as long as that of Derry, although the masonry, while solid and reasonably thick, lacked the broad earth ramparts and angle bastions to protect against siege guns. In the opening decades of the century Tallow already had 150 English households and Boyle's showpiece of Bandon 250. Shortly before the 1641 rising Boyle could boast that the latter had 'at least 7,000 souls' and 'no one Irishman or Papist' within the walls.[89] The urban artisan and merchant were more numerous than in the Ulster plantation and a sequence of urban settler communities grew up in Munster, dominating particular localities rather than a broad spectrum settler society permeating the entire region, as happened in Clandeboy and the Laggan.[90] Depositions taken from Munster Protestant refugees in 1642–43 highlight a settlement triangle with a base running the seventy miles of coastline from Clonakilty to Dungarvan and an apex touching Adare in County Limerick.[91] This triangle was shaped by native ownership and occupation of land and by proximity to ports, markets and easily tapped natural resources.

One such natural resource was the timber of the Blackwater valley: especially extensive woods lay north of the river Bride in the elbow where the Blackwater bends sharply to the west. The clearest example of an enclave and extractive economy was the iron-working industry. This was not the heavy and immobile industry of later times. Driven by deforestation, ironworkers ranged ever deeper into the backwoods looking for the increasingly scarce combination of wood and water: wood for charcoal to fire the ravenous smelters and water to drive waterwheels and to transport ore and iron.[92] Ironworking was an 'eminently wasteful' asset-stripping business that had a limited life expectancy. Given the weight and bulk of the product, transport was a critical cost and remoteness from sea or navigable river tolerable only if woodland was especially abundant. As early as 1639 Cork's agent in London reported that it was hard to undercut English iron and for similar reasons other wood-based industries like the making of planks and barrel staves, or wood processes like glass making, had a limited life expectancy.[93]

The Munster plantation was more urban than the Ulster plantation but, that said, most settlers in Munster were farmers of one kind or another. Unlike his northern counterpart, the Munster settler tended to come from relatively well-developed parts of Britain, like the English West Country, had the capital to set up families and servants in a foreign land and brought agricultural practices 'significantly ahead' of Irish ones.[94] The Munster husbandman invested heavily in the enclosure and liming of his fields, bred English cattle and sheep, and used ploughs and other English-made farm implements. Paradoxically, in light of the equation of natives with pastoralism, wherever the New English settled in Munster they tended to promote commercial pastoralism at the expense of tillage which was more associated with the natives. This may explain the frequent reports of ritualistic slaughter of English breeds of cattle and sheep during the 1641 rising.[95]

The Irish Sea was more 'of a gangway than a barrier' and planters in Munster found themselves on estates drained by rivers which had ancient port towns looking towards south-west England and Normandy, with lively markets for agricultural output, fish, tallow, timber, wool and hides.[96] Consequently, the south Munster region was 'radically and irreversibly transformed' between 1600 and 1640 and presents many indices of commercialisation.[97] Settlers built stone bridges across the Blackwater, first at Mallow then at Fermoy and Cappoquin. They also opened up the forty miles of river between Mallow and Fermoy for navigation by small boats. Most of the new markets and fairs in the region were founded by settlers like Sir Richard Aldworth, who got a patent for a Thursday market and two annual fairs at Newmarket, County Cork, the nucleus of the old MacAuliffe *oireacht*.[98]

Later plantations

Mountjoy had set up a commission for remedying defective titles as a way of stopping, once and for all, the harrying of native landowners. In practice, the commission facilitated further plantations. When a group of North Wexford landowners sought to secure their 'defective' land titles in 1610 through the commission, they were forced to concede one quarter of their lands in exchange for secure title to what was left. An Irish Catholic tract of the 1640s bitterly pointed out the 'quirks and quiddities of law' involved in discovering title and planting. Typically, packed juries awarded title to the King on the basis of some 'moth eaten record' of a medieval grant. Conveniently, all later royal grants or patents passed to the present possessors were *ipso facto* invalid.[99]

This precedent was also applied across the Gaelic midlands, to Leitrim, Longford and the unplanted sections of Laois and Offaly.[100] The midland plantations represented a 'radical break' with the Ulster plantation in that grantees did not have to settle tenants of British origin.[101] The main impetus was the dismay of Elizabethan army officers at what they considered the paltry rewards for servitors in the Ulster plantation. Chichester and his successor, Oliver St John (1616–24), were sympathetic to their fellow ex-officers.[102]

The ripples of plantation radiated beyond those regions actually planted. For example, one Charles O'Dwyer tipped off Sir Philip Perceval in 1637 to buy up land in west Tipperary from owners so disturbed by reports of plantation 'that they will sell upon very easy rates'.[103] Perceval, registrar of the Court of Wards and owner of a large estate in north-east County Cork, was no stranger to this kind of transaction. Two years earlier he had acted as a front man for Lord Lieutenant Wentworth and Sir George Radcliffe in buying the entire estate of the recently deceased Donough O'Connor Sligo at a knockdown price by letting it be known the estate would otherwise be declared confiscate to the crown in a forthcoming plantation.[104]

Case study: Leitrim

Brian O'Rourke, heir of the local lordship, was imprisoned in London prior to his coming of age, thus reducing the possibility of effective local opposition. By 1617 surveying was under way while subsequently two Palesmen were encouraged to claim possession of County Leitrim by virtue of descent from a twelfth-century grantee. Officials made good use of their title to suppress the claims of the natives, then deftly claimed it could not be asserted against the monarch's because their ancestors had been expelled two centuries before.[105] One of the officials in question, William Parsons, picked up 1,400 acres in Leitrim, having already been ideally poised as surveyor-general to pick up three separate 1,000-acre grants in the Ulster plantation, a 1,500-acre block in Wexford, along with other parcels in Kildare, Wicklow and Dublin. In County Leitrim smaller landowners were squeezed out because no one got a grant less than 100 acres.[106] On paper, native landowners were obliged to surrender only one quarter of their land, but planters ended up with well over half the total land (often due to inequality in measuring 'quarters'), lying mostly in the less barren south-east of the county. A strategic rationale of sorts underlay this: two new garrisons at Jamestown and Carrick-on-Shannon could control the Shannon crossings. Indeed, Jamestown looked set to be a successful settlement. Sir Charles Coote built an impressive circuit of walls and bastions one mile in circumference. Next in order of importance was Manorhamilton, followed by Castlefore, where thirty settler families clustered around one of Sir Charles Coote's many ironworks; he employed 2,500 workers in his three works in Counties Cavan, Fermanagh and Leitrim.[107]

Mortgage

In addition to plantation, the mortgage was an important instrument in transferring landed wealth from one community to another, and within communities. It is sometimes hard to distinguish from an outright sale because mortgaging usually led to the mortgagor getting permanent possession of the property involved and may indeed have been a legal fiction to conceal a sale of land and thereby avoid fines due when land was sold.[108] A landowner, typically a Gael, found himself overwhelmed by the need for ready money to buy off an inquisitive discoverer, pay legal fees or indulge in conspicuous consumption. He borrowed and typically could not pay the annual rent, usually equivalent to 10 per cent of the loan.[109] The sequence was broadly the same whether the lender was a New English speculator or an Old English merchant. In County Sligo in 1635, for instance, about 40 per cent of mortgage money was advanced by Old English merchants from Galway, with the bulk coming from just two members of the Ffrench family, Patrick and John, who dealt in the lands of the O'Connor Sligo family. By 1641 150 Galway merchants held around 18 per cent of profitable land in County Galway, 11 per cent in Mayo and 14 per cent in Sligo.[110]

Conclusion: plantation and the market economy

Before the Tudor conquest, Gaelic and Gaelicised Ireland had a localised and redistributive economy. The lord and his train of soldiers and hangers-on consumed through customary exactions of free entertainment such as 'cuddies' [*cuid óiche*] and 'coshering' [*cóisir*] most of whatever agricultural surplus his 'country' or *oireacht* generated. Some of the surplus found its way to the market. Though merchant vessels did put in to smaller havens like Ballyshannon or Lough Swilly, foreign trade was almost entirely in the hands of the corporate Anglo–Irish towns.[111] The staple imports were 'enormous quantities' of wine, salt and iron; the staple exports hides, linen and coarse woollens. The lord, as we have seen, did not 'own' his *oireacht* and the nexus of lord and follower was largely personal.

That lord either replaced the personal nexus with a contractual one based on market value rents expressed in cash or he lost his land through plantation or mortgage.[112] The oft-quoted estimate that the New English owned some 40 per cent of Irish land by 1641 does not capture the scale of the changeover in ownership in the first forty years of the seventeenth century. It includes those (relatively few) native landowners who conformed to Protestantism, but the figure does not include other new landowners, like the many Catholic merchants and professionals from towns like Galway, who got lands through mortgages.

In short, new landlords (or less often old lords acting as such) yanked Ireland from being a pre-capitalist to a 'market' economy. The pace and scale of commercialisation were undoubtedly impressive. Wool exports landed at Chester, for example, grew from 100–200 stone in the late 1580s to 6,666 stone in 1639; live cattle exports from virtually none to 15,814 beeves landed in 1634.[113] Another symptom of economic growth was the jump in land values. By the 1620s land was changing hands at eight or nine years' purchase, that is, for eight or nine times the annual rental income, and by the mid-1630s twenty years' purchase was common. As for the regional impact of commercialisation, it is noteworthy that, for the purpose of the Adventurer's Act of 1642, land in Leinster was valued at twelve shillings an acre, in Munster nine, Connacht six and Ulster four.[114] Commercialisation and conquest did not always march hand in hand.

Endnotes

1 Armitage et al. 2000, p. 50.

2 Canny 1976, p. 133; Morgan 1999, p. 23.

3 Lenman 2001, pp. 118–19; Coughlan 1989, p. 65; Canny 2001, pp. 47–9.

4 Litton Falkiner 1904, pp. 228–30, 261–4.

5 Foster 1988, p. 18.

6 Renwick 1970, pp. 3, 8, 12, 24, 51, 53, 95, 104.

7 Edwards 1999, pp. 127–8; Cunnane 1999, p. 8; Canny 2001, pp. 43, 51; Maxwell 1923, p. 251.

8 Noonan 1998, p. 155.

9 Myers 1969, p. 163.

10 Davies 1612, p. 5; Cunnane 1999, p. 8.

11 Myers 1969, pp. 165–6, 175–82.

12 Sir Arthur Chichester 'Certain Considerations Concerning the Plantation' (1610) *CSPI James I*, pp. 37–9.

13 Myers 1969, pp. 182, 272; Keaveney and Madden 1992, p. 81; Hinton 1935, p. 79.

14 Robinson 1984, pp. 3, 59; Flanagan 1999, pp. 171–80; Davies 1612, pp. 284–5; Myers 1969, p. 259; Canny 2001, p. 172.

15 Rhodes et al., 2003, p. 222.

16 Lenman 2001, pp. 153–6.

17 Edwards 2005, p. 191.

18 Fitzpatrick 1988, p. 26; Casway 2001, p. 53.

19 McCavitt 1998, p. 142.

20 Falls 1936, pp. 146–8.

21 O'Riordan 1997, p. 77.

22 McCavitt, 1998, p. 223.

23 Butler 1918, p. 44; Robinson 1984, p. 7; Nicholls 2004, p. 177; Clarke and Edwards 1976, p. 197.

24 Gillespie 2006, p. 45.

25 McCavitt 1998, pp. 12–13; Gillespie 2006, pp. 47–9.

26 Robinson 1984, p. 61.

27 *TCD Ms 747* f. 164v.

28 Perceval-Maxwell 1973, pp. 84, 91, 96, 98.

29 Treadwell 1998, p. 36; Barnard 1999, p. 204.

30 Ohlmeyer 1998b, p. 138.

31 Clarke 1976, p. 202.

32 *CSPI* (1874b) 'Considerations Concerning Plantation', p. 38.

33 Elliott 2001, p. 89.

34 Clarke 1976, pp. 200–4.

35 Cited in McCavitt 1998, p. 71; Falls 1936, pp. 182, 195, 217; Healy 1917, pp. 24, 31, 54–5.

36 Robinson 1984, pp. 69, 71.

37 McCafferty 2002, pp. 191–2.

38 Robinson 1984, p. 86. This may overstate the land awarded to natives and understate the amount taken by undertakers and Gillespie cites figures of over 40 per cent and 13 per cent respectively. Canny 2001, p. 209; Gillespie 2006, pp. 48–9.

39 Clarke 1976, p. 197; Robinson 1984, p. 61.

40 Canny 2001, p. 132.

41 Clarke 1976, p. 197.

42 Maxwell 1923, pp. 278–9.

43 Estyn Evans 1992, p. 78.

44 Robinson 1984, pp. 14, 26.

45 Curl 1986, p. 57.

46 Maxwell 1923, p. 292.

47 Edwards 2004, p. 294.

48 Canny 2001, pp. 434–5.

49 Robinson 1984, p. 101.

50 Hill 1877, pp. 536–7.

51 Robinson 1984, p. 98.

52 Johnston 1988, pp. 206–7.

53 Robinson 1984, pp. 98–103.

54 Gillespie 1991, p. 27; Robinson 2000, pp. 261–2.

55 Robinson 1984, p. 98.

56 Hunter 1995, pp. 295, 296, 303, 313.

57 Gillespie 1985, p. 58.

58 Stevenson 1920, p. 27.

59 Maxwell 1923, pp. 264, 302.

60 McCavitt 1998, p. 13.

61 Robinson 1984, p. 55.

62 Falls 1936, p. 156.

63 Gillespie 1985, p. 62.

64 Robinson 1984, pp. 14, 26; Gillespie 1985, pp. 57, 59.

65 McCavitt 1998, pp. 150–1.

66 Maxwell 1923, p. 291.

67 Canny 2001, pp. 433, 435.

68 Edwards 2004, pp. 285–9; Falls 1936, p. 181.

69 Moody 1939, pp. 25, 51–8, 188.

70 Andrews 2000, pp. 143–4; Hunter 1981, pp. 59–60.

71 Hill 1877, p. 101.

72 Thomas 1992, pp. 259, 274; Kerrigan 1995, p. 73.

73 Cullen 1981a, pp. 63–5.

74 Andrews 2000, pp. 144–7; Harris 1747, p. 229.

75 Kerrigan 1995, pp. 65–6; Forde Johnstone 1977, p. 157.

76 Turner 1975, p. 285.

77 Clarke 1981, pp. 42–3.

78 Butler 1918, p. 54.

79 Harris 1747, p. 234.

80 Robinson 1984, pp. 105–6; MacCarthy-Morrogh 1986, p. 260.

81 Perceval-Maxwell 1994, p. 31; Anon 1641, p. 3.

82 Canny 1988, p. 96; Canny 1994, p. 62.

83 Perceval-Maxwell 1994, p. 31.

84 Gilbert 1882–91, i, p. 13; Cox 1692, p. 150.

85 'A Plot Discovered in Ireland and Prevented without the Shedding of Blood . . .' (London, 1644) unpaginated; Canny 2001, p. 456.

86 Quinn 1966b, p. 39.

87 Canny 2001, p. 321.

88 Quinn 1966b, pp. 34–5.

89 Quinn 1966b, p. 38; Canny 2001, p. 322; Dickson 2005, p. 25.

90 Canny 2001, pp. 336–47.

91 Canny 2001, p. 337.

92 Dickson 2005, pp. 19, 22; MacCarthy-Morrogh 1986, p. 256; Cipolla 1981.

93 Canny 2001, p. 314.

94 Canny 1988, pp. 7, 77–8, 83; Canny 1985, pp. 13, 19, 29.

95 Dickson 2005, pp. 21–2.

96 MacCarthy-Morrogh 1986, p. 279; Canny 2001, pp. 360–1.

97 Dickson 2005, pp. 17, 22–3; O'Connor 2003, p. 31.

98 O'Connor 2003, pp. 34, 46, 50.

99 Clarke 1970, p. 165.

100 Clarke 1976, pp. 219–22; Butler 1918, pp. 62, 88.

101 Mac Cuarta 2001, pp. 299, 305.

102 Canny 1987, p. 159.

103 HMC 1905, p. 93.

104 Canny 2001, p. 496; O'Dowd 1991, pp. 90–1.

105 Mac an Ghallóglaigh 1971, pp. 237, 239, 240.

106 Mac Cuarta 2001, pp. 311, 313.

107 Cullen 1981a, pp. 84–8; Canny 1985, pp. 15, 21, 22.

108 O'Dowd 1991, pp. 92–3.

109 Canny 2001, p. 327; MacLysaght 1951, pp. 65, 77.

110 Gillespie 2006, p. 81.

111 Nicholls 1972, p. 119; O'Dowd 1988, pp. 17–26; Gillespie 1991, p. 24.

112 Dickson 2005, p. 191.

113 Gillespie 1991, pp. 32–3.

114 Cited in Crawford 1975, p. 9.

CHAPTER 4

English, Old and New 1613–40

Inventing Irishness

The Irish nation, contended an eighteenth-century exile, was 'one of the most ancient in Europe'.[1] It wasn't.

An island place

In the last decades of the sixteenth century and the first decades of the seventeenth, clerics and *literati* fabricated a new transcendent Irishness which could embrace Gael and the descendants of pre-Reformation settlers who had been until now '...two different Nations (like the twins of *Rebecca*) struggling in the Womb perpetually'.[2]

Such nation builders often claimed that lineage no longer mattered because there was hardly a Gael or Anglo-Irishman of higher social class who did not carry a 'mixture of blood'. The argument is unconvincing. For instance, a bewilderingly ramified network of marriage criss-crossed the Pale community and intensified inter-connectedness but included few enough surnames of Gaelic origin: Dongan, Darcy, and Hussey, to name most of them. More convincingly, the *literati* stressed identification with the shared womb, so to speak, Ireland, and shared historical experience on that island.[3] As early as 1584 Richard Stanihurst, a Dubliner, claimed in *De Rebus in Hibernia Gestis* that the name 'Anglo-Irishman' was absurd and insisted that he be known as plain 'Irishman'.[4] In 1607 the chronicler Tadhg Ó Cianáin makes the 'highly significant' association of *nasión* and the term *Éireannach* [Irishman or Irishwoman] rather than the ethnic marker *Gael*.[5] The word *Éireannach* first took on a fresh meaning in the Spanish Netherlands in the early years of the seventeenth century at the Franciscan College in Louvain and in Spain's Irish regiments.[6] The new self-definition was more general forty years later. A French traveller who traversed Confederate Ireland in 1644 found that people described themselves as 'Ayrenake', his phonetic rendering of *Éireannach*.[7] In 1662 John Lynch, a Galway cleric, insisted that 'the place [*regio*] of a man's birth is his true fatherland [*patria*]' and that 'whosoever is born in Ireland should be called Irish'.[8] Whether it is William Nugent referring to *Inse Fáil* as the land of both *Gaoidhil* and *Gail* or the Franciscan poet Eoghan O'Duffy (d. 1590) urging Ireland not to become a 'new England' (*Saxa óg*), the poetic canvas is now the whole island. Fearghal Óg Mac an Bhaird's lament on Rory O'Donnell (who died at Rome in 1608) elegises his hero as a loss to the whole country.[9] This country (the name Éire itself is the name of a Celtic goddess) is often personified as a woman: a maiden waiting for her mate, a poor widow bereft of her man, a victim abused by any and every man [*bean gach duine Éire*] or, for the clerical scholar Geoffrey Keating, writing in 1642, a harlot.[10]

Keating was born in Moorestown, near Clonmel, in south Tipperary to prosperous parents who had him educated towards a clerical career. His formative educative influences included the Mac Craiths, historians and eulogisers of the Butlers, barons of Cahir.[11] Keating reworked the twelfth-century Gaelic mytho-history of the arrival of the sons of 'Milesius' or 'Mil of Spain' [*Mil Espáinn*] in or around 1,000 B.C. His monumental *Foras Feasa ar Éirinn*, penned in 1634, implies that only the Milesians or Gaelic Irish could be fit mates for Éire.[12] Keating was touchy about racial slurs and his controversial preface to *Foras Feasa* unforgettably compared Spenser, Moryson, Davies and Giraldus Cambrensis to the beetle which ignores 'any delicate flower' and 'keeps bustling about until it meets with dung of horse or cow, and proceeds to roll itself therein'.[13] The importance of *Foras Feasa* can be gauged from the many translations, into Latin by 1674, into English in 1688 and in 1722, the latter translations attracting hundreds of subscribers from Protestant scholars and patrons who, while politically unsympathetic to the ideological stance of *Foras Feasa*, could not overlook such an important documentary source.[14]

There exist opposing views of professional bardic poets or *fileadha*, the traditional *literati* of Gaelic Ireland, as either creators of a new and dynamic Irish identity in the late sixteenth and early seventeenth centuries or as provincial, anachronistic and opportunistic time servers, glibly turning out praise poems for English settler patrons almost as easily as for Gaelic lords.[15] The latter view is, on balance, more credible. It is unsettling to see, for example, how smoothly Eoghan *Rua* Mac an Bhaird could deploy the same motifs associated with the loss of a patron to lament the absence of Rory and Niall *Garbh* O'Donnell.[16] The institution of the *fileadha* suffered a mortal blow with the Tudor conquest and the 'contention of the bards' of 1616–24 was their anachronistic swansong. The contention began when Tadhg mac Dáire Mac Bruaideadha, poet of Donogh O'Brien, fourth Earl of Thomond, fired off the opening salvo asserting the primacy of the southern half of the island. The northern *literati* were dismayed at Mac Bruaideadha's eulogy of a prominent collaborator with the new regime and Lughaidh O'Cleary, *ollamh* to the O'Donnells since 1595, retorted by asserting the north's primacy through the eldest of Míl's sons.[17] Various poets subsequently joined in the poetic ruckus until the Franciscan Flaithrí Ó Maoilchonaire sourly rebuked both sides for baying like hounds 'fighting over an empty kennel' [*ag gleic fán easnair fhalaimh*].[18]

The new national consciousness was, rather, celebrated and reinforced by amateur poets, most of them clerics, who came to the fore in the second quarter of the seventeenth century and gradually replaced the syllabic metres of the *dán díreach* by stressed metres. As the bardic schools withered, Louvain became the centre of Gaelic learning. Members of the old literary families showed a tendency to enter the religious life; examples included Bonaventure O'Hussey, Hugh Mac Caughwell (Aodh Mac Aingil), Michael O'Cleary and Ó Maolchonaire. They embarked on a deliberate project to align Gaelic culture, aspirations to political autonomy and Catholicism. The Louvain Franciscan contribution to the formation of national consciousness is personified by Michael O'Cleary (c. 1592–1643), who was sent back to Ireland from Louvain in 1626 and for the next eleven years wandered the country, collecting, transcribing and checking manuscript sources. In 1632 he began on his major work, *Annála Ríoghachta Éireann* [Annals of the Kingdom of Ireland], a history of Ireland in annalistic form from earliest times till 1616. The whole work took four years to complete and took its more popular title, *Annals of the Four Masters*, from the fact that O'Cleary had the help of three other important scholars. His research had the support of wealthy patrons, including members of parliament Terence Mac Coghlan and Sir Fergal O'Gara. This was more than an antiquarian salvage operation. The annalistic sources, for instance, are frequently rewritten or set in a Tridentine framework.[19] It was nothing less than an authoritative history for the new Irish Catholic nation.

Old English

Typically, the experience of exile or of commitment to the Catholic Reformation (and usually both experiences together) sharpened the sense of identification with Ireland: this is true of figures as diverse as Stanihurst, Nugent, Fearghal Óg Mac an Bhaird or Ó Maolchonaire. Shared historical experience of Rebecca's womb was to be the solvent of distinct Gaelic and 'Anglo–Irish' identities, while a common religion would be the main building block of a new identity. Keating's *Mo thruaighe mar tá Éire*, composed around 1642, portrays a racial triad but he insists his own *Sean-Ghaill* (as he now calls the Anglo–Irish) formed a community with the Gael through marriage ties, family links, a shared external threat and, above all, a common religious allegiance. This Old Englishness was, among other things, a way station on the journey between Englishness and Irishness. The currency of the term helps track the timing of that journey. When Sir George Carew, former president of Munster, warned in 1614 that 'until of late, the Old English race despised the mere [pure] Irish, accounting them a barbarous people', he was using a well-established term.[20] By the 1640s terms like 'new' or 'newer' Irish usually displace 'Old English', when it proves necessary to speak of a distinct subgroup at all.[21] However, the currency of the term 'Old English' can be misleading because the same words could have different meanings at different times. Settlers of pre-Reformation stock originally employed the term with an implicit weight on 'Old *English*' to emphasise their shared civility with the 'new' or Protestant English. The *Fóras Feasa* deploys *Sean Ghaill* [old foreigners] which had almost the same literal meaning as 'Old English', but Keating's intention was quite different: to reiterate that the *Gael* and *Sean Ghaill* had more in common than had the *Sean Ghaill* and *Nua Ghaill* [new foreigners]. They had religion, as discussed, but also a shared historical experience. Thus when Lynch sought to integrate the Old English culturally and politically, he accepted their prescriptive property rights; even though they originated in violence, they were sanctioned by time and long possession. Logically, there was little but time separating the claims of the Old English from those of newer arrivals.[22] But time mattered.

Old Englishness is too vague and ephemeral to be a tight ethnic or sociological definition; rather, it best serves as a label for those who professed contradictory allegiances to Pope and King and who relied on politics to redress their grievances.[23] In that sense, *all* Catholics in Ireland of any wealth or position, whatever their paternal ancestry, professed Old English politics and so were Old English. Even Catholic and Gaelic exiles at

Louvain and Rome usually professed loyalty to the Stuarts. The difference in Gaelic and old English attitudes might be the difference between the *politique* Archbishop Lombard, who believed loyalty to the Stuarts was a good in itself, and his short-lived successor MacCaughwell, who saw loyalty as a necessary expedient. This difference between tepid and warm loyalty to the Stuarts would be important during the 1640s, but before then it counted for little enough.

Finally, Old Englishness could be a plea for privileged treatment, but once the Stuart government began to treat the Old English just like Gaels, the posture had outlived its rhetorical usefulness. Before 1633 and the start of Wentworth's viceroyalty, the Old English would escape plantation. Walter *na bpaidrín* [of the rosary beads] Butler, Earl of Ormond, grumbled in 1631 when threatened with plantation that he was the 'first of the English to be ranked with the Irish'. When Lord Deputy Wentworth showed himself willing to press ahead and plant the land of the impeccably loyalist Earl of Clanricard, the Old English and the Gael became, without differentiation, 'simply so many papists'.[24]

The end point of the equation of religion and nationality is described by Sir Richard Cox, a spokesman for the Protestant interest in Ireland, in *Hibernia Anglicana* (1689–90): '. . . if the most ancient natural Irishman be a Protestant, no man takes him for other than an Englishman, and if a cockney be a papist, he is reckoned in Ireland, as much an Irishman as if he were born on Slevelogher' [Sliabh Luachra in County Kerry].' By that logic, Protestants of Gaelic background such as Donogh O'Brien, 4th Earl of Thomond (d. 1624), and Protestants of Anglo–Irish church conformist descent like James Ussher, Archbishop of Armagh (d. 1656), were not Irish.

The steadfast Catholicism of native landowners was remarkable, except for those unlucky enough to fall prey to the Court of Wards.[25] The Court, before its abolition in 1662 as 'grievous and prejudicial', brought about a slow attrition of Catholic landholding. Where a Catholic landowner was unlucky enough to die while his heir was still a minor, the Court had the right to appoint a Protestant to manage the minor's estate and to supervise his education as a Protestant. Of a half dozen noble minors James I wanted educated as Protestants under the Court of Wards provisions, two were lost permanently to the Catholic interest: David Barry Viscount Barrymore and Gerald Fitzgerald, 16th Earl of Kildare, were married off to two of Cork's many daughters.[26] The Court notched up another victory with Murrough O'Brien, who was two years old at the death of his father, 'an exceeding good Catholic', in 1624. Murrough was educated as a Protestant while his court-appointed guardian Sir William

St Leger got a lease of all O'Brien's estates during his minority and ultimately married him to his daughter.[27] 'Murrough of the Burnings' [*Murchú na dTóiteán*] would be the scourge of the Catholic Confederates in the 1640s: '*Chonaic sé Murchú*' ['he saw Murrough'] said the Munster peasant for generations afterwards of one who took a bad fright. However, such losses threatened to be more than offset by a Catholic counter-coup. 'Black Tom' Butler's Protestant heir predeceased him, leaving a Catholic relative, and a devout one at that, Walter *na bpaidrín*, next in line. However, the drowning of Walter's heir in 1619 left the youthful James Butler Viscount Thurles to be reared and educated as a Protestant in England. As the figure who dominated Irish politics in the seventeenth century he was a crucial reinforcement to the New English interest. Movement from one community to another flowed both ways:[28]

As soon as an Englishman cometh over and settleth himself in this country and hath gotten any estate, he findeth himself environed with the Irish and hath no safety for himself and posterity, but by some way to stick themselves by marriage and gossipry or the like.

There was some basis for this Munster settler's disquiet. In that province alone, he could ponder the reversion of Cormac MacDermod MacCarthy's son Cormac Óg (1st Viscount Muskerry) to Catholicism or the five Munster seignory-owning families that had turned Catholic through inter-marriage or conversion by 1641: Spensers, Cullums, Springs, Thorntons and Stephensons.[29] One Oliver Stephenson would be shot dead by a Protestant O'Brien while leading Catholic horsemen at the Battle of Liscarroll in 1642.

The parliament of 1613–15

It was necessary to call a parliament to confirm the Ulster forfeitures and put an end to speculation about the return of the exiled Ulster lords. At James's personal instigation, Carew and Davies drew up a bold plan for Protestant and governmental (the two were seen as synonymous) control over parliament.[30] James created many new boroughs. These lay mostly in Ulster, whence came nearly half the Protestant membership, and each was entitled to return two members of parliament. Eight new boroughs were also created in Munster and four each in Connacht and Leinster. This would pack the new House of Commons with a voting majority of twenty-eight pro-government members.[31] In the House of Lords the block vote of twenty bishops gave the government control.

A specific legislative programme was less important to the crown than the demonstration that it controlled the business of the Irish parliament. The government's mood of aggressive religious confrontation over the previous two years had culminated in the public execution of Bishop Cornelius O'Devany in 1612. Publicly, the bishop was convicted for aiding the flight of Tyrone, but the real purpose seems to have been to cow the County Dublin electorate and secure the return of Protestant MPs.[32] The Old English members made a concerted effort to sabotage parliament by disputing the legality of proceedings. The government proposed Davies as speaker of the House of Commons while the opposition proposed Sir John Everard. The Catholics elected Everard by acclamation, sat him in the speaker's chair and held him there. The Protestant commoners then lifted the corpulent Davies onto Everard's lap whereupon Everard and his supporters stormed from the house.[33] As they did the opposition leader Sir William Talbot jeered that 'those within the house are no house'. His parting shot hit home. In theory, government could have proceeded without the absentees, but the participation of the opposition was considered essential to give parliament the requisite authority to bind the community. Parliamentary opposition itself implied consent. Parliament was prorogued until the King could decide on the issue of legality. Talbot (onetime recorder of the city of Dublin until he refused the Oath of Supremacy) led an Old English delegation to protest in 1614 against 'miserable villages by whose votes extreme penal laws shall be imposed on the king's subjects'. In response James dressed down the delegates in front of Chichester as 'only half-subjects of mine'. The delegates would not be browbeaten and their firmness partly explains why James seemed to back down.[34] He excluded some boroughs which had received their writ of charter after the summoning of parliament. It was a shrewd move that got the opposition back into parliament at no long-term cost. The New English majority in the Commons was shaved to a half dozen members, but a solid Protestant majority for the future was assured.[35] The Irish parliament did not enact new anti-Catholic laws but James was determined to enforce the old ones, despite his public disclaimer in 1613 that he would not 'extort any man's conscience'. Moreover, plantation would be intensified as the instrument of strengthening Protestant control and influence.

The 'Graces'

However, the looming threat against Catholics began to recede before the end of the decade when religious warfare broke out again across continental Europe. James saw himself as a religious moderate, an arbiter of international peace between Habsburg and Bourbon, Catholic and Protestant, Spanish and Dutch.[36] He married his daughter Elizabeth to a German Protestant, Frederick the Elector of the Palatinate, and planned a Spanish marriage for his eldest son Henry (d. 1613) and, later, for his surviving son Charles. When the Habsburgs crushed the Czech Revolt and expelled the Elector from Bohemia and from his Palatinate, James found in 1621 that he did not have enough money to help his son-in-law.

James's reign was bedevilled by insolvency, caused mainly by his notorious extravagance, but Ireland also proved a heavy drain on revenue of over £47,000 every year. A 1622 commission set up to examine the curiously low income and inexplicably high costs of Ireland concluded that the Ulster plantation was a failure because of widespread New English corruption and also professed to be puzzled how Sir Charles Coote's Connaught composition revenue was 'strangely lost'. Coote threw no light on the mystery but skipped off to England, where George Villiers, Earl of Buckingham, James's current minion, protected him and other corrupt clients.[37] Buckingham had thrown his weight behind the plantation lobbyists in return for land grants by proxy across Ireland, his 'secret garden'.[38] But the enquiry forced even the indefatigably greedy Buckingham and his clients to slacken the pace of plantation. So, too, did the resistance of Richard Burke, Earl of Clanricard, who distrusted assurances that his estates would be secure and mobilised landowners in Connacht against plantation with the support of their provincial president, Charles, Lord Viscount Wilmot.[39]

After a decade of war it seemed that a Papist international stalked Europe. Bohemia and the Palatinate were conquered and Christian IV of Denmark beaten. Wallenstein's armies had reached the Baltic and the Emperor was demanding in his Edict of Restitution (1629) the return of all property confiscated from the Church over the preceding eighty years. With hindsight we know that the Emperor had overreached himself and that the Thirty Years War (1618–48) had many years to run. So long as the Protestants seemed to be losing what was still primarily a religious war, James would shy away from provoking Irish Catholics. Chafing at their parliamentary disempowerment, the Palesmen grasped the opportunities offered by the Spanish marriage negotiations and lobbied Philip IV to make religious toleration for Irish Catholics a condition of the match and also insist on reinstating a parliament at Dublin where the Old English would be appropriately represented alongside Catholic bishops and heads of religious houses.[40] Olivares, Philip's chief minister, wanted to disengage from the Spanish match without inflicting loss of face on the English, but this proved impossible after Charles and Buckingham turned up in Madrid to woo the princess in 1623, bearing false names and wearing false beards.[41] Humiliated and angry, the knight-errants returned to England and James opened a naval war on Spain in 1625.

Anxious not to goad Irish Catholics in wartime, James ordered Henry Cary, Viscount Falkland (Lord Deputy from 1622 to 1629), to suspend the operation of the laws against recusants, but proposals to formally suspend the collection of recusancy fines were withdrawn in the face of apocalyptic warnings from the Church of Ireland bishops against tolerating idolatory.[42] Within two months of James's death in March 1625, Richard Burke, 4th Earl of Clanricard, could report that the 'needy and greedy' were discomfited by royal promises of a 'stay' on plans to plant Roscommon, Mayo and Sligo.[43]

However, the new King Charles I (1625–49) needed more than Old English passive loyalty. Westminster, unhappy with his marriage to the French Catholic princess, Henrietta Maria, voted a sum which met only a sixth of the government's demands. The fiscal crisis worsened when Charles contrived to embroil himself in war with France as well. Naval descents on Cadiz and the Isle de Rhé were, successively, a débâcle and a disaster.[44] Ireland seemed to be the soft underbelly of the Stuart realm. Having toyed with plans to raise 'trained bands', Charles heeded New English warnings against raising what would be a mostly Catholic militia and so arming those 'of whose hearts we rest not well assured'.[45] Instead the regular army was expanded more than threefold to counter an invasion threat. This cost money, which the Old English were in a position to pay.[46] The market economy boomed in the opening decades of the century (larger port towns like Youghal and Cork probably doubled in population) and, since most Irish trade was in the hands of Old English merchants, that community accumulated wealth while it lost political clout. Like their English parliamentary counterparts, the Old English wanted guarantees in return for annual parliamentary subsidies. In April 1627, as the negotiations between Charles I and the Irish Catholic agents neared conclusion, three Church of Ireland bishops thunderously warned that God withdrew his favour from Saul when he ignored God's command to kill idolaters 'both man and woman, infant and suckling, ox and sheep, camel and ass'.[47] Despite these bloodthirsty admonitions, in March 1628 the King gave audience to a delegation from Ireland, mostly of Old English landowners, and conceded fifty-one 'Instructions and Graces' which were dispatched to his governor in Dublin.[48]

Among these, Charles offered to stop the collection of recusancy fines and relax the Oath of Supremacy as a test for public office and for taking formal possession of estates under the Court of Wards.[49] The machinations of Sir William Parsons' Court of Wards posed a potentially mortal threat to Old English landowners because by 1622 the Court was making it more and more awkward for native Catholics to inherit or sell land by insisting on the Oath of Supremacy before they could sue out livery. If the Court were allowed to continue unchecked, Catholic landowners were likely to lose control of their land piecemeal.[50] Moreover, those who had held land for over sixty years would enjoy security of title, a provision that would have halted the policy of plantation. Those Graces, then, were concessions 'of quite exceptional importance' – or might have been.[51]

Falkland assumed that Charles's agreement with the delegation constituted authority to summon parliament to confirm the Graces and he did not first consult the English Privy Council. Poynings' law demanded that a governor should obtain permission from king and council in England to call a parliament and send them drafts of any bills to be amended, sanctioned or rejected as the case might be. Falkland's administrative blunder forced a postponement of the parliament even though Falkland had already begun collecting the subsidies. The Old English protested but stumped up. This collective failure of will allowed the government to further postpone the confirmation of the key Graces which would have halted the process of plantation.[52] The only solid concession in the Graces was the dropping of the Oath of Supremacy test on landowners dealing with the Court of Wards. Then the window of opportunity for Irish Catholics closed. In 1628 Buckingham was stabbed to death by a demobbed officer and his client Falkland was exposed to New English wrath and recalled in disgrace. Charles then made peace with France and opened negotiations with Spain.[53]

The experience of the Graces was a 'defining moment' for the Old English and the Dublin administration. It demonstrated that day-to-day workings of government and defence could be agreed between both parties but also demonstrated that such arrangements could break down because mutual trust was lacking. Trust linked to the core value of honour and, in turn, service, loyalty and reputation. The government did not trust the Old English to the extent of putting weapons in their hands, while the latter resented the administration's clawing back the Graces as a breach of trust.[54] The Graces promised pragmatic recognition of Catholicism and this alleviation, even if it was something of a false dawn, helped an aspirant Tridentine church establish itself in Ireland.[55]

The Tridentine project

There would be setbacks. With Cork installed as Lord Justice alongside Adam Loftus, Viscount Ely, the New English were back in power and in December 1629 they closed sixteen religious houses in Dublin that the Catholics had cheekily opened in the 1620s. These included the Jesuit house in Back Lane within sight of the Protestant cathedral of Christ Church: this was as large as a Protestant parish church in Dublin, richly adorned with pictures, and featured a raised and railed-in altar and continental-style confessional boxes.[56] On St Stephen's Day 1629 the Mayor and the Archbishop of Dublin led a raiding party that burst into the Franciscan Church in Cook Street, scattering the congregation, smashing and tearing statues and images and carrying off vestments before a mob caught some of the raiders who were then 'thrown down, grabbed by the hair and their heads dashed against the ground until they no longer had human faces'.[57] Cork and Loftus, attending morning service in nearby Christ Church, heard the hubbub and fled to the castle. This clampdown culminated in the symbolic destruction in 1632 of St Patrick's Purgatory at Lough Derg in south County Donegal, a pilgrimage site with a European-wide reputation which had undergone a sixteenth-century revival. One wonders not why it was closed now but, rather, why it hadn't been closed before. Stuart anti-Catholic policy fell well short of systematic repression.[58]

The centralised and bureaucratic Tridentine project depended on bishops to supervise parochial priests. When David Rothe took up the see of Ossory in 1618, he was the first bishop to reside in Ireland since O'Devany's execution. Rome quickly filled vacancies in the southern and eastern dioceses and by 1630 seventeen bishops were resident.[59] This was probably enough as Ireland had a lot of bishoprics relative to its size: thirty-five sees compared with twenty-three in England.[60] Straitened for revenues, nearly all bishops lived with rich kinsfolk and relied on them for money to maintain horses and servants on visitations.[61] The burgeoning number of bishops was accompanied by a doubling in the number of priests between 1615 and 1630 in the archdioceses of Cashel and Dublin (map 9) and, a decade later, in Tuam and Armagh archdioceses. Countrywide, by the 1640s there was at least one priest for every two parishes, though numbers were regionally variable, with a pronounced gradient from the wealthier and more heavily populated south-east to the north-west. Waterford diocese in 1639 had forty-five parishes overstaffed by fifty-nine secular priests and forty-five regulars, whereas Raphoe, griped the local bishop, could support only nineteen beggarly priests while 'new colonies of heretics that come every day to live here' squeezed them ever more.[62] For Catholicism to hold its ground it needed enough priests to maintain continuity of ministry.[63] This it did. The quality of these priests was less critical. The power of the priest to administer the sacraments did not depend on his character but on his office. By saying mass and consecrating bread and wine on the altar he performed the miracle of transubstantiation, transforming the bread and wine into the body and blood of Christ.[64]

Reforming bishops tried to bolster the priest's status by regulating his behaviour and so set him up as a man apart. Much of the work of the earlier Irish synods was taken up in prohibitions of outright misbehaviour, fornication, frequenting taverns, drunkenness, gambling, keeping too many horses and servants, and so on. More positive injunctions tended to come later: while saying mass he should wear a clean black tunic, biretta and surplice and otherwise wear sober civilian clothes. The priest should be reasonably knowledgeable and should own staple books such as a breviary, catechism and New Testament.

Comerford of Waterford in 1631 acidly dismissed most of his priests as drones 'contenting themselves to say mass in the morning and until midnight playing cards or drinking or vagabonding'.[65] The bishops could not call on the secular power to back them up against troublesome priests: quite the reverse. A wayward priest or embittered friar need only complain to the authorities and the bishop could be imprisoned for exercising papal authority.[66] As bishops increasingly challenged freelance regulars officiating at burials and collecting funeral offerings, the intense and unedifying squabbles that followed supplied the most common spark for such complaints to the authorities.[67]

'Thorough'

After Falkland's recall long-standing plantation schemes were dusted off. The possibility of planting the baronies of upper and lower Ormond in Tipperary was explored though the title of the landholders, pre-eminently Walter *na bpaidrín*, was found to be too solid to be impeached. In 1630 Charles Coote, vice-president of Connacht, went to London to lobby for plantation in Mayo, Roscommon and Sligo. He envisaged avoiding Old English opposition by excluding Galway, where Clanricard's estates lay, and also exempting named Old English landowners in the other three counties. Coote was, doubtless, not acting alone but as a proxy for Cork, Parsons and Henry Jones, Viscount Ranelagh, president of Connacht.

Whitehall accepted Coote's idea in principle and he was appointed as one of the commissioners 'to secure defective titles', this being the legal mechanism whereby peacetime land confiscations could be set in train.

The belated arrival of a new governor, Thomas Wentworth, in 1633 put a stop to this for the moment. His arrival coincided with the expiry of the Graces subsidy and even after cutting back the size of the army, he faced a hefty debt and annual deficits. Initially Wentworth pretended to ally with the Old English, using two New English figures, Francis Annesley, Lord Mountnorris, and Sir Piers Crosby, as his go-betweens. Crosby was of Gaelic parentage (his father was Church of Ireland bishop of Ardfert and a scion of the bardic family of Mac Crossan) and married to a Catholic Paleswoman. Mountnorris enjoyed credibility in Old English eyes because he had a long-standing time preference for exploiting customs revenue, rather than exacting recusancy fines as a means of paying for the army.[68] Moreover, he did not favour more plantations. Implicit in this may have been some form of long-term accommodation to create one political community of Old English and some New English.[69] Wentworth, then, sought to charm the Catholics into renewing subsidies by representing himself as their friend restraining Cork's hardliners from pressing ahead with recusancy fines and plantations. Once he had secured the subsidies he brusquely rejected the Graces in August 1634. Next year Mountnorris suffered disgrace at Wentworth's hands and was imprisoned for two years.[70] Wentworth's manoeuvres were of a piece with his strategy for the forthcoming 1634 parliament, namely to 'govern the Native by the Planter and the Planter by the Native'.[71]

Wentworth and the Planter

Wentworth liked to present himself as a political idealist cutting through local vested interests and governing, in his own words, 'thoroughly'. He could ride out protests from the New English or any other interest group in Ireland and enforce a policy that was entirely conceived in England because he could count on full royal backing. This gave the deputyship a strength it had never enjoyed before. He dismissed his New English officials as 'a company of men the most intent upon their own ends that ever I met with'. But Wentworth himself was no less, or not much less, dishonest than his predecessors. He combined public and private profit from plantation by buying plantation land in Wicklow at knockdown prices. He sold judicial offices, judgeships and other offices in his gift as Lord Deputy, cheerfully mingled government finances and his personal speculation in,

for instance, the farming of tobacco customs dues.[72] He was 'violently zealous in his master's ends', said a contemporary acidly, 'and not negligent of
his own'.[73]

Wentworth's defining mix of 'cunning, idealism and self-interest' can
be seen most clearly in the story of the plantation of the O'Byrne territory
in County Wicklow. This was a fertile coastal strip coveted by Sir William
Parsons and by Lord Carlisle, a minor luminary at the Stuart court. The
perfected technique was to hand. Charles had made a grant of the land
to Carlisle if he could discover royal title, Parsons had the requisite
'proof' but insinuated that he would withhold it until Carlisle agreed to
sell the grant to him and to his crony, Ranelagh. Wentworth, a friend of
the Carlisle family, issued a commission of enquiry to investigate. Parsons,
naturally alarmed, confessed that he had been obstructing Carlisle and
proposed a 'superbly dishonest scheme'. Wentworth should dupe Carlisle
into taking a once-off payment or composition, ostensibly from the
O'Byrnes. Parsons then promised to see that royal title was then found in
Wentworth's favour, giving him lands worth £3,000 a year.[74] Wentworth
did not respond in any of the ways one might expect of a high official.
He did not round on Parsons, quietly pocket the bribe, or tip off his friend
Carlisle. Instead he told the King and used royal revenue to buy out
Carlisle's interest so the crown would get over 23,000 acres while the
O'Byrnes secured legal possession of almost 20,000 acres.[75] Wentworth
was granted as his reward two manors worth more than £1,000 a year.
The O'Byrnes were of course the biggest losers, but Carlisle had been
fobbed off with a lesser bargain while Parsons had surrendered his hopes
of profit but had not gained power over the deputy by embroiling him
in complicity.

Politics is personal. In transactions like this Wentworth drew bitter
hatred, not just as an enemy but as an unpredictable, faithless and immoral
enemy who could exploit and flout the normal social conventions. He was,
in the words of Parsons, 'that strange man'. Wentworth saw no incon-
gruity in staying in Clanricard's house in Portumna, County Galway, while
holding a kangaroo court to seize his lands. The Old English were shocked
by Wentworth's boorishness in doing so and his studied abuse of hospital-
ity when, to cite the most notorious example, he lay 'in his riding boots
upon very rich beds'.[76]

Though he helped arrange a match between Cork's eldest son and
his niece, Wentworth set Sir George Radcliffe to devise ingenious legal
challenges to Cork's titles. His viceregal court was now empowered as
the arbiter of such matters as disputed church tithes without appeal to

common law: Wentworth was complainant, prosecutor and judge.[77] Wentworth fined Cork £15,000 in his prerogative court of Castle Chamber (the Irish counterpart to the notorious Star Chamber) as a preamble to an attack on all his church land holdings. He appointed compliant bishops in Cork's backyard: Atherton in Waterford and Lismore, the happily named Chappel in Cork and Synge in Cloyne. They were not picked for their piety but were tough-minded and ambitious officials ready to resist local pressures and claw back church property and income.[78] Atherton was the pick of the bunch. He lay under a cloud of allegations of incest, infanticide, fornication, adultery, rape and simony and was executed after his patron's recall. With a touch of personal vindictiveness Wentworth also forced Cork to remove the large monument to his wife's memory from St Patrick's cathedral, Dublin in order to install a railed-in altar.[79]

What seems to modern eyes a curious fixation on church furnishings and liturgy reflected the religious reform programme of William Laud, created Archbishop of Canterbury in 1633. Laud believed that the sacraments, set prayer and ceremonial aspects of worship had been unduly neglected and that episcopal authority existed by divine right. Laud's convictions inflamed suspicions that he would 'unlock the door to popery'.[80] Wentworth's favoured bishop in Ulster, Bramhall ('Bramble' his enemies nicknamed the prickly bishop) of Derry, enforced tighter conformity and railed against the Scots as natural enemies of an orderly church. Wentworth's most flagrant measure was the infamous 'Black Oath' imposed by the army in the summer of 1639 on all adult Ulster Scots. This demanded that they abjure the covenant signed (as discussed in the next chapter) by their fellow countrymen across the Sea of Moyle and assumed *ipso facto* that they were traitors and subversives.[81]

Wentworth enforced conformity to a Laudian norm which was unrepresentative of Protestant opinion in Ireland. For all Wentworth's mastery of administrative detail, intelligence and forcefulness, he suffered from 'a total incapacity either to understand or to acknowledge the legitimacy of an opposing point of view'.[82]

Charles I's critics in England tended not to see Wentworth's policies as unique to Irish conditions but feared that Ireland was a laboratory of Stuart absolutism where Wentworth could try out solutions to common problems of religion, law or constitution before they could be applied in England.[83] There was some truth in the charge they eventually laid against him that he had tried 'to subvert the fundamental laws of the kingdom': Wentworth had boasted he would set 'his master's power' above the common law.[84] He had come armed with more power and prestige than any previous governor and used the extraordinarily wide law-giving and enforcing functions of the Irish Lord Deputy to their fullest.[85] Ireland was a conquered country that could be, and should be, governed by royal will alone because the New English had perverted the common law into an instrument of chicanery and fraud.[86] This was so because the judges who applied the common law were themselves New English looking to enrich themselves by the patronage of great landowners or by land speculation on their own account. Wentworth pulled at this web of New English cronyism like the very long leases of crown and church lands at low rents or the royal patents supplied on misinformation.

Wentworth and the native

Wentworth differed from the New English in his willingness to grant Catholics *de facto* toleration while persecuting Protestants. This toleration, however, was not based on any sympathy for the Irish, as his critics alleged. Indeed, he despised the Gaelic Irish as 'animals'.[87] But he saw little point in forcing religious compliance and expelling priests until he put the Church of Ireland on a sound financial and doctrinal basis and sapped the wealth of Catholic landowners, the patrons and protectors of the clergy.[88] Only then would he expel the Catholic clergy.[89] Nor did he encourage evangelisation. James I upbraided Trinity College in 1620 for not training Irish-speaking ministers and an attempt followed to encourage evangelisation in Irish.[90] This effort is associated with William Bedell, provost of Trinity and Bishop of Kilmore (d. 1641). Bedell was a cosmopolitan scholar and a man of wider horizons than the typical New English bishop.[91] He neither identified the Pope with the Antichrist nor went along with the common accepted New English view that salvation was impossible within the Church of Rome and urged the Church of Ireland's evangelical mission with a zeal that challenged local Protestant sensibilities.[92] Bedell laboured on a translation of the Old Testament but his death in 1641 halted work that had been delayed already when Primate Bramhall had the principal translator arraigned before the court of high commission in Dublin.[93] His notes were saved but it would be another forty years before the Old Testament translation was finally published.

In March 1635 Wentworth professed to be nettled by a complaint that he would 'proceed in the plantations with an intent to overthrow the old law and in time the old religion'.[94] The complaint was prescient.

To plant was to Protestantise. Wentworth had decided (though he did not publicly avow this) to plant nearly all land remaining in Catholic possession, a scheme as potentially sweeping as that implemented later by Oliver Cromwell's agents.[95] He pursued the long-mooted plantation of Connacht with speed and ruthlessness. Juries in Roscommon, Mayo and Sligo were bullied into finding that the monarch had title to most of the land, regardless of latter's patent or other titles.[96] At Clanricard's instigation a Galway jury stood firm and Galway landowners sent a delegation to London to present a petition directly to the King. The appeal was ignored and on returning to Ireland Wentworth threw the delegates in gaol.[97] In 1636 the jurors finally bowed to Wentworth's demands and offered to find the King's title.[98] Wentworth, characteristically, proposed to punish the recalcitrant landowners and jurors by planting half the forfeited land rather than a third or a quarter.[99] Temperamentally, Wentworth could not see the struggle between the crown and its opponents as open to compromise. He was determined that executive power would be seen to bear down with no regard for consent or negotiation and that direct appeal to Charles I would be seen to be bootless. In due course Charles did exempt Clanricard from the proposed plantation, to his viceroy's chagrin, but otherwise Wentworth made his point.[100] Wentworth went on to secure royal title to County Clare and parts of Tipperary and north Kilkenny. The localised Scottish troubles of 1637 brewed into a three-kingdom crisis over the next three years and delayed the actual implementation of most of these plantations because Wentworth was forced to try to regain the trust of the political nation in Ireland. It was too late and by the time of his recall he left pitifully few supporters in Ireland.[101]

Conclusion

On one side a self-confident, assertive and acquisitive New English community, buoyed by a powerful sense of cultural and religious mission. On the other an emergent Irish nation increasingly imbued with that most potent of all weapons, a collective consciousness. The seemingly inexorable taking and getting of land by the one from the other was the most obvious point of conflict between the two communities. Despite the superficial similarity of institutions like parliament, Ireland was crucially different from the rest of the British polity in that institutionalised land confiscation in peacetime would simply not have been seriously considered in England or even in Scotland.[102] The crown (the monarch, his courtiers, counsellors and officials) was not a neutral but, except for an enforced lull in the 1620s, drove a radical course of colonisation to reshape Irish society as a replica of England, in government, religion, language and culture. The opposition of Catholics in parliament was ineffective; having lost control of the Irish parliament in 1613 they continued to lose seats (through devices such as the suppression of Catholic-dominated boroughs) in the 1634 and 1640 parliaments.

So long as plantation lasted, no stable *modus vivendi* could be negotiated between both communities and the combustible fuel for a violent revolt piled up. As discussed later, the Ulster plantation provoked the outbreak of the 1641 rising. Moreover, the experience and threat of later plantations, including Wentworth's schemes, were undoubtedly important in explaining its wildfire spread.[103] However, it is unhistorical to retrospectively blame James I, Charles I or Wentworth for provoking a rising. Wentworth accepted 'discontentments and grumblings' as the price of radical colonisation.[104] He could hardly have foretold the collapse of Stuart authority across three kingdoms: something worse than grumbling ensued.

Endnotes

1 MacGeoghegan 1758, xxviii.

2 Deane 1991, p. 268.

3 Caball 1998, p. 112.

4 Simms 1989, p. 197; Ford 1998, p. 190.

5 Walsh 1916, pp. 42–3; Simms K. 1989, p. 196.

6 MacCraith 1996, pp. 51–2.

7 La Gouz 1653, p. 456; MacCraith 1996, p. 52.

8 Lynch 1662, p. 273.

9 Caball 1998b, pp. 66–8; 1999, pp. 74–5; Caball 1998, pp. 118–19; Caball 1998, p. 120; Leerssen 1996a, pp. 193–4.

10 Caball 1998, p. 124.

11 Cunningham 2001, pp. 20–3.

12 Canny 1982, p. 101.

13 Jones 1974, pp. 3–20; Cunningham 2001, pp. 97–8, 115.

14 Cronin 1996, p. 94.

15 O'Riordan 1990, p. 118; Dunne 1980, p. 11; Bradshaw 1978b, p. 78.

16 O'Riordan 1997, p. 76; De Blácam 1929, p. 146.

17 Leerssen 1996b, pp. 14–15; Cunningham 1986, pp. 163–4.

18 De Blácam 1929, p. 155.

19 Ó Buachalla 1982–83, p. 94; Mac Craith 1996, pp. 77–8.

20 Carew 'A Discourse of the Present State of Ireland 1614' *CSPI* (James I), p. 305.

21 Gilbert 1879, iii, p. 301.

22 Cunningham 2000, p. 145; Caball 1998, pp. 125–6.

23 Clarke 1966, pp. 19, 21; Kearney 1961, p. 15.

24 Clarke 1966, p. 110; MacCraith 1998, pp. 16–17.

25 Canny 2001, pp. 431–2.

26 Treadwell 1998, pp. 115–17, 121.

27 O'Brien 1991, p. 5.

28 *CSPI* (1647–60), p. 184.

29 Dickson 2005, p. 14; McCarthy-Morrogh 1986, pp. 277, 284.

30 Clarke 1976, p. 212.

31 Webb 1918, p. 116.

32 Edwards 2003, p. 272.

33 Litton Falkiner 1909, p. 37.

34 McCavitt 1998, pp. 190–5.

35 Clarke 1976, p. 216.

36 Kishlansky 1996, pp. 92, 97.

37 Canny 2001, p. 241; Treadwell 1998, p. 201.

38 Treadwell 1998, pp. 175, 310.

39 Canny 2001, pp. 265–6.

40 Redworth 2004, p. 258.

41 Smith 1998, p. 62.

42 Clarke 1976, p. 233; Clarendon 1807, ii, p. 528; Clarke 1997, pp. 146–7.

43 Cunningham 1996, p. 179.

44 Kishlansky 1996, pp. 110, 115; Gillespie 2006, pp. 74–5.

45 Clarke 1966, p. 35.

46 Gillespie 2006, pp. 75, 80.

47 Ford 2003, p. 134.

48 Gillespie 2006, p. 77.

49 Clarke 1976, p. 238.

50 Kearney 1961, p. 19.

51 Russell 1991, p. 381.

52 Clarke 1966, pp. 55–6.

53 Canny 2001, pp. 268–9.

54 Gillespie 2006, p. 87.

55 Hazlett 2003, pp. 110.

56 Gillespie 2006, pp. 92–3.

57 Browne 1962, p. 149.

58 Hazlett 2003, p. 111.

59 Cregan 1979, p. 85.

60 Hazlett 2003, p. 91.

61 Ó hAnnracháin 2002, p. 469.

62 Moran 1874, p. 49.

63 Connolly 2004, p. 11.

64 Russell 1996, p. 263.

65 Corish 1981, p. 29; Mullett 1998, p. 67; Moran 1874, p. 166.

66 Ó hAnnracháin 2002, pp. 42–3.

67 Flynn 1993, pp. 22, 255, 256; Ó hAnnracháin 2002, pp. 51, 54.

68 Clarke 1988, pp. 144, 149; O'Grady 1923, p. 15.

69 Perceval-Maxwell 1994, p. 15.

70 Little 2001a, pp. 556, 560–1.

71 Kearney 1961, p. 44.

72 Ranger 1967, pp. 274–5.

73 Kearney 1961, p. 172.

74 Ranger 1967, pp. 284–5.

75 Gillespie 2006, p. 99.

76 Clarke 1966, p. 97.

77 Ranger 1967, p. 282.

78 Clarke 2003, pp. 143, 149.

79 Kearney 1961, p. 118.

80 Smith 1998, p. 95.

81 Canny 2001, p. 294; McCafferty 2002, pp. 197, 200, 202.

82 Clarke 1976, p. 243.

83 Merritt 1996, p. 2.

84 Ranger 1967, p. 280.

85 Shaw 2006, p. 340.

86 Gillespie 2006, p. 95.

87 Canny 1996, p. 173.

88 Canny 1996, pp. 172–3; Lotz-Heumann 2005, p. 52.

89 Canny 2001, pp. 284–5.

90 Ford 1986, p. 62.

91 Clarke 1989b, pp. 66–7.

92 Clarke 1989b, p. 64.

93 Barnard 1975, p. 177.

94 Ranger 1967, p. 289.

95 Canny 2001, pp. 283–7.

96 Knowler 1799, i, ff. 139, 465.

97 Kearney 1961, p. 98; Clarke 1966, p. 103.

98 Clarke 1966, p. 103.

99 Kearney 1961, p. 98.

100 Canny 1996, p. 178; Kearney 1961, pp. 68, 87–93, 107; Canny 2001, p. 284.

101 Kearney 1961, pp. 219–20; Ranger 1967, p. 276.

102 Canny 1996, pp. 178–9.

103 Clarke 1976, p. 252.

104 Canny 2001, p. 283.

CHAPTER 5

Rising 1641–42

The Scottish crisis

Charles I's authority began to unravel when he foisted a set prayer book on the Scots as part of his attempted reform of the Church in July 1637. Presbyterians protested violently against the book's 'popish' rubrics and bound themselves by a solemn oath or 'covenant' to maintain the 'true religion, liberties and law of the kingdom'.[1] A Covenanter provisional government set about recalling veterans fighting in the Thirty Years War and recruiting an army to give force to their demands while Charles withdrew the book in order to buy time to mount a military attack on Scotland.[2] The showdown came, or should have come, in summer 1639. The main English army should have been capable of beating a somewhat smaller Scottish force arrayed on the northern bank of the Tweed. Fatally, the King backed down.[3]

Wentworth, latterly Strafford, was recalled from Ireland. With the successful precedent of his management of the 1634 Irish parliament in mind he persuaded his master to call an English parliament to vote subsidies for another attack on the Covenanters.[4] The precedent was misleading and the majority of the Commons were unwilling to vote monies to Charles until their various religious, legal and constitutional grievances were heard. The King promptly dissolved this 'Short Parliament' and went ahead with his plans to march an army across the Tweed. The plan included a diversionary attack by 9,000 newly recruited Irish troops encamped at Carrickfergus who were to make the short sea passage and fall on the west of Scotland.

To begin with, Irish Catholics saw opportunities rather than dangers as Anglo–Scottish conflict simmered. The king needed their goodwill and the existence of an army of Catholics at Carrickfergus, even if under Protestant officers, gave added weight to their demands which they pressed in alliance with the New English opposition in the Irish Parliament. In the first session of the Irish parliament (6 March to 17 June 1640) the Catholics could return only seventy members of the House of Commons out of a total of 240, a fall of one third in their representation since the 1634 parliament. They were the chief victims of manipulation of county and, especially, borough constituencies by Wentworth's officials who called in borough charters by royal warrant and agreed to restore some 'upon agreement to send such to the parliament as those in power should name'.[5] The interests among the Protestants in parliament were, however, exceptionally diverse. Strafford's followers formed one interest block, a second faction formed around Cork, another (hostile to the Boyle interest) around Sir William St Leger in Munster and another around Lord Lambert from County Westmeath. Strafford's followers dominated the first session and by early April when Wentworth left Ireland all seemed well. Subsidies for the war against the Covenanters had been voted and the contentious issue of plantation in Connacht and Tipperary postponed. The first sign of an anti-government realignment came in June 1640 when a bill to ratify the proposed plantations was, in effect, blocked by a New English-dominated parliamentary committee and referred to another committee dominated by Catholics.[6]

Before any Irish army embarked from Carrickfergus, the Covenanters struck and seized Newcastle.[7] Losing the Second Bishop's War meant Charles could no longer contain the crisis in one kingdom. Successful resistance to Stuart authority in Scotland would set off a 'billiard-ball effect' of rebellion in Ireland followed by civil war in England.[8] An alternative holistic view comprehends 'a single crisis, not just a series of interlocking crises'.[9] This chapter recognises this archipelagic inter-connectedness, not least because the credibility of the Stuart monarchy was an issue common to all three kingdoms, but considers events in Ireland as one of three separate histories which periodically collided.[10]

Plots

In October 1640, a humiliated Charles I agreed to foot the bill for a Covenanter army of occupation in north-eastern England until satisfactory peace terms were agreed. This would be no easy matter since the Covenanters vowed to destroy prelacy in England as well as Scotland and such terms had to be guaranteed by an English parliament in which the

Scots could expect to find a large fifth column.[11] Led by John Pym, these covert sympathisers demanded common action in 'both of your realms' (Ireland was implicitly left out) against the 'common enemies' of protestantism.[12] The 'Long Parliament' which first met on 3 November 1640 was so called because it lasted in one form or another for the next twenty years. It began by venting hysterical anti-Catholic rhetoric, thundering declarations of hostility to prelacy and starting proceedings against for a bill of attainder declaring Strafford guilty of treason.

When the Irish parliament convened in late October it adopted a remonstrance or indictment of Wentworth's government in Ireland and appointed thirteen agents to take their petition to the Long Parliament. In a show of unanimity these were drawn from diverse backgrounds and included Donough Mac Carthy, a future Confederate Catholic and royalist leader, on the one hand and Sir Hardness Waller, a future regicide, on the other.[13] The bill of attainder received Charles's reluctant consent in May 1641 and shortly afterwards Strafford was beheaded on Tower Hill in London.

In the spring of 1641, after Strafford's fall seemed certain, the Irish parliament broke up his cabal. In the fourth session which began in May 1641, a leading counsel and agent for the County Galway landowners against Wentworth's plantation five years before tried to define the limits of royal authority for his fellow members of parliament.[14] In July 1641 parliament endorsed Patrick Darcy's *Queries*:

> . . . *the subjects of this His Majesty's kingdom of Ireland are a free people, and to be governed only according to the common law of England and the statutes made and established by parliament in this kingdom of Ireland . . .*[15]

At first glance it seems 'futile' for the Old English to collaborate with the opposition in asserting legislative independence and hedging the crown about with legal constraints.[16] Their only shield, flimsy as it was, against New English avarice was the monarch's goodwill and his capacity to do them good. However, Catholic political leaders like Nicholas Preston, Viscount Gormanstown, Donough Mac Carthy, Viscount Muskerry, Nicholas Plunkett, Geoffrey Browne and Patrick Darcy were no fools. Their willingness to side with some New English parliamentarians suggests that they saw enough common ground for a long-term alliance rather than chilly and opportunistic cooperation.[17] They had grounds for such optimism: the New English constitutionalist opposition had not, after all, protested against the King's agreement in April 1641 to discontinue plantation and grant the Graces.

In July 1641 Charles agreed a comprehensive series of concessions including the regulation or suspension of extra-judicial conciliar proceedings and less onerous tenure for Ulster undertakers, though he refused to modify Poynings' law procedures so as to allow the Irish parliament to initiate legislation. The agents of the Irish parliament in London also lobbied for bills that would guarantee valid titles and, thereby, end the plantation process.

In December 1640 Charles had wanted to appoint an ally of Strafford, James Butler, Earl of Ormond, as lord deputy but was pushed into selecting Parsons and Sir John Borlase as lords justices.[18] Together with other New English plantation lobbyists such as Richard Jones, Viscount Ranelagh, they controlled the royal council in Dublin and took the opportunity to delay any settlement of the crucial issue of securing land titles. Parsons, in particular, was an 'inveterate enemy' of Irish Catholics.[19] In August they prorogued the Irish parliament until the following November in order to delay a bill ratifying Charles's concessions. Whatever pressures were needed to bend the royal will one way or the other would now come from outside parliament.

The colonels' plot

Irish Catholics needed a king who was enfeebled enough to want their support against his enemies but not so helpless that he would cave in to those enemies. The point when the dangers of royal weakness outweighed the opportunities was reached around March 1641. The Old English wanted to keep the Carrickfergus army in being but, pressed by Pym, the leader of the English parliamentary opposition, Charles agreed to disband the army from the following May.[20] Charles next licensed nine would-be colonels to recruit regiments for the Spanish service from the disbanded soldiers.[21] On the face of it, Charles dispensed with the Old English to appease the opposition in the English parliament.

Yet it was not so simple. The fact that Charles agreed to the Graces after apparently agreeing to disband the army certainly suggests that he valued continued Irish Catholic goodwill.[22] Years later Randal MacDonnell, Earl of Antrim, claimed that Charles I told Ormond (by then commander of the army in Ireland) to disband the Carrickfergus army while at the same time sending him a secret order not to do so. Antrim also claimed to be party to a plot hatched in the late spring of 1641 to seize Dublin Castle, centre of government and the central magazine of arms and ammunition.[23] The conspirators would then declare for the King in the emerging conflict with the Scots and the English parliament. Antrim is not the most credible of witnesses but Charles may well have dabbled in a passing intrigue with Ormond and some of the recruiting colonels to take Dublin Castle.[24] This kind of backroom intrigue would have been in character: Charles had been complicit in the abortive 'First Army Plot' to seize the Tower of London, release Strafford and threaten the parliament with dissolution.

Retrospective Irish justifications of the rising often claimed the implicit sympathy of the King and pleaded self-defence against the 'Puritan parliament of England' that 'would otherwise destroy them' backed by a 'Scottish army with the sword and the Bible in hand'.[25] The torrent of anti-Catholic rhetoric spewing from the English parliament gave subjective grounds for Irish Catholics to fear a Scottish–Puritan plot to 'extirpate' them.[26] Such fears began, or should have begun, to be soothed by late summer 1641 when Charles won back some support in Scotland and a backlash against religious radicalism set in at Westminster.[27] Abandoning Laudianism, and accepting the abolition of prerogative monarchy, Charles started to swing public and parliamentary opinion behind him. Time appeared to be on his side.[28]

The Ulster plot

Meanwhile, two recruiting colonels, Richard Plunkett and Hugh Mac Phelim O'Byrne, attached themselves to a shadowy second circle of plotters.[29] At the centre of the circle was Rory O'More, grandson of a government-backed claimant to the O'More lordship who inherited lands assigned by Queen Elizabeth in County Kildare. He also held an Ulster plantation estate in County Armagh. In February 1641 O'More approached Conor Maguire, Baron Enniskillen, then attending parliament in Dublin. He urged that the Anglo–Scottish crisis offered the Irish a chance to regain lost estates by force. He also reminded Maguire of his heavy debts and claimed to have secured support in Leinster and Connacht. The latter claim, while probably untrue, was credible. O'More, like Maguire, had married into a leading family of the Pale. Maguire in turn drew in Sir Phelim *Rua* O'Neill, MP for Dungannon. From September aspirational scheming hardened to an operational plot grounded in confident planning and a sophisticated political programme.

Were these plotters acting 'out of fear of what was doing in England', as was later claimed?[30] The initial decision of the insurgents to target only English settlers suggests they were keenly aware that Charles had hopes of realigning the Scots against his parliamentary enemies. Their claim to be acting on his behalf was a deception and the commission that Phelim O'Neill would flourish a forgery. The very fact that deception was useful, however, suggests that would-be followers were fundamentally loyal.[31] The plot and the parliamentary protest movement could then be seen as 'different means to the same end'.[32] Conor Maguire was a member of the House of Lords, Rory Maguire, Sir Phelim O'Neill and Philip O'Reilly were all members of the House of Commons, Hugh Mac Mahon the brother of another and Morgan Cavanagh a former member. Nor on the face of it did the Ulster plotters envisage completely overturning the plantation settlement. They were apparent beneficiaries of plantation belonging to distant collaterals of the main *derbh fine*: the nearest common ancestor the Lord Maguire could claim with the senior branch of the family dated back as far as 1430. These cadet branches had tended to side with Queen Elizabeth against the Ulster Confederates. Philip O'Reilly's grandfather *Maolmórdha* had been killed at the Yellow Ford fighting for Bagenal.

Yet perhaps the Ulster plotters were driven by 'antecedent wrongs' rather than 'anticipated oppression'.[33] They wrote to John O'Neill, Tyrone's son (not knowing of his death four months before), and subsequently solicited military assistance from Eoghan *Rua* O'Neill, Tyrone's nephew, the most senior surviving officer among the Irish mercenaries in the Spanish service. This contact surely indicates that the conspirators, most of them 'men of broken fortune', envisaged some reversal of the Ulster plantation.[34] Many native landowners in Ulster were crushed by growing indebtedness because they were burdened with higher crown rents than their Protestant counterparts and had been too slow in dropping customary tribute and levying higher commercialised rents. Their estates had dwindled steadily. In County Cavan, for instance, the amount of land owned by native proprietors fell from 20 per cent in 1610 to 16 per cent by 1641.[35] Hugh *Óg* Mac Mahon, a former lieutenant colonel in the Spanish army and son of the last Mac Mahon, was a typical case in point: piecemeal sales and mortgages had shrunk his estate by over 60 per cent.[36]

It is hard to infer what the plotters really wanted from public protestations after the failure of the Dublin *coup* when the insurgents wanted to 'put a fair gloss' on their motives in order to make terms with the government or attract wider support.[37] Even in adjacent counties the ostensible causes of alienation could be proximate or long term. Insurgents in Cavan grumbled about recent political developments in Britain while in Longford they complained of plantation. Above all, aspirations were contingent on military success or failure, a key point made by a British deponent, held captive by Phelim O'Neill for the first six months of the rising. He asked O'Neill what he wanted:

At first he told this deponent that they required only liberty of conscience, but afterwards as his power so his demands were multiplied. They must have no Lord Deputy, great officers of State, Privy Councillors, Judges or Justices of the Peace but of the Irish nation. No standing army in the Kingdom. All tithes payable by Papists to be paid to Popish priests. Church lands to be restored to their bishops. All plantations since Primo Jacobi *to be disannulled none made hereafter. No payment of debts due to the British or restitution of anything taken in the war. All fortifications of strength to be in the hands of the Irish with power to erect and build more if they thought fit. All strangers (meaning British) to be restrained from coming over. All acts of Parliament against Popery and Papists, together with Poynings' Law, to be repealed, and the Irish Parliament to be made independent . . .*[38]

O'Neill's utopian wish list still envisaged retaining Ireland within the Stuart composite monarchy. The Irish were rebelling against a puritan government in Dublin as a way of showing their loyalty to the ultimate head of that government.[39]

The prime conspirators settled on a plan to capture Dublin Castle on Saturday 23 October 1641 in concert with an uprising in Ulster. Two hundred men would trickle unnoticed (it was a market day) into Dublin where they would rush the castle led by Maguire and O'More. There was nothing inherently wrong with the plan. Numbers were small enough to maintain secrecy but large enough to hold Dublin Castle until reinforcements came from County Wicklow, a region recently planted by Wentworth and consequently discontented.[40] The 2,000-strong standing army was dispersed in garrisons across the country and would, necessarily, have been slow to react and counter-attack.[41]

Only eighty men turned up and, fatally, the plotters put off the attack until the following morning and adjourned to a tavern. One of the tipplers was Owen O'Connolly, a Presbyterian convert and foster brother to Hugh Óg Mac Mahon. O'Connolly, improbable as the coincidence may seem, also happened to be a servant to Sir John Clotworthy, who formed an important strand in the web of secret contacts between Covenanter leaders and some of Charles's noisiest opponents in England.[42] He slipped away to the castle where he blurted out his story to Parsons and next morning Maguire and Mac Mahon were picked up and the putsch foiled. O'Connolly's first statement of 22 October to Parsons was factual but his second, in response to leading questions prepared by Clotworthy along with Pym and other leaders of the parliamentary party in England, claimed that the conspirators had long-laid plans to massacre 'all Protestants', and, in a reference to the Old English, 'others of *English* Blood, tho' of the *Romish* Religion'.[43] The massacre legend preceded the massacre.

The thunderclap revelation of a papist massacre together with Phelim O'Neill's claim of royal sanction revived Pym's fortunes and supplied the issue over which the English Civil War would break out. Could Englishmen trust Charles with control of the army that would have to be raised to crush the Irish rebellion?

The rising

Late on the night of 22 October and early next morning the conspirators seized control of a block of south Ulster, stretching almost from sea to sea, from Castle Archdale on Lower Lough Erne across to Newry. A typically swift and decisive insurgent coup was the capture of Shannock Castle, near Clones. Before six o'clock on the morning of 23 October a large group of tenants brought a supposed cow-stealer to Arthur Champion, their land-lord and the justice of the peace. When the gate was opened they threw off their long mantles and stabbed Champion and three others with hidden 'skeans' and hanged others later.[44]

Forewarned of the actual date of the plot, Sir William Cole had time to gather scattered settlers at Enniskillen and tip off Robert and William Stewart of the Laggan, who commanded the only regular companies posted in north-west Ulster.[45] Elsewhere settlers were initially stunned by 'the suddenness of our surprisal' and could 'scarcely believe themselves prisoners though in their chains'.[46] Promises to spare the Scots, while insincere, helped initially to confuse and divide the settlers, particularly in east Tyrone and Cavan.[47] By beating of drum and firing of beacons the 'principal gentlemen' among the Ulster settlers elsewhere formed other, more precarious armed enclaves: Arthur Chichester at Carrickfergus, Viscount Montgomery in the Ards, the Phillips brothers in north County London-derry and Sir James Craig at Belturbet.[48]

The first place Phelim O'Neill's army 'appeared anything of a body' was at Lisburn where he massed 3,000 men on 10 November.[49] His two attacks were held off and the settler enclave of Clandeboy saved. Burning the town, O'Neill turned south. He realised that a national uprising demanded the capture of Dublin and, in the way, Drogheda.[50] By 21 November some 2,000 Ulster men and their local allies were encamped north of Drogheda, waiting for a second thrust led by Philip O'Reilly to pass south of the town and cut it off from Dublin. Eight days later a relief column from Dublin blundered into O'Reilly's men in countryside broken up by lanes and ditches and shrouded by a 'great mist'. The troops promptly fled and the Ulster men 'pursued them and all the English to slaughter'.[51] This action at Julianstown Bridge made O'More's eloquent plea afterwards to the leaders of the Palesmen at Knockcrofty all the more compelling:

... we are made incapable of raising our fortunes by serving our King in any place of honour, profit or trust, in that country wherein we were born and which God, of his providence appointed us as a part of the earth which our ancestors for so many hundred years did inhabit.[52]

Julianstown was the trip wire for a national rising. **Map 2** gives a snapshot of the high tide of that revolt in mid-February 1642 lapping around the pockets of the Laggan, Clandeboy, Dublin and Cork. By then Dublin was already reinforced by an advance party of substantial reinforcements. Meanwhile Phelim O'Neill, with no artillery to breach the thin curtain walls, was reduced to keeping a 'loose blockade' around Drogheda. On 19 February a storm broke up the boom across the Boyne channel; a relief fleet promptly broke the blockade.[53] Day to day, O'Neill had something like 5,000–6,000 men, making this the second largest Irish operation of the rising.

The largest and potentially the most decisive operation came in Munster. Old Richard Butler, Viscount Mountgarret, uncle of Ormond and a one-time son-in-law and ally of Tyrone, joined the revolt on 30 November and within two days overran virtually all the county apart from Kilkenny city, which defected a fortnight later.[54] The three Butler peers in Tipperary rose with him, revealing the extent to which he had displaced Ormond as the dynasty's real figurehead.[55] He then led a horde of soldiers, their massed pikes bristling like 'a spacious wood', across Tipperary and Limerick and into North Cork where many of the local Catholic nobles and gentry joined him. Muskerry stood back as yet and his extensive estates stand out (see **map 2**) as the largest island in the sea of insurgency. After storming a castle in Mallow, the leaders bickered about loot and precedence, whereupon Mountgarret's men turned for home. But for this unedifying squabble the whole of Munster would, likely, have fallen into the insurgents' laps.[56]

Drogheda and Mallow were unusual examples of large-scale and co-ordinated insurgent activity. The typical action was a siege, a Drogheda writ small. Protestant strongholds dotted many parts of the country (see **map 2**). Where a castle was not taken by surprise, carelessness (insurgents in Thomond took Dromoland Castle, 'knowing where the key was hid') or some obvious weakness like lack of water, it tended to hold out for weeks, indeed months.[57] The insurgents could not cast siege guns, mill gunpowder in any quantity, nor, with the Shannon estuary and Waterford harbour blockaded by English ships, could they import more than a trickle of powder. But starving out the defenders took time.[58] The numbers of civilians sheltering in such holds could be unsustainably high, with up to 1,000 settlers huddled within the walls of Newcastle West in County Limerick, for instance, or 1,300 sheltering at Limavady and Ballycastle in County Derry.[59] Ultimately so many hungry mouths could not be fed in castles beyond striking range of the major government garrisons of Dublin, Cork and Carrickfergus.[60] Defenders gave up, like those of Castle Forbes in Longford, pressed by a 'woeful want of victuals' or decimated by 'mortal and infectious sickness'.[61] The end for King John's Castle in Limerick, for example, came in the early hours of 21 June 1643 when a bulwark collapsed and smoke billowing up from the underground fires revealed that a mine had been sprung below. By then, from an estimated 600–800 refugees and soldiers crammed together for the past five weeks, at least 220 lay buried in the castle yard and many more died afterwards.[62]

Popular revolt

Quite early on a popular revolt can be distinguished from the purposeful military activity described above. The deposition of Henry Boine, a clergyman in east Tyrone, captures this phenomenon.[63] On the second morning of the rising he heard from a Scottish eyewitness that:

. . . the Castle of Mountjoy was taken by Turlough Groome Ô Quin & Phelim Coggie Ô Neile & others and [the eyewitness] related that he himself was in the said Castle at the taking thereof and was demanded what countryman he was to which hee replyed he was a Scottsman whereupon they demanded him to depart from there for they had nothing to [illeg.] who being Scottishmen but only with the English: whereupon the deponent presently departed towards his owne house; Where in the way he saw one James duffe Mc Cauwell of Mullamoile in the County of Tyrone and about forty or fifty of the Irishmen in rebellion and despoiling all the English thereabouts: beating and abusing all that offered in any way to fight. And when he came to his house he founde there an Irish

woman who was come out of Donoghmore about 6 myles distant to tell
the deponent's wiffe that it were best for him to be gone least he might
be killed: She related the Rebells had cutt off the head of one Mr Madder
a minister . . .

The capture of Mountjoy Fort was a well-organised coup. The fact that the attackers bothered to question the eyewitness and let him live suggests the band acted under discipline. Their leaders, Turlough *gruama* [gloomy] O'Quinn and Phelim *a'chogaidh* ['of the wars'] O'Neill, were scions of once locally dominant clans acting on direct orders from Sir Phelim O'Neill. Contrast this with the gang of ruffians led by James *dubh* Mac Cothmhaoil [usually anglicised as McCall and Caulfield], a descendant of a subordinate sept depressed into the ranks of the landless by the expanding O'Neill clan in the sixteenth century. The mob was not killing English settlers outright yet, though Boine was right to be afraid: the hapless Rev. Madder was one of over a dozen clergymen murdered in east Tyrone and north Armagh.[64] The clergy were prime targets of violence because many had ready cash from church fines and fees and money lending and had the records of indebtedness. Like prayer books and bibles, Protestant ministers were also hateful as visible embodiments of a despised religion.[65]

The popular revolt, then, was a spontaneous, uncontrolled and sometimes murderous outburst by the lower classes of native society. Well before Julianstown and the defection of the Pale the popular revolt caught up 'all the common people and most of the younger sons of the gentry' north of the Boyne.[66] Demobbed soldiers from Wentworth's army were especially troublesome. Foolishly, Westminster blocked nearly all of them from embarking, leaving 7,000 bored and restless men billeted in companies across the country in expectation of eventually getting permission to sail away.[67] By the end of November the revolt had flamed like a brushfire throughout Leinster, almost all of Ulster and the adjacent overspill counties of Connacht. In contrast, the Catholic 'nobility and gentry' of Munster initiated and controlled the rebellion because they claimed to fear 'the height to which the meaner sort of people might grow up'.[68]

Richard Bellings unconvincingly explains away the 'stripping and robbing of Protestants' as the response of a 'desperate multitude' to the prorogation of parliament after a one-day sitting on 17 November and the consequent absence of a parliamentary forum for their grievances.[69] Hatred of 'very nation, name and kind of the English' ran too deep for such a glib explanation.[70] This was especially so in territories planted, or threatened with plantation, by the Stuarts.[71] The effects of the first generation of rapid population growth were felt after two decades and the frontier of cheap land and economic opportunity for settlers shifted from empty lands towards lands tenanted by native Irish.[72] Consequently, the major losers in colonial expansion were the native Irish tenantry who were inexorably displaced by settlers who 'could pay higher rents, and pay more securely'. Many natives considered 'the land was theirs and lost by their fathers'. A typical illustration of such commonplace attitudes would be the remark of one Art O'Melaghlin from a planted area of County Westmeath, that the settlers 'came but beggars out of England and had nothing but what we had wrongfully gotten from the Irish nation'.[73] So it was wholly appropriate to rob English and Scots, strip them to their underclothes and put them on the road. The would-be leaders of native society could not rein in such rage, or even discipline their own soldiers. Followers of Phelim O'Neill from his *Uí hEochaidh* [anglicised Hughes or Haughey] foster family murdered his prize prisoner Lord Caulfield of Charlemont and went on to kill most of the British families whom O'Neill had planted on his lands near Caledon, County Tyrone.[74]

Like their social betters, popular insurgents sometimes claimed 'we are his true subjects for we have the King's commission' or declaimed loyalty to Charles's Catholic Queen, Henrietta Maria: they were 'the Queenes souldyers and no rebels' and they would 'display her banners on Dublin Green'.[75] Such distorted echoes of the contemporary political crisis across the water reverberated alongside wilder messianic aspirations. Insurgents as far away as Offaly and Limerick clarified that 'the King that we mean is one of our own' and cast Phelim O'Neill as the hero prophesied by the saints complete with a birthmark in the shape of a crown, while some proto-republicans wanted 'to have a free state of themselves as they had in Holland'.[76] Others 'cared not a fart for the king and his laws'.[77]

'We desire,' Sir Conn Magennis of Iveagh reassured his Protestant neighbours, 'no blood to be shed.'[78] But neither he nor his fellow insurgent leaders could control their followers.

Massacre

Sir John Temple's *Irish Rebellion*, first published in 1646, long exercised a 'strong and hateful influence'.[79] It fixed a black legend of 'barbarous cruelties and bloody massacres' which were 'the most barbarous and bloody that was ever attempted in any part of the world' and to admirers like Edmund Borlase, son of one of the two lords justices in 1641, was 'writ without passion on unquestionable proofs'.[80] A commission headed by a tireless clergymen, Henry Jones, Dean of Kilmore and vice-chancellor of Trinity College, took these sworn statements or depositions in writing mostly from Protestant refugees who had fled to Dublin by the early months of 1642. Another set of statements was collected in Munster between 1642 and 1643 by the archdeacon of Cloyne.[81] 'Examinations' of Catholics are often lumped in, though most of these were taken a decade later and, for present purposes, they are not counted as depositions. The initial purpose of the depositions was to quantify losses of property for future compensation.[82] The legend in all its graphic horror was used for so long as a stick to beat Irish Catholics that subsequent historians who professed impartiality dismissed the depositions as tainted and inadmissible. However, these statements are admissible so long as they are treated with the same caution as any other partisan source.[83] The depositions show that the massacre legend was grounded in reality, however exaggerated and selectively remembered. **Map 2** shows several collective killings (that is, where twenty or more civilians were murdered) in the first four months of the rising. Nearly all were Catholic on Protestant massacres. The first mass killing seems to have happened in mid-November. A convoy of civilian prisoners was being led from Loughgall to, most likely, Lisburn. Phelim O'Neill had already sent other such convoys safely to Carrickfergus and Newry. However, a local insurgent captain, Toole McCann, drove around 100 men, women and children of the convoy 'like hogs' onto Portadown bridge, holed the middle of the bridge, stripped the prisoners and 'thrust them down headlong' into the river Bann.[84] Though native Irish tenants at Castlereagh had already been killed, there is no direct evidence that the Portadown massacre was in retaliation for settler atrocities since the better-known killings at Islandmagee (which Irish apologists insist started the cycle of killings) and Templepatrick came later.[85]

The single most common type of Catholic on Protestant collective massacre happened when a convoy of prisoners was set upon by attackers and by their escorts. In January 1642 an arrangement was made for the transfer of seventeen settlers from Newry to Newcastle, County Down, to be swapped for Irish prisoners held by Sir James Montgomery in Lecale. Sir Conn Magennis, incensed by reports that Montgomery had killed his prisoners, brought the settlers into a wood and had them hanged.[86] Up to sixty 'old men, women and children' were killed while en route from Oldstone Castle in County Antrim to Carrickfergus.[87] Another convoy of prisoners was set upon by their guards on Shrule bridge while crossing from County Mayo to County Galway.[88] Death struck mostly in ones and twos to straggling columns of refugees trudging slowly (one deponent talked of covering just three miles a day) to a safe haven. One of the grimmest examples must be that of Ann Dodd, who recollected how thirty-seven 'poore stripped English people' set out from Leitrim in mid-winter. No more than eight made it as far as Dublin, the women and children perishing of exposure or privation and the menfolk killed.[89] Men were killed more often than women and children because in the grim calculus of a faltering insurgency it began to seem foolish to send off able-bodied men who would soon return, armed and vengeful.[90] Thus when Longford Castle fell early in 1642, the menfolk were slain while women and children were 'stripped of their apparel' and put on the road to Dublin in cold weather.[91]

The number of murdered settlers was wildly inflated. At least 600 Protestants were killed in County Armagh, probably the worst-hit county in Ireland. Even multiplying this total by nine falls well short of the estimate of 154,000 settlers killed in that province claimed by Robert Maxwell, a clergymen from Armagh, and cited approvingly by Temple.[92] That said, a minimum estimate of 600 dead represented at least 17 per cent of the British population of County Armagh.[93]

Numbers mattered less to the contemporary reader than the impression of enormity and ghastliness. The latter was conveyed by emphasising atrocities that were even more horrific than hanging, burning, drowning, shooting or clubbing. For example, Temple sweepingly asserted that 'ordinarily' the Irish 'ript open' the wombs of pregnant British captives.[94] The trope was well established before Temple's *Rebellion*. Local Irish complained that the lord president of Munster's soldiers had 'ripped up' an Irishwoman during their November 1642 rampage through Tipperary.[95] A pamphleteer in 1642 recounted how 'blood-thirsty Savages' in Kilkenny beat out the brains of one Mr Atkins after which 'they layd hold of his wife being big with childe & ravisht her then ript open her wombe'.[96] This image is a staple in most of the visual representations of the massacre, often complete with the murderer plunging his hands in the womb. The pamphleteer insisted they 'count it a meritorious worke to imbrew their hands in the blood of the poore Protestants . . .' and Cromwell used almost the exact form of words eight years later when he justified the massacre of the garrison and civilians at Drogheda. In fact Temple's evidence of what Fitzpatrick describes as 'Jack-the-Ripper' crimes consisted of two vague hearsay reports and a third more authentic-sounding report from County Donegal, naming a perpetrator (Manus Bán MacKnogher) and a victim (the wife of one William McKenny), culled from the depositions.[97] Thus what may have been a single ghoulish atrocity became, imperceptibly, commonplace fact.

Catholic apologists showed less genius for fabricating a black legend. The synod of May 1642 (which created the Confederate Catholic regime) directed that every province keep 'a faithful inventory' of the 'murthers, burnings and other cruelties' perpetrated by the 'puritan enemies' specifying the place, persons, date, 'cause' and 'manner', to be compiled and publicised 'for the comfort and instruction of our people'.[98] 'RS', the author of a 1662 *Collection of some of the murthers and massacres committed on the Irish . . .* , may have drawn on this.[99] He is not always reliable, he grossly exaggerates the numbers killed at Islandmagee, for instance. Outside Ulster he is more credible. Taking County Cork for example, he enumerates fifteen separate atrocities including one at Clonakilty perpetrated by a raiding party from Bandon where he claims 'about 238 men, women and children were murthered, of which number seventeen children were taken by the legs by soldiers who knockt out their brains against the walls'.[100] A Protestant eyewitness of this massacre confirms that government troops 'killed all, and ranged about and found some hundred more in gardens and killed all . . . old, young and none spared'.[101] RS's catalogue of atrocities in Cork tapers off, with just three after 1643, two of them involving the shooting of named individuals and only one mass killing of civilians, in 1650. The pattern of reported Protestant on Catholic massacres in 1642 is skewed towards Cork and the Pale.[102] A typical example from the Pale would be raiders from Drogheda who 'kill'd and burnt in the firres [furze] about 160 men, women and children of the inhabitants of Termonfeighin'.[103] James Touchet, Earl of Castlehaven, stumbled on the aftermath of a similarly 'considerable slaughter' near Rathcoole: 'I saw the bodies and the furze still burning.'[104]

The geographic range (**map 3**) of reported massacres of Catholics in spring and early summer 1642 represents the footprint of reinforced government armies (almost 45,000 in aggregate) striking out from Cork, Dublin and Carrickfergus deep into insurgent territory: 'Where we came against the rebels, their adherents, relievors and abettors,' admitted the Lords Justices, '[we] proceeded with fire and sword the soldiers sometimes not sparing the women and sometimes not the children . . .'[105] All the while, killings of Protestants continued in the sectarian cockpit of County Armagh. The burning of up to twenty Protestants at Shewie probably happened in mid-February while the massacre of Protestants from Armagh town can be linked to the preceding massacre of Catholics in Newry by Covenanters recently disembarked from Scotland.

Such killing of civilians sheltering in captured castles or towns was a moral grey area. A Scottish soldier who fought in Ulster in the early 1640s thought that if defenders were foolish or desperate enough to surrender without first securing an explicit promise of quarter, the besiegers were acting within the 'Law of War' to kill them outright. Yet he also believed that such killings were tainted by 'horrible cruelty'.[106] By that reckoning, the killing of women and children and of male prisoners 'first takin to mercie' (as at Augher, County Tyrone) counts as a massacre.[107]

Eoghan *Rua* O'Neill, just back from thirty years of military service in the Spanish Netherlands, in the summer of 1642 should have the last word: 'On both sides,' he exclaimed in shock, 'there is nothing but burning, robbing in cold blood and cruelties such as are not usual even among the Moors and Arabs.'[108]

Conclusion: three kingdoms, one crisis?

'I see you take your pistol in your hand, cocking it to shoot at me, in which case it is lawful for me to discharge my pistol and kill you': Catholics subsequently claimed that fear of what was happening in the other two kingdoms justified their rising in 1641.[109] Parliamentary hacks and propagandists, however, later denied emphatically there had been any 'new, unexpected and pressing' threat. The Irish had launched a 'voluntary and causeless rebellion'.[110]

The prime and long-term cause of the rising was not to be found in Covenanter and Puritan attacks on Catholicism but in the plantations *and* threatened plantations of the preceding decades. In that sense, it is hard to see how the 1630s' trend was really 'towards accommodation and away from conflict'.[111]

The short-term context and the archipelagic backdrop are important to understand proximate rather than long-term causes. By securing a position of strength from which to dictate terms to the King, the Covenanters offered a pertinent example to Irish Catholics of what they might achieve by a coup: 'The Scots have taught us our ABC,' admitted one insurgent.[112] This attempted coup in turn, as it degenerated into bloody war and massacre, supplied the issue on which, to a great extent, the English Civil War broke out. Could a man be put in command of an army to defeat Irish rebels when he had conspired, or so his opponents could plausibly claim, with those rebels?[113]

The insurgents and, later, the Confederate Catholics would conceive their strategies within a three-kingdom context.[114] Yet there can be no unitary history of the archipelago. The popular nature of the Irish rising and the atrocities that marred it set it apart from what was largely a baronial revolt in Scotland and England.[115] Moreover, the rising and the war that followed in Ireland from 1641 to 1653 was not, for the most part, a *civil* war. Rather, it was an uncompromising struggle between distinct ethnic and religious groups. An Irish priest expected there would 'be scarce an Irishman in all of Ireland that was a Catholique that should take part with the Protestants' and this expectation was reinforced by exemplary punishment of those who did.[116] While the moral context of Irish warfare would never again be as stark as in the first nine months of the rising, it was grim by the standards the English and Lowland Scots applied among themselves and against each other.[117] Ireland was different.

Endnotes

1 Russell 1991, pp. 373–400; Morrill 1996, p. 84; Bennett 1997, pp. 31–6.

2 Smith 1998, p. 102; Kenyon and Ohlmeyer 1998, pp. 17–21.

3 Adamson 1997, p. 99.

4 Bennett 1997, p. 52.

5 Cited in Clarke 1976, p. 272; Gillespie 2006, pp. 126–8.

6 Clarke 1976, p. 276.

7 Morrill 1993a, pp. 252–7.

8 Russell 1990, p. 27.

9 Morrill 1993b, pp. 8–19.

10 Morrill 1999, p. 67.

11 Russell 1990, p. 119.

12 Russell 1991, pp. 291–4, 330–7.

13 Gillespie 2006, pp. 128–9.

14 Clarke 1976, pp. 254–6; Gillespie 2006, pp. 133–4.

15 Gillespie 2006, pp. 136–7; Clarke 1976, p. 286.

16 Clarke 1966, p. 152; Russell 1991, pp. 382–5.

17 Perceval-Maxwell 1994, pp. 150–4, 160.

18 Perceval-Maxwell 1994, p. 287.

19 Bindon 1846, p. 35; O'Hara 2006, p. 24.

20 Russell 1991, p. 395; Stradling 1994, pp. 32–40; Jennings 1964, p. 37.

21 *CSPI (Charles I) 1634–1647*, pp. 281, 307.

22 Clarke 1981, p. 37.

23 According to Phelim O'Neill other strongholds countrywide were also to be seized: Hickson ii, p. 190; Gillespie 2006, p. 141.

24 Perceval-Maxwell 1994b, pp. 421–30; Clarke 1966, p. 227; Perceval-Maxwell 1994, pp. 200–4; Ohlmeyer 1992, pp. 905–19.

25 *TCD Ms 830* (County Roscommon) 'Examination of Hugh O'Connor' f. 9; 'Remonstrance of Catholics of Ireland' Dec., 1641 in Gilbert 1879, i, p. 360; Russell 1991, p. 379; *TCD Ms 832* (County Cavan) 'Deposition of George Crichtoun' f. 146v; Curry 1773, pp. 99, 108; *TCD Ms 833* (County Cavan) 'Deposition of Henry Reynolds' f. 60.

26 Perceval-Maxwell 1994, pp. 233–4.

27 Clarke 1981, p. 40.

28 Smith 1998, pp. 112, 120, 352.

29 Perceval-Maxwell 1994, pp. 204–7.

30 'The Persuasions and Suggestions the Irish Catholicks make to his Majesty' in King 1692, p. 290; Deposition of Arthur Culme, *TCD Ms 833* fol. 133r–v.

31 Clarke 1981, pp. 32–3.

32 Clarke 1970b, pp. 88, 98.

33 Clarke 1981, p. 36; Gillespie 1986, pp. 194–5.

34 Anon (nd) *An Account of the War in Ireland* f. 5.

35 Gillespie 2006, p. 140.

36 Gillespie 1991, p. 15; Livingstone 1980, pp. 103, 111.

37 Perceval-Maxwell 1994, p. 221.

38 'Deposition of Robert Maxwell' in Hickson 1884, i, pp. 326–40.

39 Fitzpatrick 1988, p. 75.

40 Gilbert 1882–91, i, pp. 13–14.

41 McKenny 2005, pp. 36–7.

42 Russell 1990, p. 27; Russell 1991, pp. 60–4, 68–70, 151–3; Fitzpatrick 1988, pp. 133–48.

43 Gilbert 1879, i, pp. 357–8; Armstrong 2005, p. 45.

44 Gillespie 1993, p. 58.

45 McKenny 2005, pp. 38–9.

46 'Relation by Audley Mervin' in Gilbert 1879, i, p. 466.

47 *TCD Ms 832* (Cavan) 'Deposition of R. Parsons' f. 89; 'Deposition of G. Crichtoun' f. 144; *TCD Ms 839* (County Tyrone) 'Deposition by Roger Markham' f. 17; Canny 2001, pp. 478–83.

48 Armstrong 2005, pp. 29, 36.

49 Hogan 1873, pp. 12–13.

50 Corish 1976, p. 292; Lenihan 2001, pp. 34–5.

51 Smith 1963, pp. 112–13.

52 Gilbert 1882–91, i, p. 36.

53 HMC 1903, ii, p. 82; Borlase 1680, pp. 61–5; Gilbert 1882–91, i,
    pp. 45–50; Gilbert 1879, i, p. 26; D'Alton 1863, i, pp. 223–53;
    Ó Dhonnchadha 1931, p. 8.

54 Edwards 2003, pp. 309–14.

55 Coonan 1954, p. 135.

56 Carte 1736, i, p. 340; Fitzpatrick 1912, p. 119; Clarke 1966, p. 196; TCD
    Ms 825 (County Cork) 'Deposition of Thomas Betteworth' ff. 261–2.

57 Gilbert 1879, i, pp. 475, 485; Gilbert 1882–91, ii, pp. 69–73.

58 TCD Ms 815 (Queen's County) Deposition of John Tucker f. 367; Lenihan
    2001, pp. 54–7; Anon (1643) Another Extract from Severall Letters from
    Ireland (London) p. 23; Cuffe 1841, p. 19; Edwards 1998, pp. 253–84.

59 Hogan 1936, pp. 3, 6, 9, 10, 13, 79, 120; TCD Ms 815 (Queens' County)
    ff. 358, 370.

60 Bennett 2000, p. 53.

61 TCD Ms 817 (County Longford) Dame Jane Forbes f. 187. See also TCD
    Ms 814 (King's County) Joseph Joice f. 259; TCD Ms 815 (Queen's County)
    Deposition of Richard Steele f. 358.

62 Wiggins 2000, pp. 157, 177; Gilbert 1879, i, p. 494.

63 TCD Ms 839 (County Tyrone) 'Deposition of Henry Boine' and 'Deposition
    of John Kerdiff' ff. 1–2.

64 TCD Ms 832 'Deposition of George Creichton' fol. 145; 'G.S' 1641, p. 5.

65 Robinson 1984, pp. 69–72; Ford 1995, pp. 85, 94–6; TCD Ms 833 (County
    Cavan) 'Deposition of William Thorpe' f. 72r; Canny 1997, pp. 44–70;
    Canny 2001, pp. 490, 513.

66 Perceval-Maxwell 1994, p. 258; Canny 1997, p. 51; HMC Ormond 1903, p. 23.

67 Russell 1991, p. 395; Stradling 1994, pp. 32–40; CSPI Charles I 1901, p. 281.

68 Canny 2001, p. 532; Clarke 1966, p. 196.

69 Gilbert 1882–91, i, pp. 31–2.

70 TCD Ms 817 (County Westmeath) 'Deposition of Thomas Fleetwood'
    ff. 764–68; TCD Ms 814 (King's County) 'Deposition of Marmaduke
    Clapham' f. 79.

71 Clarke 1981, pp. 29–45; Gillespie 1986, pp. 191–213; Perceval-Maxwell 1994, pp. 213–33; Canny 2001, pp. 469–91.

72 Gillespie 1991, p. 15.

73 Perceval-Maxwell 1978, p. 163; *TCD Ms 817* (County Westmeath) 'Deposition of Thomas Fleetwood' ff. 764–8.

74 Ó Dhonnchadha 1931, p. 7; 'Examination of William Skelton' *TCD Ms 836* (County Armagh) ff. 171–5 and 'Examination of Michael Harrison' ff. 127–36; *NLI Ms 345* p. 9; *TCD Ms 839* (County Tyrone) ff. 7, 70, 72, 74, 85, 171–2.

75 *TCD Ms 834* (County Louth) 'Deposition of John Montgomery' fol. 71v.; *TCD Ms 833* (County Cavan) 'Deposition of John Perkins' f. 47r.; 'Deposition of Robert Daye' f. 135b; *TCD Ms 814* (King's County) 'Deposition of Henry Aeyloffe ff. 61–2/175–6; *TCD Ms 815* (Queen's Co.) ff. 160, 203, 226, 229; *TCD Ms 829* (County Limerick) 'Deposition of John Potter' f. 245b; Hore 1904, v, p. 255.

76 *TCD Ms 829* (County Limerick) 'Deposition of Henry Hughes' f. 352b.

77 *TCD Ms 829* (County Limerick) 'Deposition of William Fytton' f. 310; Canny 2001, p. 486.

78 O'Sullivan 1997, p. 181.

79 Barnard 1990, p. 52.

80 Canny 2001, p. 463; Bartlett 1992, p. 7; Anon 1741, p. 118; Orrery 1662, pp. 4, 12; Lindley 1972, pp. 145–65; Shagan 1997, pp. 4–34.

81 Smyth 2006, p. 114.

82 Barnard 1997, pp. 178–9; Clarke 1997, pp. 148–9; Bennett 2000, p. 51.

83 Simms 1997, p. 137.

84 Simms 1997, pp. 126–8; Canny 2001, pp. 484–5.

85 Elliott 2001, p. 103; Reilly 1742, viii; *BL Add. Ms.* ff. 326–7 (my thanks to Kevin Forkan for bringing this to my attention); Hickson 1884, i, p. 21; Fitzpatrick 1903, p. 106; Armstrong 2005, pp. 32–5.

86 *TCD Ms 837* (County Down) 'Deposition of Elizabeth Croker' f. 4; 'Deposition of Thomas Trevor' f. 86; 'Deposition of Peter Hill' f. 36; 'Deposition of Edward Saunders' f. 59.

87 *TCD Ms 838* (County Antrim) 'Deposition of John Blaire' f. 68b.

88 *TCD Ms 831* (County Mayo) 'Examination of Lord Mayo' f. 229; 'Examination of Murtagh Duff' f. 233; 'Examination of William Ling' f. 239.

89 *TCD Ms 831* (County Leitrim) 'Deposition of Ann Dudd' f. 9; *TCD Ms 814* (King's County) 'Deposition of Marmaduke Clapham' f. 162.

90 *TCD Ms 812* (County Carlow) 'Deposition of Martha Moseley' f. 91b; *TCD Ms 814* (King's County) f. 176.

91 *TCD Ms 817* (County Longford) 'Deposition of Christopher Thomas' f. 15; 'Deposition of Lydia Smith' f. 159; 'Deposition of Elizabeth Trafford' f. 162b; 'Deposition of Elizabeth Aleyne' f. 180.

92 Temple 1646, p. 126; Smyth 2006, p. 116.

93 Simms 1997, pp. 133–7.

94 Temple refers to the daughter of one John Stone of the Grage whose belly was 'ripped up' in April 1642 at Ballincolough near Ross but he probably confused this with another allegation relating to Graige, County Kilkenny; see Dunlop 1913, i, p. 180; Temple 1646, p. 97. Temple missed at least three other such depositions referring to a woman 'great with child' who had her belly 'ript up' and the child taken out alive *TCD Ms 826* (County Cork) 'Deposition of Captain Joseph Salmon' f. 114; *TCD Ms 829* (County Limerick) 'Deposition of Elizabeth Martin' f. 329; *TCD Ms* (County Donegal) 'Deposition of Mulrony Carroll' f. 125; 'Deposition of Ann Dutton' f. 126; Temple 1646, p. 97. See also Smyth 2006, pp. 133–4.

95 Edwards 2003, p. 309.

96 O'Hara 2006, p. 36; O'Dowd 1991b, p. 101.

97 Anon 1679, p. 4; Fitzpatrick 1903, p. 195.

98 Borlase 1680, Appendix, p. 41.

99 Barnard 1997, pp. 179–80.

100 R.S. 1662, p. 24. For an account of an Irish soldier who grabbed an infant by the heels and dashed his brains out against an oak block see *TCD Ms 831* (County Leitrim) 'Deposition of James Stevenson' f. 5; 'Deposition of Susanna Stevenson' f. 13.

101 *Good News from Ireland* (London 1642) cited in Bartlett 2003, p. 25.

102 Anon 1643, pp. 26–7. The two instances in County Leitrim are extracted from Sir Frederick Hamilton's boastful *True Relation* to the English parliament. Curiously, Newry apart, RS reports no atrocities by Monro's large covenanter army as it rapidly overran Counties Antrim and Down.

103 R.S. 1662, p. 15.

104 Fitzpatrick 1903, p. 155.

105 *HMC* 1903, pp. 23, 24, 27, 30, 35, 38–9, 46, 56, 62–5, 79, 82–3, 95, 99, 130.

106 Turner 1683, p. 336.

107 Perceval-Maxwell 1978, p. 157. Lisgoole does not feature on the map since probably fewer than twenty civilians were killed. *TCD Ms 834*

(County Monaghan) 'Deposition of Charles Campbell' f. 56; Temple 1646, p. 83; Lynch 1662, pp. 93, 111.

108 Jennings 1964, p. 507.

109 Bindon 1846, p. 40.

110 Temple 1646, p. 66; Borlase 1680; Jones 1642, pp. 4, 6; Maley 1998, p. 183; Russell 1991, p. 373.

111 Perceval-Maxwell 1994, p. 285.

112 *TCD Ms 832* (County Cavan) 'Deposition of George Creichton' f. 146; Perceval-Maxwell 1994, p. 235.

113 Armstrong 2005, pp. 50–1, 59, 61–4; Barnard 1975, p. 4.

114 Ó Siochrú 1999, pp. 238–9.

115 Samuel 1998, i, p. 33.

116 Canny 2001, p. 497; Carlton 1991, p. 19; *TCD Ms 826* (County Cork) 'Deposition of Donogh McCormack' f. 86.

117 Carlton 1990, p. 243; Wheeler 2001, pp. 164–5.

CHAPTER 6

God or King? 1642–49

Confederation of Kilkenny

Claims that lords justices Parsons and Borlase deliberately goaded the Old English into rising with the Ulstermen are unconvincing because at the outset of the rising they were not secure enough to play with fire.[1] Actions such as disarming the Palesmen and describing the insurgents as 'evil-affected Irish Papists' reflected panicky bumbling rather than cold malice.[2] Flushed with the success of their counter-offensive, however, the lords justices did not encourage the individual surrenders which would otherwise have brought the rising to a quick end.[3] The *cause célèbre* of Nicholas Nettervill, Viscount Dowth, accused of provisioning insurgents near Drogheda, suggested otherwise: his plea that the besiegers had taken what they wanted 'against his will' was rejected out of hand.[4] The case suggested that a net of complicity and guilt would be thrown wide enough to catch nearly all Catholic landowners, as did Charles's formal assent in March 1642 to an act of the English parliament to fund reconquest by loans 'adventured' on confiscated estates. He signed away his prerogative rights to wage war and make peace and it would now be for the English parliament to adjudge on any pardon granted to an Irish rebel.[5] The scale of the envisaged confiscations, amounting to roughly half the land in the country, emphasised that parliament assumed collective Irish guilt.

War would go on. 'We have no choice,' clamoured a Franciscan in September 1642, 'but to conquer or be conquered.'[6]

Responding to the need for a coordinated military effort, a national congregation of Catholic clergy convened at Kilkenny in May 1642 and invited Catholic lay leaders to join them in setting up a new government for the two thirds of Ireland still under insurgent control. The participants described themselves as 'Confederate Catholics' bound as individuals by an 'oath of association' comparable to the Scottish covenant.[7] They solemnly swore, among other things, to 'bear true faith and allegiance' to Charles I and to maintain the 'free exercise of the Roman Catholic faith and religion throughout this land'.[8] The Confederate motto *Pro Deo, Rege et Patria Hiberni unanimes* [literally meaning 'Irish united for God, King and Country'] encapsulated the by now long-standing hope of reconciling religious and political allegiances. The Irish, unlike the Covenanters, had no pretensions to impose their religious preferences on the other two kingdoms: 'Our ancient Land and Faith: 'tis all we crave . . .'[9] Patrick Darcy drew up the final model of government comprising county and provincial councils culminating in a powerful 'Supreme Council' or standing executive. This government has been called the 'Confederation of Kilkenny' because the Supreme Council most commonly met in Kilkenny. This was to be nominated by, and answerable to, a 'General Assembly' which the Confederates insisted was not a parliament.[10] The unicameral nature of the assembly reflected the relative weakness and tardiness of support from the upper social strata. Some Catholic peers fought against the Confederation and many tried to stay neutral: a 1644 listing of General Assembly members recorded only 18 peers, 13 bishops and 166 others.[11] The assembly first met in October 1642 and nine were called altogether.[12]

The most urgent task for this Irish proto-state was to levy taxes, recruit soldiers and 'from a confused medley of freebooting' wage 'an orderly war'.[13]

'Conquer or be conquered': 1642–43

Four distinct provincial armies were formed under generals with long experience of continental warfare: O'Neill in Ulster, Garrett Barry in Munster, Thomas Preston in Leinster and John Burke in Connacht. This arrangement can be criticised for institutionalising provincialism and fragmenting the war effort.[14] However, a 'running' or national army may not have been feasible when fighting was necessarily localised by the lumbering slowness of large armies (cavalry raiders were another matter) marching overland. To take one example, it usually took Robert Monro's Scottish army a fortnight to march from Carrickfergus to Charlemont and back. The difficulty of scraping together much more than a fortnight's supplies for enough men to take the stronghold helps explain why Charlemont survived so long.[15] Moreover, all parts of Confederate Ireland were potentially menaced by cavalry raiders or by the English parliament's Irish Sea squadron based in Milford Haven.[16] Therefore the Confederate Catholics had to hold many local strongholds and actually manned more than they needed through logistic inertia.[17]

The lords justices harangued their troops to '. . . burn, spoil, waste, consume, destroy and demolish' in the summer of 1642. There was cold genocidal intent here and later they would decry a ceasefire with the Irish 'before the sword or famine should have so abated them in numbers as that in reasonable time English colonies might overlap them'.[18] There was also sound military strategy given that the lords justices anticipated a steady flow of supplies and fresh troops from England and Scotland and an ever-tightening naval blockade of Irish-held ports.[19] However, scorched earth made less sense after the English Civil War began in late August 1642. The flashpoint of that war is yet another reminder of archipelagic inter-connectedness and came when parliament announced its intention to transfer a magazine to London, ostensibly to equip regiments for Ireland.[20] For all Westminster's rhetoric of unrelenting war against popery in Ireland, funding war in England now came first. Agonising over the cost of a land war in Ireland, parliament accepted glib promises that a naval descent on the west coast would 'end the war before Xmas', but the murderous fatuity of Lord Forbes's cruise along the west coast did nothing of the sort.[21] Stranded and perishing of privation and disease in alarmingly large numbers, government troops stopped burning to their doorsteps and instead jostled with the Irish to secure enclaves from which to draw food and contributions.[22] The exception was Ulster, where Monro's Covenanters and the Laggan army continued to burn rather than conquer and forced desperate 'creaghts' (a collective term for wartime refugees and their herds) to migrate towards Connacht in May 1643, guarded by O'Neill's army. Laggan horsemen unexpectedly fell on the rear of his shambling column near Clones and cut down the fleeing Irish foot soldiers.[23] Government troops also won two other battles. In August 1642 the 'old and unfortunate' Barry had mustered a host of over 6,000 men and took Liscarroll castle, which guarded the northern route into the Blackwater valley.[24] Morrough O'Brien, Baron Inchiquin, with an army half the size of Barry's, challenged him 'rather than starve'.[25] In open countryside English horsemen could usually break up stands of pikemen and so it proved at Liscarroll, though the Irish suffered more than the usual handful of casualties because there were no adjacent bogs or woods to which they could run. Another battle was fought in March 1643 when Ormond, commander of the English forces in Ireland, tried to capture New Ross and choke off the Waterford estuary, the Irish lifeline to Catholic Europe. He failed and on his return march to Dublin brushed Preston aside at Ballinvegga, County Wexford.[26]

Yet the Protestant forces continued to lose ground, and subsistence room, outside Ulster in a succession of sieges, the most common military action of these wars.[27] Drawing on their experience in the Spanish Netherlands, the Irish proved to be brisk and competent in this technically demanding business. Barry, for instance, had fought with Spinola at the siege of Breda (1624–25) and penned a history of that emblematic event. Dragging a dismounted 32-pounder gun on a makeshift sled across the County Limerick and north County Cork countryside, he forced the many Protestant strongholds to surrender before Inchiquin stopped him at Liscarroll. The landing of more siege guns in April 1643 speeded the tempo of Irish operations.[28]

By the summer of 1643 Charles I was coming around to the view that he faced a long-drawn-out struggle and needed to tap Irish Catholic resources of manpower and money.[29] The truce between Protestant royalists and Confederate Catholics prompted the Solemn League and Covenant of September 1643 by which the Covenanters agreed to send a large army across the English border to fight for parliament which, in turn, nudged Charles closer to the Irish.[30] Before the dismissal of Parsons in March 1643, peace feelers bypassed the Irish Council and those, like Parsons, 'most affected to the Parliament'.[31]

Cessation

On 15 September 1643 the Confederate Catholics agreed to a year's ceasefire with Ormond, now the King's viceroy. The agreement tried to freeze the territorial status quo (**map 4**) into an untidy mix of disputed zones and straggling outposts.[32] Ormond's own forces held the old Pale and a sprinkling of outposts while Inchiquin held the coast from Bandon to Youghal with a tongue of land stretching thence almost to County Limerick. Neither the Laggan army nor Monro's Scots observed the ceasefire. The Irish toehold in Ulster was precarious and Eoghan *Rua* O'Neill's soldiers and creaghts wintered among unwilling hosts to the south and drifted north of the drumlins fleetingly each summer to graze their cattle while the grass grew.

Charles I secured the return of many of the troops sent over to put down the rebellion and opened the possibility of further reinforcement of his army in England by Irish Catholic troops. He could plausibly justify the cessation on the grounds that 'his Protestant subjects could not defend the little they had left'.[33] For Protestants outside Ulster, the ceasefire was indeed a 'good deal'.[34] For the Irish, the benefits were less apparent. They had to pay a large subsidy to the royalists and their agreement raised doubts at the Vatican, their most likely source of support abroad, about their religious commitment.[35] Above all, they were winning. Cessation broke the painfully gained momentum of victory: as the recently arrived papal envoy Scarampi put it, 'not to go forward is to go backward'.[36]

Admittedly, Ulster was lost, but the province was remote and strategically marginal. Monro posed no real threat below the drumlin belt of south Ulster because he was held back by orders from Edinburgh to stay close to Scotland, ready for recall if necessary.[37] Leinster and Munster were more populous and more densely sprinkled with towns and knit together with post roads and navigable waterways.[38] The Confederate Catholics controlled these two provinces but for the Dublin and Cork enclaves. Ormond and Inchiquin still had big armies but, starved of supplies, they were fast wasting away and would have had to send many of their troops to reinforce the royalists in England, regardless of the cessation. Ormond's quarters were being squeezed ever more tightly towards Dublin, while horsemen led by the Earl of Castlehaven pounced on a Protestant army 'in a dangerous passage' near Fermoy and routed it.[39] Cork and Dublin would have fallen to a determined attack.

Such speculation is not unhistorical because some considered territorial consolidation should take priority over schemes to help Charles in England. Scarampi, for example, admitted that if the King won an outright victory he might offend English sensibilities by showing leniency to Irish Catholics but pointed out that the Irish should plan for the more likely outcome of negotiated peace or victory for the Long Parliament.[40] Whoever won then 'will find us in arms, well provided, with increased territories, and stronger in foreign succours' and 'could not so readily invade us nor swallow us up'. Richard Bellings, secretary of the Confederation, meanwhile professed himself satisfied if Charles would merely 'tolerate the free exercise of our religion' and demand nothing more that might make them less 'serviceable to the King'. Bellings and Scarampi personify distinct political objectives, tacit religious toleration or religious freedom and distinct strategic priorities either to help Charles I unreservedly or to abandon him. They did neither. Most historians would agree that the Confederate Catholics failed because they did not definitively choose either one of these 'viable but incompatible policies'.[41]

The fracture line was not ethnic.[42] The first General Assembly resolved to avoid 'distinction or comparison made betwixt old Irish and old or new English' and redefined the political nation in confessional terms. This comprehended even English Catholics with Irish interests, such as Castlehaven, or those who saw themselves as such, like Ulick Bourke, Earl of Clanricarde, who was born in England of an English mother. The fissure opened over status and class rather than putative ethnicity. The smallish number of nobles, unsurprisingly, had most to lose from pro- longed rebellion and most to gain from a speedy settlement with the King. They were more flexible in their demands than the bulk of Confederate Catholics. With the death of Lords Slane and Gormanstown, Donough MacCarthy, Viscount Muskerry, Edmund Butler, Viscount Mountgarret, James Touchet, Earl of Castlehaven and their allies dominated the Supreme Council until August 1646. This council, whatever was set down on paper, was only imperfectly and intermittently accountable to the General Assembly.[43] They dominated not only through strength of numbers (half the council members belonged to their faction at any one time) but through their energy and the unifying web of Butler kinship, affinity and clientage. Their critics decried them as an 'Ormondist' clique (it is too early to speak of a contending faction, rather than vague and passive disquiet) and one can see why the term was so apt and has some currency among modern his- torians.[44] Muskerry was Ormond's brother-in-law, Mountgarret president of the council his great-uncle, one of Castlehaven's sisters was married to Mountgarret's son and another to Richard Butler of Dunboyne (Ormond's brother) and so on. So long as one remembers that Muskerry and his allies were not dupes and were willing to oppose Ormond when necessary, the term 'Ormondist' is preferable to 'moderate' (which carries an implied value judgement) or 'peace faction' which can be confusing.[45] The choice was not between peace and war but between a war fought in Britain or Ireland.

Talking peace

At the time, the two policies did not seem incompatible: 'the keeping of our enemies in action abroad is that which will secure us at home.'[46] Randal MacDonnell, Earl of Antrim, persuaded the Confederates to ship Alisdair Mac Colla Mac Donald with a small army to fall on the covenant- ing Campbells in the west of Scotland.[47] Castlehaven, charged in 1644 with winning back Ulster, managed to dodge a battle with Monro 'by all possible means' and duly camped his large army near Charlemont until autumnal privation and sickness forced him to pull back.[48] In contrast, Mac Colla's little army provided the backbone of Montrose's royalist army which won a string of crushing victories and immobilised the Covenanters in Ulster and in the north of England.[49] The immobility of the Scots let the English royalists recover temporarily from what should have been a crushingly decisive defeat at Marston Moor in July 1644.[50] From a royalist perspective the Confederate expeditions to Ulster and Scotland were a riposte to a Covenanter army crossing into England in January 1644.[51] Charles could also throw English troops released from Ireland onto the scales. These 'Irish' (as roundhead propaganda quickly dubbed them) fought well in North Wales and Cheshire but did not play nearly as significant a part in the First English Civil War as the Covenanters. Charles needed more men from Ireland.

The chance for a timely agreement was fleeting. It could last only so long as the existing sympathetic, at times even sycophantic, Supreme Council continued to marginalise two potentially more radical constituencies. These were, first, General Assembly members and, second, the clergy.[52] The latter were a potential counter-weight to the peers. The cadre of counter-Reformation bishops were nearly all the scions of wealthy families: four of those attending assemblies were themselves the sons of peers. They were unusually talented and enjoyed special prestige in what was, essentially, a war of religion.[53] A clerical convocation usually met at the same time as a General Assembly and this had the potential to serve as an institutional basis for opposition. Most Catholic landowners seemed content with so much religious toleration ('it was indifferent to him,' taunted Robert Talbot 'to have mass with all solemnity in Christ or St Patrick's church, as privately by his bedside') as would enable them to partake fully in public and professional life.[54] Most clergy, however, wanted religious freedom, rather than just toleration, and to keep churches and church lands seized from the Church of Ireland.[55]

Moreover, the opportunity for a definitive settlement between the Confederates and royalists would arise only after Marston Moor when Charles at last realised that if he wanted an Irish army of 10,000 men shipped to England he must promise more than bare religious toleration by connivance and address some of the items on the wish-list of Catholic envoys to his wartime capital of Oxford: these included a reversal of Wentworth's plantations, the Graces, repeal of penal laws, the right of Catholics to share office and a declaration that the Irish parliament was 'independent of, and not subordinate to the parliament of England'.[56] Agreement would have had to be reached and the army sent before the second royalist defeat at Naseby (June 1645) which made parliamentarian victory in the First Civil War 'all but inevitable'.[57] An Irish army landing in England after Naseby would have been stranded by the collapse of royalist armies and, likely, repudiated by Charles in an attempt to prise a compromise peace from his enemies.[58]

Ormond was not the man to negotiate a timely agreement. He retained little residual prestige and authority among his Catholic kin.[59] He was a zealous defender of the Protestant interest in Ireland and so was usually 'reactive, sometimes grudging, occasionally obstructive' even as an increasingly frantic king urged him in February 1645 to conclude a treaty 'whatever it cost' and get the Irish to send an army to England before it was too late.[60] Charles was privately prepared to promise the 'present' abolition of penal laws against Catholics, not just a promise of future action after he got an Irish army.[61] Ormond dithered and months later had come only so far as to offer toleration by connivance of the 'quiet exercise of their religion'. By the time he provided an answer, the question had changed. The clergy at the General Assembly of May 1645 blisteringly attacked those negotiating with Ormond and insisted on keeping 'their' churches retaken from the heretics along with other church dues and property.[62] This was absolutely unacceptable to Ormond or, indeed, to Charles. Rather than fudge such an emotive issue, as the Confederate negotiators did, Ormond publicly demanded the restoration of Church of Ireland property. His clumsiness stalled negotiations and almost collapsed them.

The King must have suspected that Ormond could not negotiate a timely peace but did not accept Ormond's resignation when it was offered in November 1644. Instead, with characteristically self-defeating duplicity, he tried to circumvent Ormond by choosing a more biddable servant, the Catholic Earl of Glamorgan, ostensibly to help Ormond convince the Confederates to make peace.[63] The newly arrived nuncio, Archbishop Rinuccini, brought guns and gold, with the promise of more to come if the Confederate Catholics held out for the retaining of Church of Ireland property and public exercise of religion.[64] The clergy duly began to assert themselves at last and Glamorgan promised them all for an army.[65]

While talking peace with Ormond, the Confederates also had to fight Protestant forces, not only in Ulster but also in Connacht and Munster.[66] Inchiquin had switched sides in 1644, 'as full of anger as his buttons will endure' at being passed over for the Munster presidency. The Supreme Council in March 1645 tried to overrun Munster before Inchiquin's small army could be reinforced by the English parliament.[67] Castlehaven picked off all the parliamentary garrisons north of the river Blackwater before attacking Youghal alongside Preston's Leinstermen: 'Thus doe they brag what they would doe,/they will have Cork and Youghall too.' With Youghal lost, Inchiquin would have held only the thin coastal strip anchored by Cork and Bandon.[68] Unexpectedly, Castlehaven broke camp and, seeing that he was now dangerously isolated, Preston also withdrew into winter quarters. It is all too easy to see treachery where there is only muddle, but on this occasion such allegations may be true. Ormond made it clear to the Supreme Council that the fall of Youghal would jeopardise continuing negotiations and one cannot discount the possibility that the council quietly told Castlehaven to abandon Preston.[69] Meanwhile, the Long Parliament's newly appointed president of Connacht, Charles Coote, landed at Derry and fell on Sligo in July 1645, thereby opening up the strategic backwater of Connacht to attack by raiders from west Ulster.[70] Gloomily prescient, Malachy O'Queally, Archbishop of Tuam, led an expedition of squabbling Connachtmen to recapture Sligo. Enniskillen horsemen surprised the archiepiscopal camp near Sligo and scattered O'Queally's followers. They caught O'Queally, hanged him and found a copy of the Glamorgan Treaty on his person.[71] When parliament published the treaty as a propaganda coup, Ormond professed to be shocked by the revelations, repudiated the treaty and imprisoned Glamorgan. Matters were further confused by the arrival of an envoy from Henrietta Maria with details of yet another peace treaty, concluded with Innocent X, offering even more generous religious concessions.[72]

Ormond had quietly released Glamorgan to continue mustering 10,000 soldiers for England and at the General Assembly of February 1645 Rinuccini supported shipping them to Chester: the royalists were desperately holding the port and adjacent North Wales as a bridgehead for Irish reinforcements.[73] It was too late. By the time Irish soldiers were waiting on the quayside in March 1646, Chester had fallen. Two months later Charles surrendered to the Scottish army at the siege camp of Newark.[74]

As he intended, his action opened a rift between the Covenanters and their Presbyterian allies in England on the one hand and the 'Independents' on the other. 'Presbyterian' in this sense was not a religious label but a description of those who favoured negotiating a compromise with the King and re-imposing ecclesiastical discipline, albeit without bishops. 'Independents' insisted that the war must first be won and the King then coerced in granting 'liberty of conscience' (except, of course, for Catholics) that let individual congregations govern themselves within the context of unity on 'fundamentals'.[75]

With the fires of war now guttering out across Britain it was time to reduce Ireland. Before 1646 it was axiomatic that this would be the work of a joint Anglo–Scottish campaign. However, the power of the independents was growing and factional distrust of the Scots meant the reconquest was to be an exclusively English affair. It would fall on Munster, the theatre of war furthest from Scottish influence.[76] Inchiquin was reinforced and was able to recoup his losses of the previous year.[77] The defection of Barnabas O'Brien, 6th Earl of Thomond, from Ormond let 1,500 parliamentary soldiers sail up the Shannon and ensconce themselves in Bunratty Castle.[78] Another erstwhile Ormondist, Arthur Jones, 2nd Viscount Ranelagh, had betrayed Roscommon Castle to Charles Coote some months before. The Confederate Catholics recaptured both that summer. Having spent Rinuccini's gold to recruit his largest ever army, O'Neill felt strong enough to march north where he found himself astride Monro's line of march towards the south-west. He drew him on to give battle at Benburb (5 June 1646).[79] After an hour's fighting the Scottish foot soldiers were herded 'by push of pike' into a tightly packed crowd and then shoved towards the Blackwater and destruction. Monro's plan to link up with the Laggan army suggests that he planned to march across the Shannon and disrupt Irish preparations to besiege Roscommon. A detailed timetable for a twelve-day march on Kilkenny found on one of Monro's colonels was probably a paper exercise.[80] It suited Rinuccini and O'Neill, however, to trumpet that the battle saved Kilkenny.

The Confederate negotiators signed a peace treaty with Ormond in March 1646, postponing publication until an opportune time. Hearing of Charles's surrender in June 1644, the council did not reappraise the treaty and conclude that pursuing an alliance with the King was now futile. Rather, the council agreed to Ormond finally publishing the secret treaty on 30 March 1646. They failed to consider the only pragmatic alternative: the insular strategy of conquering the kingdom favoured by Rinuccini. The Ormond Peace amounted to 'a poor return on almost four years of war'.[81] Gone were the religious concessions promised by Glamorgan, while the confederates agreed to dissolve with no religious guarantees beyond a promise of 'his Majesties gracious favour'.[82] A prisoner of the Scots could hardly show much favour to Papists. Rinuccini was not persuaded that such sweeping concessions were necessary in view of the King's weakness and, moreover, he was incensed by what he considered the 'deliberate deceit' of signing a secret treaty.[83]

In early August 1646 Ormond entered Kilkenny in triumph and pomp and the Supreme Council relinquished power to him. Meanwhile, a clerical congregation convened in Waterford and used their power as arbiters of the Oath of Association to fulminate with one voice that the Ormond Peace was contrary to that oath. Backed by the armies of O'Neill (recalled from Ulster) and Preston, the Clericalists routed Ormond's supporters and sent the viceroy scurrying back to Dublin. O'Neill's failure to follow up his victory at Benburb is commonly blamed on his recall, but the order did not come until nearly two months after the battle. The summer of 1646 was as close to the trumpeted *aimsear buadha* [season of victory] as the Confederate Catholics ever got.[84] Yet their victories at Benburb, Roscommon and Bunratty were defensive and reactive. They also came too late.

Confederate collapse

Back in Dublin, an embittered Ormond threatened to hand over the capital and its outlying garrisons to parliament.[85] The Catholic response was a ponderous march on Dublin by some 15,000–18,000 soldiers of the Ulster and Leinster armies, the biggest force ever mobilised by the Confederate Catholics. A campaign dogged by 'bad timing, mistrust, treason and sheer incompetence' fizzled out in pointless talks to salvage last summer's agreement.[86] Even Rinuccini parleyed with Ormond when he must have known he would not cede to demands for the 'free and public' practice of Catholicism.[87] Ormond was playing for time and intriguing to detach individual Confederates, especially Preston, into a royalist body that could join what he hoped would be a new alignment between king and disaffected Roundheads.[88] When an English troopship sailed into Dublin Bay in mid-November, an already deeply suspicious O'Neill struck camp. Soon the Supreme Council ordered Preston to ravage the Pale and retreat.[89]

The 1647 General Assembly rejected the Ormond Peace, but exonerated the peacemakers in an attempt to restore a façade of unity. Dublin remained the prize. Ormond made a last foray into Irish quarters to try to detach regiments and territory from the Confederates in north Leinster and rebuild an enclave around Dublin.[90] When this failed he went ahead with his plans to surrender the capital to the Westminster parliament despite the pleas of the royalist court in exile to unite with the Irish. He bluntly rebuffed Henrietta Maria's envoy in April 1647 and insisted he would prefer Dublin to fall 'rather to the English Rebels than the Irish Rebels': in the final analysis, Ormond's priority was 'the best interests of Irish Protestants'.[91]

Preston's orders for the 1647 campaigning season were to tighten the noose around Dublin and Michael Jones, the parliamentary commander designated to replace Ormond. George Lord Digby, the King's secretary of state (yet another royalist envoy at large in Ireland), also encouraged Preston in pursuance of a hare-brained plot to somehow strengthen Ormond (while he was still in control of Dublin) and deliver near the capital a body of troops which could then be exported by Digby to France in return for French help for the royalist cause.[92] Jones, having linked up with auxiliaries from east Ulster, relieved the besieged town of Trim whereupon Preston withdrew to the shelter of a nearby bog-island, but rather than sit in this fastness, he marched towards Dublin and its skeleton garrison.[93] Having covered only twelve miles he was overtaken at Dungan's Hill (**map 4**) on 7 August where he hastily drew up his pike and shot in an impossibly cramped field. Attacked on almost all sides the Irish fled as far as a small bog nearby where they were surrounded and 'did capitulate for quarter, as the Irish say, and the English deny it'.[94] Wherever the truth lies, at least 3,000 Irishmen were killed. A large, well-trained and well-armed force was annihilated by a bedraggled army of ex-royalists, mutinous roundheads and Ulster hirelings. Meanwhile, the new general of the Munster Catholic army, Theobald Viscount Taaffe, did not challenge Inchiquin's incursions into Catholic quarters. With the Leinster army gone, his army was to be kept intact for French service.[95] Inchiquin, however, forced battle on him at Knocknanuss (**map 4**) on 13 November 1647.[96] Taaffe posted his foot soldiers in two blocks which 'had no sight the one of the other'. Mac Colla, recently returned from Scotland, led his 'Redshanks' in their usual furious charge, broke the opposing wing and set about plundering Inchiquin's baggage train. Meanwhile, Inchiquin attacked the Munster troops who loosed a single volley and ran, Taaffe with them. The rout at Knocknanuss 'broke the very heart of the Confederate affairs'.[97] By deft manoeuvring in the depths of winter O'Neill managed to save Kilkenny, but it could hardly be expected that the Confederate Catholics could hold out against Inchiquin next summer.

Royalist resurgence

In the event they didn't have to because divisions opened up in Britain between those who favoured constitutional monarchy and peace talks with Charles (Presbyterians, most members of the Westminster parliament and the 'Engager' faction of the Covenanters) and those (the army, Independents faction and the 'Kirk' faction of the Covenanters) who pressed for radical change. As the royalist military position crumbled the French began to fret that a powerful English republic would be a more uncomfortable .

neighbour than a weak and chastened monarchy.[98] With an end of the Thirty Years War in sight, Chief Minister Mazarin promised massive military and financial aid from France.[99] Thus heartened, the royalist court in exile sent Ormond back to Ireland to detach loosening components of the Scots–Parliamentary alliance and juxtapose them in improbable new alignments.

The weakest joint of the alliance came unstuck well before Ormond's return in September. The Independents in Ireland were the political heirs of the 'Boyle group', the plantation lobbyists of the 1620s and 1630s led by Lord Broghill, one of Cork's many sons. Broghill busily traduced Inchiquin, who silenced his critics for a time by letting his men 'do all they can with fire and sword', most notoriously in sacking Cashel in 1647.[100] But with Westminster starving him of supplies, Inchiquin was driven to declare for Charles in April 1648 and to patch up a ceasefire with the Supreme Council the following month.[101] This was no Ormondist coup. The General Assembly now kept tighter control of the executive and authorised a truce with the execrated 'Murrough of the Burnings' as a pragmatic response to the collapse of the Catholic war effort.[102] The nuncio could not stop them because of the prevalent mood of defeatism, widespread dislike of his Ulster allies, disunity among the bishops about the latest excommunication decree and his inability to deliver on the promise of massive papal subsidies.[103] Eoghan *Rua* O'Neill lurked in the midlands and briefly threatened Kilkenny before being driven northward by converging counter-attacks from Inchiquin and the Confederates.[104] Meanwhile, in Britain the Engagers marched south. It would have been a 'near-run thing' but for the fact that Oliver Cromwell and Thomas Fairfax, leaders of the Independent or army faction, had already smothered brushfire royalist rebellions.[105] Cromwell intercepted and defeated the invaders at Preston in August 1648.

Negotiations between the General Assembly and Ormond ground on as they had before until firm instructions from Queen Henrietta Maria forced him to offer more attractive terms. Ormond now made concessions which marked a 'major advance' on previous offers. Catholics were promised free exercise of religion and an overwhelmingly Catholic standing army would be kept in being until the agreement was ratified.[106] Reports that the 'Rump' (the few members of the Commons left after military purges) would try Charles Stuart 'as a tyrant, traitor, murderer and implacable enemy' helped break the logjam on 17 January 1649, while the shock of his execution soon after would prompt mass defections of Protestants to the royalist cause.[107] The Irish had got their treaty and Charles II an army. Had the Confederation of Kilkenny been a success after all?

Conclusion

The Confederate Catholics embodied the collective response of a self-defined Irish nation to a mortal threat. By and large they did act collectively and it is a mistake to see them as hopelessly split into 'Gaelic' or 'Old Irish' and 'Old English' factions. The fault lines did not open around putative ethnicity alone but involved class interests, familial allegiance, individual religious conviction and pragmatic assessments of what objectives were reasonably achievable. Nor was factionalism unique to Irish Catholics; the other two constituent nations of the composite monarchy also proved to be hopelessly split on the question as to how far Charles Stuart, father and son, could be trusted on religious matters.

The regime was set up to provide effective national government, counter the immediate military threats posed by king, parliament and Covenanters, and later to negotiate a settlement with the King. By January 1649 it had signed a definitive peace with the King's heir, won significant concessions and voluntarily disbanded. In that sense the Confederation was a success. However, the catastrophic Cromwellian conquest and settlement casts a retrospective shadow over this achievement. Was there anything the Confederate Catholics could have done to avoid this worst of all possible outcomes?

The motto *Pro Deo, Rege et Patria* was more than just a rhetorical protestation of loyalty so common among early modern rebels. Many, probably most, of the Catholic leaders took it seriously so it is unfair to condemn them as 'selfish and myopic' for not pursuing policies that would have brought a final break with their monarch.[108] Yet one cannot acquit them of hopeless naivety. Reconciling political and religious loyalty was impossible in a confessional Europe where religious and political loyalties were inextricably linked and when public opinion in two of the three Stuart kingdoms was so stridently anti-Catholic. The protracted search for a definitive treaty between the Confederates and Charles I illustrates the complexity, indeed impossibility, of reconciling these conflicting loyalties. Only in the fleeting gap between Marston Moor and Naseby could Irish troops have tipped the balance. Only then was Charles ready to pay the political price to get them: or say he was ready. Charles made, complained Irish clericalists, 'many fair promises, yet when he could make better terms with any other party he was always ready to sacrifice them'.[109] The Irish could not have saved Charles I. They might have saved themselves.

Endnotes

1 Ó Siochrú 1999, p. 37; Clarke 1966, pp. 231–2.

2 Gilbert 1882–91, i, p. 226; Armstrong 2005, p. 17.

3 Clarke 1966, p. 206.

4 *TCD Ms 816* 'Extracts of Sir John Netterville's Petition' f. 202; 'Deposition of Richard Streete, Andrew Aylmer and Robert Aylmer' f. 204.

5 Little 2001c, p. 110.

6 Meehan 1872, p. 329.

7 Coonan 1954, p. 140.

8 Ó Siochrú 1999, p. 47; Meehan 1882, pp. 21–2.

9 Perceval-Maxwell 1990, p. 207; Carpenter 2003, p. 228.

10 Ó Siochrú 1999, pp. 44–6.

11 Gillespie 2006, p. 158.

12 Ó Siochrú 1999, pp. 49, 251–60; Coonan 1954, pp. 139–40.

13 Tilly 1990, p. 85; Gilbert 1882, i, p. 90.

14 Coonan 1954, p. 52; Ó Siochrú 1999, p. 51.

15 Lenihan 2001a, p. 60.

16 Kerrigan 2001, pp. 155–7.

17 Gilbert 1882–91, iii, p. 41.

18 Armstrong 2005, p. 83.

19 Carte 1736, iii, Appendix no. 60; HMC Ormond Ms (1903), pp. 63, 130.

20 Wanklyn and Jones 2006, p. 39.

21 Armstrong 2005, pp. 73, 75, 82.

22 Hogan 1936, pp. 121, 127; Shirley 1856–57, pp. 143–6, 170–88.

23 Gilbert 1879, i, pp. 49, 200–2; Ó Donnchadha 1931, pp. 20–5; Carte 1736, i, p. 433; Finch 1643, p. 12.

24 Lynch 1815, p. 56.

25 Inchiquin took over as President from his father-in-law St Leger, who died in 1642; Gilbert 1879, i, p. 38; Hogan 1936, p. 149; Hickson 1884, ii, p. 127.

26 Miller 1971, pp. 141–58; Creichtoun 1900, p. 97.

27 Hutton and Reeves 1998, p. 195.

28 *TCD Ms 815* (Queen's County) 'Deposition of Captain Richard Steele' f. 358; Gilbert 1879, i, p. 64.

29 Gilbert 1882–91, i, pp. 119, 154.

30 Ohlmeyer 1993, p. 120.

31 O'Hara 2006, p. 75.

32 Cox 1689–91, ii, 61; *TCD Ms 824* ff. 118, 374.

33 Clarendon 1807, iii, p. 266.

34 Armstrong 2005, p. 99.

35 Ó hAnnracháin 2001, p. 28.

36 Ó Siochrú 1999, p. 67.

37 Beckett 1959, pp. 60–1; Stevenson 1981, p. 128.

38 Smyth 2006, pp. 198–200; Andrews 1997, p. 144.

39 Brunicardi 2000, p. 10.

40 Gilbert 1882–91, ii, 319–27; Carte 1736, ii, p. 520.

41 Ohlmeyer 1993, p. 119.

42 Ó Siochrú 1999, p. 48; Gillespie 2006, pp. 156–7.

43 Ó Siochrú 1999, pp. 218–23, 261–8.

44 Ohlmeyer 1993, pp. 164–5.

45 Lynch 1815, p. xxvii; Ó Siochrú 1999, pp. 49, 64–7, 245–6.

46 Gilbert 1879, i, p. 666; Ó hAnnracháin 2003, p. 30.

47 Lowe 1983, p. 17; Carte 1736, iii, p. 257; Ohlmeyer 1993, pp. 129–30.

48 Lynch 1815, p. 68.

49 Reid 1998, pp. 96–9; Digby to Ormond, Oxford Feb. 1644, Carte 1736, iii, p. 243.

50 Burne and Young 1959, pp. 172–8; Stevenson 1981, p. 178; Gentles 1992, p. 54.

51 Wheeler 2002, p. 88.

52 Bindon 1846, p. 154; Ó Siochrú 1999, p. 65.

53 Ó Siochrú 1999, p. 213; Cregan 1979, p. 90.

54 Ó Siochrú 1999, pp. 57, 213–14.

55 Ó Siochrú 1999, pp. 71, 83; Ó hAnnracháin 1997, pp. 99–100.

56 Ó Siochrú 1999, pp. 71, 73, 208; Lowe 1964, p. 2; Malcolm 1979, p. 83; Bennett 1997, p. 206; Clarendon 1807, p. 446; Armstrong 2001, p. 132; Ohlmeyer 1993, p. 137.

57 Kishlansky 1996, pp. 160, 166.

58 Rushworth 1708, vi, pp. 277, 303.

59 Edwards 2003, pp. 327–9.

60 Armstrong 2005, pp. 123, 132; Ó Ciardha 2000, p. 177; Kelly 1997, pp. 43–6; Lowe 1959–60, p. 156; Armstrong 2001, p. 128; Lowe 1964, pp. 11–12.

61 Armstrong 2005, pp. 123, 131–2, 139.

62 Ó Siochrú 1999, pp. 80, 88–9; Armstrong 2001, pp. 134, 138–9.

63 Armstrong 2005, p. 141; Ó Siochrú 2005, pp. 94–5.

64 Ó hAnnracháin 2001, pp. 36–9.

65 Lowe 1983, pp. 7–8; Meehan 1882, pp. 163–4.

66 Armstrong 2005, pp. 92–3, 97, 101, 111–12, 116.

67 Gilbert 1882–91, iv, pp. 8, 148–9, 284.

68 Carpenter 2003, p. 234; Armstrong 2005, pp. 149, 163.

69 Aringhi, 1774, p. 53: My thanks to Tadgh Ó hAnnracháin for this reference; Kavanagh 1932–49, i, p. 173.

70 Ó Donnchadha 1931, p. 35.

71 Hutton 1873, p. 87; Gilbert 1879, i, p. 94; Anon 1646, p. 2.

72 Ó Siochrú 2005, pp. 98–9.

73 Hutton 1982, pp. 191, 194, 196.

74 Royle 2004, p. 387; Leyburn 1722, p. 20.

75 Kenyon 1978, p. 154; Little 2004, pp. 39–40.

76 Adamson 1995, pp. 134–5, 143.

77 Armstrong 2005, pp. 65, 73, 116; Kavanagh 1932–49, i, pp. 123, 190, 237, 575–6, ii, p. 680; Bellings to Rinuccini May 1646 in Kavanagh, i, pp. 236–7; Ormonde to O'Neill, May 1646 in Gilbert 1879, i, p. 672.

78 Armstrong 2005, pp. 155, 166.

79 Casway 1984, pp. 129–36.

80 Kavanagh 1932–49, ii, pp. 185–91, 240; HMC 1905, p. 303; Stevenson 1981, p. 224; Hogan 1873, p. 52.

81 Ó Siochrú 1999, pp. 106–7, 111.

82 Ó Siochrú 1999, pp. 110–12.

83 Ó hAnnracháin 2002, pp. 128, 135.

84 Ó Dhonnchadha 1916, p. 92.

85 Stevenson 1981, pp. 239–40; Adamson 1995, p. 32.

86 Ó Siochrú 1999, p. 118; Armstrong 2001, p. 138.

87 Lowe 1983, p. 307.

88 Carte 1851, vi, p. 450; Kavanagh 1932–49, ii, p. 416; Gilbert 1879, i, part 2, p. 711; Ó Siochrú 1999, p. 120; Kavanagh 1932–49, ii, p. 426; Carte 1736, i, p. 587; Lenihan 2001, p. 98; Armstrong 2005, p. 184.

89 Lowe 1983, p. 337, 340–41; Carte 1736, i, p. 592.

90 Armstrong 2005, pp. 193, 202.

91 Leyburn 1722, p. 45; Ó Siochrú 2005, pp. 77, 147; Meehan 1882, p. 213.

92 Ó Siochrú 2005, pp. 150–4.

93 Gilbert 1882–91, vi, p. 30; Lenihan 2001, pp. 99–100, 197–9; Borlase 1680, p. 242.

94 Borlase 1680, p. 242; *CSPI (1633–47)*, p. 740; Gilbert 1882–91, vi, p. 32, vii, pp. 32–3; Gilbert 1879, i, pp. 154–5.

95 Ó hAnnracháin 2002, pp. 188–9; Ó Siochrú 1999, p. 157; Mc Neill 1943, p. 277.

96 Ó Siochrú 1999, p. 58; Gilbert 1882–91, vii, p. 34; Anon 1647, p. 7.

97 George Leyburn cited in McKenny 2005, p. 82.

98 Wedgewood 1958, pp. 571–2.

99 Ohlmeyer 1995, pp. 101–2; Ó hAnnracháin 2002, pp. 140–3; Ohlmeyer 1998a, pp. 94–5.

100 Armstrong 2005, pp. 204, 206, 212, 217.

101 Little 2004, p. 51; McKenny 2005, pp. 82–3.

102 Gilbert 1882–91, vi, p. 271.

103 Ó hAnnracháin 2002, pp. 193–5; Ó Siochrú 1999, pp. 191–200; Casway 1984, p. 208.

104 McKenny 2005, pp. 100–1.

105 Wheeler 2002, p. 188.

106 Ó Siochrú 1999, pp. 198–200.

107 Wheeler 2002, p. 205; McKenny 2005, pp. 89–91.

108 Casway 1984, p. 117.

109 Ohlmeyer 1993, pp. 224–5.

CHAPTER 7

Cromwellian conquest and settlement 1649–59

Cromwell in Ireland 1649–59

Oliver Cromwell hated the Irish. The prejudice of the *de facto* head of the Commonwealth was common among Englishmen of his generation and was quite different from his feelings towards the Scots, who were basically God-fearing, if 'deceived'. Indeed, Cromwell was initially prepared to leave Scotland as a separate state.[1] He also had reason to fear that Prince Charles would pick Ireland rather than Scotland (where the Kirk party had ousted the Engagers) as a base for resistance and, ultimately, invasion: all six ships of the royalist navy were berthed at Kinsale.[2] The Commonwealth's armies were bled white by defections to Ormond's royalist alliance and it looked like Jones would not be able to hold on to Dublin. Worry about Ireland is reflected in the unprecedented volume of reports from Ireland carried in English newsbooks.[3] Levying of troops for Ireland began in April 1649 with army regiments picked by lot. Many soldiers mutinied, however, and would not embark until they were paid arrears of wages. Meanwhile, a delegate from Rinuccini's erstwhile clericalist followers held several meetings with parliamentary negotiators (including Cromwell and his son-in-law Henry Ireton), who promised religious toleration.[4] It is likely that the negotiators had no real interest in compromise and were buying time until the army mutinies were put down. The campaigning season slipped by.

Ormond frittered away that time mopping up outlying garrisons instead of marching directly on Dublin.[5] Fretting that Cromwell would land in Munster, Ormond sent Inchiquin south and encamped at Rathmines (**map 5**) without enough men to properly besiege Dublin.[6] One morning Michael Jones's horsemen overran the royalist camp and, literally, caught Ormond napping. Ormond's cavaliers fled and his foot soldiers, many of them English troops who had defected from parliament, surrendered en masse.[7] Apart from the incalculable 'dejection it brings upon the best inclined', to quote Ormond, the defeat handed Cromwell a suitable base for invasion and in September 1649 he disembarked.[8]

Drogheda and Wexford

Cromwell first marched on Drogheda in order to cut off the pro-royalist Scottish settlers in east Ulster.[9] His capacity to ship and deploy heavy 48-pounder siege guns, too heavy to drag over land, meant that the medieval curtain walls of Drogheda were soon breached. After a 'hot dispute' the attackers poured over the breach, bypassed the palisades topping the steep-sided Mill Mount and raced across the river before the defenders could pull up the drawbridge behind them. 'I forbade them to spare any that were in arms in the town,' admitted Cromwell, 'in the heat of the action.' Sir Arthur Aston, the English Catholic governor of Drogheda, had 'his brains beat out' with his own wooden leg.[10] On the face of it Cromwell's order was unexceptionable according to the grim usages of siege warfare. He had invited Aston to surrender: 'If this be refused, you will have no cause to blame me.'[11] Both men knew what this meant. Cromwell had not acted dishonourably if one discounts royalist claims and accepts that soldiers huddled atop the Mill Mount and elsewhere surrendered without securing promises of 'quarter' beforehand.[12] That said, mass killing of prisoners was unusually severe. Of all the officers captured at Drogheda, only one was let live (ensign Richard Talbot, of whom much more later), whereas of the 300 officers who submitted to mercy to Fairfax after the siege of Colchester, the year before, only three were shot.[13]

More morally suspect was the killing of an unknown number of women and children in and around St Peter's Church. In 1663 Anthony Wood recounted what he claimed his brother Thomas, an English soldier who was there, told him:

. . . that when they were to make their way up to the lofts and galleries in the church and up to the tower where the enemy had fled, each of the assailants would take up a child and use it as a buckler of defence, when they ascended the steps to keep themselves from being shot or brain'd. After they had killed all in the church, they went into the vaults underneath where all the flower and choicest of the women had hid

themselves. One of them a most handsome virgin and arrayed in costly and gorgeous apparel, kneeled down to Thomas Wood with tears and prayers to save her life; and being stricken with a profound pity, he took her under her arm, went with her out of the church, with intention to put her over the works and let her shift for herself; but then a soldier perceiving his intentions, ran his sword through her belly or fundament whereupon Mr. Wood seeing her gasping, took away her money, jewels &c., and flung her down over the works.

Some historians object that this eyewitness report was a fabrication: would women hiding or fleeing in a storm really 'array themselves in jewels or costly apparel'?[14] This and similar objections are unconvincing. A fleeing woman would carry whatever valuables she could and that included her best clothes. It is likely that civilians were killed in the storm but, given that the north side of the town was not blocked off by the besiegers before and during the storm, many or most of the townspeople probably contrived to escape.

Cromwell wrestled with his conscience and won, as usual, by casting himself as God's instrument acting without volition.[15] Any killings were a 'righteous judgement' on 'barbarous wretches who have imbrued their hands in so much innocent blood'.[16] The retributive justification was nonsensical. Many of the royalist defenders were English and Drogheda had never fallen into insurgent hands. More convincingly, he claimed that the example of frightfulness would terrify other towns and so 'save much effusion of blood'.[17]

Relying on his navy to carry food, munitions, clothing and heavy siege artillery, Cromwell hugged the coast (**map 5**) in his march on Wexford. This had been the main base for privateer frigates that preyed on English shipping over the previous seven years.[18] Wexford should have been a far harder nut to crack than Drogheda. The walls were backed by thick earthen ramparts and the gun bastion of Rosslare Fort covered the channel into the harbour. Unless ships could anchor there, Cromwell admitted, 'neither had we cannon for batter, nor provisions to subsist'.[19] But the defenders fled the fort and showed a strange lack of spirit during the brisk siege. While the governor was negotiating a capitulation, the English clambered over the walls and swept through the streets. Reports that they cut down 300 women gathered about the cross in the bull ring were probably well founded.[20]

The Earl of Antrim had concluded a secret deal with Henry Ireton, Cromwell's son-in-law, and may have (using a municipal official Hugh

Rochford as his go-between) been involved in sapping the town people's will to resist. He certainly did the Cromwellians a 'singular service' in securing the surrender of New Ross shortly afterwards.[21] Many Irish Catholics seem to have believed that the Commonwealth's 'liberty of conscience' rhetoric encompassed them and only at New Ross did Cromwell make it that 'liberty to exercise the mass' would be forbidden.[22]

'Like a Lightning through the Land': winter 1649 to spring 1650

Ormond 'was not a great military commander' but he cannot be altogether blamed for the faltering war effort. He had more men under arms than Cromwell but, drawing only on Irish resources, could not mobilise a field army big enough to oppose him. Moreover, Rathmines showed that his men could not sustain the onset of English horsemen. He put them behind walls and trusted 'Colonel Hunger and Major Sickness' to wear down Cromwell's forces in the hardships of long marches and wet siege encampments.[23] Normally, the campaigning season closed towards October, at about the time when Cromwell left Wexford, but a winter 'fairer than in man's memory' gifted Cromwell an extra six weeks' campaigning and an exceptionally early start the following spring.[24] He did not break off the siege of Waterford and withdraw into winter quarters until 2 December 1649 when his guns began to sink into the wet ground.[25] By then Cromwell and most of his men were sick and he could have drawn only 5,000 effectives into the field, less than one third of the number he had disembarked.[26] He was saved from the consequences of pushing his luck too far by the sudden revolt of Inchiquin's garrisons in Munster: Cromwell had reason to thank Broghill for proving 'most eminently serviceable' in suborning most of them.[27]

Even before the end of January 1650 Cromwell was on the march again, racing with 'audacity and military skill' ahead of his siege train and snapping up Fethard and Cahir.[28] The push brought Cromwell and a converging column from Dublin right to the gates of Kilkenny (**map 5**) by late March, while Castlehaven lay to the north still waiting for his troops to congregate from winter quarters. God gave a further display of partiality to Cromwell when more than two thirds of the Kilkenny garrison perished of epidemic disease before a shot was fired. Enough survived to pour a hail of musket shot into densely packed attackers storming a breach in the walls of the High Town. The governor prudently capitulated when a second breach was broken in the walls. The initial repulse of a bull-headed attack at Kilkenny was repeated on a much bloodier scale at Clonmel on 17 May. The Ulster army had at last joined the royalist war effort and Hugh *Dubh* O'Neill, Eoghan *Rua*'s nephew, prepared an entrenchment inside the breach. Into this pound the attackers twice pressed and some 1,500 tightly packed men were cut down by chain-shot and musketry in a single bloody day which saw off 10 per cent of the entire English army in Ireland. O'Neill's ammunition was exhausted and he slipped away in the night, leaving the mayor to negotiate surrender.

When Cromwell left Ireton to carry on and returned to fend off a threatened Scottish invasion, his forces had overrun the shores of Ireland (apart from a hopelessly isolated Waterford) from Bandon, County Cork, right around to Letterkenny, County Donegal, and inland to a depth of some thirty miles.[29] Only wild-eyed Levellers questioned the assumption that the Irish must be invaded, but not everyone was as committed as Cromwell to unconditional victory. Even before invasion a committee of senior army officers agreed that a commander-in-chief should not be bound by harsh terms 'as either to eradicate the natives, or to divest them of their estates'.[30] Had the reconquest presented unacceptable costs, Irish Catholics might have extracted reasonably favourable terms from a war-weary and distracted Commonwealth.[31] Cromwell showed, or seemed to, that unconditional conquest could be cheap. As it was, royalist resistance in Ireland left the English Commonwealth's resources stretched thin when Scotland prepared for war in the spring and summer of 1650 and significantly increased the odds of a victory for royalism.

An Irish war 1650-52

But such a victory would not have been a triumph for the Irish because, in late summer 1650, Charles II repudiated his alliance with Irish Catholics in return for support from the Kirk party in Scotland. This, the haemorrhage of Protestant royalist desertions, and Castlehaven's failure to relieve Carlow (which fell in July 1650), prompted the Catholic clergy to move against Ormond. The prelates met at Jamestown, County Leitrim, in August and wrote to the Lord Lieutenant asking him to 'speedily repair out of the country'. The following December he complied, having got permission to do so from Charles, and nominated Clanricarde as his successor.[32] All this redefined and clarified the overriding objective of the war: Catholic self-defence. Cromwellians like Colonel Richard Lawrence could now anticipate a more congenial Irish war that 'will end where it did begin, betwixt the English Protestant and the Irish Papist'.[33]

At the ford of Scariffhollis on the river Swilly in June 1650 Charles Coote goaded the Ulster army into rushing downhill from their secure encampment. On the 'more commodious' plain the English and settler cavalry broke and scattered them. It is too early to say that Irish military prospects 'were next to hopeless' after Scariffhollis and the Scottish defeat at Dunbar in September.[34] Continuing to tie down so many Commonwealth soldiers in Ireland allowed the Scots to stubbornly resist Cromwell until their last desperate throw of a march on England the following year. Negotiations between the Stuart court in exile and Charles Duke of Lorraine might yet have secured a foreign patron.[35]

In 1651 the Irish still held a sizeable chunk of contiguous territory in Connacht and Clare but could not support enough men to hold the line of the Shannon. Indeed Clanricarde sent home reinforcements from Leinster (behind the somewhat notional enemy front lines), they being 'not able to subsist'.[36] In a lightning march from Ulster by 'strange and unexpected ways', Charles Coote crashed right into the heart of Connacht (**map 5**), thereby making the Shannon Line irrelevant at a stroke.[37] The governor of Athlone promptly surrendered on 18 June and Coote was able to link up with troops detached from the ongoing second siege of Limerick and partially encircle Galway.[38]

The twin sieges of Galway and Limerick stretched Ireton's army beyond breaking point. Coote was forced to raise the siege of Galway while Ireton could only sit and wait at Limerick, his army spread dangerously thin all around the city. While the English army grew to 25,000 men in 1650 and to 35,000 men by July 1651, at least 12,000 of them were scattered in garrisons, with the balance pinned down at Galway and Limerick.[39] So long as Limerick held out from May to October 1651 surviving fragments of the royalist provincial armies frequently coalesced to raid, and sometimes overrun, English garrisons and interrupt their communications. John Fitzpatrick overran slumbering English garrisons covering the Shannon passes of Rachra (Shannonbridge) and Meelick and put all the soldiers to the sword, while Broghill blocked Muskerry's determined advance on Limerick only after hard fighting (**map 5**) at Knockniclashy. A countrywide wave of attacks by 'tories', as the English increasingly called the Irish guerrillas, may have been timed to coincide with the Scottish invasion of England that came to an end with crushing defeat at Worcester in September 1651. Even Dublin was on the front line. Tories swooped on Baggotrath, not much more than a stone's throw from the castle, stole horses and led pursuing soldiers into a bloody ambuscade.[40] This 'tedious' war had already cost the Commonwealth 'vast numbers' of men lost through sickness; some 2,000 soldiers (including Ireton himself) perished before Limerick alone even in an unusually 'dry and gentle' summer and autumn of 1651.[41] What hardships and dangers would a wet and cold winter siege bring?

The Irish bellowed from the walls that 'they would beat us away with snowballs', reported Ireton. The Irish still had enough munitions and their governor, Hugh *Dubh* O'Neill, the hero of Clonmel, was ready to exploit any thinning of the line encircling his city.[42] However, most of the city councilmen wanted to surrender and at their instigation one Colonel Fennell mounted the citadel at St John's Gate on 27 October 1651, turned the guns on the city and forced O'Neill to capitulate.[43] The soldiers piled their weapons and marched out, some dropping dead of plague as they marched. Civilians were given three months' notice to leave town and two dozen named leaders were hanged for inciting such obstinate resistance, though O'Neill's life was spared.

'All is lost here,' Muskerry conceded.[44] Worcester and Limerick ended any realistic prospect of Irish victory. Edmund Ludlow, who replaced Ireton as commander-in-chief, rebuffed Clanricarde's offer of negotiated surrender, insisting that he would not 'capitulate with those who ought to submit'.[45] The demand for unconditional surrender dragged out a war in which the Irish fought on, no longer to win but to extract tolerable collective terms.[46] While English forces sat before Galway, large swathes of countryside (**map 5**) were dominated by tories. For instance, islands in the extensive bogs of Laois, Offaly and North Tipperary 'into which they have passes or causeways where no more than one horse can go abreast' provided secure bases for wide-ranging raids.[47]

The Cromwellian response was to draw a 'line of protection' around their quarters outside of which crops were liable to be burned, cattle driven off and peasants killed as spies and enemies.[48] The northern fringe of one such no-man's land included Dundrum and Rathfarnham, within sight of Dublin Castle.[49] Colonel Cooke, governor of Wexford (who was shot not long after by tories), exulted after one sortie in March 1652: 'In searching the woods and bogs we found great store of corn, which we burnt, also all the houses and cabins we could find; in all of which we found plenty of corn: we continued burning and destroying for four days . . .'[50] This counter-insurgency strategy forced civilians to cluster in designated villages of a minimum of thirty households at least half a mile within the 'line' and so denied provisions to the tories.[51] That same month converging columns carried fire and sword across frost-hardened bog to the stronghold of a leading tory, John Fitzpatrick, near Nenagh. Soon after,

Fitzpatrick asked for terms.[52] To begin with, he asked for 'liberty of our religion' and security of property for his officers and himself but settled for liberty to transport himself and his band 'beyond the seas' and an under-the-table promise that he could keep his lands. The commonwealth commissioners hoped that Fitzpatrick's surrender would lead to the 'breaking of the Irish confederacy and to their insisting on national conditions'.[53] So it did.

A scramble to secure the best conditions followed. The burgesses of Galway capitulated soon after on condition that they could keep their property within the town and two thirds of their land outside. This concession would have had far-reaching implications for any land settlement since the burgesses owned so much land in Connacht, but the proviso was later repudiated by the commonwealth commissioners.[54] The terms accepted by Fitzpatrick, less the promise of keeping his land, formed the basis for the landslide of submissions that followed. Most members of the especially troublesome Leinster army had submitted by May 1652. The last major action of the war happened the following month when, pressed by hunger, Richard Grace led a column of around 1,500 diehards across the Shannon. He lingered for ten or eleven days near Loughrea, County Galway, until a large force of English horsemen scattered his band.[55] All that remained were mopping up operations: the sieges of Ross Castle near Killarney in County Kerry, Clogh Oughter in County Cavan and Inishbofin off the Galway coast.

A blank sheet

Ireland seemed like a blank sheet, 'ready to have anything writt in it'.[56] The Irish soldiers had surrendered and embarked. It was unconditional victory. Cromwell, proclaimed as Lord Protector in 1653, could do what Spenser had urged.

Retribution – people

In the first instance, the purpose of reconquest had been to exact war reparations by repaying the 'Adventurers' and soldiers owed arrears of pay. Ominously, 'to retribute to England' also had a wider meaning of paying for collective guilt for England's 'deep expenses of blood'.[57] The blood guilt debt was levied in full. Between one tenth and about one fifth of the population perished from epidemic disease during the reconquest, with only Ulster escaping.[58] From the year Oliver Cromwell landed in Ireland 'plague and famine ran together' [*Do rith pláig is gorta in n-aonacht*].[59] The poetic link of the Protector with famine and epidemic disease is accurate enough.[60] Over four years from 1650 to 1654 most of the reported urban outbreaks betray the seasonal footprint of bubonic plague, breaking out around May, peaking in August and waning in September.[61] Some of these outbreaks jumped from town to countryside.[62] Airborne infections transmitted directly between people or diseases, like typhus, spread by human parasites showed a strong positive correlation with increasing population density. Bubonic plague was different and once it broke out in a village or hamlet fatalities would be proportionately much the same as in towns and cities.[63] The punctuation of the reconquest with long sieges helps explain why bubonic plague raged so fiercely. A siege trapped wealthier citizens (the poor usually could not flee anyway) in a pestilential city. One fifth of the citizens, soldiers and refugees crammed into Limerick during the siege of 1651 had perished by the time the city surrendered in October.[64] In a city like Dublin that escaped siege after 1649 it took four successive summer outbreaks before the cumulative death toll reached one fifth.[65] Otherwise the link between war and plague was indirect because, while a chronically hungry population was less resistant, plague was not a classic famine disease.[66] The connection between war and other components of the epidemic was clearer. These included the classic 'famine fevers' of typhus, relapsing fever and dysentery. The tory war, transplantation to Connacht and expulsion of Catholics from towns all set refugees on the roads and so accelerated the spread of those famine fevers that flared up wherever the uprooted, hungry, demoralised and unwashed huddled, be it a nineteenth-century workhouse or a seventeenth-century shanty town.[67]

The war dragged on so long because Cromwell would offer nothing more than unconditional surrender. He had political room for manoeuvre and could have offered some security of land ownership, as he would ultimately do in Scotland. The Protector's war guilt should be judged by his personal commitment to vengefulness at a policy level, rather than what he did or did not do at Drogheda or Wexford.

The preamble of the 1652 'Act for the Settling of Ireland' disavowed any intention to 'extirpate this whole nation' and offered 'life and estate' to 'husbandmen, plowmen, labourers, artificers and others of the inferior sort'.[68] But once the conquest was complete the authorities increasingly blamed the 'commonality' alongside the 'nobility, gentry, clergy' as 'all engaged as one nation in this quarrel'.[69] Richard Lawrence, for instance, rejoiced to see Ireland as 'an empty prepared hive' ready for 'swarms' of English settlers. Only through numbers and rigid segregation could future

English settlers be safe. The natives were first to be driven out of the towns and from a new pale bounded by 'one entire line' (first mentioned in January 1652) of the Boyne and the Barrow. The pale was somewhat shrunken by the exclusion of County Meath when it was decreed in May 1655 that 'all persons of the Popish religion' be gone by 20 October.[70] More expulsions were to follow when English immigration picked up until, ultimately, the natives were to be corralled by the Shannon into a native reservation.[71] It was also briefly proposed to move the entire Presbyterian population of Counties Antrim and Down to Counties Kilkenny, Tipperary and Waterford and also to transplant 'delinquent' Protestant landowners in north-west Ulster who had sided with Ormond and had not realigned quickly enough with parliament afterwards. The Protector vetoed this and, in July 1654, instructed Fleetwood to apply transplantation to Irish Catholics only.[72]

Vincent Gookin, a Munster 'Old Protestant' (as pre-1641 settlers were increasingly known) and one of six members summoned from Ireland to Barebones' parliament, Cromwell's puppet assembly, fired off a riposte that mixed moral and practical arguments against mass transplantation.[73] Retribution was misguided and one should not act 'because a fault is done but that it may be done no more'. The native population was leaderless and 'scarce the sixth part' of their pre-war numbers through 'famine, pestilence, the sword and foreign transplantations', so the few 'useful, simple creatures' surviving posed no threat unless goaded into guerilla warfare.[74] Incensed by this 'strange and scandalous book', Lord Deputy Charles Fleetwood ignored the Protector's hints that he should quietly drop transplantation. He exempted few Irish, not even a Protestant minister named Jeremiah O'Quinn who had, Fleetwood remarked with apparent surprise, 'become somewhat bitter against the interest of England'.[75] Both the first deadline in May 1654 and the second in March 1655 passed. In July of that year Fleetwood issued new, more trenchant, instructions for transplantation, following rumours that an Irish Catholic regiment was involved in the reported massacre of Piedmontese protestants.[76] Landowners left, some taking servants and labourers, but otherwise the lower classes of the countryside stayed on. Orders of May 1653 to transplant Presbyterians to Counties Kilkenny, Tipperary and Waterford were also quietly disregarded.[77] The arrival of Henry Cromwell to take effective control of the Irish administration signalled a relaxation in the drive to Connacht.

Expulsion from the towns was more thoroughgoing. The 1650s were one of two peak decades for British immigration, 'unprecedented in scale', which mostly decanted into urban Ireland.[78] Where English or Scottish immigrants arrived in large enough numbers they could push out the natives. In April 1657, for example, the Protestant coopers in Dublin had their Catholic counterparts removed from the city and on 10 October the Protestant shoemakers obtained a similar order against their Catholic rivals. Dublin was now an English and Protestant city and would stay so for the best part of a century: 'The Cromwellian conquest was, above all, a conquest of Dublin, all port-cities and county towns . . . by immigrant elites and peoples'.[79] Waterford may serve as an example. Cromwell had hoped to colonise the city with protestants from New England. They never came and Ireton accepted a proposal to colonise the city with 1,200 soldiers. In March 1651 Catholics were duly ordered to leave within three months but most did not leave until 1655. Some soldiers settlers did arrive, as did some merchants from Bristol, drawn by 'hopes to have dwelling houses without rent'. Though the settlers complained of competition from Catholics underselling them and exploiting their better foreign trading connections, the bulk of trade passed to protestant hands and a settler enclave was scooped out within the walls, with the Catholics extruded to the suburbs.[80] Trade recovered rapidly in late 1650s Dublin, providing a sound base for the city's dramatic growth later in the century. However, the expulsion of Catholic merchants disrupted trade in the port towns of Cork, Waterford, Limerick and, especially, Galway. In terms of wealth, population and trade all slipped relative to Dublin, while Galway never recovered its former prosperity and stature in the period under review.[81] Their corporations were extinguished and when restored the new mayors or sovereigns were army officers.[82] The political capture of the boroughs would be crucial later.

While settlers trickled into Ireland, natives flowed out in greater numbers. Some 34,000 Irishmen took ship abroad, over half of them to Spain.[83] Another 12,000 Irish were transported to the plantations of the West Indies, most of them to Barbados.[84] Those transported included prisoners of war and 'recalcitrants' such as natives rounded up as collective reprisals after tory attacks. But most of the youths, old men and women doomed to back-breaking labour in the plantations were 'idle and vagrant persons': the displaced poor.[85] The scale of depopulation and economic dislocation is to be seen in plummeting land values. In the mid-1630s twenty years' purchase (a sum equivalent to twenty times the rental income) was being demanded but this slumped in some cases to only three years' purchase in the 1650s and thirty years later had still not reached pre-war levels.[86]

Retribution – land

Irish land would be 'the great capital out of which all debts were paid'.[87] First in the queue was the government, which reserved all towns, church lands, tithes along with Counties Dublin, Kildare, Carlow and Cork. Next came over 1,000 'Adventurers', or their assignees, who had lent or 'adventured' money to finance conquest. Over half were wealthy London merchants; the rest came from all over England, with a disproportionate number from the West Country, long identified with Munster colonisation.[88] The Commonwealth Commissioners for Ireland proposed on 1 January 1652 that the Adventurers should cast lots for land in ten specified counties throughout all four provinces: plans to keep Connacht and Clare for native landowners emerged by the end of that year.[89] All 35,000 serving soldiers were to be paid off at a rate of 1,600 statute acres for every £600 of arrears and their baronies were to be interspersed within the territory assigned to Adventurers in order to protect them, rather as the servitors were supposed to shield undertakers in the Ulster plantation.[90] Those due back-pay for service in England before 1649 were next in line and after them those soldiers, like the veterans of Sir Charles Coote's regiment, who were owed back-pay from service in Ireland before 1649.

The Commonwealth land settlement was quite different from the Ulster plantation. The scale was bigger, there was no requirement on grantees to actually plant British settlers, the servitor element was more lavishly rewarded and it was rational in that spoils were divided among those to whom the regime, in one way or another, was indebted rather than among court favourites. The administration of the Commonwealth land settlement was thorough when it came to finding out how much land was available to be confiscated and where it lay.

The Civil Survey compiled between 1654 and 1656 was an estimate (indeed a serious underestimate) of acreage as well as value, name, use, boundaries and ownership taken from local juries of 'the most ancient and able inhabitants' empanelled for that purpose. The survey covered all or parts of twenty-seven counties.[91] The illustrative extract opposite relates to the townland of Ballyculhane, parish of Kildimo, in County Limerick belonging to Patrick.[92]

Purcell had been second-in-command of the Munster Confederate army during the 1640s. He was one of the Irish leaders Ireton hanged after taking the surrender of Limerick. Unlike the others, the hapless Purcell did not die with exemplary fortitude; his feet gave from under him and he had to be manhandled to the makeshift gibbet.[93] Ballyculhane's boundaries are

Names of proprietors and qualification	Denomination of Lands, and their meetes, and Bounds	Number of Acres by Estimation	Lands profitable & ye quantitie of them	Lands un-profitable & wast	Value of the whole in 1640
Major Gnrall Patrick Purcell deceased Irish Papist	*Bally Cullane one plowland having upon it a Castle, a Bawne, three greate houses, and ten Cottages, one Mill seate, one Salmon weare in repayre, besides other weare Seates, mearing with ye River of Maige on ye East; On ye west with Beolane, Ballynehally, & Ballyassie; on ye South Ballyvoddanewth Faha, Courte, Killdimo, & Ballyvrrne on ye North wth Ardlaghan, oweing a penny, and a red rose p Ann to the Mannor house of Adare.*	850	*Marshland 250 Arable 400 meddow 6*	*Red bogg 90 Woody bogg 100 Shrubby wood 4*	*li160*

not accurately described, but the survey was rather better at weighing the land's productive potential. For instance, the jurors carefully distinguished turf bog and scrub from more valuable Shannonside summer meadows or callows. In contrast to the Civil Survey, Dr William Petty's 'Down Survey' was map based: it was so called from his continued reference to it as 'by survey laid down'.[94] Petty was a true renaissance man, physician-in-chief to the army, statistician, scientist, cartographer and manager. He deployed a 1,000-strong army of surveyors in December 1654: they were not the 'nimblest wits' but demobbed soldiers capable of enduring the hardships of winter in the open and the danger of tory attack and they finished surveying in just thirteen months.[95] A typical parish map sketches sparse pictorial information; settlement features such as mills, castles, churches and slate-roofed houses are carefully noted, with cabins scattered about. The boundaries of townlands are carefully drawn, numbered and cross referenced to an accompanying table of landowners.[96]

Davies had manipulated the legal mechanism of attainder as a straightforward way to spread blanket guilt and open up Ulster for plantation. The Commonwealth's attribution of guilt to landowners was more cumbersome. The 1652 Act for the Settling of Ireland distinguished the 'qualifications' of landowners in Ireland and their relative 'demerits' during the rising.[97] The clauses condemned some protestant landowners who took the royalist side, amounting to about a tenth of protestant landowners in Counties Donegal and Tyrone implicated by the Laggan army siege of Derry in 1649.[98] In 1654 such delinquent protestant landowners who were not following the royalist court in exile were allowed compound for their estates in the same way as royalist landowners in England by paying a fine. In the case of the Laggan officers this fine was equivalent to two years' purchase. In effect, then, the Act, as applied, condemned Catholic landowners only.

In theory Catholic landowners who managed to show 'constant good affection' to the English parliament and commonwealth could have kept their estates. This was extremely difficult when the landowner failed to display such affection by staying quietly at home in the Confederate Catholic quarters and paying taxes.[99] It was somewhat easier for Catholic landowners in what had been wartime Protestant territory. This partly explains why the proportion of confiscated land was relatively low in County Dublin compared with adjacent County Meath: 46 per cent compared with 76 per cent.[100] One Dublin landowner escaped because he spied for Jones on the royalist camp at Rathmines and another escaped because his wife was the sister of a prominent Presbyterian MP.[101]

Famously, Spenser's grandson evidently was not considered English. He lost his estates even though he was seven years old at the time of the rising, had 'utterly renounced' his childhood Catholicism and secured Oliver Cromwell's personal recommendation.[102] Nonetheless, it could be helpful if the landowner could downplay his or her Irishness. The Commonwealth also took some trouble to set aside lands in Connacht for Catholic widows of English extraction.[103] Furthermore, a study of the land settlement in west Ulster notes that of the dozen Catholics who kept all or part of their estates, half were Scots and one was English.[104]

In the final analysis nearly all Catholic landowners forfeited at least one third of their estates. The act also named 105 leaders to be 'excepted from pardon for life or estate', while anyone who took up arms before 10 November 1642 would lose all their lands. The date was chosen to mark the end of the rising and those who fought for the Confederate Catholics after that date (and by implication enjoyed some belligerent status) would escape more lightly by losing 'only' two thirds of their estates. On the face of it, this seems more favourable than the treatment of England Catholic royalists who *ipso facto* lost all their estates as obdurate royalists. Most, however, seem to have kept their lands by compounding or got them back by repurchase.[105]

Forfeiting Irish landowners would have to vacate their estates and get another 'in such place in Ireland as the parliament shall think fit to appoint' (Connacht and Clare it emerged) equivalent to one third or two thirds, as the case might be, of their estate. The knock-on impact would be to displace Connacht landowners who would in turn forfeit and move elsewhere in the province. Later, as the chimera of mass transplantation gripped Fleetwood's imagination, forfeiting landowners were ordered to transplant themselves, their families, dependants, livestock and goods before 1 May 1654 beyond the Shannon.[106] Cromwellians did not proclaim 'to Hell or Connaught' and Connacht and Clare were chosen as a native reservation not because the land was poor: the Commonwealth rated Connacht above Ulster in this respect. Rather, the region was chosen because of exaggerated respect for the impermeability of the Shannon Line.[107] In addition, Connacht was the furthest point from Scotland and from the Catholic mainland of Europe whence a royalist fleet might conceivably sail. To make doubly sure, a four-mile band of land was reserved for soldier-settlers to cut the Irish off from possible relief by sea. In directing transplanting landowners to settle in particular parts of what was left of Connacht and Clare (**map 6**), the plan seems to have been to remove them as far as possible from their old homes and to disperse them.[108] In practice this plan was not rigidly followed: in County Clare only one third of the transplanters were settled in their designated baronies, in County Roscommon one quarter, in County Galway one fifth, in County Mayo a mere twentieth.[109]

Later the four-mile line contracted to one mile and the barony of Clare was assigned to the Irish while all of Sligo and one third of County Mayo was clawed back from them.[110] The available land was cut back further when some commissioners helped themselves to estates and some natives condemned to death and forfeiture of all their lands, like William Nugent, Earl of Westmeath, nonetheless received large awards in Connacht.[111] Other areas forbidden to Irish transplantees included circuits of varying sizes around Galway, Athenry, Athlone, Portumna, Killaloe and Limerick and the mile line.[112] Close on 30 per cent of Connacht was either allocated to the army or acquired/retained, mostly by Old Protestants.[113] Transplanters would not find enough land to satisfy them.

What followed was a 'meer scramble' which can best be reconstructed from a local study.[114] In the winter of 1653–54 only seventy-two out of the 256 Catholic landowners in the barony of Bantry in County Wexford delivered a 'particular' of property, family members and servants to the headquarters of the local military precinct.[115] Most took their chances and remained as tenants at home. Having registered their details, those intending to go were given a 'Transplanter's Certificate'. Somewhere between half and two thirds (to judge from the experience of other regions) actually crossed the Shannon.[116] Proffering their certificate at Loughrea, County Galway, they obtained a provisional allocation of land in Connacht and Clare 'proportionable to their respective stocks and tillage'.[117] Here they threw up bothies and waited for their families and servants to join them.[118]

A second set of commissioners sat at Athlone from December 1654. They had before them the Civil Survey and the 'Black Book of Athlone' which included copies of 'examinations' taken in standard format from informers who had tattled on the political and military activism of their neighbours during the 1640s. On that basis they decided on the proportion of land to be confiscated and issued the transplanter with a decree, which was to be presented to the commissioners in Loughrea, who then issued a certificate of final settlement. Staying with the Bantry case study, sixty-four of the seventy-two landowners who transplanted actually got certificates for land in Connacht, most of them for the equivalent of about one fifth of their former holdings.[119] A half century later only eight of their descendants were noted by the books of survey and distribution as owning land in Connacht and three of those were absentees.[120] The biggest landowner in Bantry secured multiple grants equivalent in size to half his Wexford estate, presumably through bribing the commissioners.

By June 1657, when the confiscations were declared to be 'duly executed and performed', the Catholic share of land ownership had plummeted from almost 60 per cent to not more than 9 per cent.[121] One has to look far afield to find a disaster comparable to that which befell Irish Catholic landowners. On the other side of the confessional fault line, the Habsburgs arrested fifty of the defeated Czech leaders and confiscated their estates, while 730 pardoned aristocrats and gentry had their estates confiscated in whole or in part. By 1627, the year that Ferdinand decreed the expulsion of all nobles who did not become Catholics, around 150,000 Czech refugees had fled, drawn in disproportionate numbers from the cultural leaders, nobles, intellectuals and clergy.[122]

Religion

Ireland's new rulers disavowed the Episcopalian Church. In 1647 Anglican ceremonies and the Book of Common Prayer had been banned, the latter replaced with the Directory of Common Worship. They promised more vigorous evangelisation in Ireland but were divided, uncertain and incoherent about what doctrine and practice to impose.[123] Parliamentary commissioners were empowered in 1650 to enforce English ordinances abolishing the hierarchy and Common Prayer Book. However, the Church of Ireland enjoyed general support among the Old Protestant laity, except in Ulster. Ussher's 1615 Articles had entrenched Calvinist and anti-Catholic doctrine until replaced by Bramhall with the 1604 English Canons and lay control of the church remained strong despite the efforts of Wentworth and Bramhall. The Church of Ireland served the purposes of the settler community quite well.

In Ulster, Presbyterianism had restructured itself in the 1640s into something like its Scottish counterpart and put down deep roots in local communities to the point of setting up a parish structure.[124] They were split between the majority supporting Charles who subscribed to the Covenant and was crowned at Scone and the minority (the Presbyterian minister Jeremy O'Quinn was one such) who decried royal authority in religious affairs as contrary to the Covenant in all its purity.[125] Even though the Commonwealth accepted a Presbyterian congregational structure, Fleetwood persecuted the Ulster Presbyterians because of their royalism.[126] In 1653 he dramatically reversed this and announced his willingness to pay salaries to Presbyterian ministers. Possibly in response to this, the presbytery passed the Act of Bangor forbidding any reference to divisions in Scotland between those who supported King and Covenant and those who supported the Covenant alone.

By then the Baptists had replaced the Presbyterians as the most acute threat to Commonwealth rule in Ireland. In the absence of legislation on religion, much latitude was left to Lord Deputy Charles Fleetwood. He subscribed to Independency which was, in effect, the 'official' religion of the Commonwealth and Protectorate. Nonetheless, his governorship allowed radical sects to flourish. Ireland produced few such before 1649 and novel sects like Baptists, who refused to accept infant baptism as true baptism, were introduced from England by soldiers and chaplains. They directed missionary efforts exclusively towards English garrisons and showed no interest in pre-1640 settlers or the native Irish. The military government which prevailed in most Irish towns until 1656 gave the

Baptists unique opportunities to advance their sect.[127] Highly placed officers probably embraced Baptism so readily because its exclusive doctrine attracted those anxious to retain their distinct identity as the elect in the land of the unregenerate papist. Setbacks like the unexpectedly slow progress of reconquest and the spread of plague to English quarters tended to discredit mainstream Independency. Fleetwood failed to see that the sect, in England and Ireland, attracted the politically disaffected and provided a cover for opposition which aimed at the overthrow of his father-in-law's protectorate. Oliver Cromwell sent his younger son to assess the threat in 1645 and Henry Cromwell recommended that Fleetwood be sacked for allowing English government in Ireland to be identified with an exclusive and extreme sect. Oliver Cromwell adopted the compromise of commissioning Henry as major-general and adding him to the Irish council and it was only in 1657 that Henry Cromwell officially displaced Fleetwood as governor. The authorities withdrew their favour from the Baptists: some preachers had their salaries reduced or stopped while others were moved from populous towns to where they posed less of a political threat. Having failed to dislodge Henry Cromwell, the leading Baptist officers in Ireland resigned their commissions in November 1656 and transferred their opposition to England.

With the Baptist menace receding, Quakers seemed to retain a potentially threatening foothold in the army, especially in Limerick. In the course of 1655 Henry Ingoldsby, governor of the city, had some success in stemming the growth of the sect. Quakers strained any policy of toleration by their socially radical theology. They would not take oaths or acknowledge superiors in the accepted language or behaviour of deference. Their active witness, notably street preaching and disrupting traditional worship, also posed problems of public order.[128] However, like the Baptists, the Quakers did not win over a numerous body of civilian converts.

As regards papists, the Protectorate primarily targeted the clergy and it became settled policy from 1653 to exile them. There was nothing particularly new in such decrees of banishment except that now they were rigorously enforced. Of the twenty-seven bishops, only one, the aged and bedridden MacSweeney of Kilmore, stayed in Ireland. At least 1,000 priests fled into exile and more were rounded up. At first such captured priests were given passes to ship for continental Europe, but at the beginning of 1655 it was ordered that priests under forty who had refused to go into voluntary exile should be concentrated in prisons on Inishmore and Inishbofin islands to await shipment to Barbados and hard labour on the plantations.[129]

Why was the Cromwellian banishment so effective, compared with the many similar decrees in the past? There was no bloodbath. Most of the bishops and priests who died were killed during or following military actions and this is reflected in the annual numbers which spiked at around nineteen in 1649 and twenty-two in 1651, before falling to single figures. Enough priests were executed to give teeth to the banishment decrees. A typical example of a peacetime execution would be that of Tadgh Moriarty, a fifty-year-old Dominican who ignored the most recent banishment order of June 1653 and continued to say mass at a rock (the tradition of mass rocks surely dates to this decade) in Kilclohane Wood, two miles from Castlemaine. Following a dawn mass on 15 August he was arrested, imprisoned for two months and hanged on Fair Hill, Killarney. The decrees were also effective because, complained a priest on the run, they had nowhere to shelter with so many settlers moving into the houses of their wealthier co-religionists and the towns emptying of Catholics. Moreover, heavy penalties of death and forfeiture of property deterred those left from harbouring priests. Movement near roads was constrained by soldiers who actively hunted priests and mounted frequent check points, eager for the bounty of £5.[130] A Capuchin reported to Rome in 1654:

So vigilant are the eyes of the persecutors that our fathers, seculars and regulars alike, who almost all live in the countryside, hardly dare to spend the night in a Catholic's house. We mostly live on mountains, in woods, and in the middle of the many bogs where the horsemen of the heretics cannot go . . .[131]

Fewest clergy seem to have survived on the run in the ecclesiastical province of Dublin. In 1653 French of Ferns counted only one sixth of his pre-war clergy as still active and they were thin on the ground in the other Dublin bishoprics also: four in Leighlin, six in Kildare and just seven in Dublin.[132] In contrast, Meath had plenty of priests, sixty in all, by the end of the decade, while in Armagh, around twenty to thirty secular priests lived with their relatives throughout the 1650s and a dozen regulars, mostly Franciscans, lay low in the neighbourhood of their former convents.[133] The disparity probably resulted from a more intense effort to eradicate priests in the province of Dublin which was practically coterminous with the zone that was to be entirely cleared of natives by October 1655.[134] Active persecution abated after the effective beginning of Henry Cromwell's governorship in 1657, though orders banishing priests would issue as late as August 1659 and a proposal to impose an oath of abjuration on Catholic lay people was mooted.[135] 'The trial, though sharp, was short': too short.

Catholics conformed in apparently large numbers, mostly from the Dublin province, during the interregnum and this conversion experience was probably not unrelated to the fact that persons could be dispensed from transplanting if they gave proof of 'real renouncing the Popish superstitions'.[136] The significance of this should not be understated because outward compliance could be a decisive first step towards conversion, if this were consolidated by evangelisation.[137] This was not to be. Nothing was done towards translating the Directory of Worship into Irish, whereas in Wales a translation had been set afoot in 1644. Hostility towards Irish was not total. Godrey Daniel, a former Church of Ireland minister, translated *The Christian Doctrine* into Irish in 1652, but when the single fount of Irish type mysteriously disappeared afterwards, no replacement fount was cast.

The authorities were not sufficiently interested to bother evangelising the natives. Fundamentally, they believed the Irish to be unregenerate and converting them 'a waste of time'. Here the attribution of general guilt for the 1641 massacre exercised a powerful influence.[138]

Conclusion

The death of so many native civilians followed by unconditional and complete conquest seemed to proffer that 'blank sheet on which the English commonwealth could write what it wished'.[139] Responding to this opportunity, Fleetwood's retributive scheme was genocidal in scope. He wished to ultimately drive all natives to Connacht, beginning with a Boyne–Barrow pale. Policy towards Catholics and Catholicism was really just another aspect of Fleetwood's scheme, with priest hunting, its most notable feature, most intensive and successful in the new pale. Tacitly, the more humane and saner counsels of Old Protestants prevailed, their practical arguments given force by the lack of immigrants to replace labourers to be transplanted.

The new plantation failed on the gigantic scale originally envisaged.[140] In 1670, when the estates of the Cromwellian settlers were confirmed they numbered 8,000 as against 36,000 in the original scheme.[141] Many Adventurers had been reluctant to settle their land and most soldiers sold their debentures at a discount to their officers for ready cash.[142] In the countryside the Protectorate created 'not a protestant community, but a protestant upper class'. Banishment of natives was more effective in towns and cities which were mostly captured by mercantile and artisan immigrants. When it came to identifying, mapping and dividing confiscated land, the Protector's agents displayed consummate energy and administrative skill, but the land settlement failed as an exemplary exercise in retribution. Degrees of guilt and appropriate punishment counted for little in the corrupt and creaking process of assigning land west of the Shannon.

Endnotes

1 Wheeler 2001, pp. 163, 167; Smith 1998, p. 175; Gardiner 1903, pp. 197, 237.

2 Gardiner 1903, pp. 6, 25, 92; Stevenson 1990, p. 156; Firth 1900, p. 257.

3 O'Hara 2006, p. 191.

4 Miller 1973, p. 43; Hill 1970, p. 121.

5 Scott 2004, pp. 196–7.

6 Woolrych 2003, p. 468.

7 Hayes-McCoy 1969, pp. 210–11.

8 Gentles 1992, p. 357.

9 McKenny 2005, p. 103.

10 Cited in Reilly 1999, p. 81.

11 Murphy 1885, p. 92.

12 Gardiner 1903, p. 117.

13 Gardiner 1903, p. 125; Burke 1990, p. 7.

14 Gardiner 1903, p. 122; Schama 2001, p. 205.

15 Barber 2001, p. 184; Hill 1970, p. 109.

16 Burke 1990, pp. 9, 10, 13; Corish 1976, p. 340.

17 Stevenson 1990, p. 157; Firth 1900, p. 257.

18 Murphy 1885, p. 160; Lydon 1998, p. 192; Ohlmeyer 1989, pp. 34–7.

19 Cited in Wheeler 1999, p. 96; Gilbert 1879, p. 226.

20 Burke 1990, p. 264; Gale 1834, p. 124.

21 Carte 1736, ii, pp. 2, 43, 72, 90–3, 100, 106, 107, 108; Ohlmeyer 1993, pp. 232–3; Dunlop 1913, i, p. 124.

22 Reilly 1999, p. 294.

23 Wheeler 1999, pp. 178, 164; Simms 1973–4, p. 215.

24 Gilbert 1879, ii, p. 466.

25 Murphy 1885, p. 228.

26 Murphy 1885, p. 218.

27 Little 2004, pp. 60–1.

28 Wheeler 1999, pp. 128, 135–9, 151–8.

29 Burke 1907, pp. 72–4; Corish 1976, pp. 336–8.

30 Gentles 1992, p. 352; Gardiner 1903, i, p. 27.

31 Wheeler 1993, p. 65.

32 Wheeler 1999, pp. 173, 175–7, 179, 188, 190; Corish 1976, p. 349.

33 Lawrence 1649, p. 8.

34 Wheeler 1999, pp. 158, 170; Gilbert 1879, iii, part one, p. 167; part two, p. 274; Borlase 1680, p. 312.

35 Ó Siochrú 2005b, pp. 905–32.

36 Gilbert 1879, ii, pp. 158, 192–3.

37 Gilbert 1879, ii, p. 233.

38 Gilbert 1879, ii, pp. 161–2.

39 Wheeler 1999, p. 192.

40 Dunlop 1913, i, pp. 27, 33, 38, 48–50, 63, 69, 71, 74.

41 Dunlop 1913, i, pp. 74, 134; Wheeler 1999, p. 194.

42 Simms 1986, pp. 26–7.

43 Wheeler 1999, p. 219.

44 HMC 1874, p. 571.

45 Wheeler 1999, p. 222.

46 Dunlop, 1913, i, pp. cxxix, 147, 150–1, 155–7.

47 Dunlop 1913, i, pp. 115, 119, 134–6, 140, 248; Gilbert 1879, iii, pp. 69–70, 274, 281, 283, 297, 301, 303; CSPI 1903, pp. 385, 393; Ludlow 1698, i, pp. 392–3, 402–3, 408–9, 424–5; McNeill 1943, pp. 336–7, 338, 342, 344, 349, 357.

48 Prendergast 1875, pp. 326–7; Dunlop 1913, i, pp. 27, 33, 38, 42, 50, 119; ii, p. 321; Burke 1904, pp. 81–2; Hore 1904, iv, p. 495; Ludlow 1698, i, p. 391.

49 Gilbert 1879, iii, part one, p. 203.

50 Gentles 1992, p. 381.

51 Dunlop 1913, ii, p. 425, 514–15; Berresford-Ellis 1975, p. 37; Kelly 1848–52, iii, p. 193.

52 'Ballybawn', probably Bawn, near Nenagh. Burke 1907, p. 82; Dunlop 1913, i, p. 128.

53 Dunlop 1913, i, pp. 147, 155, 157.

54 Dunlop 1913, i, pp. 169–71, 175–6; Kavanagh 1932–49, v, p. 22.

55 Gilbert 1879, iii, pp. 113, 128; Berresford-Ellis 1975, p. 42.

56 Gentles 1992, p. 383.

57 Waring 1650, p. 27.

58 Dickson 2005, p. 4; Cullen 1976, p. 389; Lenihan 1997, pp. 1–2; Smyth 2006, p. 159; Gillespie 2006, p. 184; Kavanagh 1932–49, v, p. 175. For a comparative figure, population loss of 15–25 per cent hit the territories of the Holy Roman Empire during the Thirty Years War: Ruff 2001, p. 61; Tallett 1992, p. 161; De Vries 1976, p. 4.

59 O'Rahilly 1952, pp. 71–5.

60 Wheeler 1999, p. 230; Gillespie 1995a, p. 180; Gilbert 1882–91, vi, p. 207.

61 Moran 1874, p. 432; Ramsey 1949, pp. 170, 171, 178; Kavanagh 1932–49, v, p. 80; Clarkson 1975, pp. 60–2; Dunlop 1913, p. 33.

62 Browne 1962, p. 156; Lawrence 1655, pp. 86–7; Gilbert, 1879, iii, p. 372; Hore 1858–9, p. 451.

63 Slack 1985, pp. 109, 120; Benedictow 1987, pp. 401–31.

64 Kavanagh 1932–49, iv, p. 643; Gilbert 1879, iii, pp. 266, 270; Benedictow 1987, p. 426.

65 Smyth 1988, p. 55; Moran 1874, p. 432; Dunlop 1913, p. 33.

66 Cipolla 1973, p. 17.

67 Walter 1989, p. 18; Robbins 1995, pp. 22–3; Outram 2001, p. 159; Post 1985, p. 220.

68 Gillespie 2006, p. 186.

69 Lawrence 1655, p. 12; Lawrence 1656, pp. 3, 21–3; Stevenson 1990, p. 166.

70 Dunlop 1913, ii, p. 544.

71 Barnard 1975, pp. 91–6, 102–21; Dunlop 1913, i, p. 120.

72 Stewart 2001, p. 88; Gillespie 2006, p. 188; McKenny 2005, p. 122.

73 Gillespie 2006, p. 194.

74 Berresford-Ellis 1975, p. 126; Gookin 1655, pp. 21–2, 25.

75 Berresford-Ellis 1975, pp. 131–2.

76 Gillespie 2006, p. 190.

77 Gillespie 2006, p. 186.

78 Cullen 1974–5, p. 154.

79 Smyth 2006, p. 299; Smyth 1997, fig. 7.2.

80 Barnard 1975, pp. 52–4.

81 Gillespie 1991, p. 40.

82 Barnard 1975, pp. 63–6.

83 Stradling 1994, p. 139.

84 Corish 1976, p. 364.

85 Kelly 1851–62, iii, p. 183; Moran 1874, p. 411; O'Callaghan 2001, pp. 78–9, 81, 104.

86 Gillespie 1991, p. 59.

87 Cited in Corish 1976, p. 360.

88 Bottigheimer 1971, pp. 64–6, 75.

89 Smyth 2006, p. 168.

90 Prendergast 1875, pp. 82–3, 93–4, 187, 191.

91 Prunty 2004, p. 49; Corish 1976, p. 362.

92 Simington 1938, p. 346.

93 Dowd 1890, p. 52.

94 Berresford-Ellis 1975, p. 122.

95 Prunty 2004, p. 51.

96 Smyth 2006, pp. 175–8.

97 Corish 1976, iii, p. 347; Gentles 1992, pp. 351–84; Wheeler 1990, p. 38; Stevenson 1990, p. 166; Dunlop 1913, ii, p. 378; Simington 1970, vii.

98 McKenny 2005, pp. 112–15, 123.

99 Butler 1918, p. 132.

100 Corish 1976, p. 358.

101 Arnold 1993, p. 33.

102 Fraser 2001, p. 503; Dunlop 1913, ii, p. 659.

103 Dunlop 1913, ii, pp. 494–5.

104 McKenny 1995, p. 195; Dunlop 1913, ii, p. 355; Prendergast 1875, p. 214.

105 Hutton 1989, pp. 7, 38.

106 Simington 1970, vii; Dunlop 1913, ii, p. 355.

107 Stewart 2001, p. 87.

108 Dunlop 1913, ii, pp. 387–8.

109 Smyth 2006, p. 183. For a local example in the barony of Kenry County Limerick see Simington 1970, pp. 41, 49–50, 52–3, 56, 49, 252, 255; Begley 1927, p. 235.

110 Clarke 1999, p. 223.

111 Dunlop 1913, ii, pp. 524, 570; Corish 1976, pp. 365–6.

112 Dunlop 1913, ii, pp. 524, 56–7, 608–11.

113 Smyth 2006, p. 185.

114 Airy 1890, p. 201.

115 Simington 1970, p. xviii.

116 Smyth 2006, p. 186.

117 Simington 1970, p. xviii.

118 Ramsey 1933, p. 47.

119 Goff 1990, p. 172.

120 Goff 1990, pp. 177, 181; Corish 1976, p. 370.

121 Corish 1976, p. 368; Simms 1969, p. 4.

122 Kamen 1971, p. 471.

123 Barnard 1975, pp. 91–7.

124 Gillespie 2006, pp. 188, 203.

125 Kilroy 1994, pp. 16–17.

126 Corish 1976, pp. 376, 379.

127 Barnard 1975, pp. 98, 100, 104–5, 108.

128 Gillespie 2006, p. 203; Barnard 1975, p. 109; Kilroy 1994, pp. 139–40.

129 Corish 1976, pp. 382–3; Dunlop 1913, ii, pp. 436, 477, 549, 675.

130 Moran 1874, pp. 389, 408–9.

131 Moran 1874, pp. 407, 418.

132 Giblin 1956, pp. 52–5; Corish 1981, p. 49.

133 Ó Fiach 1957, p. 185; Dudley Edwards 1952, p. 102; Ó Fiach 1957, p. 192; Moran 1874, p. 391.

134 Dunlop 1913, ii, p. 544.

135 Barnard 1975, p. 296; Dudley Edwards 1952, p. 71.

136 Dunlop 1913, ii, pp. 413, 660; Corish 1981, p. 55; Barnard 1975, p. 298.

137 Murphy 1990, pp. 82–3; Corish 1976, p. 384; Barnard 1975, pp. 178–80.

138 Stevenson 1990, p. 174; Barnard 1975, p. 91.

139 Corish 1976, pp. 357, 362.

140 Simms 1969, p. 4.

141 Bottigheimer 1971, p. 140.

142 Canny 1987, pp. 220–1; Moody 1967, p. 203; Barnard 1975, p. 34.

CHAPTER 8

Charles II 1660–85

Restoration

Only Oliver Cromwell's formidable personality and the menace of his army held the Protectorate together because his regime did not enjoy the support of the gentry in England, or still less, Scotland or Ireland.[1] As the Old Protestants had been mostly royalists who switched to the winning side quite late, they were regarded with suspicion, excluded from political life and threatened with composition fines as a condition of keeping their estates.[2] Henry Cromwell repudiated Fleetwood's alliance with the Baptists and Independents and tried to broaden the regime's base by, among other things, quietly dropping composition fines to attract Old Protestant support.[3] Simultaneously, Broghill, the Protector's man in Scotland, tried to draw more locals there into cooperation with the regime.[4] This policy of co-option and compromise moved from the fringes to the heart of the realm in February 1657 when Broghill led a majority of the Commons in proposing to reinvest authority in a king, parliament and a national church bound by common doctrine. The 'Humble Petition and Advice' proffered by Broghill and Henry Cromwell begged Oliver Cromwell to declare himself that king. While he took on some of the style and forms of monarchy, Cromwell reluctantly turned down the crown, fearing the hostility of the army generals.

'The man who destroyed the Protectorate was Oliver Cromwell.'[5] He bequeathed near-bankruptcy and made no arrangements for a successor other than to nominate his son Richard on his deathbed in September 1658.[6] The army and the politicians failed to work out a working compromise in the third Protectorate parliament summoned in January 1659. Defiant colonels and generals deposed 'Tumbledown Dick' and tried to turn the clock back to the Rump parliament and Commonwealth.[7] The Rump was the remnant of the Long Parliament that had been thoroughly purged in 1648 by Colonel Pride.[8] Westminster recalled Henry Cromwell, replaced him with parliamentary commissioners and purged the army of many Old Protestant officers. Disgusted at their want of religious radicalism and their failure to make good arrears of army pay, Major General Lambert locked out the members of the Rump in October and thereby precipitated greater administrative disorder, constitutional uncertainty and royalist intrigue.[9]

Dreading a return to the army radicalism of the early 1650s, Old Protestant officers and ex-officers struck against Lambert's partisans. Sir Hardness Waller and Theophelus Jones (a brother of Michael Jones, hero of Dungan's Hill and Rathmines) took Dublin Castle in December 1659.[10] The irrepressible Broghill joined them in Dublin and the plotters summoned a General Convention or quasi parliament to meet at Dublin in February 1660.[11] This was in no sense a royalist coup: Waller was a 'regicide' who had signed Charles's death warrant and could expect no favour from his son, while Broghill remained uncommitted to Charles until his restoration was a foregone conclusion.[12] The conservative nature of the coup became apparent and Waller tried to arrest Coote but was himself put behind bars. At some point the members were persuaded that only a restoration of Charles Stuart could secure their long-term interests. It is unlikely that General Monck would have led his army from Scotland to topple Lambert without knowing that he had the tacit support of Coote and the army in Ireland. In that sense, it has been argued, '. . . the Restoration was made in Ireland'.[13] Ostensibly, Monck was for a Commonwealth but the parliament he restored began, increasingly, to utter pro-monarchical sentiments.[14] Sensing the mood, Charles II issued the Declaration of Breda in April 1660. This was the manifesto for a restored Stuart constitutional monarchy, in which he promised that none of his subjects would suffer the 'least endangerment . . . in their lives, liberties or estates' except for the regicides. Monck agreed and Charles II was invited home.

'All wish'd the King restor'd, but none could do't/Till *Scotland* found her Monk, & *Ireland* COOTE.'[15] In reality, neither Charles Coote nor any other 'slippery time-servers' among the Old Protestants played anything more than a negligible role in Charles II's return.[16] But reality was less important than the widespread perception, shared by influential figures like the Earl of Clarendon, Charles's chancellor, that Old Protestants had made 'the earliest advances towards his Majesties Restoration'.[17]

The Convention was elected through the normal parliamentary constituencies and Old Protestants comprised about ninety-eight of the 138
delegates known to have been returned. Munster was a Boyle fiefdom
and Charles Coote dominated Connacht and much of Ulster.[18] Perhaps
significantly for the future religious settlement, only two of the Ulster
representatives had a Scottish background. However, the fact that the
Convention chose a Presbyterian minister to preach before it at its opening
session seemed to bode well for the Presbyterians and the Convention's call
for a learned and orthodox ministry made no mention of episcopacy.[19]
Coote and the other power brokers took their cue from the exiled king's
preference for a 'narrowly Episcopalian' settlement, that is, a return
to the forms of worship and church government of his father's reign.[20]
The argument seemed settled when Henry Jones, now addressed by his
former title as Lord Bishop of Clogher, was asked to preach at Christ
Church in Dublin on the day that Charles was proclaimed king in the
city on 14 May 1660.

The members of the Convention, both 'Old' and Cromwellian
Protestants, buried their differences on matters of religion and acted
as one in identifying their essential interest: land. They sent commissioners in May 1660 to ask the King to confirm the massive
transfers of land over the preceding decade. Responding to royal hints,
the commissioners quickly requested the Church of Ireland's re-
establishment.

Ormond's second viceroyalty 1662–69

Where English politicians were content to let Scotland look after itself,
a wealthy and populous Ireland (Dublin doubled and may even have
tripled in size between 1660 and 1685 to become the second city of the
Stuart kingdoms) was a more important prize. The spoils of Irish land,
revenues and offices were too important to be let slip by one court faction
to another without a contest. High politics, the comings, goings and
doings of governors, can be understood only in the context of the rise
and fall of these contending factions at Whitehall Palace. The period
of 'Clarendonian' dominance lasted from the Restoration until Lord
Chancellor Clarendon was hounded out of office in 1667 and lasted in
Ireland until his ally Ormond was dismissed from the viceroyalty in 1669.
This was the most formative period of Charles II's reign in Ireland when
the big question was answered: to what extent would the land confiscations of the interregnum be reversed?

The land settlement

Ireland's Case Briefly Stated (1695) by Hugh Reilly, master in chancery and clerk of the council in Dublin during the fleeting Jacobite regime, was the nearest the Irish Catholic community came to producing a popular equivalent to Temple's *Irish Rebellion*.[21] Reilly spent over half this little book railing against the 'settlement of rebels and traitors' in the early 1660s. That Cromwell's followers stole Irish land was to be expected, but Charles II's failure to undo this loomed in the Catholic consciousness as the most traumatic betrayal of the century.

His 'betrayal' was implicit in the Declaration of Breda and explicit in his Declaration Regarding the Settlement of Ireland, issued in November 1660, which promised that the Cromwellian adventurers and soldiers could keep their gains. Stuart amnesia was not peculiar to Irish royalists. English cavaliers forced to sell off land to pay composition fines and punitively heavy taxes found these sales irreversible.[22] Most of the commissioners appointed to implement Charles's wishes had a vested interest in keeping the land settlement intact: included were Broghill and Coote (newly created Earls of Orrery and Mountrath, respectively) and Sir William Petty.[23] In the event the law courts refused to enforce their decisions and Charles was forced to defer the land question to an Irish parliament that sat from May 1661 until August 1666. The Commons was returned on the Cromwellian franchise and so was an all-Protestant assembly; members successfully challenged the election of the single Catholic, Geoffrey Browne MP, for the borough of Tuam. The Protestant character of the House was further assured by having the oaths of allegiance and supremacy administered to members.[24] Unsurprisingly, parliament was hardly more sympathetic than the commissioners to Catholic demands. The preamble to the parliament's draft bill for an Act of Settlement invented an agreeable past where the King's Protestant subjects in Ireland subdued Irish rebels during his 'absence' and deprived them of their estates as punishment. Having done so, they promptly recalled their king as soon as they could. Orrery glibly explained away any apparent inconsistencies: if his fellow 'Old Protestants' might be 'seemingly rebels', they were driven by 'a necessity only created by the Irish Papists themselves'.[25] It was all the fault of the Papists. Adventurers and soldiers had loaned money or risked their lives to reduce Papist rebels to obedience to the crown and so deserved Charles's favour alongside these hardy Old Protestants.[26] The bill was sent, in accordance with Poynings' Law, to be ratified by the English Privy Council.

Agents for Irish Catholics at court lobbied furiously against the bill but failed to block it. The chief agent, Nicholas Plunkett, probably made a tactical mistake in hectoring Charles that he was 'obliged in honour' to make good the treaty concluded on his behalf with the Confederate Catholics in 1649.[27] 'Kings,' demurred Ormond's biographer Carte, 'do not care to be taught their duty in such a manner.'[28] Moreover, Orrery, the man who had pressed Cromwell to assume the crown of three kingdoms, was able to impugn Plunkett's loyalty by producing a letter from the Confederate Catholic Supreme Council, co-signed by Plunkett, that purportedly offered Ireland to the Pope in exchange for military aid.[29] The subsequent Act of Settlement of 1662 confirmed virtually all the Cromwellian land grants.

Yet if Charles had little apparent sympathy for Irish Catholics as a body, he felt obliged to individuals who had helped him and his father.[30] His Declaration of November 1660 listed, first, thirty-nine persons who, 'in an especial manner merited our Grace and Favour'. This list was headed by top-ranking nobles such as the Earls of Clancarty, Clanricard, Fingal and Westmeath and also included others who earned Charles's gratitude in exile.[31] A good example would be Theobald, Viscount Taaffe, who commanded the Confederate Catholic army so ineptly at Knocknanuss. In exile Taaffe had become the King's boon companion, master of revels and protector of Charles's then mistress, Lucy Walter.[32] Taaffe was eventually restored to all his own estates by 1667 and, in addition, was granted the estates of Taaffe kinsmen in Louth and Tyrone who had been implicated in the rising. In second place came an altogether longer list of well over 200 Irish officers or 'ensignmen' who served in royalist regiments in exile. Most of these, men like Arthur Magennis, Viscount Iveagh, or Dudley Costello (who, in disgust, turned tory in the 1660s), did not get their lands back. The catch was that the act allowed such 'ensign men' to get their lands back without having to prove their innocence only if the Cromwellian grantee was fully 'reprised' or compensated beforehand by getting the same acreage elsewhere. In third place, Charles professed that he felt 'obliged to perform what we owe' to the far greater number who had subscribed to the 1649 Articles made with Ormond on his behalf; 'we could not forget the peace'. Louis XIV put diplomatic pressure on Charles on this very point, since he had been the guarantor of that treaty. But such 'articlemen' were caught by the same clause: Cromwellian grantees had first to be reprised.

'There must be new discoveries made of a New Ireland,' concluded Ormond.[33] Charles had allowed himself to be convinced by Orrery's specious assurances that there was a land bank big enough, comprising mainly regicide's estates, to confirm the titles of soldiers and adventurers and still leave enough for deserving Catholics.[34] Other persons and parties snapped up the land bank before the ensignmen and articlemen. For instance, James, Duke of York, was granted the regicide's estates giving him almost 170,000 acres in Ireland, while officials in Dublin such as Ormond and Arthur Annesley, Earl of Anglesey, vastly increased their estates.[35] So-called '49 officers' (any Protestant officer who fought for the Stuarts in Ireland and was owed arrears of pay) mopped up most of what remained, except for the Munster Protestant officers whose claims were 'postponed' (Stuart euphemism for not granted) as punishment for defecting to Cromwell in the winter of 1649.[36] If Cromwellian grantees had to be reprised and there was not enough land to reprise them, the Irish would get little or nothing back: so far, so bad.[37]

There was one loophole in the Act of Settlement. So-called 'innocent' papists could get their lands back right away without having to wait for the occupant to be reprised. 'Innocents' were those who could be deemed never to have taken up arms against Charles I. There should have been only a tiny number of them because the Act excluded any person, or their heirs, who was involved in the Confederate government or anyone who 'enjoyed their estates' in its territory, some two thirds of the country.[38] Charles took the implementation of the Act of Settlement away from the Irish parliament and, in January 1663, entrusted it to a court of claims made up of seven English commissioners without any direct interest in Irish land. The commissioners took an unexpectedly generous definition of 'innocence' and issued 564 decrees to Catholics from a total of 820 adjudications.[39] Those who got a hearing were mostly Palesmen. Perhaps the commissioners called the most likely looking category of innocents first, namely those who lived close to hand and in what had been the English quarters during the 1640s. At any rate, they did relatively well. In County Dublin, for instance, the original landowners clawed back two thirds of their pre-1641 landholdings.[40]

The Irish House of Commons was enraged and threw out a Bill of Explanation (a sequel to the Act of Settlement), tried to narrow the definition of innocence and demanded that land claims be reserved to local and reliably Protestant juries. For his part, Charles's anger was comparably intense and he threatened the House with armed action.[41] The impasse was broken by a conspiracy in May 1663 to seize Dublin Castle, kidnap Ormond, reinstate the Solemn League and Covenant and secure all Protestant land from the court of claims. Ormond found the tentacles of the plot so 'far spread' that he was afraid of what he might find if he were to dig too deeply. The ringleaders were known to be Cromwellian veterans – Colonel Thomas Jephson MP for Trim and the melodramatically named Lieutenant Thomas Blood, who later stole the crown jewels from the Tower of London.[42] Eight MPs were known to have been involved and the other members, eager to show off their loyalty, shied away from confronting Charles over the court of claims.

The court continued until Randal MacDonnell, Marquis of Antrim, strained the concept of innocence until it snapped in August 1663. He was not even an articleman but had actively opposed the second Ormond Peace in 1649 and had been lucky to be acquitted of well-founded charges of collaborating with the Cromwellians.[43] Badgered by Antrim's wife, a niece of Sir Daniel O'Neill, groom of the bedchamber, Charles peremptorily declared Antrim innocent and instructed Ormond to make this known to the court of claims commissioners.[44] By a narrow majority they ordered Antrim restored, though Charles later publicly reversed the verdict (Antrim still won his estates back) to calm Protestant outrage.[45] Shortly afterwards the commissioners wound up their hearings after only eight months, leaving several thousand claims unheard.[46] Instead, Anglesey and Ormond drafted another explanatory bill which envisaged Cromwellian grantees voluntarily surrendering one sixth of their estates. Charles kept himself well briefed about the bill and invited comments by Plunkett and other Catholic representatives.[47] The wrangling dragged on interminably and as late as April 1665 the Catholics clamoured for full restoration. The following month they reluctantly acceded to a new and somewhat more favourable formula whereby most soldiers and adventurers surrendered one third, rather than one sixth, of their holdings and the land thus freed should be used to reprise displaced Cromwellian grantees.[48] The resultant Act of Explanation of December 1665 was all of 200 folio pages long, largely because the provisos named individuals to be granted estates.[49]

The rise of Richard Talbot, the busiest of the many brokers peddling influence and access, illustrates how such provisos were obtained. A Palesman, his father had been leader of the Catholic opposition in Parliament half a century before. Taken prisoner at Dungan's Hill, and ransomed in time to be captured at Drogheda, his life was spared 'by a providence that marked him out for greater things': so claimed a pamphleteer celebrating his later career as the first and only Catholic governor since the Reformation.[50] Through the influence of Daniel O'Neill and one of his brothers, Father Peter Talbot, an envoy to Spain for the Stuart court in exile, he secured an *entreé* to Charles's court in exile and volunteered to go to London to assassinate Cromwell.[51] Captured with other would-be assassins, he mysteriously escaped from the Tower and made his way back to court where he charmed his way into the circle of Charles's younger brother, James, Duke of York, the future James II. During the debates over the Act of Explanation Talbot journeyed indefatigably between the two realms, arguing cases before the court of claims or at Whitehall. His two most influential court patrons were in the bedroom cabal of Barbara Villiers, the King's mistress. These were Clarendon's main rival, Secretary of State Henry Bennet, Earl of Arlington, and Charles Berkeley, Earl of Falmouth, the 'most absolute' of Charles's personal favourites.[52] Talbot acted as a go-between for Arlington in getting part possession of the estate of O'Dempsey Lord Clanmaliere, whose claim of innocence went unheard. The name of the town of Portarlington, County Offaly, marks the success of this typically crooked conveyance.[53] Talbot harboured an abstract desire to see justice done to his co-religionists but, as Ormond quipped, he and his brothers had not 'omitted to consider themselves'.[54] By then Talbot had fallen out with Ormond over his handling of the land settlement and publicly threatened his life.[55] The threat was taken seriously: 'everybody knew the man had courage and wickedness enough,' fussed Clarendon. Talbot was subsequently thrown into the Tower but was released early in 1665 after Berkeley pleaded that these were just 'hasty and unadvised words'.[56] Talbot was 'full of cunning' and had 'courage aplenty'.[57] He would need both for the ups and downs to come.

Where Catholics had held less than 9 per cent of land at the Restoration, their share began to climb after 1663 until it reached around 22 per cent by the end of Charles's reign.[58] Bribery, family influence, luck and court connections all helped. It is significant that Catholics who got their land back still tended to identify with their dispossessed co-religionists. For instance, while Ormond warned his nephew off from identifying with the Irish and reminded him who had secured the restoration of his inheritance, young Muskerry still fumed about the injustice of rewarding 'the scum of Cromwell's army'.[59] The Irish Catholic community as a whole, and it is now possible to speak of such an entity, did not accept the settlement as final and blamed Ormond for breaking faith with them over the 1649 treaty.[60] The most authoritative statement of Catholic disenchantment with Ormond came in the lengthy preamble inserted by the Jacobite House of Commons before the bill to repeal the Acts of Settlement and Explanation in 1689. The Jacobite author of the 'Light to the Blind' also wondered why Charles had abandoned them: 'We cannot assign any other reason for this poverty of spirit than a certain inbred loathing to involve himself in new troubles, which he falsely conceived might be raised by the Cromwellian Protestants of Ireland.'[61]

'Falsely conceived'? Clarendon ostensibly worried that it would be 'dangerous' to reverse the land settlement and so provoke the still powerful army in Ireland and one can certainly argue that the 'mechanic bagmen', 'scum', 'fanatic scabs' and 'bloody traitors' (to pick out just some of the choice Catholic epithets) were so well entrenched and cohesive that it was prudent and politic to follow the line of least resistance and let them keep their new estates.[62] But, politic or not, Clarendon did not want a general restoration of Catholic estates.[63] Nor did Ormond: at the outset Ormond accepted Orrery's premise that 'it must be laid as a ground, that no adventurer or soldier shall be removed from his lot' and he no longer regarded himself as bound by the treaty he had concluded in 1649.[64] Handpicked Catholics might deserve their estates back. Such persons included members of the minor Butler houses of Mountgarret, Ikerrin, Dunboyne and Galmoy (even though Galmoy and Ikerrin's grandfather had collaborated with the Cromwellian authorities), together with families linked by marriage alliance, especially the Fingals, Clancartys and Clanricardes.[65]

The Remonstrance

While possession of their lands hung in the balance, Irish Catholics embroiled themselves in an untimely religious squabble. It began in December 1661 when a letter from one priest to another discussing a forthcoming rebellion was 'discovered' in a Dublin street.[66] Parliament was already mindful of the last rebellion and would later enact that the 23rd of October be commemorated annually to perpetuate memory of 'a conspiracy so generally inhumane, barbarous and cruel, as the like was never before heard of in any age or kingdom'.[67] The forged letter precipitated government into rounding-up Catholic clergy, mobilising the army and transplanting many gentry to Connacht. The squall of persecution drove many Catholics to petition for royal protection. Richard Bellings (one-time secretary of the Catholic Confederation and a client of Ormond and Clarendon) drafted an abject appeal or 'Remonstrance'.[68] Almost ninety years earlier the Pope justified the excommunication of Elizabeth I in 1570 on the basis that he had the right to depose a monarch and absolve subjects from allegiance to that monarch. In the Remonstrance Irish Catholics professed obedience and disclaimed 'all foreign power, be it either Papal or Princely, Spiritual or Temporal, in as much as it may seem

able, or shall pretend to free, discharge or absolve us from this obliga-
tion'.[69] Attempts like this to define the Pope's vague claim of secular
authority into a concordat on the Gallican model were hopeless and raised
the same insoluble questions as they did for the French church.[70] Rome
was embarrassed by public discussion of such anachronistic claims but
would never formally renounce what Protestants regarded as a 'damnable
doctrine'.[71]

The Remonstrance could not fail to divide and weaken Catholics.
A number of clergymen and nobles, including Taaffe, Clancarty and
Inchiquin (the scourge of Catholics had experienced a Pauline conversion
while in exile), signed the Remonstrance but the prestigious college of Irish
Franciscans in Louvain censured it as offensive to the dignity of the
Papacy.[72] The maverick Franciscan Peter Walsh, like Bellings an Ormond
client, continued to push for a general convocation of clergy in order to
debate the issue. His persistence paid off when he persuaded Ormond in
1666 to permit the Catholic clergy to hold a national meeting. The 100
or so priests who attended conceded the substance of Walsh's demands
but stopped short of accepting a form of words that the Vatican had
specifically condemned. This was not enough for Walsh.[73]

On the face of it, Ormond had prompted Walsh and Bellings as a way
of distinguishing between disloyal and loyal Catholics.[74] This was but a
pretext. Ormond did not need a remonstrance to distinguish hostile from
friendly clergy, nor were the latter picked out for special favour.[75]
Ormond, ever 'a great bramble scratching and tormenting the Catholics of
Ireland', fomented divisions with the primary purpose of weakening a
church which was the only surviving institution capable of rallying Irish
Catholics.[76] It was what a prudent governor did: Essex, a later Lord
Lieutenant, boasted of how he exploited the 'little wrangles' of the clergy
in order 'to keep these men divided'.[77]

Ormond out of favour 1669–77

Recovering from a false start in 1663, a diverse coalition of enemies led by
George Villiers, 2nd Duke of Buckingham, hounded Clarendon out of
office and into exile by 1668.[78] As an identifiable Clarendonian, Ormond's
days as Lord Lieutenant were now numbered. Ormond was also vulnerable because of his free spending and careless approach to revenue.
Sniffing the wind, Orrery promised enough proofs of Ormond's financial
irregularity to provide plausible grounds for dismissal.[79] Having first
disarmed him with fulsome compliments, Charles duly recalled Ormond.

But the probable underlying reason for recalling Ormond was that Charles already planned to announce religious toleration and needed a 'less inflexibly Anglican' successor.[80]

The replacement of the Clarendonians by Buckingham and Arlington's faction was more than a matter of personal rivalry; it formed part of a seismic reorientation of English foreign and religious policy. Charles signed the Treaty of Dover with the French in 1670 in which he agreed to join with France in attacking and carving up the United Provinces and in return he was promised a massive annual bribe that would free him of the need to call parliament and seek subsidies. In a secret proviso Charles claimed to be 'convinced of the truth of the Roman Catholic religion' and promised to publicly say so 'as soon as his country's affairs permit'.[81] The next step on what appalled old cavalier Anglicans saw as the road to Rome came in March 1672 when Charles issued a Declaration of Indulgence, announcing his intention to suspend penal laws against dissenters and Catholics. Charles's offer of toleration was cynically calculating. He disliked dissenters but was prepared to grant them religious toleration as a way of splitting protestant opposition to toleration for Catholics.[82]

Government in Ireland followed the drift towards toleration. Catholics and dissenters were vulnerable if Anglican bishops and magistrates chose to enforce the 1666 Act of Uniformity. Neither Lord Lieutenant Robartes (1669–70), a Presbyterian sympathiser, nor Lord Lieutenant Berkeley (1670–72), close friend of the Duke of York, was committed to curbing religious dissent.[83] The latter encouraged the admission of Catholic merchants to borough corporations and some 150 Catholic gentlemen were appointed magistrates. Orrery's Munster presidency court, based at his new town of Charleville, County Cork, had been a scourge of dissenters and Catholic ecclesiastics. Having misread the drift of Charles's religious policy, Orrery prohibited Catholic worship throughout Munster in 1670 and ordered several churches to be demolished. The following year the Munster presidency court was abolished and Orrery humiliated. By now the Catholic church had climbed back to the staffing levels of the late 1630s. The average conceals significant regional variations. A priest writing in 1668 of the 'mountainous and less cultivated' area of Achonry (**map 9**) complained that the 'labourers are few', but Oliver Plunkett could complain of Meath in 1673 that he had 'too many' priests.[84] Plunkett probably meant that too many priests were drawing from the same depleted well of lay patronage. For that reason the build-up of numbers would stall at a point where there was roughly one priest for every two parishes. The supply of priests was kept up by the practice of ordaining young men who could read Latin. Some of these men later went to one of the Irish seminaries abroad to be educated in philosophy and theology and, if they came back, comprised between one third and one quarter of all Catholic clergy.[85] Even if they were not all intellectual high-fliers, their intellectual and moral formation was, by Tridentine standards, more satisfactory than the rest. Continentally trained priests (**map 9**) were least common in Ulster and Connacht at the end of the century and so there was something of a contrast in priestly behaviour between regions more and less thoroughly exposed to Trent. Oliver Plunkett of Armagh was something of a martinet and his 1671 visitation uncovered two clerics in Raphoe who were in sexual relationships, two drunks and three more of weak learning from a total of fourteen priests.[86] Yet Plunkett found fault in Armagh with only one of his priests, tempted by women and drink, from a total of fifty-six. What emerges from reports of priestly behaviour and education and from other indices of Tridentine reform is the familiar binary of the wealthier south-east contrasted with the poorer north-west.

During Berkeley's short stay in office the political climate was sufficiently favourable to allow a general synod by a new cadre of Catholic bishops to be held in Dublin. They were a talented but quarrelsome group. The dispute between Peter Talbot, the new Archbishop of Dublin, and Archbishop Oliver Plunkett of Armagh over diocesan precedence reflected a personal feud between, on the one hand, Richard Talbot and, on the other, John Fitzpatrick, who was allied to the Ormond interest.[87] Richard Talbot, bearing a formal request from fifty-eight Irish Catholic gentlemen to represent their interests at Whitehall, now styled himself 'agent general of the Roman Catholics of Ireland'.[88] Against the advice of Berkeley and the Irish Privy Council, Charles heeded Talbot's pleas and set up yet another inquiry into the injustices of the land settlement.[89]

But the dominant court faction, the so-called 'Cabal', proved unstable, the Dutch fleet blocked any English descent and the French did not stump up the promised subsidies.[90] The free-spending monarch consequently had to call a parliament and the Commons promptly tore into his Declaration of Indulgence. Members were all the more sensitive to the religious question because they looked with foreboding to a Catholic succession and dynasty, with James, Duke of York, now openly professing Catholicism and married to a pious young Catholic princess.[91] Desperate for a supply bill, Charles withdrew the Declaration and reluctantly agreed, in early 1673, to a Test Act as a way of weeding out Catholics, including York, from public office. The successor to the Cabal, the ministry of Lord Treasurer Danby, opposed religious toleration and advocated a pro-Dutch foreign policy.

Government in Ireland was impossible unless a governor was 'thoroughly countenanced' at Whitehall, according to Arthur Capel, Earl of Essex, and he remembered the lesson well enough to last as governor from 1672 to 1677, even surviving the eclipse of his patron Arlington for a time.[92] Before taking office Essex received private directions to allow full liberty of conscience and he kept up Berkeley's discreet friendship with Plunkett, the Catholic primate. Matters changed with the disintegration of the Cabal. The House of Commons quickly moved to condemn Talbot in March 1673 as a 'chief promoter' of Popery and insisted that he be stripped of his captaincy (he was the sole Catholic in the standing army) and banished from court.[93] Charles yielded on this and parliament's other demands for persecution of Catholics and dissenters. Presbyterian meeting houses were closed and in October 1673 Essex ordered all Catholic clergy to leave Ireland by the end of the following December. The fact that the order was twice repeated (in 1674 and 1678) suggests it was ineffective.[94]

Essex was an unusually honest Lord Lieutenant and this 'exactness' was to prove his eventual undoing.[95] The smooth-talking Roger Jones, Viscount Ranelagh, had taken the farm of the whole Irish revenue and promised to pay off debts, meet current expenditure and pass money under the counter to Charles's privy purse.[96] Ranelagh was helped by buoyant revenues but pulled off the shady scheme only by neglecting the pay of the army. In disputing Ranelagh's falsified accounts, Essex inadvertently threatened to expose the complicity of those higher up. He had to go. Charles was expected to appoint his illegitimate son, the Earl of Monmouth, as Lord Lieutenant but York was reluctant to see his dashing nephew and potential rival for the succession awarded such an honour. Instead, he persuaded Charles to play safe and reappoint the ageing Ormond. This he did, on condition that Ormond passed Ranelagh's accounts. It was a timely and opportune appointment.

The Popish Plot

Hatred of Roman Catholicism was 'the strongest, most widespread and most persistent ideology in the life and thought of seventeenth-century Britain'.[97] The tiny Catholic community (and a fortiori Irish Catholics) conveniently fitted into conspiracy theories. It was commonly believed, for example, that papists set the Great Fire of London of 1666.[98] Consequently, James, Duke of York's publicly professed Roman Catholicism scandalised the enfranchised classes and the public at large. This was the context of the 'Popish Plot'.

In 1678 Titus Oates, a defrocked Church of England clergyman, claimed knowledge of a Jesuit plot to kill the King, replace him with York and pin the blame on Presbyterians.[99] Oates proved a slippery perjurer throughout the judicial circus that followed and his allegations brought Danby to the Tower and saw York packed off to Scotland, out of sight. Those who wanted him excluded from the succession coalesced into an agglomeration of groups and individuals soon to be known as the 'Whigs', whose anti-Popery papered over the many contradictions and divisions among them.[100] Public hysteria peaked in the summer of 1679 when fourteen Catholics (Oates's web of fabrications would ultimately claim thirty lives) were executed. The Whigs appealed to opinion out of doors through pamphlets, petitions and processions and consciously invoked the memory of the 1640s.[101] But a Popish plot without an Irish massacre was a pallid production to set before the English public. When the Whigs abused their opponents as 'Tories', they were repeating an accusation of complicity with Irish rebels that had been levelled so devastatingly against Charles I. The speed with which his son's supporters adopted the name shows how easily they could shrug off the accusation because no credible plot emerged in Ireland.

Early attempts at talking up an Irish dimension to the plot petered out. In October 1678 a London correspondent breathlessly informed Ormond that Oates's revelation 'seems impossible to be a fiction' and told of an Irish sideshow to 'bring in popery by the sword' in which Peter Talbot, now Archbishop of Dublin, and his brother Richard were the main actors.[102] Ormond seems to have been sceptical from the beginning: Talbot's supposed Lieutenant General was none other than the ninety-year-old Lord Mountgarret, one of his Butler kin. Orrery, now allied with Shaftesbury, the leader of the Whigs, tried to whip up fears of a French invasion of Munster.[103]

Ormond's response to Popish Plot murmurs was calm and steady.[104] He did the things one would expect of a Lord Lieutenant in a crisis: locked up the Talbots, closed Dublin mass houses and ordered bishops and regular clergy out of the country. Yet he trod warily lest he provoke a violent reaction that would be seized on as proof that Ireland was dangerously unsettled.[105] As the crisis in England intensified, Shaftesbury complained bitterly of what he claimed was Ormond's negligence in rooting out the plotters. By riding out such criticism, Ormond stopped the billiard ball, so to speak, from rolling again across three kingdoms as it had in 1641 and 1642.[106]

By March 1680 Shaftesbury and Essex had collected enough enemies of Archbishop Plunkett, mostly renegade priests and friars from Armagh diocese whom he had had occasion to discipline, to lay evidence of yet another Irish plot before the English Privy Council and thereby force an investigation into Ormond's supposedly lax handling of the Catholic threat.[107] The 'MacShams', as sceptics dubbed them, accused Plunkett of raising an Irish army to assist a French landing, this time at Carlingford in County Louth. The Lords voted in January 1681 to affirm their belief in the Irish plot, but this backing for Shaftesbury's scheme to exclude York from the succession came too late in the game. Still resisting an exclusion bill, Charles dissolved parliament later that month and called a new one to meet at Oxford.[108] The Tory reaction had begun. Yet Plunkett's prosecution had gained a momentum of its own. Nobody, not even Shaftesbury, had much interest in continuing it, but no one cared enough to stop the trial and execution of a man who was, even the contemporary Whig historian Bishop Burnet conceded, a 'wise and sober man'.[109]

Charles was able to ride the wave of support for church and crown that swept away the increasingly demoralised and desperate Whigs. Oates was committed to prison in May 1682, Shaftesbury was driven into exile later that year and Essex was imprisoned in the Tower in 1683 for purported complicity in the 'Rye House Plot', the Tory riposte to the Popish Plot.[110] Wholesale government restructuring of boroughs secured Tory control over many Whig strongholds, including London.

As for Ireland, by early summer of 1684 it seems Charles had already decided to replace Ormond with Henry Hyde, Earl of Clarendon, York's brother-in-law. It would be 'too hard', Charles apologised, to ask Ormond to preside over the 'many and almost general alterations' he had decided upon.[111] The alterations involved restructuring the army to dismiss Cromwellian officers and intrude deserving Catholics like Ormond's old enemy Richard Talbot. Charles evidently wanted to forestall a Protestant revolt in Ireland at his brother's succession. In the event James II succeeded peacefully.[112]

Conclusion

The New English or Old Protestants, together with more recent arrivals, managed to present the Cromwellian land settlement as an unassailably accomplished fact. Their parliament of 1661-66 wrote the enabling law and one of their own, Ormond, was governor for most of the reign. Charles quailed at any outright attack on that settlement, feeling no debt was owed to Irish Catholics collectively.

Yet the King, his brother, mother and others in his circle felt deeply indebted to a number of individual Catholic aristocrats. Consequently, the court of claims used 'innocence' to batter a dangerously wide breach in the legislative wall surrounding the land settlement. The outcome was that the Protestant position looked a lot less secure a decade after the Restoration. Demographically they were still a minority and the natural leaders of the majority still held significant estates across three provinces (the Earl of Antrim was the only really significant Catholic landowner in Ulster). Those Catholics who got their estates back were the natural leaders because they tended to identify with the interests of a disinherited and revanchist community.

Worse, the monarch preferred a French paymaster to parliamentary bills of supply and favoured religious toleration as a back door to help Catholics. When Charles indulged these preferences there was nothing the Protestants of Ireland could do to stop him. Since Irish revenue was generating a modest surplus from about 1670, Charles did not need to call any parliament in Ireland for a money supply bill after 1666. When he wanted to indulge in a pro-French and pro-Catholic policy he promptly dismissed Ormond. If this policy were to be blocked, the impetus would have to come from Britain, as happened after 1673 and the disintegration of the Cabal. Charles 'could see things if he would', observed Buckingham. His brother James was conscientious but less astute: he 'would see things if he could'.[113] He would press on where his brother had stopped and try again to impose religious toleration.

Endnotes

1 Kishlansky 1996, p. 190.

2 Barnard 1973, p. 35.

3 Barnard 1973, p. 57.

4 Mitchison 1983, p. 64.

5 Hutton 1989, pp. 15, 41.

6 Kenyon 1978, p. 161.

7 Hutton 1989, p. 38; Brady 2003, pp. 25–6, 38.

8 Gillespie 2006, p. 216.

9 Keeble 2002, p. 9.

10 Clarke 1999, pp. 3, 251–2.

11 Barnard 1995, pp. 231, 234–5.

12 Little 2004, p. 175.

13 Harris 2005, p. 89.

14 Keeble 2002, pp. 23–5.

15 Haukes 1661.

16 Barnard 1973, p. 35; Barnard 1995, p. 247.

17 Harris 2005, p. 88; Orrery 1662, pp. 17–18, 26–7; Barnard 1995, p. 232; Clarke 1999, pp. 4, 247, 299.

18 Barnard 2004, p. 31; Gillespie 2006, pp. 217–18.

19 Gillespie 2006, p. 219.

20 Harris 2005, p. 90; Hutton 1989, p. 149; Clarke 1999, pp. 302, 312–13, 316.

21 Later reprinted as *The Impartial History of Ireland*.

22 Jones 1978, pp. 135–6.

23 Little 2001b, pp. 941–61.

24 MacCurtain 1972, p. 165.

25 Brady 2003, p. 52; Boyle 1662, pp. 17–18, 26–7.

26 Carte 1736, ii, pp. 357–8.

27 Simms 1976, p. 424; Carte 1851, iv, pp. 66–7, 71.

28 Carte 1736, pp. 233, 235.

29 Arnold 1993, p. 47; Hutton 1989, p. 174.

30 Hutton 1989, p. 456.

31 O'Hart 1884, p. 427; Crist 1974, pp. 1–6.

32 Wilson 2003, p. 70.

33 Cited in Beckett 1990, p. 80; Hutton 1989, p. 173.

34 Arnold 1993, p. 41.

35 Harris 2005, p. 94.

36 McKenny 2005, pp. 134, 144–5, 147, 158.

37 Reilly 1742, pp. 36–53.

38 Burghclere 1912, p. 16; Arnold 1993, pp. 44, 72; Reilly 1742, pp. 44, 51.

39 Butler 1917, p. 188.

40 Simms 1969, p. 144; Arnold 1993, pp. 34, 45.

41 Hutton 1989, p. 200.

42 Harris 2005, p. 96; Lydon 1998, p. 201; Hanrahan 2003, pp. 37, 39, 40.

43 Ohlmeyer 1993, pp. 267–70.

44 *CSPI* 1905, p. 643.

45 Ohlmeyer 1993, p. 263.

46 Simms 1976, pp. 424–5.

47 Hutton 1989, pp. 209, 236.

48 Arnold 1993, p. 37.

49 Aylmer 2000, p. 90.

50 Anon 1688, p. 3; Lytton Sells 1962, p. 245; Petrie 1972, pp. 39–57.

51 Creighton 2004, p. 20.

52 Keeble 2002, pp. 96–7; *CSPI* 1905, pp. 531, 612, 641–3, 647, 663–4, 666–7; *CSPI* 1907, pp. 17–18, 80, 134, 674.

53 Bennet to Ormond, 6 August 1662 MS. Carte 221, fol(s). 5–6; Oldmixon 1716, p. 5.

54 Arnold 1993, p. 73.

55 Carte Ms 215, fol(s). 24–5; Carte Ms 48, fol(s). 179; Clarendon 1729, p. 687.

56 Hartmann 1951, pp. 48, 51, 76–7; Clarendon 1729, p. 693.

57 Berwick 1780, ii, pp. 103–4.

58 Lydon 1998, p. 201; Simms 1956, p. 196.

59 Carte Ms 128 ff. 388–9.

60 Simms 1969, p. 5.

61 'A Light to the Blind'. Attributed to Nicholas Plunkett c. 1715 in Gilbert 1892, p. 25.

62 Arnold 1993, pp. 76, 147; Ó Ciardha 2000, p. 180; Reilly 1742, p. 56; Anon *A Letter from an English Gentleman to a Member of Parliament, shewing the Hardships, Cruelties and severe Usage with which the Irish Nation has been treated,* in Taaffe 1810, p. 377; Stewart 2001, p. 91; McGuire 1989, p. 76; Beckett 1990, pp. 88–9.

63 McKenny 1995, p. 198.

64 Bindon 1846, pp. 101, 103–7; Ó Ciardha 2000, p. 181; Ohlmeyer 1993, p. 284.

65 Brady and Ohlmeyer 2005, pp. 14, 20; Smyth 2006, p. 299.

66 Hutton 1989, p. 177.

67 Barnard 2004b, p. 114; Carte 1736, pp. 223, 231, 239.

68 Reilly 1742, p. 72.

69 Walsh, 1674, pp. 8–9.

70 Briggs 1998, p. 156.

71 Miller 1973, p. 31.

72 Briggs 1998, p. 156; MacCurtain 1972, p. 170.

73 Miller 1973, p. 95; Fitzpatrick 1988, p. 229.

74 Burghclere 1912, ii, pp. 48–51; MacCurtain 1972, p. 169; Simms 1976, p. 429.

75 Creighton 2004, p. 36.

76 Ohlmeyer 2000, p. 26; Bindon 1846, p. 15; Creighton 2004, pp. 19–20, 37.

77 Airy 1890, pp. 137–8.

78 Keeble 2002, pp. 96–7; Carte 1851, iv, pp. 297–8, 303.

79 Aylmer 2000, p. 125; Burghclere 1912, ii, pp. 144, 146–7.

80 Simms 1976, p. 421; Aylmer 2000, p. 124; McGuire 1973, pp. 310–11; Beckett 1990, p. 96.

81 Smith 1998, p. 226.

82 Petrie 1972, p. 99.

83 Dickson 1987, p. 134; Simms 1976, pp. 421, 430–1.

84 Forristal 1998, p. 41.

85 Fenning 1974, p. 78; Moran 1874, p. 215.

86 Forrestal 1998, p. 183; MacLysaght 1979, p. 288.

87 Airy 1890, p. 76.

88 Simms 1976, p. 426.

89 Hutton 1989, p. 274.

90 Marshall 1999, pp. 41–3.

91 Spurr 2000, p. 45.

92 Airy 1890, p. 224; Hutton 1989, pp. 323–39.

93 Airy 1890, pp. 60, 61, 75.

94 Jennings 1937, p. 81.

95 Stackhouse 1906, p. 144.

96 Simms 1976, pp. 441–2; Hutton 1989, pp. 312, 323–42.

97 Jones 1987, p. 190.

98 Tindal 1751, ii, p. 643.

99 Kenyon 1972, p. 74; Kishlansky 1996, p. 253; Tindal 1751, ii, pp. 688, 710; Smith 1998, p. 251.

100 Miller 1973, p. 170.

101 Smith 1998, p. 256.

102 HMC 1906, pp. 221, 222.

103 Oldmixon 1716, p. 24; HMC 1906, p. 350; Simms 1976, p. 432; Samson 1680, pp. 5, 11–13, 22, 24; Harris 2005, pp. 381–4; *HLJ* 1680. vol. 13, 6 November 1680.

104 Barnard 2004b, p. 79; Carte 1851, i, p. 4.

105 Beckett 1990, p. 116.

106 Simms 1976, pp. 432–3; Harris 2005, p. 381.

107 Hutton 1989, pp. 392, 397.

108 Hutton 1989, pp. 395–7; Harris 2005, pp. 239–40; Smith 1998, p. 258.

109 Stackhouse 1906, p. 182.

110 Kenyon 1972, p. 281.

111 Beckett 1990, p. 133; Simms 1969, pp. 17–18.

112 Schama 2001, p. 207.

113 Keeble 2002, pp. 61–2.

CHAPTER 9

James II 1685–91

The 'glorious revolution'

James II believed that God had brought him to power in the face of so many obstacles for the great purpose of converting England. Time was short. He was in late middle age and had no legitimate Catholic heirs and so he set a breakneck pace of religious change. His consistent objective was to 'establish' Catholicism: that is, to secure legal toleration that would survive his death and the Protestant successors, namely his daughter Mary and her husband (and James's nephew) the Dutch *stadholder* William of Orange.[1] His means of achieving that objective changed over time.

James's natural supporters, the Tory-Anglicans, were motivated less by personal loyalty to the monarch than by acceptance of a symbiosis of crown and church. James alienated them by relentlessly promoting Catholicism, especially at a time when Louis XIV's persecution of the Huguenots increased popular fears of resurgent popery and persecution. James's Declaration of Indulgence of April 1687 was a desperate attempt to forge an alternative alliance with dissenters and Whigs: dismay that indulgence would extend to papists outweighed any dissenter gratitude for their own toleration.

James could have limped along, unpopular but unassailable, to his death. Even the birth of a Catholic heir (the future James III or 'Old Pretender' was born in June 1688) and the disagreeable prospect of a Catholic dynasty did not make his collapse inevitable. James's former Tory supporters feared anarchy and abhorred the idea of active resistance. Whig accusations that James was bent on creating a despotic monarchy were implausible and reflect an instinctive linking of popery and absolutism, but his regime was absolutist to the extent that its bedrock was an army of 20,000 regular soldiers.[2] No purely domestic revolt could succeed against them.

To understand why James II's regime collapsed in November 1688, then, it is necessary to privilege the wider European context. The War of the Grand Alliance (1689–97) subsumed two conflicts. One was yet another round of the century-old Bourbon–Habsburg contest, the other a Franco–Dutch war sparked by Louis XIV's expansionism in the Rhineland and his resumption of economic warfare against the Dutch in the autumn of 1687. James wanted to stand aside from this looming conflict, but English neutrality raised the spectre of a renewed Anglo–French alliance.[3] Consequently the States-General embarked on a 'risky and momentous enterprise' to force a man they saw as Louis XIV's English stooge to back the Grand Alliance.[4] Some of James's disillusioned Tory supporters went so far as to make common cause with the Whig opposition and invite William of Orange to lead an expedition to England, supposedly to secure a free parliament and investigate the legitimacy of James's heir. It was in reality an invitation to invade England.

After disembarking in November 1688, William of Orange waited in the West Country as his uncle's larger army disintegrated through pre-arranged defections. At this point James II suffered a psychological breakdown and retreated towards London. The trickle of defectors grew to a flood and included his daughter Anne. With William's connivance, James fled London on his second attempt in December 1688. By fleeing the country and his supporters, it could be claimed by a plausible constitutional fiction that he had abdicated.

William's motives for invading were essentially European: '. . . he took England on his way to France. About Ireland, he knew and cared still less.'[5] The latter island would not fall into William's lap. This was largely due to the energy and politic subtlety (or to his enemies, 'Falshood' and 'Flattery') of one man, Richard Talbot, the recently created Earl of Tyrconnel.[6]

Tyrconnel

Tyrconnel was 'more courtier than colonel', not just a regimental commander but *de facto* commander-in-chief of the army before Lord Lieutenant Clarendon arrived in early 1686.[7] Tyrconnel had seized on Argyll's Covenanter rising in May 1685 as an excuse to disband protestant militia companies in the north and purge the standing army. In the three months following his formal confirmation as lieutenant general of the army in Ireland in June 1686, Tyrconnel dismissed protestant soldiers *en masse* (Clarendon complained of 400 men being turned out of one regiment in a single busy day) until the rank and file were over two thirds Catholic.[8] *Caithréim Thaidhg* by the Munster poet Dáibhí Ó Bruadair captures the symbolic importance of the despised 'Mountainy Teague' [*Tadhg ón sliabh*] having the army, the ports and the towns [*Go bhfuil fórsa, port is bailte aige*]. Teague is the sentry challenging *Seón* or John the Englishman '*Cia súd?*' or 'Who's there?'[9] He packed the standing army with Catholics and disbanded the militia to give the king ready-made military support in the event of further internal dissension in Britain, on the lines of Argyll's and Monmouth's rebellions in Scotland and England.[10] In the event Irish regiments could not prop up James in late 1688 and over a third of the Irish regular infantrymen found themselves stranded in England, from where most were shipped off to the Emperor to fight the Turks.[11]

With the army purge in full swing Tyrconnel returned to court in August 1686, intent on displacing Clarendon. The fatal weakness of the Hyde brothers, Clarendon and Rochester (the latter was now James's chief minister), was that they refused to convert to secure their positions.[12] Tyrconnel adroitly sided with Sunderland, Rochester's deviously opportunistic rival, and got away with repeatedly and flagrantly undermining Clarendon. As well as relentlessly importuning him, Tyrconnel was able to dominate James face to face and to appeal to his Catholic scruples. Finally he replaced Clarendon in January 1687, though with the face-saving lesser title of Lord Deputy, 'to the astonishment of all sober men and to the evident ruin of the Protestants in that kingdom'.[13] Thomas Wharton's satirical *Lillibullero* which swept England during the Revolution and 'sung a King out of three kingdoms' takes this appointment as the crowning indignity:[14] 'Ho brother Teague,/Dost hear de decree?/Lilli burlero, bullen a la;/Dat we shall have a new debbitie/Lilli burlero, bullen a la;/Ho! By my shoul it is a Talbot;/And he will cut all the English throat.'[15] In his later political testament James advised that only a disinterested Englishman should be made viceroy of Ireland and this advice suggests that he regretted having appointed Tyrconnel.[16]

One can see why appalled Protestants could fear that James and his lord deputy in Ireland intended to 'utterly ruin the Protestant interest and English interest in Ireland'.[17] Tyrconnel accelerated the pace of Catholicisation of central government, army, judiciary, magistracy, commissions of the peace and parliamentary boroughs.[18] The Church of Ireland was not yet attacked. However, the re-consecration of chapels in Dublin Castle and at the Royal Hospital Kilmainham and the appointment of a Catholic archbishop as Chaplain-General of the Army can only be seen as precursors to eventual disestablishment.[19] The bedrock of the Protestant interest was, of course, the Cromwellian land settlement. 'His Majesty,' Clarendon had placated Protestants, 'hath no intention of altering the Acts of Settlement.'[20] Sunderland, too, was conscious of settler fears and proposed to offset the shock of Tyrconnel's appointment with a proclamation guaranteeing the land settlement unambiguously.

To counter this proposal Richard Nagle, Tyrconnel's attorney-general, penned the 'Coventry Letter' insisting that the only way to establish Catholics securely before a Protestant succession was 'to make Catholics there considerable in their fortunes as they are in their number'.[21] Tyrconnel's own hope was that James would divide disputed estates equally between Cromwellian grantees and displaced Irish owners and he browbeat James into accepting this compromise and repudiating his categorical assurance.[22]

For a time Tyrconnel may have wanted to go much further. According to Thomas Sheridan, secretary of state and first commissioner of the revenue, Tyrconnel wanted the Irish to 'set up a king of their own'.[23] James Fitzjames (later Duke of Berwick), a Catholic and one of James's illegitimate sons, was the likely choice. Tyrconnel, perhaps fearing that James was about to sack him, probably went so far as to seek secret assurances from Louis XIV in August 1687 that he could count on his support if he severed the Anglo–Irish connection.[24] James may even have known of this overture.[25] French envoy Bonrepaus was unequivocal. In the expected event that James died without a Catholic heir:

I know for absolute certain that the King of England intends to detach this kingdom [Ireland] from his successor and to fortify it so that all his Catholic subjects may have a safe asylum there. He wants to do so within five years.

An heir arrived, the Glorious Revolution followed in November 1688 and Tyrconnel shelved any 'go it alone' plans.

After James fled to France, Tyrconnel wavered 'between his hopes and his fears' and hinted that he would come to terms with William III on the basis that Catholics would be no worse off than at the end of Charles's reign.[26] The arrival of the capable Major-General Richard Hamilton, one of Ormond's Catholic nephews, encouraged Tyrconnel to hold out. After that, Tyrconnel spun out negotiations with William to gain time. Time until Louis XIV sent James II (apparently content to hunt, pray and wallow in self-pity) to head the resistance there.[27] 'I hope,' confided Louis, 'we

shall never see each other again.'[28] The apparently disinterested bene-
volence of his parting words to James II is misleading.[29] James saw Ireland
as a stepping-stone towards his other two kingdoms but Louis simply
wanted, confessed war minister Louvois, a 'diversion' or proxy war.[30] In
contrast, the English saw Ireland, in the words of the *philosophe*
Montesquieu, as 'urgent business'.[31] William might not share this concern
but, given his financial dependence on the English parliament, he knew he
must do what they wanted.[32]

A 'patriot parliament'

On 24 March, just a day after he arrived in Dublin, James issued a proclamation calling a parliament for 7 May.[33] Uneasily conscious of the linkage
his enemies made between popery and arbitrary government, he wanted
revenue to fight a war to be seen to be voted by a parliament.[34] Again with
an eye to a British audience, James was careful to present 'liberty of conscience' as the central theme of his opening speech to parliament. His
religious toleration was genuine: 'Our Blessed Saviour whipped people
out of the temple, but I never heard he commanded any should be
forced into it.'[35] The problem for James, of course, was that parliament
clamoured for redress of Catholic sectional grievances. Tyrconnel had
succeeded all too well in packing the House of Commons. Tyrconnel
called in borough charters and issued new ones in order to purge them
of disloyal members and secure the admission of a Catholic majority in
the corporation membership. He also appointed Catholic sheriffs who
would act as returning officers at elections. Newly admitted Catholics
now dominated most of the close and rotten boroughs which returned
most members of parliament.[36] The Counties of Donegal, Fermanagh and
Londonderry, and a number of boroughs, mostly in Ulster, did not return
any members and this left an overwhelming Catholic majority in a
depleted House of Commons, seventy short of its full quota.[37] As for the
Upper House, only a handful of Protestant peers took their seats. Even
before the war all but nineteen of the Protestant lay peers were absentees,
whereas all but two of the thirty-seven Catholics lived in Ireland.[38] The
only body of parliamentary opposition came from four spiritual peers who
were, at James's insistence, bishops of the Established Church.[39] Indeed,
the Act of Uniformity, which recognised the Protestant established church
alone, was left on the statute book and the Church of Ireland kept its
churches and glebes, though landowners would now pay tithes only to
their own clergy.

The members of parliament began by condemning James's treasonous subjects because they 'forced him to withdraw' and reiterated the classic theories of hereditary right and divinely ordained monarchy.[40] More controversial was the land settlement. The House of Commons and most of the Lords favoured complete restoration of confiscated land and voted down the compromise proposal that Tyrconnel favoured, whereby old proprietors would get back just half their estates. One of the Protestant bishops jeered that his fellow lords were squabbling about 'the skin before the beast had been slain' and sneered that they had justly forfeited their lands because of bloody rebellion.[41] The repeal of the Acts carried with it the rejection of the Protestant interpretation of the 1641 rebellion and, unsurprisingly, parliament repealed the act for the annual commemoration of the rebellion. In repealing the Acts of Settlement and Explanation there was no question of turning back the clock further to restore pre-1641 proprietors or their heirs, other than a special clause annulling James I's grant of County Londonderry to the London companies. This was done to create a land bank from which to compensate 'new interest' Jacobites who would necessarily lose lands they had bought since 1660.

The sweeping bill of attainder is best understood in the context of this complete reversal of the Cromwellian land settlement: only the confiscated estates of 2,000 attainted 'rebellious and traitorous' Williamites would supply enough land to restore the Irish landowners. The best that can be said for the attainder is that it was not avowedly sectional because the yardstick for confiscation was not religion but loyalty. The object of that loyalty wanted no attainder or repeal or anything, snapped one of his officers, 'that might dissatisfy his Protestant subjects in England'.[42] But it was made clear to James that if he did not consent, parliament would not vote him taxation. James climbed down: 'he is in their hands and must please them.'[43] The *State of the Protestants of Ireland under the late King James' government* (1692), written by William King, Bishop of Derry and later Archbishop of Dublin, would run through ten editions by 1768, putting it up with Temple's *Irish Rebellion* as a definitive text of Protestants in Ireland.[44] For King, repeal and attainder justified withdrawing allegiance to James:

The immediate end of Government is to protect Property; where therefore a Government, instead of preserving, entirely ruins the Property of the Subjects, that Government dissolves itself.[45]

Since the reign of Charles I, Irish constitutional lawyers such as Patrick Darcy objected both to claims of the English parliament to negotiate for

Ireland and to Poynings' Law. Such was James's obstinacy and the importance he attached to English public opinion that he successfully opposed
the repeal of Poynings' Law. Reluctantly, he had to accede to parliament
trumpeting a resounding declaration of independence from the English
parliament: 'Ireland is, and hath been always a distinct kingdom from that
of his majesty's realm of England.'[46] For a nineteenth-century nationalist
like Thomas Davis, this declaration set the seal on the Jacobite parliament
as a 'Patriot' body and the true precursor to the Anglo–Irish patriots,
Molyneaux, Grattan and Flood.[47]

Parliamentary rhetoric remained to be tested in battle and siege. Twelve
days after parliament was dissolved on 18 July, the Jacobite siege of Derry
was broken.[48]

The war of the kings

1689: Derry, Newtownbutler and Dundalk

Before James landed, the Irish had secured control over all Ireland except
for west Ulster and at first it seemed they would sweep up this enclave. On
15 April 1689 Richard Hamilton's cavalry plunged into the river Finn at
Clady (**map 7**) and scattered a large settler host which promptly streamed
back to Derry. Robert Lundy, governor of the maiden city, opened negotiations during which the Jacobite army was to be kept back from Derry.
Then James appeared in sight of the walls with part of the army. The
apparent breach of faith strengthened the resistance party. Lundy fled, his
name to become a byword for treachery among Ulster protestants.

Strictly speaking what followed around Derry was not a siege. 'Far
from being besieged,' groaned a French engineer on 3 June, 'it is not even
well blockaded.' The Irish, he said, had two unserviceable guns and one
mortar. There were just 3,000 troops, with another 4,000 raw and mostly
unarmed recruits on the way.[49] Hamilton built a camp and siege works in
the modern Bogside, thereby cutting off the town from Donegal, while a
boom covered by gun batteries blocked ships sailing upriver from Lough
Foyle. The blockade might have been more effective if Hamilton had not
indulged in quixotic chivalry by letting thousands of civilian 'useless
mouths' slip out of the city.[50]

At the outset the besieged had more troops and, it is argued, showed
'remarkable lack of initiative and enterprise' in letting themselves be
cramped into a narrow space about 500 yards long by 300 yards wide.[51]
The judgement is too harsh. The defenders, amateur soldiers most of them,

showed spirit at the beginning of the siege, sweeping the Irish out of their newly dug trenches on Windmill Hill to the south-west.[52] Slowly, their numbers were thinned out by disease and their spirit sapped by hopelessness and hunger: 'A certain fat Gentleman conceived himself in the greatest danger, and fancying several of the garrison looked on him with a greedy Eye, thought fit to hide himself for three days.'[53] The grim humour of Governor Walker's diary and his notorious price list of dogs and cats confirm that the defenders were half-starved. In the three weeks before the relief fleet tied up at the quays, the strength of the garrison fell by almost a fifth to 4,456 soldiers.[54] For their part the Irish launched just two serious attacks, both in June. A storm of Windmill Hill was beaten back and many officers, leading from the front, cut down. Towards the end of the month a regiment fresh from Munster tried to pack a cellar near Butcher's Gate with gunpowder and spring a mine. After desperate hand-to-hand fighting the Irish were driven off.[55] All the while the relief fleet under Major-General Percy Kirk stood off, daunted by the guns of Culmore Fort covering the boom. Not until a month later, on 28 July, did Kirk sail up the Foyle and burst through the flimsy boom past Jacobite gunners who shot wide. After 105 days Derry was relieved and the Irish retreated south.

Whether or not the siege was really 'the most memorable in the annals of the British Isles', it is the most remembered.[56] The siege legend has it all: defiance, solidarity, sacrifice and deliverance. It perfectly epitomises the state of unending siege which many Unionists saw, and see, as their bleak historical reality and evokes only one appropriate response: 'No Surrender.'[57] It is going too far to assert that William's ultimate survival 'was due in no small measure' to Derry holding out as long as it did.[58] John Mackenzie, writing a Presbyterian view of the siege in opposition to the Anglican churchman Walker, came nearest to grasping its real importance. If Derry had not been a 'sacrifice to the fury of the Irish', he claimed, James might have sent more than just 300 'very indifferent' Irish infantry to aid his supporters in Scotland. Such reinforcements would not have won him Scotland but they might, at the very least, have turned Scotland 'into a field of blood' and delayed William's attack on Ireland.[59]

The failure of the siege of Derry is partly to be explained by horsemen from Protestant-held Enniskillen, County Fermanagh, who threatened communications between Dublin and Derry: they 'scoured the country' far about and once raided as far as Kells, fifty-five miles distant and over halfway to the capital.[60] Converging attacks on Enniskillen led by Patrick Sarsfield, Berwick and Lieutenant-General Justin MacCarthy, Viscount Mountcashel, did not, after all, converge.[61] Realising this, Mountcashel began to pull back from Crom Castle on Upper Lough Erne but was forced to turn about and stand near Newtownbutler. A smaller army of 2,000 Enniskillen frontiersmen swarmed 'very smartly' towards him over a bog and up a steep hillside. The Irish infantry fired once and fled, fatally, westwards towards Lough Erne rather than south to safety and 'most of them were cut down or drowned in Boggs and Loughs'.[62] Following this disaster, Enniskillen forces overran County Sligo and lapped around the Shannon Line.

A week later, in early September 1689, the seventy-four-year-old Protestant refugee Schomberg, regarded as the 'ablest soldier of his age', disembarked at Bangor.[63] His multinational army of at least 14,000 men linked up with local irregulars and if he had marched straight on Dublin, rather than huddling in a fortified camp near Dundalk, he would have finished the war at one blow. A disheartened James wanted to flee the country and his troops were scattered and disorganised. Schomberg's later pleas that he was crippled by re-supply difficulties are unconvincing.[64] Of course he suffered from an incompetent and possibly corrupt commissary, not enough carts and draught horses, and supply ships delayed by contrary winds: this was the seventeenth century. A baffled French envoy d'Avaux wondered why he didn't push a little further south where his men and horses could have battened on the rich and (much to his disgust) still unburned harvest of the Pale.[65] While Schomberg waited for reinforcements to embark from Britain, James recovered his nerve and insisted on marching north in late September 'to looke the enemie in the face'.[66] He then retreated slowly, destroying the horse forage on his way and forcing Schomberg to disperse his cavalry. A month later William reluctantly accepted that nothing more would be done that winter and ordered Schomberg to disperse his army into winter quarters. This he did, but too late. Early modern armies had to move camp every few weeks in late summer and leave behind their privies, dirty straw and befouled drinking water.[67] Ultimately one half of Schomberg's men perished from a 'flux and feaver' that stalked the shanties and tents, packed hospital ships and squalid base hospital at Belfast.[68] This episode was more costly than any siege or battle of the War of the Kings except, perhaps, Derry and Aughrim.

1690: the Boyne and Limerick

'Unless I go to Ireland,' grumbled William III, 'nothing worthwhile will be done there.'[69] His personal drive ensured that a well-supplied Allied force of 36,000 men, the largest army to tread Irish soil, debouched from the

Moyry Pass in early July 1690. William could be 'confounded without striking a stroke', wrote Tyrconnel as he begged in vain for a French squadron to prowl the Irish Sea to cut off the invader's supplies.[70] Rather, French advisors favoured burning Dublin and pulling the main Franco–Irish army behind the Shannon. James's unwillingness to face William near Moyry, the 'Gap of the North' of Tyrone's time, left only the river Boyne as a possible defensive position north of Dublin. James, elated by one of his sudden mood swings, was all for fighting on the riverbank rather than 'lose all without a stroke'.[71] It was not a rational decision. The Williamites had a third more men and their foot soldiers were mostly equipped with the flintlock musket and socket bayonet, thus anticipating eighteenth-century warfare. In contrast, the Irish foot soldier trailed the obsolescent pike or, if he had a working musket at all, hefted the slower-firing and more cumbersome matchlock.

The smaller Franco–Irish army sat in a forward loop described by the river Boyne which invited the bigger army to peel off some men to cross upstream and cut behind, or 'envelop' them. The Allied army did just that and the Jacobites, in turn, split to meet them.[72] William did not close the pincers in time, in part because brave and dashing Jacobite horsemen swept down again and again on his troops at Oldbridge Ford and Donore Hill and bought time for the Franco–Irish army to come together again and squeeze across the Nanny River more or less intact. The body count was low: the Allies lost about 800 dead, the Jacobites less than twice that. Indeed, by contemporary standards the Boyne was hardly a battle at all but some half-dozen rearguard skirmishes.

Did the outcome of these skirmishes matter? Surely, whoever won or lost, 'in the long run' Britain's massive fiscal and logistical superiority would have ground down the Jacobites?[73] But there would have been no 'long run' for William if the cannon ball that grazed his shoulder had passed an inch or two closer to his head. William was far more than a figurehead to the Grand Alliance and his death, at this stage of the war, would have unravelled the loose coalition. Moreover, William's grip on Britain was 'highly precarious' until the Boyne 'decisively tilted the balance'.[74]

In a war of propaganda, perceptions mattered. James handed his enemies material for a myth of providential victory against the odds that could be trumpeted across Europe, drowning out the reality that the Allied war effort went badly elsewhere on land and sea.[75] More than just a propaganda boost, the Boyne represented an important source of legitimacy for those Irish Protestants who were still troubled with the implications of having disclaimed loyalty to James II. A clergyman defending the actions of the Enniskillen men claimed the allegiance of crown subjects in Ireland automatically switched from James when the English Convention declared William and Mary the new sovereigns.[76] Like the members of the English House of Commons, William King, albeit in different words, accused James of 'breaking the original contract'.[77] However, Whiggish constructs of social contracts and conditional loyalty did not ease the consciences of all Irish Protestants. Where English Tories could console themselves with the constitutional fiction of James's 'voluntary desertion' of the throne, no such rationalisation was possible in Ireland whence he was, evidently, driven by force of arms.[78] Consequently, the most popular and coherent justification by Protestants who neither fought James nor fled from him was providential. Bishop Wetenhall of Cork and Ross called on subjects to recognise that Providence had intervened at the Boyne.[79] God had spoken. James, personifying the losers, implicitly accepted this by fleeing Dublin the next morning and telling his followers to 'shift for themselves'.[80] The disintegration of the Franco–Irish army followed the moral collapse that percolated from the top.

William, however, believed his own propaganda and the euphoria of this normally frosty little man probably explains the uninviting peace terms he offered from his camp at Finglas a week after the battle. He excluded landowners from pardon and expected unconditional surrender and a mass forfeiture of Jacobite estates that he could then use to pay for the campaign and to reward his favourites.[81] This was a mistake because Tyrconnel 'sank prodigiously' after the Boyne and would have grasped at more attractive peace terms.[82] Three years of war would cost more than twice the value of all Catholic-owned property.[83]

The French expeditionary force marched to Galway to take ship but the Irish straggled to Limerick, key to the Shannon Line. During this coldest and wettest decade for centuries past and to come, large armies could not safely campaign outside about ten weeks of high summer. So, William needed to take the city and break the Shannon Line quickly. He could not push inland with his entire army in hot pursuit because he would then be marching away from his seaborne supplies and leaving his fleet exposed to the French, 'now masters of the sea'.[84] He had to first secure ports facing the Irish Sea and St George's Channel. It was unavoidable, then, that the Jacobite army should gain a forty-day breathing space after the Boyne.

When William did appear he no longer had the overwhelming numerical advantage needed to storm Limerick and was short of cannon shot and gunpowder, the last because Irish cavalry raiders swooped on the siege artillery train on 12 August at Ballyneety. Consequently his guns could not batter down a wide enough stretch of wall near the 'black battery' in the south-east corner of the city. Weather was a more pressing worry for the besiegers. One of the besieged, writing on 22 August (1 September in 'new style'), looked forward to 'heavy rain, high winds and long nights'.[85] But William's failure to take Limerick cannot be explained by too little powder and shot, too few men, or too much rain.

His assault on the afternoon of Wednesday 27 August was bungled. 'There were no orders given to enter the breach but the contrary,' claimed William's Principal Secretary of State for Ireland Robert Southwell.[86] Be that as it may, storm troops clambered over the rubble into a pound covered by a *retirade* or makeshift internal rampart wall where musketry and guns firing case and chain shot scythed through them. The Irish drove out the survivors and stood fast atop the breach, 'filling the gaps with willing soldiers as fast as they were shot down'.[87] It was like Clonmel a half-century before. The rest of the attackers, thousands of them, bunched up outside:[88]

From half an hour after Three, till after Seven, there was one continued fire of both great and small Shot without any intermission, insomuch that the Smoke that went from the Town reached in one continued Cloud to the top of a Mountain at least six Miles off.

The attackers were not pulled back quickly once it was clear that they could not hang on atop the rubble and they lost well over 2,000 in one day's work. Autumn rains were too close to allow another attack and within two days the Williamites decamped hastily.[89] It took John Churchill, Earl of Marlborough, to show how a siege should be executed. Just after Ballyneety, Marlborough got the go-ahead for a naval descent on Cork and Kinsale. A walled port on a marshy island, Cork was Ireland's second city and provided the shortest crossing from France.[90] In capturing both and bagging 5,000 Irish prisoners, Marlborough displayed that genius as an administrator and logistician that neither Schomberg nor William could match.

1691: Athlone, Aughrim and Limerick

The departure of William and Marlborough left a ponderous Dutchman, Godard de Ginkel, in charge. Ginkel clustered his men during the winter of 1690–91 in large 'frontier garrisons' forming a rather porous defensive line (**map 7**) while Jacobite partisans or 'raparees' ranged across the large no-man's land between the frontier and the Shannon.[91] Patrick Sarsfield, hero of Ballyneety and *de facto* leader of the army, tried to maintain an active defence during the winter but the land west of the river could not feed the army and a civilian population swollen with refugees. By April 1691 most of the soldiers had scattered to scavenge for food, leaving the Shannon crossings thinly guarded. Just in time, on 19 May, a convoy sailed into Limerick bringing a French commander, Saint Ruth, to take control of the Irish war effort, enough grain to feed an Irish army until the autumn, 'a small matter of money, and a great many fine promises'.[92]

Ginkel's lumbering columns almost reached the Shannon before Saint Ruth. What followed, recollected Major General Hugh Mackay, was 'one of the most perilous actions of the war'.[93] Ignoring Mackay's advice to feint at Athlone and cross elsewhere, Ginkel had his siege guns and mortars pound the 'narrow compass' of the western side of Athlone for ten days. 'With the balls and bombs flying so thick,' said a defender near the town's bridge, 'that spot was hell on earth.'[94] Yet the Irish clung to the bridge. On 28 June the Allies laid planks over a broken arch but volunteers unflinchingly ran into the firestorm to tip the beams into the water. Their courage deserved a better outcome. Two days later, Ginkel belatedly realised his soldiers could ford the river downstream of the bridge. In a surprise attack Ginkel's grenadiers waded across, stormed the banks and drove the Irish out over the ramparts facing towards Connacht. Saint Ruth had made an appalling blunder and left those ramparts standing: sheltering behind them the attackers could hold out against Irish counter-attacks.[95]

The loss of Athlone and the breaking of the Shannon Line brought the endgame. By this time 4,000 Jacobites had been outlawed and their estates, amounting to 1.7 million statute acres, declared forfeit.[96] William had been persuaded to let Jacobites keep their estates as the price of extricating himself from Ireland by the argument that one month of war cost more than all the forfeitures would be worth.[97] At this critical juncture Ginkel now published new and more attractive peace terms.

Ten miles west at Aughrim, Saint Ruth chose 'such a piece of ground as nature could not furnish him with better'.[98] This was a long ridge (*Each Dhroim* in Irish means 'horse's back') along which Saint Ruth's main battle lines stretched for about a mile and a half southwards from the hamlet of Aughrim. A stream and a bog formed a major obstacle to his front, while the passes at either extremity were guarded by Jacobite cavalry.[99] Here, Saint Ruth planned a do-or-die last stand to redeem his reputation after Athlone. Both Sarsfield and Tyrconnel, for once in agreement, thought this too risky and suggested splitting the army, holding Galway and Limerick in strength and sending Jacobite cavalry to raid deep into enemy-held territory.

In the battle that followed Huguenots and Danes pushed through a ford on the Tristaun stream river pass on the southern, and weaker, of Saint Ruth's flanks. Their attack was broken up in close-quarter fighting among hedgerows running down 'to the very edge of the bog'.[100] 'Never did the Irish fight so well in their own country as they did this day . . . ,' admitted an enemy soldier.[101] Ginkel then sent four English regiments against the middle of the Irish position where the bog was widest. After dragging themselves across 'up to their middles in mud and water' to the lower slopes of the ridge, they were overwhelmed. 'The day is ours, boys!' Saint Ruth is said to have cried.[102]

Meanwhile, by late evening, Williamite horsemen cavalry were trickling across a causeway leading to the left-hand or northern part of Saint Ruth's battle line and ignoring scattered musket fire from a tumble-down castle that stood near the mouth of the pass. Henry Luttrell's two dragoon regiments and Major General Dominic Sheldon's cavalry facing them should have charged the Williamite cavalry before they had a chance to consolidate on firm ground. As Saint Ruth rode over towards that causeway, a cannon ball shot off his head. Mysteriously, Luttrell's and Sheldon's horsemen melted away, exposing the northern flank of the Irish battle lines. Sheldon displayed a lamentable want of initiative and the one-time fire-eating Luttrell may have, literally, sold the pass. He was subsequently awarded a government pension and thrived until assassinated many years later: 'He'd sold his country to preserve his class, /the gutters hissed: but that was done/Twenty-six years ago, he said, /Had they not buried Aughrim's dead? /Standing under grey cut stone/A shadow cocked a gun.'[103] Once the horsemen fled, the battle, as a contest, was over. The thin and elongated battle lines of the day faced front and could not easily face left or right to meet a flank attack: horsemen facing the right way would always run down foot soldiers facing the wrong way. Many were caught in the little fields on the ridge, their corpses heaped by the ditches, while others were ridden down by the cavalry for miles around until darkness put an end to the butchery.[104] At least one fifth of the estimated 20,000-strong Irish army perished along with at least 1,200 Allies killed in the opening attacks.[105] It was the bloodiest day in Irish history.

Galway, which had held out for nineteen months against Charles Coote in 1652, now surrendered 'without a stroke' just over a week after Aughrim.[106] Had Ginkel been forced to wait for his artillery train and spend ten days knocking a breach in the ramparts, the capture of Galway would, likely, have been the last action of the campaigning season and the war would have dragged on into 1692. Relieved at the pliability of the townspeople he granted generous articles to the mercantile elite or 'tribes', Ffrenches, Lynchs and the rest.[107]

Next, a year to the day that William had abandoned his siege, Ginkel marched on Limerick.[108] Ginkel's mortars lobbed bombs into the city, laying it into 'a heap of rubbish', and his guns battered the ramparts of the Irishtown, the lower part of the hourglass-shaped city.[109] However, thick banks now lay behind the Irishtown's walls, a deep ditch and massive bastions protruded in front of them and, beyond, a covered way bristling with sharpened palings atop a fire-swept sloping *glacis*. Ginkel had to switch his attack and battered the Englishtown (the upper part of the hourglass) on its island, for five days.[110] After opening a wide breach Ginkel evidently considered bridging a river and sending his men across 300 yards of boggy ground to the breach. An Irish sortie overran his forward positions and dissuaded him from what was likely to have been a blood-soaked failure.

Next, on 22 September, Ginkel led most of his horsemen and somewhat less than half his infantry over a pontoon bridge into County Clare and around to the other side of Limerick. The Jacobite cavalry, true to form, recoiled.[111] After heavy fighting, the Allies began pushing the Irish back across Thomond Bridge. A French officer panicked and raised the drawbridge, leaving over 600 Irish to be trapped and killed, their corpses piling up higher than the parapets of the bridge. This discredited d'Usson, the French governor, and disheartened the Irish officers, from Sarsfield down. The city was completely cut off, Tyrconnel had just died and the French re-supply fleet had not yet appeared. Yet Ginkel was uneasily aware that it was very late in the campaigning season, he had fewer men than William had had the year before and they were dangerously overstretched on two sides of the river.[112] Even after the débâcle on Thomond Bridge he thought the Irish troops were 'very steady' and that an outright attack would be 'impracticable'.[113] That very evening the Jacobites beat the chamade.

The Treaty of Limerick

The first question the Irish asked was whether they could go 'wherever they had a mind'. This was the deal-breaker because Sarsfield wanted to land in France not as a lone refugee but at the head of a large body of recruits. Ultimately the Articles not only allowed the Irish to take ship for

France but even, in an act of almost unprecedented generosity, promised them ships in which to embark: so much for the military articles of the 'Treaty' of Limerick. The civil articles would be far more controversial.

'Treaties made, Promises given, and Capitulations sign'd . . . should be clear, sincere, and candid.'[114] Article one of the Treaty was anything but:

The Roman-Catholics of this Kingdom, shall enjoy such privileges in the exercise of their Religion, as are consistent with the Laws of Ireland; or as they did enjoy in the Reign of King Charles the II.

The words artfully gave the impression that, at worst, the Catholic religion would be connived at as it had been in Charles II's reign. But the laws of Ireland were not consistent with any 'privilege' towards Catholicism, while the modifier about Charles II's reign was meaningless in the absence of a specific year, given the up and downs of his reign. Article one was not 'warily drawn' and it was all the easier to wriggle out of it afterwards, as may have been the intention all along.[115]

Article two initially offered guarantees of property only to 'persons in the city of Limerick and in the Irish army that is in the counties of Clare, Kerry, Cork and Mayo . . .'. But the Jacobite negotiators insisted this article also embrace 'all such as are under their protection in the said counties'.[116] At this point the Articles of Limerick look less like a normal capitulation by a town or fortification, where articles referred to the garrison and townspeople only, than a wider agreement between sovereign powers; a 'treaty' in the modern sense of the word. The latter was a point the English were reluctant to concede and somehow this clause was left out from the transcribed copy sent to Dublin. The Articles as passed by the Irish Parliament in 1697 also omitted the clause.

Berwick accused the Irish negotiators of stupidity and selfishness for not insisting on property guarantees for all Irish Catholics, officers and civilians everywhere. But could the negotiators really 'have gotten much more'?[117] Ginkel might well have agreed to more extensive guarantees of property but the episode of the 'missing clause' of Article two suggests that a subsequent Irish Parliament would have repudiated such guarantees and William, however reluctantly, would have gone along with the parliament. Moreover, one could hardly expect the Irish negotiators to exert themselves on behalf of Catholic landowners who had taken protection under the terms of the Declaration of Finglas.[118] It is more puzzling that the negotiators should not have looked out for prisoners and the heirs of those who died fighting.[119] The net effect of wartime forfeitures was to cut the proportion of land owned by Catholics from 22 per cent in 1688 to

14 per cent by 1703.[120] The landowners who forfeited were overwhelmingly those caught by the Declaration of Finglas, those outlawed for foreign treason by following Sarsfield to France, like Piers Butler, Viscount Galmoy, or prisoners like Donough MacCarthy, Earl of Clancarthy.

Conclusion: what if?

Ginkel could not have stayed another week and the Allied squadron in the Shannon estuary was not big enough to block the French relief fleet which was on the seas. His quite generous promises in the Limerick capitulation reflect the projections of plausible futures by both negotiating teams. The failure to keep those promises reflects the factual future. French dominance of the high seas, confirmed by naval battles off Bantry Bay (1689) and Beachy Head (1690), was lost after the battles of Barfleur and La Hogue (1692) and subsequent famine and financial collapse forced them to choose land war over fleet action. Even if the Irish had hung on grimly for the winter of 1691–92, they would not have lasted another campaigning season without French provisions. Nor would tying down 20,000 Allied soldiers in Ireland for the summer of 1692 have made a difference to the main theatre of war in the Spanish Netherlands. In the event, most of Ginkel's troops spent that campaigning season waiting in England to embark for a descent on Brittany that never happened.[121] It was as well for the Irish that they capitulated when they did.

Endnotes

1 McGuire 1990, p. 46.

2 Miller 1973, pp. 148, 197.

3 Gibbs 1990, p. 17.

4 Israel 1996, pp. 82–3.

5 Miller 1990, p. 39.

6 King 1692, p. 112.

7 Dickson 1987, p. 23.

8 Miller 1977, p. 817.

9 Béaslaí n.d., p. 124; Mac Erelean 1917, pp. 129–33; Ó Ciardha 2002, pp. 79–80.

10 Miller 1990, p. 56.

11 Murtagh 1990, p. 33.

12 Hutton 1997, p. 84.

13 Bray 1907, p. 264; McGuire 1990, p. 48.

14 Macaulay 1858, iii, p. 170; Stackhouse 1906, p. 284.

15 Carpenter 1998, p. 37.

16 Clarke 1816, ii, pp. 636–7; McGuire 1990, p. 54.

17 McGuire 1990, p. 45.

18 McGuire 1990, pp. 46–8.

19 McGuire 1990, pp. 52–3.

20 Dickson 1987, p. 23; McGuire 1990, p. 50.

21 Gilbert 1892, p. 194; Simms 1976, p. 481.

22 McGuire 1990, p. 51; Anon 1763, ii, p. 142; Beckett 1969, p. 126.

23 Ó Ciardha 2002, pp. 59–60.

24 Miller 1977, p. 821; Pillorget 1995, p. 3.

25 Miller 1977, p. 821; Macaulay 1858, iii, p. 44.

26 Dalrymple 1773, p. 331; Simms 1969, p. 51.

27 Childs 1996, p. 198.

28 Simms 1969, p. 62.

29 Murtagh 1990b, p. 61; Lenihan 2003, pp. 64–5; Hogan 1934, pp. 638–9; Clarke 1816, pp. 351–2.

30 Rousset 1891, pp. 187–8, 542–3.

31 'l'affaire capitale': Berwick 1780, p. xx.

32 Japikse 1937, p. 158; Simms 1969, p. 135.

33 Hogan and Plunkett 1894, p. 5.

34 Gilbert 1892, p. 70; Harris 2006, p. 438.

35 McGuire 1990, p. 54.

36 Simms 1986, pp. 66–8.

37 Hayton 2004, p. 19; Harris 2006, p. 437.

38 Barnard 2004, p. 29.

39 Harris 2006, p. 438.

40 Harris 2006, p. 439.

41 Ó Ciardha 2002, p. 64; Rolleston n.d., pp. 45–6, 50, 64.

42 Hogan 1894, pp. 5–6; Simms 1986, p. 78.

43 MacCurtain 1972, p. 182; Harris 2006, p. 442.

44 Lydon 1998, p. 220.

45 King 1692, p. 109.

46 Davis 1893, p. 43; Simms 1974, p. 27.

47 Rolleston n.d., p. 35.

48 Bagwell 1916, p. 237.

49 Mulloy 1983, pp. 223–4; Gebler 2005, p. 208.

50 Simms 1969, p. 105; Gilbert 1892, p. 64.

51 Childs 1996, p. 199; Simms 1969, p. 96; Doherty 1998, p. 58.

52 Gebler 2005, p. 91.

53 Hempton 1861, p. 131; Fraser 2001, p. 12.

54 Doherty 1998, p. 69; Simms 1969, pp. 109–10.

55 Doherty 1998, p. 68.

56 Macaulay 1858, iii, p. 237; McBride 1997, pp. 10–11, 15.

57 Smyth 2001, p. 19.

58 Fraser 2001, pp. 379, 381, 385; Hempton 1861, p. 152.

59 Lenman 1984, pp. 47, 49.

60 Latimer 1896, p. 30.

61 Gibson 1989, p. 129.

62 Story 1691, p. 5.

63 Glozier 2005, p. 2; Fréderic Armand Vicomte de Schomberg or Friedrich
    Hermann graf von Schönberg or Frederick Duke (an English title) of
    Schomberg.

64 Ferguson 1990, pp. 67, 77–9.

65 Hogan J. 1934, pp. 465, 469.

66 Kazner 1789, pp. 307, 311, 314, 319.

67 Pringle 1764, p. 100.

68 Childs 1996, p. 195; Story 1691, pp. 38–9; Ferguson 1990, pp. 67, 77–9;
    Richard 1968, p. 228.

69 Miller 1990, pp. 32, 195.

70 Cited in Lenihan 2003, pp. 68–9; Kerrigan 2001, pp. 172–4; Mulloy 1990,
    p. 30.

71 Doherty 1998, p. 107; Clarke 1816, p. 393.

72 Berresford-Ellis 1976, pp. 68–9.

73 Kenny 1991, p. 179.

74 Israel 1995, p. 853.

75 Simms 1969, p. 144.

76 Harris 2006, p. 451.

77 Stackhouse 1906, p. 293.

78 Harris 2006, p. 451.

79 Connolly 2000, pp. 83–104; Hayton 2004, p. 145; Eccleshall 2001, p. 63.

80 Baxter 1966, p. 290; Harris 1747, p. 123; Bagwell 1916, p. 299; Harris 2006, p. 456.

81 Simms 1986, p. 186; Lenihan 2003, pp. 250–2.

82 Berwick 1780, i, pp. 69–71; Mulloy 1983, ii, p. 454; Ranke 1875, vi, pp. 124–5.

83 Dickson 1987, p. 40.

84 Story 1693, p. 31.

85 Murray 1912, p. 142; Irwin 1995, pp. 114–15; Chandler 1976, p. 308; Mulloy 1983, iii, pp. 136, 139.

86 Kemmy and Walsh 1990, pp. 154, 172; Murray 1912, pp. 177–8; Mulloy 1983, ii, p. 106.

87 Story 1691, p. 130; Gilbert 1892, p. 264.

88 Kemmy and Walsh 1990, pp. 120, 126, 154.

89 Gilbert 1892, p. 266.

90 Simms 1969, pp. 174–85; Doherty 1998, p. 142.

91 Story 1691, pp. 46–7.

92 Parker 1757, p. 28.

93 Murtagh and O'Dwyer 1991, p. 59.

94 Murray 1912, p. 208; Lenihan 2001b, pp. 146–7; Wauchope 1992, p. 212.

95 Haddick-Flynn 2003, p. 169; Murtagh and O'Dwyer 1991, p. 50.

96 Harris 2006, p. 501.

97 Simms 1986, p. 194.

98 Story 1691, p. 122.

99 Hayes-McCoy 1969, pp. 250–4.

100 Story 1691, p. 122.

101 Parker 1757, p. 36; Wauchope 1992, pp. 224–9.

102 Simms 1969, p. 224; Doherty 1998, p. 182.

103 Murphy 1968, pp. 57–8.

104 Story 1691, p. 137.

105 Doherty 1998, p. 181; Simms 1969, p. 219.

106 Hogan and Plunkett 1894, p. 96.

107 Simms 1951, p. 72.

108 Danaher and Simms 1962, pp. 126–8, 310; Mulloy 1983, ii, pp. 160, 206, 216, 259, 280, 535–3; iii, pp. 85–8; Burke 2001, p. 281.

109 HMC 1899, p. 279; Story 1691, pp. 220–1.

110 Burke 2001, p. 286.

111 Story 1691, pp. 207, 216, 225; Doherty 1998, pp. 190–2; Gilbert 1892, p. 296.

112 Mulloy 1983, ii, pp. 401–2, 410–11, 540–1.

113 HMC 1874, p. 323; Ginkel to Lords Justices 23 September 1691.

114 Turner 1683, pp. 342, 345; Anon 1692, p. 19; Claudianus 1718, p. 134.

115 Hogan and Plunkett 1894, p. 107; HMC 1899, pp. 280–1.

116 Simms 1956, p. 56.

117 Berwick 1779, p. 178; Gilbert 1892, p. 178; Simms 1969, p. 257.

118 Simms 1951, p. 48.

119 Simms 1956, pp. 19, 87; Simms 1969, p. 181.

120 Maguire 1990, p. 156.

121 Parker 1757, p. 38.

CHAPTER 10

Parliament, patronage and 'patriots' 1692–1727

Protestant, Catholic and Dissenter

The tripartite ethnicity of New English, Gael and Old English discussed earlier was no more. The latter two markers had been subsumed in an inclusive Irishness.[1] The 'New English' of the early decades of the century, or the 'Old Protestants' of the 1650s, had displayed cohesiveness and unity of purpose at critical junctures that overrode differences of theology or church organisation. Nearly a half century later this protestant community was bigger than ever and growing by the day. It probably comprised about a fifth of the population in the latter years of Charles II, rising to about 27 per cent by 1715.[2] A countrywide statistical survey commissioned by the Irish parliament showed (**map 9**) in 1732 that protestants dominated five Ulster counties and the capital.[3] Dublin was a city of protestants, with their numbers growing from about 51,000 in 1695 to about 75,000 in 1733 to outnumber Catholics by almost two to one.[4] Yet that community had sundered and a new tripartite religious (and arguably ethnic) division had emerged of (English) Protestant, (Irish) Catholic and (Scottish) non-conformist. This chapter largely concerns a Protestant minority within a protestant minority: members of the Church of Ireland.

Protestant power rested on wealth and office. Yet the creation of Catholic office holders and the repeal of the Acts of Settlement and Explanation under James II were shocking reminders that office and wealth conferred no security against a monarch who would attack 'the English Interest in Ireland' and 'alter the very Frame and Constitution of the Government . . .'.[5] Protestants in Ireland could not afford to scruple about swearing allegiance to William and Mary and disavowing their oath to James II. The muted debate on non-resistance in Ireland, in contrast to

England, reflects Protestants' longstanding response of pragmatic support for whatever power effectively controlled England and could protect them in Ireland:[6] 'No man,' reasoned Bishop Dopping of Meath, was 'bound to obey a power that either cannot or will not protect him in his life and fortune.'[7] For their part, it would no longer be feasible for English monarchs to play off one religious group in Ireland against another because of the exclusively Protestant character of the monarchy, confirmed by the English Act of Settlement of 1701.[8] English government must, necessarily, depend on a Protestant ruling class.

This *élite* went from wanting a Protestant ascendancy, in the original meaning of the term, to *being* the Protestant ascendancy.[9] One cannot restrict the term 'ascendancy' just to peers and members of the House of Commons and those (not many more than 100 persons) who exercised significant influence over the return of such members.[10] It certainly embraced the 5,000 or so landed families, or those of them that were Protestant, who formed the core of the small group monopolising power and wealth.[11] One should go even wider because such landowners were not cut off from below by impermeable class barriers. They might be of modest origins given the surprising degree of upward social mobility within Protestant Ireland and would certainly feel the pull of vertical ties from poor relations or clients.[12] Moreover, the many 'middlemen' across the countryside made for subtle gradations of landed wealth within the Protestant squirearchy. The origins of many middlemen lay in the decades just after the War of the Kings when many landlords granted long leases at low rents to attract Protestant head tenants who would guarantee cash rent payments and would covenant to improve the estate.[13] The typical middleman was Protestant, often a younger son or scion of a cadet branch of a gentry family, though Catholic or crypto-Catholic landowners were numerous in the dairying districts of Munster. A local study of seven County Wexford estates shows that the middlemen living among the tenantry carried out important social functions like keeping a watchful eye on Catholics and encouraging Protestants. Even a nominally resident big landlord could not hope to emulate such localised social control and leadership because the pull of politics, business and sociability drew him away.[14] Finally, it is difficult to draw a clear-cut distinction between landlords and middlemen because many landlords who held lands in fee also held lands on lease.[15]

One could widen the definition of 'ascendancy' even further to include poorer Protestants who benefited from systematic preference and the exclusion of Catholics: doormen in the office of the linen trustees, Dublin porters and hackney coach drivers who lobbied parliament claiming they 'could hardly get bread' because of pushy papist competitors, and tradesmen who enjoyed full, rather than quarter, membership of a guild with associated civic and political privileges.[16] In the countryside, all things being equal, the Catholic living 'in a miserable and sordid manner' would undercut the Protestant in competition for leases. But all things weren't equal.[17] Protestant landlords shared an almost universal belief that industriousness and Protestantism were naturally linked while many also strove to have enough Protestant families to raise a troop of horsemen at moments of crisis, or to provide jurymen and parish constables, or to be biddable 'forty shilling freeholder' voters at election time.[18] Consequently, they often displayed a systematic preference for Protestant tenants.[19] The Protestant tenant who got a longer lease at lower rent than the Catholic would get was, by that reckoning, a member of the ascendancy.

The members called themselves the 'Protestants of Ireland', the 'English of this kingdom', even the 'People of Ireland': any circumlocution except 'Irish'.[20] Jonathan Swift, for instance, did not regard birth in Ireland as making him an Irishman: 'I happened to be dropped here.'[21] Indeed, their members of parliament were reminded in a 1698 sermon that 'they lived in an Enemies country'.[22]

Papists and Presbyterians

The reminder implies that Ireland was somehow different to other European societies of the time. Historians often try to capture this difference by calling Ireland a 'colony'. This is unfortunate because 'colony' is a semantically slippery term.[23] When, for instance, Henry Cromwell mused that 'we are but a kind of colony' in the dying days of his governorship, he was apparently using the term in its original Latin sense to distinguish watchful and armed Englishmen set down in an alien and hostile environment.[24] Yet when contemporaries wanted to point up similarities between Ireland and North America, for instance, they tended to call Ireland a 'plantation'. For present purposes the term 'colony' or 'colonial' serves as an unsatisfactory but inescapable synonym for Europeans inflicting violence and expropriation on natives set apart by barriers of language and culture. In that sense:

A history of conquest followed by plantation and the expropriation of native proprietors gave Ireland some of the features of a colony. Yet geography and ethnography ensured that the indigenous population, at any social level, could not in the long term be treated as the native peoples of colonies usually were.[25]

Tudor commentators portrayed the Gaelic Irish as subhuman and barbarous, often drew explicit and unflattering parallels with American Indians and pagans, and sometimes acted as if these parallels were true. This changed from about 1615 to a predominant, if still hostile, English view of the Irish manning a northern outpost of Catholic Europe.[26] Ireland clearly lacked many of the eighteenth-century colonial stereotypes, including distance from the mother country, exotic produce, extreme temperatures and slavery.[27]

Catholic Irishmen like the Earl of Antrim or the Talbot brothers could enjoy privileged access at court. If they converted then Gaelic antecedents presented an inconsiderable barrier to social and political acceptance. Not many people thought it odd that a 'natural' Irishman like Murrough O'Brien led the parliamentary armies in Ireland during the 1640s or that another pure-bred Gael like Daniel O'Neill was a groom of the bedchamber to both Charles I and his successor and, consequently, an important power broker. Old English and Irish saw themselves as subjects of the crown rather than victims of colonisation.[28] The native Irish were different from, say, the colonised Native American, then, in that the line between coloniser and colonised was far more permeable and it was possible for an Irish person to, in effect, cease to be Irish by passing for a Protestant. Indeed, it will be argued that the central thrust of the penal laws was to force landed Irish Catholics to do just that.

The majority Irish population was ruled by a privileged class or group different in religion, ancestry and (albeit decreasingly) language.[29] A society in which power and wealth were monopolised by an *élite* was the contemporary norm. Less common was rule by a religious and racial minority. The analogy of the cosmopolitan Habsburg nobility imposed on the Protestant Bohemians from 1627 is incomplete because the Habsburgs wanted to Catholicise but not necessarily Germanise the Czechs.[30] Charles O'Hara, a County Sligo landlord of Gaelic descent, castigated the 'spirit of domination' of most of his fellow landlords who were 'the descendants of adventurers'.[31] The hostility of the Protestant ascendancy to the Irish was both religious and cultural. The usual complaints one expects about the lower classes by the comfortable and well fed had an edge of contempt when the masses were papist as well as poor.[32] It is this persistent antipathy and contempt that cannot be normalised and gives to Ireland the whiff of a colonial frontier.

The revived 23rd of October public holiday remained the most significant of several 'rites of exclusion' of a majority and fed morbid fears of massacre.[33] The tories and rapparees who ranged quite widely after the war had been killed, captured or scattered by the late 1690s.[34] After that Ireland was at peace.[35] Less irrational than the spectre of massacre were periodic invasion scares.[36] Between tentative descents on Scotland in 1708 and 1719 came a display of 'massive military strength' in 1715 that faltered only because Scottish Jacobites were so ineptly led.[37] All the while a large body of well-regarded Irish troops, the 'Irish brigade', fought for Louis XIV and was topped up by a steady trickle of 1,000–1,500 recruits a year. It would be naïve to discount the lure of pay and uniform, but there remained for recruits a tangible sense of commitment to the Stuart cause. Invading soldiers could have been disembarked in wintertime when it was almost impossible for the Royal Navy to intercept troopships from Brest.[38] We know with the benefit of hindsight that the Jacobite court in exile never seriously intended to do so, but nervous Protestants in Ireland were denied this comfort.[39]

To generalise, this was a 'colonial settler community' frustrated that William's ministers were so soft on the potential Catholic threat.[40] Yet the community was no monolith. Not all Protestants felt equally menaced by papists or responded in the same way.[41] Clergymen like William King, Archbishop of Dublin, and Edward Synge, Archbishop of Tuam, tended to prefer 'soft laws and strict execution'; in other words, enforcing existing laws against Catholics and not introducing new ones that might breach the Articles of Limerick and so impugn 'the King's Honour'.[42] It was no coincidence that clergymen, in particular, urged moderation against the papist threat; many of them were more preoccupied with a menace on another flank altogether.[43]

When a deputation of Ulster ministers reminded Charles soon after his restoration that he had signed the Solemn League and Covenant, he received them coldly. The Church of Ireland, as re-established in 1661, was no longer inclusive and accommodating to varieties of protestant practice and organisation and by enforcing tighter religious conformity it pushed dissenters and nonconformists out from what had been a theoretically comprehensive church.[44] Bishops ejected ministers who refused to publicly assent to all parts of the Book of Common Prayer – Taylor of Down and Connor evicted no fewer than thirty-six Scots from livings in a single heady day.[45] Some isolated prosecutions against ministers for officiating without a licence came before Anglican church courts.[46]

Yet Dublin Castle was sceptical that shutting meeting houses and breaking up congregations would achieve anything more ephemeral 'than scattering a flock of crows', to quote Ormond.[47] There was no Irish equivalent of the English act of 1673 whereby office holders had first to qualify themselves by taking communion in the established church.[48] From 1672 the government even undertook to pay the royal bounty or *regium donum* to technically illegal Presbyterian ministers in Ulster while their congregations did not suffer persecution nearly as acutely as their brethren in Scotland had during the 'Killing Times' of the Tory reaction.[49]

Tacitly, government policy towards dissenters and nonconformists was one of containment.[50] It worked with many dissenters, mainly Baptists and Independents, who were slowly absorbed by the established church.[51] They were loosely organised, many of their ministers did not see their differences as presaging a permanent break with the Church of Ireland, and they were also tainted by association with the republicanism of the interregnum. Nonconformists, especially Presbyterians in Ulster, proved more cohesive and resilient. The number of Presbyterian ministers and congregations mushroomed by half between 1689 and 1707 and jumped another 30 per cent between then and 1716.[52] In 1672 Presbyterians probably accounted for no more than one third of all protestants, but fifty years later they accounted for well over half.[53] The dominance of Presbyterians, often seen as clannish and surly by other protestants, was now overwhelming in east Ulster and increasing in west Ulster.[54] An estimated third of the entire population of Tyrone in 1712 were recent (and mostly Scottish) immigrants or their offspring.[55] Between 1663 and 1740 there was a fourfold jump in the number of people of settler (and mostly Scottish) extraction in north-west County Londonderry and an eightfold explosion in the southeast of the county.[56]

There was more to the Presbyterian threat than a sudden spurt of immigration. The Glorious Revolution had overthrown episcopacy in Scotland. As Presbyterians came to outnumber Protestants of the established church they also came to dominate a number of northern corporations and so return members of parliament from these boroughs. Moreover, the English parliament's repeal of the Elizabethan Oath of Supremacy in 1691 opened the door for Presbyterians to take office. The wartime mood of toleration and protestant union quickly dissipated.[57] For many clergy, like Jonathan Swift, distrust of dissenters was sharpened by personal experience; in his case the 'lonely futility' of his early ministry to some half dozen Anglican families in the overwhelmingly Presbyterian parish of Kilroot near Carrickfergus.[58]

In England, dissenters provided crucial support for the Whigs, especially in borough constituencies, thus prompting English Whigs to defend dissenter interests. In Ireland, the concentration of dissenters in the north made them more electorally marginal than English dissenters and nonconformists. Nearly all Protestants in Ireland were whiggish in their unambiguous support for the Glorious Revolution, but their whiggishness did not extend to agreement on the relative seriousness of the threat from popery, on the one hand, or from dissent, on the other.[59] English party labels were, as yet, irrelevant.

The nature of the relationship between Anglicans and, in particular, the papist bulk of the population is but one aspect of the question: was Ireland a colony? Another aspect concerns the nature of Ireland's political, constitutional and economic relationship, its subordination to England or, later, Britain.[60] In that respect by the last decade of the seventeenth century the Irish parliament was a more 'colonial' institution than the representative assemblies in English America: here settlers enjoyed greater de facto control over the internal government of their territories.[61]

Parliaments 1692–99

Parliament was virtually a Protestant monopoly. The Presbyterian presence in the Commons was always small: no more than a dozen in 1715, for instance.[62] Office and a seat in the Commons were shut even more tightly against Catholics by the requirement, imposed in 1691, to swear an oath abjuring transubstantiation and (that old sticking point of the remonstrance controversy) the Pope's temporal power.[63] A secure majority of Lords was Protestant and from 1716 Catholic peers were excluded from the House of Lords simply for being Catholics.

It was by no means certain that an Irish parliament would be called after the war. Only four parliaments had sat in the century if one discounts the Jacobite assembly, as Protestants did with a shudder: 1613–15, 1634–35, 1640–41 and 1661–66.[64] Westminster had effectively legislated for the country for some years past and there was a strong possibility that the English parliament would settle forfeited estates without reference to an Irish parliament.[65] In the end William felt he had to call an Irish parliament in October 1692 to have it ratify the Treaty of Limerick and vote additional revenues. The hereditary revenues voted by Charles II's parliament (customs, excise, rents and hearth tax) had slumped and could never meet the spiralling costs of waging a war against Louis XIV that would drag on until 1697.[66] Afterwards the burden of national debt bequeathed by the War of the Grand Alliance would force monarchs to call regular parliaments.

Williamite armies had delivered Protestants from disaster just a year ago, but Lord Lieutenant Sidney found their representatives in the Commons 'in a mind to be angry'.[67] Their main gripe was that the Treaty of Limerick was too open-handed in promising liberty of conscience and treating the Jacobite army so generously. Worse, with no windfall of forfeited Catholic estates, there were disappointingly fewer chances to snap up confiscated lands, the traditional spoils of victory.[68] Members regarded the lords justices who had signed this treaty as untrustworthy, Sir Charles Porter because they tarred him as a crypto-Jacobite and Thomas, Baron Coningsby, because they assumed (probably rightly) that he was a corrupt and self-serving trimmer.

In a thinly veiled attack on Coningsby and Porter, the Commons set up a committee to investigate claims that government officials 'encouraged the papists' and embezzled forfeited Jacobite estates.[69] Members also laid down what seemed a direct constitutional challenge.[70]

'Sole right'

On paper the subordinate position of this institution was codified in a medieval statute known as Poynings' Law, which was originally intended as a brake on an over-mighty viceroy. It prevented the summoning of a parliament in Ireland until the lord lieutenant and council in Ireland had informed the King and Privy Council in England why the parliament was necessary and what specific bills would be laid before it. Consequently, the Irish parliament could not initiate legislation but members could introduce 'heads of bills', in other words draft bills, without prior permission of the King or the English Privy Council. They were bills in fact, if not in form, differing from English bills only in the wording of their preamble. If approved in England, the heads of bills were returned to Ireland as bills and once more laid before the house to be either approved or rejected, but not amended. A memorandum of advice drawn up in 1690 spelled out the implications of Poynings' Law to William: to present a government bill to the Irish parliament 'was no more in effect than referring it to yourself'.[71]

Poynings' Law stipulated that some bills had to be ready before a parliament was called. In obstructive mood, MPs objected to the inclusion of a money bill on this list for the 1692 session and provocatively claimed the 'sole and undoubted right' to decide how much money to vote and the 'ways and means' such taxes should be taken up.[72] The clear implication was that Poynings' Law, so far as the Commons was concerned, did not apply in the case of revenue legislation. Members had no long-term scheme in mind, though some leading members of the opposition, notably Alan Brodrick, were aware that parliamentary control of the purse strings would force regular meetings of parliament.[73] With his money bills thrown out, Sidney brought the session to an early conclusion. Ostensibly the sole right challenge was the reason for prorogation, but it was a smoke screen. The pressing reason was the enquiry by the parliament's committee of grievances into allegations of corruption and mismanagement of forfeited estate revenues.[74]

'Capel's expedient'[75]

The first step on the road to a negotiated compromise was to dismiss Sidney, who had never enjoyed the monarch's confidence: 'he will do till I find a fit man,' William is reported to have said.[76] Sidney was duly recalled in July 1693. Henry, Baron Capel, one of the three lords justices who replaced him, was an altogether abler politician with impeccable Whig credentials. He was a younger brother of the Earl of Essex who was Lord Lieutenant in the 1670s, defected to Shaftesbury during the Exclusion crisis and later died a prisoner in the Tower. In the winter of 1694–95 Capel hammered out a deal with the leading members of the opposition so that a new parliament could be summoned to meet next summer. He would concede the sole right of the Commons to raise the bulk of revenue while saving face by initiating a token money bill.[77]

Parliament voted revenues for only two years in advance, thereby ensuring that, so long as spending outstripped hereditary revenue, the Irish parliament would have to meet regularly. The constitution that thus emerged 'as much by mistake as by intention' may be summarised as follows.[78]

Capel took two of the main opponents of the government into the castle administration, Alan Brodrick, head of a Munster-based network of influence, as solicitor general and Robert Rochfort as attorney general. One could see this as the first step towards the so-called 'undertaker' system. The 'ways and means' of raising taxation in Ireland were to be the preserve of the parliament to which the executive was to be accountable for income and expenditure. Parliaments could initiate legislation by heads of bills procedure and vote a money bill, normally to last two years, ensuring that Irish parliaments would meet regularly every other year. If it appears in retrospect that the 1695 session established the pattern whereby

Ireland would be governed for the next century, the permanence of the arrangement was not apparent at the time.[79]

Ratifying Limerick

Subsequent conflict between the followers of Porter and Capel, for and against ratifying the Treaty of Limerick, was a no-holds-barred contest in which there was a significant correlation between the respective partisans and later Tory and Whig groupings. Strongly anti-Porter groups dominated Munster, centred on the over-represented county of Cork, and Ulster: the latter grouping may have originated in the Williamite volunteer corps of 1688–89.[80] The House voted down an attempt to impeach Porter as 'generally in favour of the Catholics'.[81] Capel died in office in May 1696 and a few months later Porter died suddenly of apoplexy. Incipient party rivalry outlived them both.[82]

William had rejected a 1695 draft bill from the Irish Commons to banish all regular clergy (overwhelmingly Franciscans) after representations from his ally Emperor Leopold. However, Porter's death removed the most powerful opponent of anti-Catholic measures while, with the winding down of the Nine Years War, William could ignore Leopold's protests.[83]

The Treaty of Limerick was at last ratified in the 1697 session. Missing was the clause extending protection to Catholic civilians living in Jacobite quarters. Curiously, Irish landowners in Mayo and Clare (the counties potentially most affected) seem nonetheless to have enjoyed the protection of the missing clause. Under Porter and Coningsby, 491 claims under the Treaty had been heard up to the end of 1694, of which all but seven were adjudged to be within the Treaty.[84] When the hearing of petitions resumed in 1697–98 the outcome was hardly less favourable to Catholics, with only eight petitions rejected out of 791. The ratifying act also eroded the wartime indemnity clause and left out the article promising Catholics the same religious liberties that they had enjoyed under Charles II. Neither was Article 9 included, under which Irish Catholics would have to swear only a simple oath of allegiance.[85]

The need to appease the Protestant *élite* arose largely out of the fact that Ireland was, after the Treaty of Ryswick, the barracks of the peacetime army. William suspected that war with France would soon be renewed and did not want his army disbanded. However, the English parliament, pleading fear of a standing army, would supply only a tiny force of 7,000 men. Some 12,000 additional soldiers were, however, placed on the Irish establishment.[86]

With the Commons baying for tougher measures against Catholic clergymen, the price for confirmation of this watered-down version of the Treaty was a law banishing regular clergy and bishops. This was the first of the major penal laws. Parliament had already passed two relatively minor ones forbidding Catholics to seek education on the continent and disarming Catholics (except for Jacobite army officers at the time of the Treaty) and forbidding them to own a horse of cavalry charger quality. Banishment reflected long-standing Protestant phobia about bishops and 'strolling friars' who took their orders directly from Rome. Consequently, to banish bishops and regular clergy was seen not as an act of religious persecution but as a blow in self-defence against fifth-columnists working for a hostile system of 'government and polity'.[87] This perception was not altogether delusional when one considers the Dominican provincial Ambrose O'Connor snooping around Connacht in the summer of 1708 and writing to Mary of Modena about plans to raise an army and hold the Shannon Line.[88]

So popular were the anti-Catholic policies, and so secure the Irish administration, that in the summer of 1697 English ministers seem to have contemplated Anglo–Irish union. Irish MPs coming to London, so the 'junto' assumed, would reinforce the Whig interest at Westminster. Such complacency was premature and a serious Anglo–Irish crisis erupted the following winter with threats to the ruling *élite* in Ireland, not from papists but from parliament across the water.[89]

The Woollen Act

The first threat arose out of a legal dispute between the Bishop of Derry and the Irish Society of London over land and fishing rights. The Irish House of Lords decided in favour of the bishop, whereupon the Society, in a direct challenge to the final appellate jurisdiction of the Irish Lords, appealed to the English House of Lords. This flash point was subsumed within a second and wider controversy of constitutional and economic significance.

Mercantilism

Rather than try to pin down the multi-faceted theories, beliefs and prejudices that constituted 'mercantilism', one can deduce its core assumption as it applied to Ireland from an open letter penned in 1673 to the Lord Lieutenant by Sir William Temple, diplomat and essayist: If 'the Trade of

Ireland comes to interfere with any main branches of the Trade of England', claimed Temple, 'the encouragement of such Trade ought to be either declined or moderated'.[90] Temple was writing after the Cattle Acts of 1664 and 1667. Sectional lobbyists secured an act at Westminster banning livestock, beef, pork and bacon imports from Ireland as a 'public nuisance', a legal device used to stop the King from exercising his prerogative to circumvent the ban.[91] New outlets like the salt beef trade took up a little of the slack as it became apparent that it was more economic to work black slaves on the West Indies' plantations to produce sugar and nothing else. They could be fed on cheap imports of beef, salted to preserve it in the warm waters of the mid-Atlantic crossing. However, the Atlantic and continental trade was too slow-growing and too subject to the vagaries of war to absorb all the cattle on offer, so livestock exports fell by half between 1665 and 1683.

Nonetheless, overall exports jumped significantly as trade turned to butter, wool and, latterly, woollen goods.[92] South Munster sustained a lively export trade in West Country types of cloth using English immigrant workers and techniques at a time when the parent region was badly hit by the War of the Grand Alliance. Coins were set at relatively high values in Ireland (for instance, the guinea passed for 26 shillings) and this 'weak' currency, together with low wages and material costs, let Irish exporters undercut English cloth. Merchant clothiers in the West Country complained to the English parliament in 1697 and again in 1698 that Irish wool exports 'prejudiced' English exports in third country markets.[93] William III bowed to the English wool lobby and the Irish parliament responded to his wishes by slapping heavy duties on Irish exports of woollen goods, 'that the same may not be injurious to England'.[94] But the English Commons still pressed ahead with the Woollen Act of 1699. This sweeping restriction forbade the export of Irish woollen manufactures to any country other than England, where prohibitive duties were already imposed, and reasserted England's monopoly on Irish exports of raw wool.

The Irish linen industry did not compete with English commercial interests and in 1696 'brown' or unbleached Irish linen had been freed of all English import duties. This advantage and lower production costs at once gave linen from Ulster (where flax growing and many steps in the manufacturing process were concentrated) a distinct edge over German and Dutch cloth on the English market. The Irish parliament also nurtured linen, paying the Huguenot Louis Crommelin to establish a colony of skilled weavers in Lisburn in 1698 and setting up the Linen Board in 1710 to distribute grants, subsidies, export bounties and spinning wheels. But from the point of view of Protestant Ireland, encouraging Scottish immigrants at the expense of the Protestant towns in Counties Cork and Waterford and, indeed, Dublin was but a poor exchange for a thriving woollen industry.[95]

Polemicists, economists and historians from Swift to Froude presented the Act as the clearest example of mercantilist restrictions stunting the English colony in Ireland: '. . . fuller of greediness than good policy' fulminated Swift nearly thirty years later.[96] The Act may not have been as economically damaging as all that. English woollen manufacturers did not corner supplies of Irish raw wool, always in more demand than coarser Spanish and French wool: imports from Ireland plummeted tenfold between 1703 and 1729.[97] While official figures suggest a sharp fall in exports of woollen goods to third countries, they do not capture goods smuggled abroad.[98] The Woollen Act was only one of several shocks alongside coinage revaluation and the later outbreak of the war of the Spanish Succession which plunged the Irish economy into long-term stagnation, broken only by the export boom of 1713–15. Whatever its economic effects, the Act was of enormous political and symbolic importance.

Molyneux and patriotism

At the time the proposed Woollen Act and the Irish Society appeal to the English House of Lords evoked a ringing assertion of Anglo–Irish 'patriotism'. As the title of his polemic suggests, William Molyneux's *Case of Ireland being bound by Acts of Parliament in England stated* of 1698 denied the right of the English parliament to legislate for Ireland. Grounding his argument in historical and legal precedents, Molyneux claimed Ireland was a separate kingdom, subordinate to the crown but not subordinate to the English parliament. Ireland emphatically was not a colony.[99]

Does it not manifestly appear by the constitution of Ireland, that it is a complete kingdom within itself? Do not the kings of England bear the style of Ireland amongst the rest of their kingdoms? Is this agreeable to the nature of a colony? Do they use the title of kings of Virginia, New-England, or Maryland?

Hence an English parliament ought not claim the right to make laws binding 'the great Body of the Present People of Ireland' who as 'the progeny of the English and Britons' (clearly Molyneux was speaking of his fellow

Protestants) enjoyed the rights of Englishmen and crown subjects.[100] In addition to citing precedents, Molyneux anticipates later Patriot thinking in the way he draws on the natural right ideas of Locke's *Two Treatises on Government* (1690) and the Whiggish argument that laws enacted by the English parliament were illegal because this 'people' of Ireland had no representation in the body that enacted them.[101] Molyneux was no dogmatic separatist and his arguments were equally capable of being used to justify complete union with the English parliament. The libertarian discourse in the *Case* represented an enduring legacy to later 'Patriots' but in the shorter term Molyneux outraged English political opinion. In the Irish Society appeal to the English House of Lords the peers not only assumed final appellate jurisdiction but denied the Irish Lords any role in appeals from the court of chancery.[102]

Other snubs followed. In 1700 the English parliament set a body of trustees to recover and resell, without compensation, all confiscated property assigned by William, most controversially the enormous grants to his Dutch favourites Bentinck and Keppel and to his mistress Elizabeth Villiers.[103] Irish Protestants resented the trustees for a number of reasons. The trustees personified the power of the English parliament exerted successfully and insultingly against the monarch and against the Irish parliament; they even set themselves up in Chichester House, the parliament's meeting place, to hear the claims of ex-proprietors and new purchasers. William Conolly, a Donegal lawyer already famed for his mushrooming fortune, was the largest buyer of forfeited estates and he rallied other MPs against the trustees.[104] These supporters included an incandescent Alan Brodrick, who railed against the 'vipers' admitting the claims of many former Catholic proprietors or their heirs pleading an interest in forfeited lands on the basis of leases or family settlements. Indeed, 12 per cent of the land held by Catholics in 1703 had been secured on the basis of such claims.[105]

Tory ascendancy 1702–14

The government had dissolved the 1698–99 session of parliament because it was dissatisfied at the renewal of debate on the English parliament's right to legislate for Ireland. Naively, as it seemed in retrospect, parliament had voted generous duties and other revenues that were not due to finally expire until the end of 1703. Consequently a parliament was not called until then, leaving the longest gap without a session of parliament between 1692 and 1800.[106]

Brodrick's followers, now in opposition, advocated more frugal and shorter-term money bills. Still smarting from the forfeitures resumption and other grievances, the Irish parliamentary session of 1703–04 was almost of one voice in petitioning for either Anglo–Irish union or 'full enjoyment of our constitution', free from what members saw as misguided or mischievous intervention by the English parliament subverting Protestant liberties and damaging the economy. Westminster was not interested in union, yet somehow had to forge anew a working relationship with the Irish parliament.[107]

The opening of party fissures helped. King William died in 1702 after his horse stumbled on a molehill (Jacobites toasted the mole, the 'velvet gentleman' for many years afterwards). His successor Queen Anne (1702–14) favoured the Tories. Consequently, between them, James Butler, 2nd Duke of Ormond, grandson of the first Duke, and Sir Constantine Phipps as Lord Justice dominated Ireland for most of her reign with only one short Whig intermission in 1709–10.[108] There were plenty of individuals driven by nothing more than 'opportunism, ambition or pique' but most members, then and for the next decade, were identifiably Tory or Whig.[109]

Why had party come to Ireland? Ormond was a strongly partisan Tory and his appointment probably guaranteed that Irish politics would polarise around him. Moreover, the forfeitures trustees had been Tory appointees and so opponents like Brodrick and Conolly bound themselves more closely to the Whig Junto at Westminster. Finally, Church of Ireland bishops and representatives of lower clergy met in 'convocation' for the first time in almost half a century during the 1703–04 session and the extreme anti-Presbyterian rhetoric of some speakers also heated the partisan atmosphere.[110]

The 1704 'Act to Prevent the Further Growth of Popery' was the cornerstone of the penal edifice. The lengthy and convoluted passage of a bill with 'no single guiding hand, no one purpose' illuminates the complex interrelationship of Whitehall, Westminster, Dublin Castle and Chichester House.[111]

Before parliament met, Ormond and the Irish council prepared a draft popery bill to prevent Catholics from buying or taking long leases on land, inheriting land from protestants or disinheriting protestants. The draft was inspired by a recent Westminster law and the many claims submitted to the forfeiture trustees.[112] It was intended as a popular measure that would reassure the Irish parliament that Tories were not soft on Catholics and so grease the wheels of a sorely needed money bill. The council draft also proposed to banish Catholics from Limerick and Galway.[113]

London preferred just to prevent Catholics from buying land and delayed a bill considered too draconian. Brodrick's impatient 'Cork Squadron' managed to have a new heads of bill passed which again included a clause preventing Catholics from inheriting from Protestants and further stipulated that Catholic land inheritance should be subject to 'gavelkind' or partible inheritance. The Commons attached great importance to the heads of bill and the entire house carried the text to the Lord Lieutenant. A cowed Irish Privy Council sent the heads of bill to London in December 1703 without further amendment. The Catholic Lords Antrim and Fitzwilliam of Merrion condemned the heads of bill as contrary to 'the plain intent and meaning' of the Treaty of Limerick and specifically Article 3 which conceded that beneficiaries 'shall hold, possess, and enjoy all and every their estates of Free-hold and Inheritance'.[114]

Presbyterians and the test

When the bill came back across the Irish Sea it included the stronger anti-Catholic clauses and, unexpectedly, a sacramental test that demanded Dissenters take communion according to the rite of the Church of Ireland or face exclusion from public office. Stronger laws against Catholics were a sweetener for passing the test while those churchmen most likely to oppose them on conscientious grounds were most likely to be gratified by a clamp-down on Presbyterians.[115] It was a master stroke that gave the bill a fairly easy passage through both houses. Presbyterians remained subject to bad-tempered sniping during Queen Anne's reign; the *regium donum* was stopped and marriages carried out under the forms of the Church of Scotland were not recognised, so legal problems of legitimacy and inheritance ensued. Repeated attempts to repeal the Test failed, even when backed by Westminster, but from 1719 a Toleration Act and a series of short-term Indemnity Acts alleviated restrictions on Presbyterians.[116] By then the spectre of Presbyterian expansion was dissipating.

Gratifyingly, most peers and gentry in the Presbyterian heartlands, Massareenes, Donegalls or Mongomerys, quietly conformed to the established church; when County Antrim landowners worth more than £100 per annum were enumerated in 1720, sixty-one were found to be members of the Church of Ireland as against only eighteen dissenters.[117] Ulster Presbyterian emigration to north America began in 1718 from Londonderry, the frontier of settlement.[118] Much of the early exodus was led by ministers and its tone was set by the minister of Aghadowney parish (about ten miles south of Coleraine), whose farewell sermon thundered that his flock was driven into exile by 'oppression and cruel bondage'.[119] Emigration was more likely driven by the fact that the generous leases granted to attract settlers began to expire and, as they did, many landlords doubled or tripled rents. After a brief lull, Ulster emigration picked up again, with 4,000 departures in 1728 alone following a run of poor harvests and a depression in the linen trade.[120] From 1724, Philadelphia and the other Delaware ports received the bulk of what would be called the 'Scotch–Irish'. In all, some 200,000 Presbyterians emigrated from Ulster before 1776. This amounted to about three fifths of all emigrants from Ireland to North America and was a massive drain from a community that numbered only two or three times that during the whole period.[121]

The 'Act to prevent the further growth of popery': purpose and effect

The Banishment Act of 1697 had been quite effective and by July of the following year between 700 and 1,100 regular clergy and bishops had fled the country.[122] Of the thirteen bishops, five were already in exile, five more exiled themselves in accordance with the Act and only three stayed in Ireland illegally.[123] After a further crackdown in 1708, none was left. By then the Franciscans had begun to reorganise. They held only one chapter in Ireland between the years 1690 and 1702 but thereafter they resumed regularly, if discreetly.[124] However, it was a decade later before large numbers of Franciscans began to slip back to Ireland.

The Popery Act of 1704 allowed one registered parish priest to remain in each parish, a *de facto* conferral of legal status. All of 1,089 'parish priests' (some of them regulars in disguise) did register.[125] Unregistered clergymen were *ipso facto* illegal and as the present generation of priests died off, as an estimated two thirds of them did by 1724, it could be expected that they would not be replaced.[126] Catholicism would wither on the vine.

Where some historians doubt many of the lawmakers seriously intended this outcome, others insist such laws were 'enacted in sincerity and enforced with conviction'.[127] Since cutting off the supply of replacement priests would slowly strangle the Catholic Church, a want of intent might be inferred from the failure to apprehend and severely punish unregistered priests.

However, apprehending and punishing were not as simple in practice as it might appear, especially after the authorities imposed an oath of abjuration in open court on registered clergy in 1709. Only thirty-three took the oath, leaving all the rest illegal. Such a sweeping extension of the category of unregistered clergy undermined the principle of registration and created legal confusion.[128] Was a non-juring priest *ipso facto* illegal, or was he so when he said mass, or was he so when he said mass outside the parish for which he was registered? In 1723 Bishop Nicolson of Derry thought the law 'makes it death' for a non-juring priest to say mass, while a 1718 account of the trial of a non-juring priest convicted of saying mass in 1718 assumed that he would have been left alone if he had confined his ministry to his own parish.[129]

Though the Irish parliament passed the laws, it had no power to enforce them.[130] The executive in Dublin Castle controlled the officials, mayors of towns, sheriffs, magistrates, justices of the peace and constables. If a magistrate happened to be zealous he could not always count on armed men to back him because in time of war and threatened invasion the army was not dispersed in small detachments across the country.[131] Intercepting a priest coming from abroad depended largely on the vigilance and honesty of port officials, assuming he was not smuggled with illegal cargoes of brandy, wine, tobacco or tea into some western creek. These officials were part-time, unpaid and busy. The unsavoury alternative was the private priest-hunter. The short career of the most notorious of them, Edward Tyrrell, was terminated by his execution for bigamy in 1713.[132] Another, the ex-priest Garzia, trapped Edmund Byrne, Archbishop of Dublin, in June 1718 during the Spanish invasion scare.[133] When Byrne was finally put on trial a year and a half later, Garzia did not appear as prosecutor (probably acting on instructions from Dublin Castle) and the trial collapsed.[134]

The Irish Privy Council grumbled in 1719 that the penalty of deportation for unregistered clergy was too light, yet there is no evidence that the authorities executed any transported priest who returned, as they were legally empowered to do.[135] The only priest to be killed was a Dominican in Fahan, County Donegal, killed by a raiding party of soldiers in 1711.[136] The Irish House of Commons forwarded a heads of bill in 1719 proposing, among other measures, to brand the letter 'P' on the cheeks of all priests before they were deported so that they would be recognisable if they came back. The Irish privy councillors fretted about passive resistance by Catholic laymen displaying the brand in order to 'destroy the distinction it was intended' and, in a splenetic outburst, substituted castration.[137] Happily, the English privy councillors binned this grotesque proposal.[138]

If the early eighteenth-century Catholic Church in Ireland was still 'thinly manned' by comparison with the Catholic mainland, this was a result of poverty rather than penal laws.[139] A 1743 report to Rome claimed that a priest needed at least two parishes to maintain a reasonable standard of living because of the poverty of his parishioners who were also squeezed by clergy of the established church for tithes. The supply of priests was kept up by the practice of ordaining young men who could read Latin. Some of these men later went to the continent to be educated in philosophy and theology.[140] The jerky growth in the number of parish priests in Elphin (**map 9**) was probably fairly typical of most dioceses in the poorer north-western half of Ireland: 1625, 13; 1637, 42; 1668, 38; 1704, 56; 1731, 66. The ceiling on the number of priests in Elphin, admitted the bishop ruefully in 1753, arose because 'parochial clergy have no tithe income and must rely on their parishioners' goodwill'.[141] Yet he had enough. He bitterly regretted losing a trickle of wealthier Catholics 'seduced by greed' but consoled himself that he was winning many more converts than he was losing 'perverts' (to use the robust language of the time). If what was happening in Elphin was at all representative, then the Protestant Archbishop Boulter had reason to fret in 1731 that 'we are daily losing many of our meaner people, who go off to popery'.[142] The Elphin figures exclude the 'scattered friars' in the diocese, perhaps up to forty in 1731. The sharp decline in the numbers in regular orders, if not in their quality, post-dates the period under study.[143] Decrees drawn up by Propaganda (the Congregation whose task it was to organise all the missionary activity of the Church) in 1743 and 1751 settled the long-contentious issues between friars and bishops decisively in favour of the latter. Bishops were granted exceptionally wide powers over them in the matter of appointments and transfers, the pastoral powers of the regulars were limited and they were forbidden from receiving novices in Ireland. Consequently, the number of friars fell into a long-term and irreversible decline.[144]

Much more effective than the attack on the clergy was the Popery Act's attack on Catholic landowners. Before 1704 Catholic landowners enjoyed much the same rights of land ownership as Protestants, though wardship provisions could discriminate against them.[145] But the 1704 Act clamped additional severe restrictions on Catholic landowners. Section 3 tempted an eldest son to conform by promising reversion of the estate in fee. The section withstood legal challenge in *Blake v Blake* (1724) when Sir Walter Blake of Menlo, County Galway, was so incensed at his son's change of religion and marriage to a Protestant that he mounted two lengthy hearings in chancery and an unsuccessful appeal to the House of Lords. Section 6 stipulated that a papist could not buy or otherwise acquire land, other than by inheritance, or take out a lease longer than thirty-one years.

Section 7 stipulated that any Catholic who took property by devise, descent, gift, remainder or trust from a Protestant had six months in which to conform to the established church and, failing that, the interest was to be transferred to the nearest protestant relative. Section 10, the gavelling clause, insisted on fragmenting estates in equal shares among all sons, or daughters if there were no sons. The underlying idea was to fragment and dissipate the Catholic landed interest.

An 'explaining and amending' Act of 1709 conferred *locus standi* on any protestant 'discoverer' whatsoever to sue in respect of property transactions forbidden to Catholics. An unusually low rent in a lease to a Catholic, for example, might suggest that the purported Protestant landlord was a decoy holding the land in some form of collusive trust. If the discoverer proved his case, he would get the property in question for himself.[146] Parliament believed the discovery clause 'would animate our popery laws'. So it did. In the decade after 1709 the number of converts jumped to 150 from a mere 36 between 1704 and 1709.[147] In other respects, too, the land provisions of the 1704 Act were rigorously enforced and the courts went to some lengths to bind them ever tighter. The *cause célèbre* of *Tomlinson v. Farrell* (1758–61) shows just how rigidly the courts interpreted the requirements of legal conformity. In *Low v Espinasse* (1762) the courts made it easier for the discoverer by holding that 'parol' or spoken evidence of a collusive trust would suffice.[148]

This Penal Law, in particular, chipped away at the surviving Catholic *élite*. In 1681 the Irish peerage comprised 38 Catholics and 79 Protestants. A half century later, in 1749, only 8 Catholic peers survived to 106 Protestant peers.[149] A disproportionate number of converts, 1,700 of the approximately 4,000 Catholic men who conformed between 1703 and 1789, were members of gentry families, so it is safe to infer that the great majority who conformed did so for political or economic reasons.[150]

'There never was nor is any design that all should be Protestants,' Archbishop William King concluded gloomily.[151] There is little doubt that the members of the Irish parliament were not aiming at 'wholesale conversion' in passing the 1704 Act, but there is no mistaking their urgent desire to force the conformity of the remaining Catholic *élite*.[152] In doing so they were not naïve. They knew or suspected that converts almost invariably remained sympathetic to their former co-religionists.[153] Robert French of Monivea, County Galway, is the only example that springs to mind of a second-generation convert who was zealously Protestant, marrying a bishop's daughter, founding a Protestant colony and building a charter school on his estate.[154] Only in the nineteenth century did convert and Protestant families blend into a common interest.[155] But the fall in the Catholic proportion of land ownership from 14 per cent in 1702 to 5 per cent by 1776 was more than a 'statistical trap'. The old regime derived status and legitimacy from the possession of property over time. The landowning convert, however sympathetic he remained to his erstwhile co-religionists, was co-opted to the Protestant ascendancy and thereby helped legitimise it.

George I (1714–27)

Before William's death the English parliament had ensured a Protestant succession by settling it on a cousin of James II which left her son, George of Hanover, as the nearest Protestant heir (otherwise he would have been 52nd in line) on the death of Queen Anne. James III ignored feelers from Tory leaders in March 1714 promising to support his return if he changed or dissembled his religion. Consequently, a Hanoverian succession was inevitable. Less inevitable was the long-term eclipse of the Tory party. The discrediting of Robert Harley, Earl of Oxford, the previous winter cost the Tories a leader who could have led them successfully after the accession of George I. Oxford was discredited, in part, because his conciliatory posture towards moderate Whigs backfired spectacularly and lost him control of the Irish Commons.[156] Moreover, the later flight of Ormond to the Stuart court in exile hit Irish Toryism especially hard.

How was the Lord Lieutenant to secure votes when he could no longer appeal to abstract principle and party loyalty? 'Court' supporters on the one hand and 'country' or Patriot men on the other were, most of the time, loose and shifting associations of hard-nosed men 'bound together in pursuit of power, place and profit'.[157] There were relatively few lords and since the government could create peers and nominate bishops, the upper house was usually easier to control. Moreover, the Lords spent much of their time on comparatively trivial matters. In holding the purse strings the Commons, in contrast, enjoyed the substance of power. Controlling the Irish parliament meant managing the Commons. In all, 300 members were returned for 150 double-member constituencies. Of these MPs, 182 sat for boroughs. Some of these were quite insignificant places: plantation settlements that had never taken off like Jamestown, County Leitrim, or decayed medieval villages like Bannow, County Wexford, that now lay under windswept sand dunes. Most boroughs were under the thumb of a single landowner whose 'friends' and dependent tenants controlled the membership of the borough. Even in an unusually heated election like that of 1713, half of these borough seats were uncontested.[158] The faces in the house changed only slowly through death and by-elections, with only one general election during the thirteen-year reign of George I.

In this arena the Lord Lieutenant had to get as much money as he could voted in taxes while giving away the fewest possible *douceurs* to borough proprietors. That was government in a nutshell. But he could not attend meetings of the house himself and he was always, except for Ormond, a stranger to Ireland and an absentee for much of his viceroyalty.

Undertakers and parliamentary management

Even before the collapse of party discipline, governors needed 'undertakers' of one kind or another to manage the House of Commons.[159] Now they needed a new kind of undertaker. William Conolly first entered parliament for the town of Donegal in 1692 and first rose to prominence as an opponent of the forfeiture trustees. Afterwards he was able to reacquire disputed lands on fairly easy terms. He ostentatiously displayed his 'very great fortune' with Castletown House, County Kildare.[160] Built between 1719 and 1722, one characteristic of this 'large heavy building' can be traced to Conolly: its size.[161] Castletown was somewhat similar in design to Carton, the home of Henry Ingoldsby, a one-time leading Tory and son-in-law of the combative Tory Lord Chancellor Sir Constantine Phipps: both comprised a central block linked by curving colonnades to flanking pavilions. Where Carton's main block had just nine bays, Castletown had thirteen.[162]

Conolly's pre-eminence as a parliamentary manager arose from holding three offices that had never before been united in one man. From 1715 he was Speaker of the House of Commons, a post that gave him control of the order of business in the House. He also held the prestigious post of lord justice on nine occasions in the absence of the Lord Lieutenant. Finally, he was 'first' commissioner of the revenue, a post his enemies alleged he bought in 1709 for £3,000 from the Whig Lord Lieutenant Wharton. He was dismissed as commissioner by the Tories but regained the commissionership in 1714. By then the revenue had over 1,000 salaried agents, making it an important source of patronage, especially with the wholesale dismissal of Tory placemen after Queen Anne's death, and one entirely outside the jurisdiction of a Lord Lieutenant.[163]

The Speaker had to contend with a rival Munster-based network of clients led by Alan Brodrick, now Viscount Midleton. Patronage was now the 'single most important factor influencing the behaviour of Irish politicians' and the rivals strove to display their 'credit' with whatever

Whig ministry was in power and their consequent capacity to deliver rewards for their followers.[164] The display of credit was especially important in the power-broker's own bailiwick. For example, in 1720 Midleton, though temporarily out of favour, was greatly relieved that his suit on behalf of a relative for the deanery of Cork was successful. The post was a small plum but it would have been an 'indignity' to have his views ignored 'in a country where our estate and friends are'.[165]

However, in displaying his credit Conolly could never admit to being an 'undertaker' – for Brodrick to accuse Conolly in 1719 of undertaking to deliver a repeal of the sacramental test was a calculated smear. A member of parliament prided himself on his independence and would have been insulted if someone publicly dared 'undertake' for his vote in the house. 'Honour' would not permit a gentleman to openly admit such dependence. This was not always self-righteous posturing. Principle could sometimes force a gentleman to act against his patron and his self-interest. 'I have put honour and integrity in one scale and find it vastly to outweigh convenience,' announced Midleton when he voted in 1719 against the government's Peerage Bill. His vote brought a permanent breach with Lord Lieutenant Bolton and the revival of Conolly's political stock.[166]

For all the attractions of patronage, a member who pretended to 'honour' could not always ignore the occasional upsurge of patriot sentiment among the wider Protestant community.

Patriotism and the Declaratory Act

Five years after the Irish Society judgment the Irish Lords took the opportunity to reaffirm their position as the final arbiter of cases adjudicated in Irish courts. Conflict was postponed rather than resolved until 1717 when a widow, Hester Sherlock, appealed from the Court of Exchequer to the Irish House of Lords in a case of forfeited lands. Her opponent, Maurice Annesley, appealed to the English House of Lords.[167] The latter dignitaries ruled that the Irish House of Lords could not act as an appeal court. The Irish Lords were furious with this ruling and during the parliamentary session of 1719 William King drafted an address to George I. This 'Humble Representation' resurrected the version of the Anglo–Irish relationship outlined by Molyneux twenty years earlier. John Toland put it succinctly: 'There is a vast difference between Ireland's being annext to the crown of Great Britain, and being subject to the Lords of Great Britain.'[168] But there wasn't. The assertion ignored the diminution in the power of monarchy at the expense of the English parliament and executive over the preceding three decades. The British Lords responded to what they saw as provocation by passing the Declaratory Act asserting the constitutional reality that a monarch acting

. . . by and with the advice of the lords spiritual and temporal, and commons of Great Britain in parliament assembled, had, hath, and of right ought to have full power and authority to make laws of sufficient force and validity to bind the kingdom and people of Ireland.

Chief Minister Lord Sunderland considered using the power theoretically available by the Dependency Law to override the Irish parliament and have Westminster pass laws to tax Ireland. However, the soon-to-be Prime Minister Robert Walpole rejected the idea, thinking that the Duke of Grafton as Lord Lieutenant could manage the Irish Commons.[169] Walpole would be proved wrong.

Patriotism and Wood's halfpence

'Wood's halfpence' drove home the reality of what might otherwise be an abstract subordination and managed to offend most of the sensibilities of Protestant 'patriots' in Ireland. First was the incompetence and lack of consultation. The Irish economy was short of silver coinage, yet the English government proposed to supply copper halfpennies and farthings. Next came the taint of corruption in the way the first Lord of the Treasury obtained a patent to mint coins for King George's cast-off mistress, the Duchess of Kendal. She sold her licence in 1722 to William Wood, an iron monger.[170] A flood of inflammatory pamphlets during the winter of 1722–23 warned that so many base metal coins would drain Ireland of gold and silver, but such economic arguments (mostly specious) usually covered resentment at the real grievance of political subordination.

The four best-selling *Drapier's Letters* written by Dean Swift in the guise of a Dublin shopkeeper were exceptional in their polemical power and down-to-earth writing (2,000 copies of the first letter were dispersed across the country in a month). Swift, a propagandist for the Tory ministry that collapsed at the Hanoverian succession, had been rewarded in the eleventh hour with what he considered a less than glittering prize: the deanery of St Patrick's Cathedral in Dublin. He had already developed the libertarian ideas advanced by Locke and his *Proposal for the Universal Use of Irish Manufacture* (1720) and in his fourth *Drapier's Letter* he baldly challenged any law that purported 'to bind men without their own consent'. Though he based this claim on shared Englishness, the axiom was universal and capable of being used to support a radical claim for self-determination: 'You are and ought to be as free a people as your brethren in England.'[171] He scoffed at the notion of Ireland as a colony or a 'dependent' kingdom. 'I am so far depending upon the people of England,' he blustered, that he would fight them if they should 'fix the Pretender on the throne of England.'[172]

The mobilisation of Protestant public opinion in Ireland and the limits of parliamentary control came as an unpleasant surprise to the English ministry. Against his better judgement Conolly undertook in 1723 to secure a majority for the Duke of Grafton, the floundering Lord Lieutenant derided by Secretary of State Newcastle as 'the child'. Conolly failed and Grafton reluctantly wrote to Prime Minister Robert Walpole advising that the coinage scheme be dropped. Instead Grafton was dropped.

The new Lord Lieutenant John Carteret, Earl of Granville, was one of the few examples of an able politician who actually took up his post.[173] He tried to press ahead promising to cap the quantity of the new coinage. No less an eminence than Sir Isaac Newton, Master of the Mint, delivered a report confirming the metallurgical content of the coins. But all three lords justices, Conolly, Brodrick and Henry Boyle (Boyle was a Brodrick protégé and the undertaker who would dominate parliament for twenty years after Conolly's death), rejected Newton's report and refused to endorse the coinage.[174] Carteret resided constantly in Ireland from October 1724 to April 1726, fruitlessly trying to cajole the opposition and open up a split between the opponents. In the end Prime Minister Walpole had to back down and in 1725 Wood's patent was rescinded. Midleton, as the man most responsible for forcing Wood's patent to be rescinded, knew he could not 'retain his majesty's favour' and his resignation was welcomed in London.

The moral that Walpole and others drew from the experience was that it had been a mistake for Grafton to let himself be 'Irishly governed' and only English-born men could be trusted in high office.[175] With Midleton's faction in full-throated opposition, Carteret nonetheless kept Conolly at arm's length and tried to act 'as one capable of doing all himself'. But, faced with the threat of the Commons voting down a money bill, he belatedly turned to Conolly to re-establish the ministry's control. The lesson of Wood's halfpence was that a lord lieutenant could govern only through an 'undertaker'.

All would-be undertakers died not long afterwards. Leaders of the opposition Brodrick (or Midleton as he now was) and his son St John Brodrick passed away in 1728, while Conolly followed them to the grave the following year.[176] It would take four years for a successor to emerge, namely Henry Boyle, a one-time follower of the Brodricks. He was a grandson of Orrery and scion of the junior Castlemartyr branch of the Boyle family and controlled a large parliamentary following through his management of the estates of the absentee Earl of Cork and Burlington.

The political weight of the Boyle interest was a constant of the long seventeenth century, from the Great Earl through Orrery to Henry Boyle.

Conclusion

The Williamite settlement tied together English government and a Protestant ascendancy as never before.[177] Most members of the ruling class accepted the Glorious Revolution wholeheartedly, were bent on erasing the Catholic landed interest and regarded dissenters with suspicion. They were a 'Protestant settlement' rather than an Irish nation, to use the words of Henry Grattan in 1782, who were colonials in the sense that they saw themselves as 'settlers' from a mother land surrounded by a sullenly hostile population.[178] Their 'patriotism' was less a coherent body of thought than a wish to be endowed with the same 'natural' rights, to use the fashionable language of John Locke, as their English fellow subjects. They aspired to full union with England as the constitutional status that would best serve their interests but accepted with misgivings a vague constitutional status as a sort of dependent kingdom over which the parliament of England asserted the right to pass binding laws. Such political subordination did not, of itself, make Ireland a colony any more than other territories under the dominion of foreign rulers: Finland under Sweden, Norway under Denmark.[179]

King William's wars transformed the Irish parliament, like its English equivalent, 'from an event into an institution' – an institution of Protestant ascendancy.[180] Members of the lower house learned to exercise tighter control of the purse strings of government and to use heads of bill procedure to, in effect, make laws. While parliament sat they did not have to submit to treaties, laws or governors that fundamentally offended their interests, ideals or prejudices. That was the lesson of the 1704 Popery Act and the Wood's halfpence controversy.

At the end of the 1731–32 session members of parliament occupied the as yet unfinished neo-classical Irish parliament building. The big questions had been answered. For the next twenty-three years Boyle would guide the members uneventfully through the hazy borderland between practical independence and theoretical subordination.

Endnotes

1   Harris 2006, p. 141.

2   Morrill 1996, p. 387; Connolly 1995, pp. 145, 159–61; Greaves 1997, p. 9.

3   Connolly 1995, p. 146.

4   Fagan 1998, p. 44.

5   Cited in Harris 2006, p. 459.

6   Connolly 2000, pp. 83–104; Hayton 2004, p. 145; Eccleshall 2001, p. 63.

7   Harris 2006, p. 454.

8   Hayton 2004, pp. 33–4.

9   Connolly 1995, p. 194.

10   Malcolmson 1978, p. xix. For the later eighteenth century it is calculated that 109 individuals were involved in returning 215 M.P.s; Johnston 1974, p. 59.

11   Connolly 1992, p. 110; Connolly 1996, pp. 15–33.

12   Connolly 1995, pp. 61–4.

13   Whelan 1998, pp. 118–19.

14   Gahan 1990, pp. 107–8; Cullen 1981a, p. 104.

15   Cullen 1981a, p. 99.

16   Gillespie 1995b, p. 33; Barnard 2003, p. 144; Dickson 1987, pp. 136–7; Scott 1925, p. 263; Barnard 2004, p. 49.

17   Whelan 1998, p. 140.

18   Whelan 1998, pp. 119, 141; McNally 1997, p. 20.

19   Dickson 2005, pp. 176–7, 186.

20   Noonan 1998, p. 166; Connolly 1995, p. 119.

21   Foster 1988, p. 178.

22   Eccleshall 2001, pp. 74–5; Ó Ciardha 2002, pp. 102–3.

23   O'Hearn 2005, p. 5.

24   Ramsey 1933, p. 239.

25   Connolly 1992, pp. 113, 115.

26   Clarke 1997, pp. 142–4.

27   Bartlett 2004, p. 61.

28   Ohlmeyer 2004, p. 26.

29   Leighton 1994, p. 33.

30 Petráň and Petráňová 1998, pp. 149–50; Evans 1979, pp. 70, 118, 123; Sturdy 2002, pp. 42–3.

31 Charles O'Hara 'Description of County Sligo' MS20.397.

32 McNally 1997, p. 20.

33 Barnard 1991, p. 914; McNally 1997, p. 26.

34 Connolly 1995, pp. 203–9.

35 Cullen 1981a, pp. 199, 246; Garnham 1999, pp. 337–9.

36 Colley 1992, p. 23.

37 Pittock 1998, pp. 33, 41.

38 Petrie 1953, pp. 142–3; O'Callaghan 1869, pp. 216, 226, 246, 321, 325, 327.

39 Ó Ciardha 2002, pp. 106, 119, 129.

40 Morrill 1996, p. 388.

41 Doyle 1989, p. 49.

42 McNally 2004, pp. 55, 58; Troost 1983, p. 181; Canny 1988, p. 120.

43 Doyle 1989, p. 34.

44 Lockyer 1985, pp. 400–1; Gillespie 1995b, pp. 11–12.

45 Simms 1976, p. 434; Morrill 1996, p. 387.

46 Greaves 1997, p. 198; Airy 1890, pp. 124–5.

47 Gillespie 1994, p. 15.

48 Connolly 1995, p. 162.

49 Simms 1976, p. 437.

50 Gillespie 1995, p. 12.

51 Greaves 1997, p. 27.

52 Harris 2006, pp. 507–8; Connolly 1995, p. 167.

53 Simms 1976, p. 437; Connolly 1995, pp. 159–62.

54 Connolly 1995, p. 167.

55 Macafee 2000, p. 436.

56 Currie 1997, pp. 327–8.

57 O'Regan 2000, p. 56.

58 Glendenning 1999, p. 50.

59 O'Regan 2000, p. 175; Hayton 2004, pp. 36, 39–40.

60 Connolly 1995, p. 110.

61 McGuire 1979, p. 2.

62 McNally 1997, p. 54.

63 Dickson 1987, p. 40.

64 McGuire 1979, p. 1.

65 O'Regan 2000, p. 63.

66 McGrath 2000, pp. 64–5, 78; McNally 1997, p. 37; McGuire 1979, p. 5.

67 McGrath 2000, p. 80.

68 Hayton 2004, p. 42.

69 McGrath 2000, pp. 87, 89; Hayton 2004, p. 49; Troost 1983, p. 85.

70 Hayton 2004, p. 49.

71 McGuire 1979, p. 5.

72 McGrath 2000, p. 85.

73 McGrath 2000, p. 90.

74 Troost 1983, pp. 64, 68–9, 153, 156; McGuire 1979, p. 20.

75 McGrath 2000, p. 149.

76 McGuire 1979, p. 10.

77 Connolly 1995, pp. 75–6.

78 McGrath 2000, pp. 22–3.

79 McNally 1997, p. 40; McGrath 2000, pp. 116–17.

80 Dickson 1987, p. 43; Hayton 2004, pp. 36, 64.

81 Dickson 1987, p. 43.

82 Hayton 2004, pp. 94–5, 121, 154; Connolly 1992, p. 83.

83 Burke 1914, p. 134.

84 Simms 1956, pp. 45–51; Dickson 1987, p. 44.

85 Troost 1983, p. 164; Connolly 1990, pp. 161–2.

86 McGrath 2000, p. 135.

87 Rafferty 1994, p. 74.

88 Fenning 1990, pp. 52–3.

89 Hayton 2004, p. 66.

90 Temple 1680, p. 111.

91 Cullen 1972, pp. 4, 17.

92 Cullen 1976, pp. 393–5; Dickson 1987, p. 46.

93 Cullen 1986a, p. 131.

94 Bindon 1731, p. 6.

95 Dickson 1987, p. 47; Hayton 2004, p. 69.

96 Scott 1925, pp. 157–62.

97 Bindon 1731, pp. 10, 13, 17.

98 Cullen 1986a, p. 138.

99 Molyneux 1698, p. 149.

100 Molyneux 1698, pp. 34–5.

101 Burns 1989, p. 11.

102 O'Reagan 2000, pp. 106, 108.

103 Simms 1956, pp. 88–9, 93; Hayton, 2004, pp. 75, 79, 81–2.

104 Hayton 2004, p. 82; Dickson 1987, p. 50.

105 Connolly 1995, p. 230.

106 McGrath 2000, pp. 151, 153.

107 Hayton 2004, p. 90; Dickson 2000, p. 56.

108 Dickson 2000, pp. 56–7; Johnston 1974, p. 65.

109 Hayton 2004, pp. 87–8, 94–5.

110 Kilroy 1994, pp. 190, 200–1; Doyle 1989, p. 35.

111 Bartlett 1992, p. 21.

112 O'Reagan 2000, p. 138.

113 Simms 1986, pp. 263, 266; Dickson 1987, p. 53.

114 Simms 1986, pp. 217, 220.

115 Fagan 1998, p. 57.

116 Johnston 1974, pp. 32, 64, 68.

117 Gillespie 1995b, pp. 33–5.

118 Miller 1985, p. 138.

119 Miller 1985, pp. 152, 158–9.

120 Philips 1770, pp. 202, 209–11, 230–1.

121 Miller 1985, p. 161.

122 Millet 1970, pp. 66–9.

123 Rafferty 1994, p. 59.

124 Burke 1914, pp. 142, 327, 430; Giblin 1956, pp. 280–323.

125 Doyle 1989, p. 29.

126 Burke 1914, p. 197.

127 Burke 1914, p. 163.

128 Leighton 1994, p. 6.

129 Burke 1914, pp. 195, 198; Millett 1969b, pp. 50–1.

130 Wall 1961, pp. 26–7.

131 Wall 1961, pp. 28, 32.

132 Brady and Corish 1971, pp. 20–1.

133 Fagan 1989, p. 134.

134 Corish 1981, p. 83; Wall 1961, pp. 45–6.

135 Burke 1914, p. 201.

136 Rafferty 1994, p. 74; Wall 1961, p. 28.

137 Burke 1914, pp. 200–1.

138 Fagan 1998, p. 60.

139 Connolly 1992, p. 150.

140 Fenning 1974, p. 78; Moran 1874, p. 215.

141 Fenning 1977, pp. 22–4.

142 Wall 1961, p. 11.

143 MacLysaght 1979, pp. 290–2.

144 Brady and Corish 1971, pp. 42–3.

145 Hill 1873, p. 269; Fagan 2001, p. 12.

146 Osborough 1990, pp. 24, 25, 27, 36.

147 Brennan 2003, p. 263.

148 Osborough 1990, pp. 36, 43.

149 James 1973, p. 25; Lawrence 1682, pp. 63–8.

150 O'Byrne 1981, p. xiv.

151 Rafferty 1994, p. 59.

152 Brennan 2003, p. 263; Leighton 1994, p. 8.

153 Cullen 1990, p. 57.

154 Barnard 2004, p. 131.

155 Cullen 1986b, pp. 27–8; Cullen 1990, p. 124.

156 Hayton 2004, pp. 180, 185.

157 Hayton 1979, p. 47; Hayton 2004, p. 217; Johnston 1974, p. 59.

158 Connolly 1992, p. 98; Dickson 2000, p. 62.

159 Hayton 1979, p. 33.

160 Philips 1770, p. 267; Barnard 2004b, p. 273.

161 Day 1991, p. 33.

162 Barnard 2004c, pp. 69–72.

163 Hayton 1979, p. 49; McNally 1997, p. 107.

164 McNally 1997, p. 117; McCracken 1986, pp. 61–3.

165 McNally 1997, pp. 108, 112, 122.

166 Connolly 1992, pp. 91–2.

167 Hayton 2004, pp. 222–3; O'Regan 2000, pp. 100–3.

168 McNally 2004, p. 67; O'Regan 2000, pp. 108–11.

169 Hayton 2004, pp. 228–9.

170 Burns 1989, pp. 134–5, 153.

171 Ehrenpreis 1968, pp. 59–73; Fabricant 2003, pp. 55, 57; O'Regan 2000, p. 316.

172 McNally 2004, p. 50; Dickson 2000, p. 71.

173 Hayton 2004, pp. 111, 215.

174 O'Regan 2000, pp. 307, 313, 315.

175 Burns 1989, pp. 195–6; McNally 1997, pp. 130–2.

176 Hayton 2004, pp. 250, 252.

177 Hayton 2004, p. 33.

178 Anon 1784, p. 258.

179 Connolly 1992, p. 111.

180 Speck 1988, p. 246.

CHAPTER 11

Land and people

This chapter will present a snapshot of peasant society in the opening decades of the eighteenth century as a product of developments over the preceding half century or more. It will also attempt to delineate the connections between an apparent jumble of loosely related agrarian phenomena: price moves on the market, farming practices, diet, the press of numbers, settlement patterns, class structure and even language. The picture changes slowly enough over time to be caught to within a decade or two. The spatial dimension presents more problems than the temporal dimension. The picture is stubbornly and significantly different across the island in two, and latterly three, distinct agrarian regions defined by climate, topography and distance from ports, towns, roads and navigable rivers.

Tillage and pastoral Ireland

From Newry to Limerick and thence to Cork meandered the bounds of the late medieval lordship. Within this region of well-drained soils, tillage was more important than across the rest of the island. That said, the country as a whole was overwhelmingly pastoral.[1] The Boyne was described in 1690 as the northern 'frontier of the corn country', but even within the Pale strangers remarked how hard it was to find good wheaten bread. A French official turned his nose up at the 'pitiful' bread doled out to Jacobite soldiers before the Boyne: 'barley, oat and rye meal, peas and all sorts of grains mixed together'.[2] 'Transplanter's Certificates' handed up by landowners in County Wexford, another tillage region, claimed 5,099 head of livestock and 3,748 cropped acres. Only when the south-eastern baronies of Bargy and Forth are taken in isolation can one find many more

– between two and three times more – acres under tillage than heads of livestock.[3] Strictly speaking, then, it would be more accurate to refer to the tillage region as a mixed-farming zone. Growing crops was labour intensive and so this zone was amply populated and studded with nucleated villages centred on parish church, tower house and, often, water mill. The prevalence of mills is a good marker of cereal growing and the Civil Survey notes quite a few in the tillage zone: ninety-one in County Kildare, for instance.[4]

Wetter, boggier and hillier land elsewhere supported a thinly scattered, more pastoral and poorer population.[5] This pastoral zone encompassed Connacht, the Gaelic midlands, west Munster and most of Ulster: it is somewhat too early to speak of a definable proto-industrial zone emerging in the 'linen triangle' of north Armagh and the parts of Counties Down and Tyrone. The skewed distribution of post roads and urban centres in the seventeenth century captures the reality of the two Irelands.[6] The contrast between the tillage zone and the pastoral north and west fits into a wider contrast between the Atlantic fringes of north-west Europe and the tillage-based agriculture of the European lowlands.

Agricultural output grew explosively in the first forty years of the seventeenth century from an economy suddenly hitched to the demands of the market. Demand for pastoral produce such as live cattle and wool from London, the biggest and fastest growing city in the world, was choked off by mercantilist restrictions in the later half of the seventeenth century. Such Atlantic and continental markets that remained were vulnerable to wartime interruption. In the 1690s the Irish economy began to move away from live cattle to processed goods, especially butter, barrelled beef and wool. With this diversification began a stable marketing network, a market economy, increased monetisation and regional specialisation.

Consequently, the pastoral zone fragmented, during the period under review, into two regions. The first was a residual small farm and predominantly subsistence region to the west and north, with tenuous links to the market through the sale of young cattle 'from wet hills by the sea' to be finished on the fat grasslands of the intermediate zone of commercialised pastoralism that emerged in the seventeenth and early eighteenth century. This second zone had a fairly stable dairying component centred on the hinterland of Cork city while the regions dominated by the other components, sheep, cattle rearing and cattle fattening, pulsed and subsided in response to price movements.[7] This dry stock or grazier belt overran extensive swathes of the tillage regions. By the second half of the seventeenth century, County Tipperary could be described as 'all pasture, and employed in sheep walks and feeding black cattle': Irish cattle of the time were hardy, black and smallish compared with their English counterparts; the 'Kerry' is the only relic of that breed.[8] At its widest and longest by the 1720s, the grazier belt formed a more or less contiguous block, running from County Tipperary through the alternating bogs and meadows of County Offaly to the great maghery (plain) of south-east County Mayo, east County Galway, north County Roscommon and County Sligo. Counties Westmeath, Longford and much of Meath were also swallowed up in this zone of transitional pastoralism: it was transitional because much of it had switched from tillage and would switch back again during the end-of-century corn boom.[9]

This expansion of pastoral farming was problematic. Charles O'Hara's account of County Sligo in the opening years of the eighteenth century bears out the extent to which the peasantry still lived in a subsistence economy:[10]

The whole country was covered with cottage tenants, who, having no foreign demand for the produce of their farms, mostly paid their rent in kind, in duties and in work. The only money brought amongst us was by means of the army and some very few lean cattle sold to the Leinster graziers.

A chronic 'want of markets', in the words of a County Galway land agent, 'to convert the cows to currency' was one drawback of the pastoral economy.[11] Moreover, unlike tillage, ranching did not need many hands. When '. . . the demands for store cattle for the south had reached us', recollected O'Hara, 'many villagers were turned off, and the lands which they had occupied stocked with cattle'.[12] Archbishop Boulter hammered home criticism of graziers in the hungry winter of 1727–28: 'In some of the finest counties, in many places there is neither house nor corn field to be seen in 10 or 15 miles travelling.'[13]

The Irish economy rested on a narrow range of primary products and was exceptionally exposed to the vagaries of war and mercantilist legislation. The evidence of economic stagnation in the first decades of the eighteenth century is unmistakable. Rental values slumped and did not generally pick up until the later 1740s.[14] Shipping tonnage tells much the same story: non-coastal shipping tonnage in and out of Cork showed a sharp pick-up from around 1710 but little subsequent expansion for the next forty years and this trend is also reflected in export returns for most of the pillars of Cork business: beef, tallow, hides and butter.

Long-term trends towards low product prices left an impoverished, underemployed and debt-ridden peasantry. Consequently, there loomed the 'danger of famine among the poor upon any little miscarriage in our harvest'.[15]

Demography and diet

It is generally accepted that fewer than 1 million people lived in Ireland in 1600 and around 2 million a century later. When one allows for mass inflows of settlers on the one hand and the heavy death toll of 1649–54 on the other, the doubling in population implies significant natural increase or excess of births over deaths.[16] The rate of natural increase in England averaged less than 0.5 per cent between 1541 and 1751, but to guess a credible Irish rate of natural increase one must allow for the peculiarity noticed by no less than Oliver Cromwell himself: '. . . the poorer sort of Irish in Ireland do, as well as the rich, abound in children.'[17] Travellers would often express pained surprise that the Irish poor 'breed as rabbits'.[18] More telling is statistical evidence from the middle of the seventeenth century that Irish women married two years younger than their English counterparts. This, in turn, would imply around five births per marriage, as against an average of around four in seventeenth-century England.[19] There is no reliable way of converting this difference into a measure of the rate of natural increase.[20]

'Hajnal's line' cut across nineteenth-century Europe from St Petersburg to Trieste. West of that line a relatively high proportion of women married late or not at all.[21] This created a 'preventative check' on population whereby the labouring classes had relatively few children because they were most likely to defer marriage longest.[22] The age of marriage was a barometer of perceived economic opportunities and so a 'tight relationship' existed between long-run price fluctuations and the rate of population growth.[23] When population growth accelerated to a rate above around 0.5 per cent a year, food prices rose, real wages fell, marriage was deferred or never happened and population growth rates fell back. Ireland, along with Finland, southern Iberia and southern Italy, were exceptional areas west of Hajnal's line then and, likely, back in the seventeenth and early eighteenth centuries.[24] In these circumstances the pressure of rising numbers brought the guillotine of the Malthusian 'positive' check slamming down.[25] As the Irish population grew it pressed against a ceiling imposed by the amount of food the country could produce and the poor could afford to buy whereupon food crises, famines and disease epidemics thinned the population. The size of the 'positive' relative to the 'preventative' check diminishes as economic development increases, market integration intensifies, the transport network improves, capital accumulates to import grain during poor harvest years and superior agricultural technology brings higher yields and greater diversity of crops.[26] Little enough of this was happening in the early decades of the eighteenth century.

The shape and scale of the preventative check varied according to the agrarian and dietary region. Along with oatcakes, 'sweet and sower, thick and thin' milk in its many forms, as curds, 'banniclabber' [*bainne clábair*], butter or soft cheeses formed the staple of the 'moist' diet of pastoral Ireland.[27] Butter passed as currency in Gaelic Ireland: Hugh O'Neill's curiously named 'butter captains' or mercenary officers were so called because they were paid in firkins of butter. A drier diet of bread and gruels made from cereals, peas and beans was typical of the zone where tillage was more common.[28] Pastoral and tillage zones suffered hungry months at different seasons: winter and summer respectively. Cows dried up in the autumn until the grass began to grow again the following April and in dairy regions wintertime diet relied heavily on butter, often buried in bogs to keep, and oatmeal roasted together into cakes before the fire. Barley which ripened in July and peas picked in early summer could bridge the gap to the main harvest in arable regions. The poorer sort would hit the Malthusian limit during those months.

A New World wonder crop seemingly had the potential to cheat Malthus. A family of six could subsist with a little milk, after a fashion, on the quantity of potatoes that could be grown on one and the same acre.[29] The earliest documentary reference to the potato comes from the first decade of the seventeenth century and it is noted in several incidental references four decades later.[30] English soldiers in 1642 killed thirty peasants 'digging of potatoes in their own gardens' at Tullow in County Tipperary. Other scattered wartime references come from as far afield as Counties Laois, Wicklow, Carlow and Kerry.[31]

It is generally believed, however, that the potato began its long march in the dairying region, specifically the coastline of Counties Cork and Waterford.[32] Here, butter was rapidly becoming a commercial product. With increased commercialisation peasants could eat more potatoes and release more butter for the market. The importance of the potato as a supplementary winter food in the dairying zone probably dates from the 1670s.[33] Local peasants told a Danish officer quartered in Munster in the winter of 1690–91 that they had adopted the *erdt appel* just sixteen years before.[34] Remarks by other officers and chaplains suggest that this had not yet happened elsewhere: a Swiss cadet who spent a hungry winter in east County Tyrone makes no mention of potatoes but lovingly describes oatcakes as the Ulster peasants' *pain ordinaire*.[35] Nor did the potato take root, so to speak, in Connacht or the midlands to judge from the absence of references by Roderic O'Flaherty or Henry Piers: the latter, writing in the 1680s, notes that the winter diet in County Westmeath was based on bread.[36] The potato may have been radiating unobtrusively from the Munster heartland to the core tillage zone of the Pale by the late 1690s when the garden crops to be seen in lowland north County Kildare were oats, peas and 'their dearly beloved potatoes'.[37]

Yet three and four decades later the potato, while spreading slowly, was still limited by class, season and region: '. . . the winter subsistence of the poor', especially in Munster, 'is chiefly potatoes.'[38] Even assuming that potatoes were eaten for nine months of the year, per capita consumption was no more than a third of what was common on the eve of the Great Famine and the potato did not become a staple food of the mass of the population until the last quarter of the eighteenth century.[39]

It did not forestall the looming preventative check. Hearth tax returns indicate sharp falls in the number of households in most counties in the 1730s.[40] This fall culminated in famine conditions that were at their worst from the winter of 1740–41 through to the following autumn.[41] Severe frost destroyed much of the potato crop in early 1793: a north County Cork land agent reported that 'the eating potatoes are all destroyed'.[42] This forced many to eat a portion of the seed potatoes reserved for planting. The arctic cold also took a heavy toll of animals in the field, as did drought in the spring: a report from County Wexford in April 1740 tells that 'their little cows are daily and hourly dropping for want of grass'. Fewer potatoes planted, a poor harvest of drought-stunted wheat and a somewhat better oat crop could ease the food shortage only temporarily. The absence of external food supplies until the summer of 1741, because of continent-wide harvest failure and war, created a truly horrific catastrophe.

Deaths peaked in the spring of 1741 due to 'flux' (dysentery and famine diarrhoea) and to 'fever'. The biggest killers were, likely, louse-borne relapsing fever and its deadlier cousin, typhus. Typhus spreads quickest in conditions of wet, cold, crowding and privation. Inclement weather encourages the constant wearing of clothing and huddling together indoors for warmth, crowding lets the insects crawl from one to another, privation makes it less likely that there would be a change of clothes or the chance or inclination to wash.[43] Estimates of deaths in contemporary correspondence vary from a third to a half of the 'labouring people' or 'cottiers': mortality was class specific.[44] Hearth-tax returns suggest that Munster and Connacht, where recent population growth had been strongest, suffered the greatest loss of life. It was the worst human cataclysm for a century.[45]

There would be no comparable disaster for another century and the underlying explanation for the gap between the famines was economic growth. To take just one aspect of that growth: outworked or cottage-based linen weaving grew steadily. It is therefore no accident that County Armagh, the centre of linen weaving, was the most densely populated county in Ireland by 1841. The earlier parts like flax growing, scutching, hackling and spinning all rippled well beyond the 'linen triangle' to encompass almost the northern half of Ireland.[46] That cushion against scarcity explained, for instance, why a County Sligo landlord could take comfort from the fact that the labouring poor, just fifteen years after the famine of 1740–41, 'grow more above small accidents'.

The market drove dietary change to the potato. The traditionally self-sufficient Irish peasant was drawn into the cash economy by new wants, needs and desires: cash to pay rent and to buy luxuries such as snuff and tobacco. With the potato the peasant's family could eat less or none of the cash crops and products: butter, pork, beef or grain.[47] The potato did not encourage the labouring class to marry earlier and have that extra child. They were going to anyway. The potato let that child survive.[48] If the primary impact of the potato was on death rates, it also indirectly boosted the birth rate. The potato, along with the spread of domestic textile work in the later eighteenth century, transformed domestic service from a 'live-in' and largely celibate experience. Typically, the servant or 'tied cottier' of the later eighteenth century was married and not co-resident in the employer's household. This opened the possibility of earlier marriage and parenthood to poorer women.[49]

Social class

The economic stagnation of the early eighteenth century shaped not just diet and demography but also the class stratification of rural society, land-holding arrangements, housing and settlement patterns.

Perched atop the apex of the pyramid were the most affluent Irish peers, like James Butler, 2nd Duke of Ormond, or Richard Boyle, 4th Earl of Cork and 3rd Earl of Burlington, who passed as grandees in England where most of their interest lay. Smaller proprietors might also be frequently absent from any one estate, dividing time between widely scattered estates and Dublin, drawn by the glitter of the social season and the business of parliament.[50] Given the scale of absenteeism, the resident 'middleman' represented the squirearchy across much of the countryside. To call someone a 'middleman' was to imply that he was a drone 'who lives upon the product of an estate, without the right of property or the merit of labour'.[51] In fact if not in name, they had been around for a while. The Earl of Clanricard griped in 1623 about his head tenants subletting at double the rent and exactly a century later Viscount Molesworth complained of grasping tenants subletting ('In England you seldom or never hear of such a thing') to 'one or more Partners or Cottagers, who shall pay him one third more per Acre than he pays by his Lease'.[52] The middleman was a social type peculiar to, and essential to, a half-capitalist society. He functioned as a broker between the cash-starved rural economy and the monetised market.[53] In addition to taking on the drudgery of collecting multiple rents from poor tenants on large or fragmented estates, he often supplied the chronic 'want of capital'. In the emerging dairying districts of south Munster, for instance, he might sublease the land, supply the milch cows, accept payment in butter, transport and sell this to the merchant in Cork, Waterford or Limerick, and pay a money rent to the landlord in due course.[54]

The middleman, then, was a symptom of economic backwardness, not a cause. Also seemingly symptomatic of a sluggish and largely subsistence economy was an apparently indistinguishable mass of poor peasants. In the later seventeenth century William Petty reckoned that around 86 per cent of the total population lived in a 'brutish nasty condition', holding little or no land and perhaps only two or three cattle.[55] About half of the rest were landlords and middlemen, leaving only a small middle peasantry or yeomanry, amounting no more than 7 per cent of the whole. How accurate is this reconstruction of a homogenous peasant class?

Scológ and gníomhaire

Cannier peasants probably took advantage of the labour shortage caused by the Cromwellian demographic catastrophe. Indices such as horse ownership and tobacco smoking point to modest peasant prosperity.[56] This is likely what Aodhagán Ó Rathaille meant when he declaimed sarcastically: 'More power to you Cromwell, O King who took notice of every *sgológ*.'[57] The *scológ* was a 'substantial fellow' who owned six or eight horses and half a dozen cows and who could pay by his ploughing £12–14 in rent annually.[58] The Munster 'gneever' or holder of a *gníomh* (roughly 25 acres of tillage or good pasture) was also a solid working farmer.[59] Because they lived so frugally their existence can easily be overlooked. They dressed more 'for use than for pomp', a chaplain with the Danish troops noted approvingly.[60] Even the wealthiest peasants lived in small, thatched, mud-walled cabins.[61]

A 1749 religious headcount of Elphin lets us interrogate Petty's gener-
alisation about a uniformly poor peasant class and allows us to reconstruct
the social stratification of agrarian society in one region. The parishes
of Tisara and Taughboy in the County Roscommon 'panhandle' could
be considered outliers of tillage Ireland. They returned 121 'tenants' as
against 203 'labourers'. The epithets 'labourer', 'cottager', 'cottier' and
'villager' in the census all seem to have been synonyms for poorer peasants
holding land in exchange for rent or, perhaps, labour services.[62] The distinction between 'tenant' and the various synonyms of 'labourer' was real
and is captured, for instance, by gravestone inscriptions in Tisara cemet-
ery. Of the thirteen inscriptions that can be tied to persons named in
the census, six were tenants, five were artisans or merchants, one was a
'farmer' (locally this meant a middleman) and one a priest. None was a
'labourer'. Further north in the diocese, the census of the grazier districts
shows a much more attenuated, and starkly two-class, social structure of
middlemen and 'villager' or poor peasant. This was probably representative of the commercialised pastoral region and the subsistence region, with
the stronger peasant surviving only in tillage regions.

Looking forward, the late eighteenth-century economic boom brought
a much different two-class system in the countryside. Middlemen declined,
while some peasants grew more prosperous and emerged as the strong
farmer class who would ultimately inherit the earth. Other peasants remained at, or sank to, the level of landless labourer or cottier.

Farming, settlement and housing

Farming practices tended to compact this homogenous peasant mass that
characterised much of the island.

The seventeenth-century Irish countryside was not broken up into the
familiar patchwork of small rectangular fields but lay open, though the
enclosing 'ditch' (usually an embankment topped by a straggling
hedgerow) was becoming more common.[63] The lowland tillage zone
of Leinster, for instance, was enclosed by the middle of the eighteenth
century.[64]

'Rundale' was the best known Irish variant of open-field and often
common-field farming widely practised in early modern Europe.[65] Rundale
functioned within the joint farm framework leased to partnership tenants
bound by kinship or the need to pool their meagre resources. They were
poor: Molesworth excoriates such partnership tenants as 'Beggars and
Thieves'.[66] The partners often lived in a formlessly clustered settlement or

'clachan', a name retrospectively borrowed from Scots Gaelic. Raven's survey of Farney shows countryside dotted with amorphous groups of two to six cabins, usually without any nucleating features like church, castle or mill. The rarity of the latter reflected the comparative unimportance of the grain economy in this traditionally pastoral region.[67] Nearest the clachan was the large open 'infield' of arable land and meadow. Usually this was held jointly, though each tenant held distinct individual strips intermingled and widely scattered to include lands of different quality. Furthest from the clachan was the 'outfield' with its rough grazing land or summer pasture: 'he who holds the greatest number of acres in the arable, is supposed the more able farmer, and consequently is allowed to have more cattle on the pastures of the town . . .'[68] While rundale allowed for some sorting out of richer and poorer peasants, it tended, like all forms of common field agriculture, to make it difficult for any one peasant to get too far ahead of his neighbours. How could he, for instance, try out a new crop without the agreement of his partners? Rundale favoured collective over individualistic values and solidarity and security over innovation and risk-taking.

Rundale could be found on about three quarters of Ulster estates in the mid-eighteenth century. However, there is no firm evidence for the practice in County Cork.[69] It is hard to be more precise about its prevalence because, confusingly, components of the rundale system were often associated with individualistic farming systems. Such components included the joint management of lands, clubbing together to pay rent and sharing plough teams.

Nor is it possible to delineate the boundaries of rundale regions by the prevalence of the clachan, as opposed to the nucleated manorial village. An Englishman traversing County Limerick in 1620 noticed nucleated villages dotted evenly across the county: 'In every village is a castle and a church, but both in ruyne.'[70] 'In ruin': the seventeenth century saw the shattering of the village system by the cumulative shocks of the Reformation and the displacement of the old landowning *élite* and their dependants. One third of nucleated settlements in County Limerick had an 'unrepaired', 'decayed', 'ruinous' or 'broken' castle and often a roofless church.[71] Protestant landlords usually placed Anglican churches on fresh sites. In idealised form the principal focus of their estate villages was the big house and demesne, with a wide street fronted by two-storey slated houses running from an Anglican church to a market cum courthouse. The Restoration period saw the first wave of estate towns: in County Cork alone one finds Midleton, Charleville, Castlemartyr, Kanturk, Newmarket and Doneraile. Sometimes the medieval human landscape was obliterated by settler landlords. For example, in 1640 the village of Loughcrew in County Meath still possessed the twin axes of an intact church and castle of the Plunkett family. By 1720 an English landlord family, the Nappers, had emptied the village, dispersing the villagers to the hillside and dissolving the village into their demesne.[72] The impersonal agency of spreading pastoralism also helped dissolve old tillage villages by scattering the workforce: this accounts for most of the 100 deserted village sites in County Tipperary. Such abrupt breaks in continuity of settlement blur the contrast of clachan and village regions. Nevertheless one can see a striking concentration of clachans west of the Shannon and, elsewhere, a thickening near the Atlantic coastline.[73] Clachans, and the rundale and social homogeneity their presence implies, were most common in the small farm/subsistence zone and in marginal and less favoured parts of the spreading commercial grassland zone.

Housing was another marker of an apparently indistinguishable poor peasantry. Thomas Raven's 1634 map of Farney in County Monaghan depicts a thin sprinkling of two-storey slated houses likely with 'cagework' or wooden frame and a stone or brick chimney.[74] In the overwhelming preponderance of single-storeyed thatched cabins we seem to see the cartographic imprint of the skewed class pyramid, too wide at the base and too narrow at the apex.[75]

That said, housing can be an unreliable guide to wealth. Generalisations about Irish cabins often confound permanent dwellings with temporary huts thrown up by herders 'booleying' in remote summer pastures or by wartime 'creaghts'. The latter was a collective term for a group of refugees and their cows. Such dwellings were likely the huts 'of a round form and without chimneys' that 'resemble so many hives of bees' and prompted unflattering comparisons with native American huts.[76] Moreover, such generalisations about permanent dwellings often obscure real differences in quality, structure and materials. Broadly speaking, two house types corresponded to the core pastoral and arable zones. In the former the 'gable hearth' type predominated. This was a long house built on a sloping site, with cattle occupying the lower end furthest from the hearth.[77] The central hearth type built elsewhere did not easily accommodate livestock in the house. Countrywide, the most common material was clay, mixed with straw. The mud-walled cabin was not as poor as it might seem. It was, admittedly, gloomy. The walls had to be thick and low so doorways were narrow and window openings set high in the walls under the overhanging thatch, like eyes glinting beneath shaggy eyebrows.[78] Yet with amenities like a stone chimney flue, half-door and frequent whitewashing, the mud cabin could be 'durable and comfortable'.[79]

Popular culture: language and religion

Moving from the material aspects of popular culture like housing to less tangible aspects of daily life, it is helpful to recollect each of the three major regions: tillage, pastoral/commercialised and pastoral/subsistence. Each experienced a different timing, pace and intensity of externally imposed changes. This differential exposure helps to explain the regional pattern of continuity and change in popular culture.

Language

The decline of the Irish language is the most important cultural change in Irish history and some increments in that weakening came in the long seventeenth century.

Gaelic was spoken across the entire island in the closing decades of the sixteenth century and had conquered the hybridised Hiberno–English cultural zone of the Pale and the little urban oases of civility whose inhabitants 'commonly speak Irish among themselves'.[80] The only places where English was the dominant spoken language were the city of Dublin, 'Fingal' or north County Dublin and south Wexford, especially Bargy and Forth in the south-eastern nook of the county where a 'mingle mangle' of Irish and archaic English was spoken.[81] To judge from surname evidence, most of the peasantry of south Kilkenny, east Waterford (Gaultier and Middle Third baronies) and the eastern fringe of Tipperary (Slievardagh barony) were of English descent but they were no longer English-speaking, despite suggestions to the contrary.[82] Here was the region that produced Keating and Hackett and was still Gaelic-speaking (**map 10**) well into the nineteenth century.

The geographic extent to which Irish retreated from this strong position over the next two centuries can be seen from a map (**map 10**) compiled by back projection from later census data that shows the proportion of Gaelic-speaking to anglophone children in the 1790s.[83] A comparable exercise in back projection using the known association of English speech with high levels of literacy in the English language yields a somewhat similar spatial pattern.[84] Connacht and Munster where Irish was spoken by more than 60 per cent of children (and an even larger proportion of the whole population) forms a solid-looking mainland, with peninsulas stretching to County Kilkenny and Donegal and a rather small offshore island in north Meath and the adjacent parts of Cavan and Monaghan. Bigger towns and cities embedded in the Gaelic continent, except for

Galway, stand out as shallow anglophone pools.[85] There were three regional dialects of Irish by the closing decade of the eighteenth century: Connacht, Ulster (including Leitrim, Louth and north Meath) and Munster (including County Kilkenny). Countrywide, half of all children spoke one of these dialects.[86] The geographic range of Irish-speaking districts was, of course, rather wider than the map implies. Thus, for instance, even if children no longer spoke Gaelic by the 1790s, the adult poor of west and south Offaly still spoke Irish and English 'with equal fluency'.[87]

The 'tipping point'

Since most people still spoke Irish at the outset of the nineteenth century one can understand why scholars traditionally treated the decline of Irish mostly as a phenomenon explicable by the Great Famine, National Schools, Daniel O'Connell or whatever. Yet they were mistaken.

By 1800 Irish was no longer spoken by 'those who had already achieved success in the world' or by those who hoped to get ahead.[88] The 'tipping point' in the displacement of Gaelic was reached some time earlier when a critical mass of Irish people discarded their excess linguistic baggage and so set up a momentum that would overcome the inertia of conservatism, linguistic loyalty and, indeed, laziness. Learning a new language is hard: learning English and unlearning Gaelic 'harder still'.[89] The tipping point came when a smallish minority of opinion leaders and cultural gatekeepers ('early adaptors' in the jargon of diffusion studies) bridged the chasm to the 'early majority' of adaptors. The rest, the late majority and laggards, typically follow sooner or later.

In 1787 a Dublin tenor named Michael Kelly, a minor celebrity in his day, gained an audience with Joseph II. He found the Habsburg Emperor attended by three of his Irish generals, Dalton, Dillon and Kavanagh. The latter greeted a clearly mystified Kelly in Gaelic: 'What, Kelly.' Emperor Joseph challenged: 'Don't you know the language of your own country?' Kelly replied: 'Please Your Majesty, none but the lower orders of the Irish people speak Irish.' Gaelic was for losers: the politically literate and the socially ambitious did not speak it any more.[90]

When?

The momentum of mass linguistic change had not begun before the Confederate and Cromwellian wars. The depositions and other sources would suggest that Irish was spoken everywhere, right up to the walls of Dublin, and imply sturdy linguistic loyalty among the natives, alongside widespread bilingualism among natives and settlers.[91] Vincent Gookin's boast in 1633 that he would not let his children learn Irish implicitly accuses many of his fellow settlers of doing otherwise.[92] Irish subsequently receded at 'overwhelming speed' across much of the midlands, east and north, an area roughly co-terminous with the unshaded regions on **map 10**.[93] The linguistic transition was already over by the 1790s and must, therefore, have been well advanced by the early decades of the eighteenth century. Irish had, according to Cullen, almost completely receded from Counties Westmeath, Laois, Wicklow and north Wexford by the end of the seventeenth century. However speedy, language change in the late seventeenth and early eighteenth centuries was not so fast as to cause a 'great silence' of abrupt language change from one generation to another, with parents and children scarcely able to communicate.[94] Likely, the transition took two or three generations to conclude, with an intermediate period of bilingualism. The comic stage Irishman's brogue is first parodied in the latter part of the seventeenth century. A typical example would be the perjuring witness (legal process was an important point of contact for language change) in the *True discovery of the Irish popish Plot* who offers that he and his ilk 'to shave themselves from de gallows, dey will come to London and be your Kings Evidence'.[95] The inability to pronounce 'th' is still a Hiberno–English shibboleth, though the supernumerary 'h' in words like 'shave' has long gone. The appearance of this brogue probably reflects the first time that lower-class Irish people spoke English in any numbers.

Using the 1659 census, the historical geographer William Smyth plotted the extent to which the 'O' and 'Mac' in Gaelic surnames were dropped in different parts of the country and ingeniously used it as an early warning of the fissures along which the English language would spread into solidly Irish-speaking regions.[96] However, the areas where the 'O' and Mac in Gaelic surnames were most completely dropped (across Leinster and the eastern fringe of Munster) and most retained (Ulster) in 1659 do not obligingly coincide with regions where the Gaelic receded earliest and most completely. The Elphin 'census' of 1749 captures the almost total anglicisation of Christian names and surnames in a region that was still Gaelic-speaking and would remain so for another century. Surnames are overwhelmingly rendered in their familiar modern corrupted forms: Moran, Fallon, Naughton, Hynes and so on, with just a few odd-looking phonetic renderings like 'Kinoyster', subsequently anglicised as Nestor. Christian names are overwhelmingly English, John, Patrick, James and Thomas being the most common for men and Mary, Catherine, Margaret and Bridget for women.[97] Comparison with a specific parish in the

County Sligo portion of the diocese where some householders are listed for hearth tax purposes in the 1660s shows that men's Christian names had then been almost all Gaelic: Manus, Laughlin, Teige (of course) and Shane, among others.[98]

The change is quite startling but quite what it means is another matter. Perhaps, as Smyth suggests, it represents a preliminary phase of linguistic transition, though the timing and incidence have little predictive value in guessing the tempo of decisive language change. These are people who can speak English: even forty years before it was 'universally spoken by the young' of County Sligo.[99] To say they could speak is not to say that they ordinarily did so. They had not yet abandoned Irish, but the adoption of English surnames and the mutilation of something as personal as a surname suggests that they aspired to do so.

Why? The market

The basic structural cause of language shift is usually taken to be economic: 'as markets and other anglicising influences penetrated deeper, Irish retreated'.[100] On this reading, the persistence of Irish was due to slow economic growth before 1750 and the localism of the countryside reinforced by poor communications and widespread illiteracy which insulated Irish speakers from English influences.[101] Dublin city's ascendancy as centre of state, law and commerce (crucially including publishing and book distribution) opened corridors of English speech flowing out of the burgeoning capital city as trade and traffic intensified on the new turnpike roads radiating from Dublin.[102]

There are problems with this assumption. If language shift was just a way of reducing transaction costs it would be more rational for the English tobacco pedlar Robin to speak Irish than for Tomás and his company of boors in *Páirlimint Cloinne Tomáis* to stutter ludicrously broken English: 'What is the bigg greate órdlach for the what so penny?'[103] If one concedes that, for some unknown reason of economic rationality, the market in its entirety could operate only in English, then involvement in commercial transactions was bound to lead to the acquisition of English. But that does not account for the loss of Gaelic. The common response to linguistic pressure is the retirement of one language from certain public domains such as the market, or law, administration, courts, schools, literature and religion. For instance, Hugh MacCurtin, or Aodh Buí Mac Cruitín, wrote poetry in Irish but when he responded in 1717 to Richard Cox's *Hibernia Anglicana* (1689) with his *Brief Discourse in Vindication of the Antiquity of Ireland*, he wrote in English, the language of the public domain of power and intellectual credibility, to reach a wider readership.[104] Children are urged to learn the more prestigious language that opens more avenues to social mobility but usually practise diglossia: using different languages with different people in different domains.[105] However, the longer-run Irish pattern was an exceptional one of total displacement of the less prestigious language from all domains.

Moreover, a glance at the map will show that the geographical patterns of language shift and commercialisation do not match. For instance, the dairying regions of Munster were Gaelic-speaking *and* commercialised. Where Art Mac Cumhaigh (c. 1715–73) of south Armagh lamented 'when I hear Irish all abandoned' [*nuair a cluinim an Ghaelige uilig á tréighbheáil*] he was speaking of *his* people, Irish Catholics. Ó Tuama of Croom in the Golden Vale of County Limerick is in a more comfortable position in his formulaic hope that the 'vain rabble of English speakers' will be expelled.[106] English speakers are the 'other' and still identifiably foreign. That said, by the 1750s as turnpike roads spread in mid-Munster, a linguistic fissure opened up along a line from Limerick to the expanding provisioning port of Cork.[107]

Why? Plantation and changing land ownership

Ulster regions where a significant part, say more than 30 per cent, of the population was of immigrant stock correspond quite closely to the unshaded regions of the linguistic map (**map 10**) where Irish had receded earliest and most completely.[108] On both the linguistic and ethnic/religious maps south and west Ulster stand out as Irish and Catholic, with the latter linked tenuously through Castlederg to the mountainy spine of the Sperrins. The match is not complete: Iveagh was, and would remain, strongly Catholic but had evidently experienced early linguistic transition.[109] In Leinster, too, the most anglophone rural districts generally coincide with the planted lands of Gaelic Leinster, Longford, Offaly, parts of Westmeath, Laois, Wicklow, north Wexford and the O'Brennan *oireacht* in the north-east corner of County Kilkenny, planted in the 1630s.[110] Francis Molloy presumably draws on personal knowledge of his native Offaly in writing the preface to his *Grammatica Latino-Hibernica* (Rome, 1677), which shows a pained awareness of his native language in mortal danger. On the face of it, something about plantation was a more likely culprit for language change than market forces. But that something was not mass immigration of English speakers. While settlers outnumbered

natives across much of Ulster, nowhere in Leinster, except Wicklow, did
the settler proportion of the population approach Ulster levels.

The retreat of Irish must be seen in the context of cumulative shocks,
including the displacement of the native landowning *élite*, massive immigration and spasmodically rapid commercialisation.[111] Native landowners,
be they of putative Gaelic or Old English descent, could be viewed as
'cultural gatekeepers' and their progressive attenuation through expropriation, exile or conversion mattered. Seeking shelter in wartime Laois,
Brian Mac Giolla Phádraig's (c. 1580–c. 1652) 'Faisean Chláir Éibhir'
drips with contempt for 'servants in every home with grimy English'
[*smáilBhéarla*] who despise his learning and show him the door *'hob
amach 's beir leat do shárGhaelgsa'* [Out! and take your precious
Gaelic with you!].[112] Servants comprised around 10 per cent of the total
population.[113] Irish servants, especially household servants, were perhaps
quickest to ape their English-speaking masters and cultural influences
may have flowed downstairs and over the demesne wall. There was some
backwash. Whoever penned the 1675 poem the 'Moderate Cavalier',
satirising the oily flattery the household servant administers to his master's
children, knew enough phonetic Irish ['Agramacree': 'Cade poge': 'Nah
tousa Shane oge'] to capture Teige's patter.[114] One spots Irish words
creeping into Swift's *Gulliver's Travels* – the 'luhimus' that the Yahoos eat
derives from 'luch' and 'mus', the Irish and Latin respectively, for 'mouse'.[115]

The regional pattern of surviving Catholic land ownership in the early
decades of the eighteenth century is a yardstick of social discontinuity. A
rough match can be discerned between such discontinuity and linguistic
change, albeit with exceptions, such as the solidly Irish-speaking counties
of Sligo and Leitrim which, in terms of land ownership, belong to Ulster
rather than Connacht. Elsewhere the match is better. In County Kilkenny
and south Tipperary the protective umbrella of the various Butler houses
sheltered the area from plantation and nurtured a local culture that
was prosperous, self-assured and durable. Even after most of the cadet
branches of the Butlers conformed, head-tenants like the Keatings, Freneys
and Walshs stayed on and stayed Catholic.[116] The Catholic landowning
interest restored after the Cromwellian confiscations was strong in County
Cork, boosted by the enormous Clancarty estates in Muskerry, estimated
at 135,820 acres.[117] The Mac Carthys and many other County Cork and
County Kerry Jacobites lost their estates in the second round of mass forfeitures, this time for good. For whatever reason, perhaps because the
confiscated estates came on the market at knock-down prices in the commercial depression of the first decade of the eighteenth century, the renting

of these forfeited lands to the existing head-tenants seems to have been 'widespread and enduring'.[118] Therefore, a resident Catholic middleman gentry survived not just in remote regions, like the O'Mahonys, Leynes and O'Sullivans on the Landsdowne and Kenmare estates, but in more favoured regions like Muskerry. The best known example of the type was Art O'Leary, a former officer in the Austrian army and a dairy middleman living in a substantial two-storey slated house at *Carraig an Ime* near Macroom. The *Caoineadh Airt Uí Léire* lamenting his shooting dead by a Protestant neighbour is attributed to his wife Eibhlín *dubh* Ní Chonaill. The *Caoineadh* lists the material comforts her husband gave her, the painted parlour, furnished rooms and hot oven: *Chuiris parlús á ghealadh dhom, / rúmanna á mbreacadh dhom / bácus á dheargadh dhom . . .*[119] This hidden gentry gave Irish a window on a world of material comfort and modest social status and supplied modest patronage to Gaelic poets and scribes by employing them as tutors and clerks.[120] Simmeringly resentful of the roadblocks strewn across most avenues of social advancement in the English-speaking world, they had no reason to adopt anglophone culture and discard Gaelic culture. They were quick enough to do so when the Penal Laws were relaxed. Eibhlín *dubh*'s nephew, the 'Liberator' Daniel O'Connell, who could famously 'witness without a sigh' the demise of Irish, neatly symbolised the generational gap to a world of individualism and unreflective practicality.[121]

The Munster poets, in turn, nurtured cultural solidarity and a shared Jacobite loyalty between native gentry and the common people. The recruiting grounds of Irish soldiers in the French service suggests that Jacobitism was countrywide and that the Jacobite counter-culture was strongest in Munster and, above all, in Cork.[122] The best known practitioner of the Jacobite *aisling* was Aodhagán Ó Rathaille (1675–1729), born in the *Sliabh Luachra* district and buried in Muckross Abbey with his erstwhile MacCarthy patrons, 'those kings my people served before Christ died' [*Na flatha fá raibh mo shean roimh éag do Chríost*].[123] The *aisling* was a dramatic dialogue between the poet and a beautiful *spéirbhean*, a female personification of Ireland. She is a beautiful maiden distinguished by attributes such as a sweet voice [*beol ba bhinn, a glór ba chaoin*], but she will not lie with another man [*gan luí le fear*] until her mate comes back. The absent mate is usually the Stuart king in exile who may be referred to by the lexicon of Stuart legitimacy and monarchy [*mac Shéamais, prionsa, an rí ceart*], by Jacobite cant and symbolism [*an brícléir*], by the language of love [*mo ghille mear, stór mo chléibh*] or of mythology [Mars, *Aonghus Óg*].[124] The reverie usually ends with a note of hope that the exiled hero, the 'lion beyond the seas' [*an leon thar lear*], will come back to deliver his woman from bondage.

The *aisling* has been dismissed as irrelevant pub talk and as formulaic: 'a literary form, not a message for the people'.[125] Yet the reverie showed an acute awareness of contemporary politics. For instance, the literati quickly grasped the implications of Louis XIV's death and turned their attention to more likely backers in Spain.[126] It is clear, moreover, that the message was intended for the 'people', the Gaelic-speaking peasantry of Munster. *Mac an Cheannaí*, Ó Rathaille's best known *aisling*, is written in popular song-rhythms rather than bardic syllabic verse. While the *spéirbhean* is often Éire, Cliodhna or some other traditional female personification, she is often given a deliberately common, even plebian, Christian name and surname like Caitlín Ní Uallacháin or Móirín Ní Luinneacháin, doubtless to help the listener identify with her. For a people who lacked the artefacts to commemorate the Stuarts and to reiterate the icons of Jacobite counter-culture, the oak, the rose, the rising sun, the green branch and so on, the *aisling* served an educational function and represented a creative and vital convergence of Gaelic culture and popular protest.[127] On James III's birthday in 1724, 'a woman dressed in white on horseback' led a group wearing white roses in procession around St Stephen's Green on James. The Jacobites then routed an attack by a Whig mob, fatally beating one man, all the time shouting Tory party catch cries.[128]

There 'is no reason why a literary form cannot carry a message'.[129] The message, the form and, perhaps, the language in which it was written seemed relevant so long, but only so long, as there existed a realistic hope of outside deliverance. After the '45 and Culloden, the *aisling* hardened into a barren and formulaic exercise. The language of United Irish republicanism and of nineteenth-century nationalism, the manifestos, the speeches and ballad poetry would be in English; where echoes of an older *aisling* vocabulary survived, like the *Shan Van Vocht* ['poor old woman'], they were likely to be in the mouths of people who knew no other Irish than that.

Why? The Catholic Church

The Welsh language successfully negotiated the vital transition from a largely oral culture, but if the Bible had not been translated, the Welsh language would have been 'gravely weakened' and might very well have gone the way of Cornish and Manx.[130] The New Testament was translated into Welsh in 1567 and the complete Bible followed in 1588, the latter almost a full century before the Irish Old Testament was printed. The Bible provided a yardstick for what would otherwise have been an assorted mass of dialects. As the native gentry grew more anglicised, Protestant ministers provided the only educated class with a vested interest in publicly using the Welsh language.[131]

It has been argued that a comparably vital link between language and religion was not forged in Ireland, that the Catholic Church made little 'positive contribution' to the Irish language, used it only grudgingly, was otherwise 'indifferent when not contemptuous' and crucially (except of course the Franciscans) failed to publish in Irish.[132] This is simply not true of the period under review. As discussed in Chapter 3, the project of inventing Irishness, and doing so in the Irish language, was to a great extent a clerical achievement. There existed a significant devotional literature. For example, Francis Molloy wrote a book of popular religious instruction, *Lucerna Fidelium* (1667), and Bishop James O'Gallagher (d. 1751) of Raphoe and later Kildare wrote the very popular *Sermons*, first published in Dublin in 1736, that went through many editions. O'Gallagher's language was printed in Roman characters and conformed closely in pronunciation to the spoken vernacular of Donegal.

However, a lack of printed material in the Irish language was a fatal weakness in the longer run. The Irish moved in one generation between 1790 and 1820 from haphazard education to virtual mass instruction. The decline in Irish, 'rather gradual' before then, accelerated dramatically. Gaelic fell victim to the prestige of written over oral culture and the demand for literacy. English was the gateway to literacy while the amount of Irish in printed form was very limited: in 1806 only 20,000 out of an estimated 1.5 million Gaelic speakers were found to be able to read their language.[133]

In the longer run, too, Catholic churchmen neglected Gaelic. Maynooth seminary was founded in the 1790s at a time when most of the population was still Gaelic-speaking but made no provision whatever for teaching the language. This startling oversight is compelling evidence that the priests of the latter part of the century, like the rising farming class that produced them, did not support the surviving Gaelic *literati*, thus denying them even a small high-status niche.

Why? Summary

There is no single explanation for the receding and the survival of Gaelic. It did not fall victim to some sort of linguistic Darwinism and the survival of the language fittest for the market. It was as good a language as English, to paraphrase the poet Michael Hartnett, to use when selling pigs.[134] That said, the remoteness of the subsistence and small farming zone insulated it from linguistic pressures and the later runaway population increase in that region masked the decline of Irish in the early decades before the Great Famine. By then there were more Irish speakers than there had ever been. They were, overwhelmingly, the poor. Elsewhere the key factor in explaining the survival of Gaelic was a stratum of resident gentry of native stock.

Popular religion

Doctrinal ignorance was the despair of energetic priests everywhere and the Irish were probably no worse off than the Catholic mainland; maybe better.[135] Papal envoy Massari was impressed to find 'among the mountains and barren places' of Kerry 'not a man or woman or any little boy who could not recite in Latin the Lord's Prayer, the Hail Mary, and the precepts of the holy church'.[136] Early seventeenth-century Irish Catholic bishops seem to have been most troubled, to judge from clerical condemnation, with (in descending order of frequency) unlawful marriage, adultery, theft, usury, enmity and disobedience to lawful authority.[137] While the Tridentine bishops and priests managed to stamp out the most florid of these excesses, they were less thoroughgoing than Protestant reformers in supplanting indigenous folk beliefs, however much they aspired to transform the religious sensibility and practice of their flocks. They could not, in particular, draw as sharp a line between sacramental and popular magic or between Christian and pagan.[138] They wanted to suppress outright certain practices that reeked too strongly of paganism like, for instance, the carving of female fertility symbols or 'Sheelanagigs' on buildings. Catholic reformers usually tried to harness other practices with pagan roots like 'pattern' days to holy wells while discouraging their carnivalesque aspects.[139] They also hoped to replace the social functions of sacraments like marriage or baptism with spiritual ones. Another recurring worry was that the mass, the sacraments, fasting, holy water and penance were popularly perceived as having folk-type magical qualities.

Irish Catholic religious practice grew as the outcome of a dialogue or compromise between laity and clergy. Consider, for example, funeral rites: Protestants were shocked to see the dead interred without what they saw as due solemnity, 'cast into the ground like dogs'.[140] Such abhorrence missed the point that the Irish customarily emphasised pre-burial rituals of separation, the wake, the removal from the house and the journey to the graveyard. A Protestant landowner writing of County Westmeath in 1682 conveys the lively juxtaposing of the sacred and the profane:

They set up commonly in a barn or large room, and are entertained with beer and tobacco; the lights are set up on a table over the dead; they spend most of the night in obscene stories and bawdy songs, until the hour comes for the exercise of their devotions; then the priest calls on them to fall to their prayers for the soul of the dead, which they perform by repetition of Aves and Paters on the beads, and close the whole with a de profundis, *and then immediately to the story or song again, till another hour of prayer comes; thus is the whole night spent until day, when the time of burial comes.*

Not just Protestants but most Catholic reformers doubtless found the wake distasteful or suspect. Yet the Catholic bishop had to recognise the peculiarly Irish conditions on which he could not impose his will, where his continental counterpart could. Bishop Mac Mahon of Clogher reveals this helplessness in apologising to Rome for allowing cousins to marry each other:

There is no use arguing with these people and no way of bringing compulsion to bear on them. In fact it is a crime in the eyes of civil law to denounce a marriage entered into before a Protestant minister. If, on the other hand, they are excluded from the Sacraments and plied with censures, there is the danger they might pervert. [141]

The fact that a bishop like Mac Mahon could not bring compulsion to bear may not have been a weakness after all. Irish Catholicism was untidy and folkish but deep-rooted. It may have drawn this strength from its enforced failure to fully conform to the continental Tridentine model.[142] If one takes, for instance, mass attendance as a basic requirement, the physical conditions varied enormously between the wealthier south-eastern part of the country and the poorer north-west, though that familiar gradient is also affected by the relative size of Protestant and Catholic communities.[143] Meath in 1731 was endowed with 103 mass houses and several 'huts and hovels'. Raphoe had two mass houses, a cabin and no fewer than twenty-three mass rocks and temporary shelters.

Conclusion

The ubiquity of the middleman, the persistence of communal farming practices and the poverty of a seemingly undifferentiated peasant mass all remind us that the half capitalist agrarian economy was stagnant in the opening decades of the eighteenth century. The stagnation may be judged from the fact that, leaving linen aside, there was little change in the overall volume of exports over the first forty years of the century. Partial, regional and class-specific diffusion of the potato was a response to increasing market demand for butter and notwithstanding that diffusion the under-employed, impoverished and vulnerable population was pressing against a Malthusian ceiling. The horrific and inevitable consequence of that vulnerability came when freakish weather hit the commercialised pastoral zone especially hard in 1740 and 1741. Commercialisation and the three agrarian zones also help to explain the regional incidence and tempo of other social changes such as linguistic transition. The market was the prime mover – when it moved.

Endnotes

1   Andrews 1976, p. 457.

2   Whelan 2000, p. 190; Mulloy 1983, i, p. 437.

3   Hore 1904, vi, pp. 502–3; Prendergast 1875, pp. 363–8.

4   Cullen 2003, p. 40.

5   Aalen 1997, p. 19.

6   Andrews 1976, p. 470; Smyth 1988, p. 77; Smyth 2006, p. 406; Whelan 1997, p. 185.

7   Whelan 2000, pp. 189–91.

8   Gleeson 1938, p. 100; Anon 1763, p. 9.

9   Dickson 2005, p. 219; Lecky 1892, p. 223.

10   Simms 1986, p. 309.

11   Cullen 1986a, p. 144.

12   Taaffe 1761, p. 11.

13   Philips 1770, pp. 178–9.

14   Crawford 1975, p. 13; Johnston 1970, pp. 105–6; Dickson 2005, pp. 124–5.

15   Philips 1770, p. 179.

16   Cullen 1981b, p. 93; Cullen 1986a, p. 161; Foster 1988, pp. 217–18.

17   Houston 1992, p. 28; Dunlop 1913, ii, p. 584.

18   MacLysaght 1982b, p. 55; Mc Manus 1939, p. 106; Bindon 1736, p. 11.

19 Houston 1992, p. 36; Wrigley and Schofield 1989, pp. 189–90.

20 Hore 1904, vi, pp. 307–8; Ford 2003, p. 129.

21 Dickson 1991, p. 225.

22 Galloway 1988, pp. 275–302; Kamen 1984, p. 29; Wrigley 1987, pp. 229, 282.

23 Wrigley 1987, p. 226.

24 Bacci 2000, pp. 102–3.

25 Wrigley 1987, p. 236.

26 Galloway 1988, pp. 281–2.

27 Clarkson 1999, pp. 32–3; Petty 1691, pp. 81–2; Murray 1912, p. 139.

28 Cullen 1981a, pp. 148, 164; Clarkson and Crawford 2002, p. 25.

29 Johnston 1974, p. 89.

30 Clarkson and Crawford 2002, p. 61.

31 'R.S.' 1662, p. 20; McNeill 1943, p. 265; *TCD Ms 815* (Queen's County) f. 370; *TCD Ms 812* (County Carlow) f. 24; *TCD Ms 811* (County Wicklow) ff. 63, 82; Hickson 1884, ii, p. 116.

32 Whelan 1997, p. 87.

33 Cullen 1981a, p. 145; Dickson 2005, pp. 237–8.

34 Danaher and Simms 1962, p. 15.

35 Jullien 1915, pp. 90, 93; Simms 1991, p. 17.

36 Hardiman 1846, pp. 58–9.

37 MacLysaght 1982b, pp. 19, 44, 917; Connolly 1995, p. 47.

38 Clarkson 1999, p. 35; Philips 1770, i, p. 178; Post 1985, p. 96.

39 Salaman 1949, p. 255.

40 Dickson et al. 1982, pp. 155, 159; Clarkson 1981, p. 17.

41 Post 1985, pp. 97, 219–20.

42 Macafee 2000, p. 436; Dickson 1997, pp. 20, 23.

43 Post 1985, pp. 230–3.

44 Dickson 1997, pp. 49, 62.

45 Macafee 2000, p. 436.

46 Crawford 1968, pp. 27, 31.

47 Bliss 1976, p. 556; Connell 1950, p. 122; Cullen 1981a, pp. 151, 152, 159, 164–5; Cullen 1981b, pp. 94, 96.

48 Cullen 1981b, p. 94; Clarkson 1981, p. 31.

49 Dickson 1991, p. 232.

50 Barnard 2003, pp. 30, 34, 38, 208, 249.

51 The quote is from Samuel Johnson and refers to the Scottish counterpart, the 'tacksman'; Greene 1984, p. 632; Dickson 1979, p. 163.

52 Cunningham 1996, pp. 183, 190; Molesworth 1723, p. 11.

53 De Vries 1976, pp. 68–9, 83.

54 Dickson 1979, pp. 165, 167.

55 Cited in Dickson 1987, pp. 111–12.

56 Cullen 1976, p. 401.

57 Dineen 1911, pp. 66–7.

58 MacLysaght 1982b, p. 45.

59 Dickson 1979, p. 162; Dickson 2005, pp. 197–9.

60 Danaher and Simms 1962, p. 17.

61 Whelan 1998, p. 135.

62 Bartlett 1982, p. 42; Legg 2005, pp. 479–85.

63 Estyn Evens 1957, p. 111.

64 Aalen 1997, p. 138.

65 Butlin 1976, p. 150.

66 Molesworth 1723, p. 11.

67 Duffy 1983, pp. 251, 254.

68 Vallancey 1770, pp. 116–17.

69 Whelan 1997, pp. 140–3; McCourt 1981, pp. 120–1; Dickson 2005, p. 241.

70 Falkiner 1904, p. 231.

71 O'Connor 1987, p. 32.

72 Whelan 1997, pp. 70, 184–6.

73 Whelan 1997, p. 79.

74 Horning 2001, p. 378.

75 Duffy 1983, pp. 245–56.

76 Falkiner 1904, p. 231; Horning 2001, p. 392; Andrews 2001, pp. 167, 277; Andrews 1976, p. 464.

77 Estyn Evans 1992, pp. 41, 63–4; Aalen 1997, pp. 145, 151.

78 Anon 1699, p. 5.

79 Estyn Evans 1957, p. 46.

80 Falkiner 1904, p. 262; Carey 1999b, pp. 48, 50.

81 Lombard 1632, p. 7; Maley 1997, pp. 35–7.

82 Aalen 1997, p. 23; Ellis 1995, p. 33.

83 Fitzgerald 1984, Map 3.

84 Smyth 2006, pp. 411–13.

85 Ó Cuív 1986, p. 387; Fitzgerald 1990, p. 63.

86 Williams 1994, pp. 447, 467; De Fréine 1965, pp. 125–9.

87 Williams 1998, p. 543.

88 Wall 1969, p. 82.

89 De Fréine 1965, p. 136.

90 Duffy 1977, p. 28; Wall 1969, p. 89; Hindley 1990, pp. 6, 8, 12.

91 Canny 2001, pp. 450–5; 'Deposition of Fergus Fullerton' *TCD Ms 838* (County Antrim) f. 56; 'Examination of James Slevin', 'Examination of William Behon', 'Examination of Patrick Murray', *TCD Ms 813* ff. 76, 81, 83; Lombard 1632, p. 7.

92 *CSPI* 1903, p. 185.

93 Cullen 1981a, pp. 88–90, 107.

94 De Fréine 1965, pp. 125–9, 139–41.

95 Gillespie 2006, p. 25; Connolly 1992, p. 23.

96 Smyth 2006, pp. 398–9; MacLysaght 1973, p. xi.

97 Gacquin 1996, pp. 15–16.

98 MacLysaght 1967, pp. 5–16; Legg 2005, pp. 275–86, 373–9, 479–85.

99 Barnard 2004b, p. 196.

100 Barnard 2005, p. 182.

101 Miller 1985, pp. 70–1, 78.

102 Smyth 2006, pp. 406, 413.

103 Bliss 1976, p. 556; Ó Ciosáin 2005, p. 141.

104 Cronin 1996, p. 92.

105 Burke 2004, pp. 71–2.

106 Ó Fiach 1969, pp. 106–7.

107 Smyth 2006, p. 414.

108 Barnard 2003, p. 290.

109 See Bardon 1996, p. 153.

110 Fitzgerald 1990, p. 2; Cullen 1981a, p. 107.

111 Cullen 1981a, p. 89; Ó Cúiv 1976, p. 529.

112 Kinsella and Ó Tuama 1981, pp. 90–1.

113 Barnard 2003, p. 297.

114 Prendergast 1875, pp. 264–5.

115 Glendenning 1999, p. 164.

116 Whelan 1998, pp. 121, 127–8, 136.

117 Simms 1956, pp. 87, 150–1.

118 Dickson 2005, p. 63.

119 Kinsella and Ó Tuama 1981, p. 199; Dickson 2005, p. 261; Cullen 1993, pp. 23–7.

120 Dickson 2005, p. 262.

121 Ó Cúiv 1986, p. 381.

122 Ó hAnnracháin 2001, pp. 249–65.

123 Ó Tuama 1965, p. 79; Dineen 1911, p. 113; Corkery 1979, p. 129; Ó Beolan 1979, pp. 79–80.

124 Ó Buachalla 1996, pp. 553–7.

125 Cullen 1969, p. 18; Dickson 2005, p. 263.

126 Ó Ciardha 2002, p. 224; Ó Buachalla 1992b.

127 Ó Buachalla 1996, pp. 553–7; Pittock 1998, p. 89.

128 Ó Ciardha 2002, p. 210.

129 Ó Ciardha 1998, p. 81; Ó Buachalla 1996, p. 606; Leerssen 1996a, p. 380.

130 Barnard 2004b, p. 184.

131 Williams 1999, p. 405.

132 Barnard 2004b, p. 107; Ó Cúiv 1986, p. 379.

133 Ó Cúiv 1986, p. 381.

134 Palmer 2001, p. 14.

135 Cited in Doyle 1991, p. 152.

136 Ó hAnnracháin 2002, pp. 63–6.

137 MacLysaght 1979, pp. 286–7.

138 Gillespie 1997, pp. 6–8.

139 Forrestal 1998, p. 65.

140 Tait 2002, p. 53.

141 Flanagan 1955, pp. 39–42.

142 Corish 1981, pp. 41–2; Bossy 1971, p. 70.

143 Smyth 2006, p. 372; Whelan 1988, pp. 257, 259; 'Report on the State of Popery' in *Archiv. Hib.*, iv, p. 173.

Wars and peace

Conclusion

When William King concluded grimly that '. . . either they or we must be ruined' he was referring specifically to the relationship of Catholics and Protestants under James II.[1] However, the mindset can be applied across the whole Stuart century since the default setting of that relationship was enmity, latent or manifest, and the black legend of 1641, in particular, fixed protestant responses to Catholics.[2]

So my organising grand narrative of the seventeenth century has been a story of 'conflict and dispossession' as a native *élite* was progressively displaced by a new colonial ruling class.[3] It was by no means that grindingly inevitable one-way progression after each of three wars that it seems in retrospect. Nor is a narrative of conflict necessarily confined to war and the three associated staples that dominate Irish historical writing: 'politics, land and religion'.[4] The struggle had cultural, religious and social reverberations. Even without such conflict trade would have grown and the mechanisms of trade, towns, markets, commercialised farming and so on would have sprung up. Associated changes would have followed in diet, settlement, class structure, perhaps even in language and religion. The abruptness with which Ireland was yanked from the medieval to the modern sets Ireland apart.

And it did stand apart from other societies in western Europe, whether one calls it a 'kingdom' or a 'colony'. The 'peculiar polity' that was the English state in Ireland did not have to rely on the support of indigenous landed society and was bent, whether by force, fraud, laws or constitution, on transforming the country into another England. The only question was whether that was best done by squeezing the raw material into English moulds or diluting that raw material with infusions from the larger island.[5] On the latter point: in crude terms the population of 'British' origin had grown from virtually nothing to around 27 per cent in the century before 1733. By any European standard this was a 'quite dramatic' change of ethnic composition.[6] Forget the modern piety that ethnic diversity is always good and more diversity even better. Such a dramatic change could only be associated with, and accomplished through, conflict. The century of conflict, in Macaulay's words, faded after Limerick into the 'ghastly tranquillity' of Irish 'exhaustion and despair'.[7] Could it have ended any other way?

Speculation about an independent Ireland may be foregone as anachronistic. Even at the peak of insurgent success in the winter of 1641–42, leaders like Sir Phelim O'Neill, while donning the mantle of Gaelic Irish kingship for lower-class political illiterates, still saw Ireland as part of three kingdoms.[8] The Confederate Catholic *régime* mounted, relative to available financial resources, a creditable effort at state-building: it raised taxes, called general assemblies, minted coins, levied armies and, in short, possessed all the attributes of contemporary statehood. Yet most Confederate Catholics never seriously considered life without the Stuarts, to the bewilderment and annoyance of foreign sympathisers like Scarampi. It was a fatally blinkered outlook because only if Charles had won a clean victory over his enemies with no peace deals and no promises would he have dared to offend English sensibilities and show favour to Irish Catholics. But such an unambiguous royalist victory would have been the longest shot of all.

Speculation about a client state is less nebulous. Had Kinsale ended in Mountjoy's defeat, a Spanish client state might well have emerged and faced down the rickety early Stuart state for many years. The outlook would have been rather less attractive for a French client state trying to hold out against repeated attacks by the much more formidable English state of William and Anne. 'He that will Old England win, must first with Ireland begin' – Englishmen saw Ireland as the open flank of their archipelago.[9] Strategically this was nonsense, but such persistent fears meant that Englishmen would fight far more strenuously to regain Ireland than a Spaniard or Frenchman would fight to hold it. English control of Ireland was inevitable.

The form of such control was not inevitable. A more benign mutual accommodation between Catholic and Protestant, for instance, could have emerged but for the persistence of acts of war in times of peace.

Why could not the English interest be maintained in Ireland without
extirpation, as well as the Spanish interest is preserved in Naples and
Flanders, the French in Roussillon and Alsace, the Swedish in Bremen
and Pomerania, the Danish interest in Norway . . . ?[10]

The question, posed by an Irishman in 1667, clearly implies that the
King of England should rule Ireland through a native *élite*, as kings ruled
subject territories elsewhere in Europe. He lays the blame for conflict on
plantation but ignores the blindingly obvious singularity: the Irish *élite*
and their monarch professed different religions. The Old English were
pathetically optimistic to expect their sovereign to recognise them as loyal
subjects even though they declined to recognise him as head of the Church.
James I was not content with half-loyalty; nor would any contemporary
monarch have been.

It is indeed likely that an accommodation of sorts could have emerged
if plantation had been permanently discontinued after Ulster and Gaelic
Leinster had been planted and Munster replanted. The Old English could
have accepted these as accomplished facts if they had got full benefit of
the Graces. With the New English no longer occupying Dublin Castle in
the 1630s, the unrelenting pressure for inquisition, confiscation and plantation should then have eased. A Wentworthless history would have stopped
the clock at around 1630 and left the office-holding New English in control of the Irish parliament and the Old English and Gaelic Irish together
(as they increasingly were) retaining the edge in land ownership and mercantile wealth. Charles I could then have played divide and rule, alter-
nately encouraging one or other community. While the dominant New
English faction led by Richard Boyle implacably pushed plantation, there
were enough New English pragmatists – Charles Wilmot and Francis
Annesley for instance – to cooperate with the Old English and mount joint
opposition in parliament. Such an alliance actually emerged in the parliament of 1640–41. In time the edges of the Protestant–Catholic dichotomy
might have blurred. But Wentworth was bent on a programme of wholesale plantation and enjoyed his master's backing.[11] Thereby Charles let slip
a real chance of a more peaceful and, for him, safer Ireland.

Ormond dominated the forty years after the Restoration. He has been
fortunate in his biographers and he appears as a decent man and a unifying
figure, in sharp contrast to Wentworth, in whose shade Protestant and
Catholic might have reached an accommodation. Ormond was no bigot;
defending his partiality to Catholic kinsmen he opined that '. . . difference
in opinion concerning matters of religion dissolves not the obligations of

nature'.[12] His calm and steady handling of the Popish Plot likely stopped a re-run of the crisis that convulsed three kingdoms in the winter of 1641–42. Precisely because Ormond was so respected by many Irish Catholics, he was a more dangerous enemy to that community than Cork could ever have been. He repudiated his treaty of 1649 and could never support a general reversal of the Cromwellian land settlement. Catholics (by now thoroughly disenchanted with Ormond) would settle for nothing less, as was apparent in the Jacobite parliament of 1689.

The subsequent victory of Protestant over Catholic was unexpectedly complete because of contingent factors. The Revolution knitted together English government and the Protestant interest in Ireland more closely than ever before. King William's wars made the Irish parliament, a Protestant parliament, the indispensable institution of government. The members of the House of Commons tightened control of the purse strings and manipulated heads of bill procedure to, in effect, legislate. What Protestant Ireland wanted badly enough, it got.

Endnotes

1 King 1692, p. 270.

2 Lietchley 1987, pp. 13–14.

3 Barnard 1999, p. 207; Brady and Ohlmeyer 2005, p. 6.

4 Barnard 1999, p. 207.

5 Armstrong 2005, pp. 3–4.

6 Cullen 1981b, p. 87.

7 Corish 1981, p. 78.

8 For example: *TCD Ms 833* (County Cavan) 'Deposition of Elizabeth Gough' f. 118.

9 Anon 1690, p. 3; Ó hAnnracháin 2001, p. 26.

10 *CSPI* 1908, p. 553.

11 Canny 2001, p. 281.

12 Cited in Sergeant 1913, p. 122.

Bibliography

Primary sources

Airy, O. (ed.) (1890) *Essex Papers i 1672–1679* (London)

Anon (1610) *Conditions to be Observed by the British Undertakers of the Escheated Lands in Ulster* (London)

Anon (1641) *Last Newes From Ireland* (London)

Anon (1641) *A Bloody Battell: Or the Rebels Overthrow, and Protestants Victorie* (London)

Anon (1642) *A Declaration of the Commons Assembled in Parliament . . . Concerning the Rise and Progress of the Rebellion in Ireland* (London)

Anon (1643) *Another Extract of Several Letters from Ireland . . .* (London)

Anon (1646) *Good News from Ireland Being an exact Relation of the late good successe at Sliggo* (London)

Anon (1647) *A Perfect Narrative of the Battle of Knocknones* (London)

Anon (1679) *An account of the bloody massacre in Ireland: acted by the instigation of the Jesuits, Priests, and Friars* (London)

Anon (1688) *A Vindication of the Present Government of Ireland under his excellency Richard, earl of Tirconnel* (London)

Anon (1690) *A Letter from Monsieur Tyrconnel . . . to the Late Queen* (London)

Anon (1692) *A Diary of the Siege and Surrender of Lymerick with the Articles at Large, both Civil and Military* (London)

Anon (1699) *A Trip to Ireland Being a Description of the Country, People and Manners* (London)

Anon (1730) *The Present State of Ireland Consider'd* (Dublin)

Anon (1753) *The Journals of the House of Commons of the Kingdom of Ireland* (Dublin) vol. 2

Anon (ed.) (1763) The State Letters of Henry Earl of Clarendon, ii (2 vols, Oxford)

Anon (1784) *The Parliamentary Register or History of the Proceedings and Debates of the House of Commons of Ireland 1781–1782* (Dublin)

Anon (ed.) (1916) 'Miscellanea Vaticano-Hibernica' *Archiv. Hib.* v.

Anon (ed.) (1973) Edmund Tighe 'Report on Visitation of the clergy of Elphin' *Collect. Hib.* no. 16

Berwick, James Fitz James Duke of (1780) *Mémoires* (2 vols: Paris)

Bindon, S.H. (ed.) (1846) *The Historical Works of Nicholas French* (2 vols, Dublin)

Bindon, D. (1731) *Some Thoughts on the Woollen Manufactures of England* (London)

—— (1736) *An Abstract of the number of protestant and popish families in the several counties and provinces of Ireland* (Dublin)

Boate, G. (1652) *Ireland's Naturall History* (London)

Borlase, E. (1680) *History of the Execrable Irish Rebellion* (London)

Boyle, R. (1662) *An Answer to a Scandalous Letter* (Dublin)

Bray, W. (ed.) (1907) *The Diary of John Evelyn* (London)

British Library. Add. Ms 4819, ff. 326–7: A list of murders committed by Ulster Scots on Irishmen c. 1641

Browne, P. (ed.) (1962) 'Brevis Relatio' in *Anal. Hib.* xxv

(1874a) *Calendar of State Papers Ireland (James I) 1606–08*

(1874b) *Calendar of State Papers Ireland (James I) 1608–1610*

(1877) *Calendar of State Papers Ireland (James I) 1611–1614*

(1880) *Calendar of State Papers Ireland (James I) 1615–1625*

(1901) *Calendar of State Papers Ireland (Charles I) 1634–1647*

(1903) *Calendar of State Papers Ireland (Charles I) 1647–1660*

(1905) *Calendar of State Papers Ireland (Charles II) 1660–1662*

(1907) *Calendar of State Papers Ireland (Charles II) 1663–1665*

(1908) *Calendar of State Papers Ireland (Charles II) 1666–1669*

Carpenter, A. (1998) *Verse in English from Eighteenth-Century Ireland* (Cork)

Carte Ms. 48, 215. Bodleian Library, Oxford

Carte Ms. 512. Bodleian Library, Oxford

Carte Ms. 128. Bodleian Library, Oxford

Clarendon, E. Hyde, 1st Earl of (1729) *Continuation of the Life of Edward Earl of Clarendon*, iii (3 vols, Dublin)

Clarke, A. (ed.) (1970) 'Discourse Between Two Councillors', *Anal. Hib.* no. 26

Clarke, Rev. J.S. (1816) *The Life of James the Second*, ii (2 vols, London)

Claudianus, A. (1718) *Mavor Irlandicus sive Historia de bello Hibernico* (Copenhagen)

Cox, T.E. (ed.) (1843) *Works of Thomas Cranmer* (Cambridge)

Cox, R. (1689–91) *Hibernia Anglicana*, i (2 vols, London)

Creichtoun, G. (1900) 'A Faithful Account by G. Creichtoun chaplain to his Lordship's Regiment' in P.H. Hore, *History of the Town and County of Wexford: Old and New Ross* (London)

Crist, T. (1974) *Charles II to Lord Taaffe: Letters in Exile* (Cambridge)

Cuffe, M. (ed.) (1841) 'The siege of Ballyally castle in the county of Clare' in T.C. Croker (ed.) *Narratives illustrative of the contests in Ireland* (London)

Danaher, K. and Simms, J.G. (1962) *The Danish Force in Ireland 1690–1691* (Dublin)

Davies, J. (1612) *A Discoverie of the True Causes why Ireland was never entirely Subdued, nor brought under Obedience of the Crowne of England, until the beginning of his Majesties happie Raigne* (London)

Day, A. (ed.) (1991) *Letters from Georgian Ireland* (Belfast)

Deane, S. (ed.) (1991) *The Field Day Anthology of Irish Writing*, i (Derry)

Dunlop, R. (1913) *Ireland under the commonwealth: being a selection of documents relating to the Government of Ireland* (2 vols, Manchester)

Edwards, D. (ed.) (1998) 'The Ship's Journal of Captain Thomas Powell', *Anal. Hib.* no. 37

Falkiner, L.C. (ed.) (1904) Luke Gernon 'A Discourse of Ireland' (1620) and Fynes Moryson 'The Commonwealth of Ireland' in *Illustrations of Irish History and Topography* (London)

Fenning, H. (ed.) (1974) 'John Kent's Report on the State of the Irish Mission, 1742', *Archiv. Hib.* xxviii

—— (ed.) (1977) 'Two Diocesan Reports Elphin (1753) and Killaloe (1792)', *Archiv. Hib.* xxx

Finch, Captain Henry (1643) 'Letter from London-derry', *Another Extract of Several Letters from Ireland* (London)

Fitzpatrick, T. (1912) *Waterford during the Civil War* (Waterford)

Flanagan, Rev. P.J. (ed.) (1955) Report by Hugh McMahon, Catholic Bishop of Clogher (1714) in *Clogher Record*

Giblin, C. (ed.) (1956) *Liber Lovaniensis A Collection of Irish Franciscan Documents 1629–1717* (Dublin)

Gilbert, J.T. (ed.) (1879) *A Contemporary History of Affairs in Ireland* (3 vols, Dublin)

—— (1882–91) *History of the Irish Confederation and the War in Ireland 1641–1649* (7 vols, Dublin)

—— (1892) *A Jacobite Narrative of the War in Ireland 1688–1691* (Dublin)

Gookin, V. (1655) *The Great Case of Transplantation in Ireland Discussed* (Dublin)

Greene, D. (ed.) (1984) *Samuel Johnson: A Critical Edition of the Major Works* (Oxford)

G.S. (1641) *A briefe declaration of the barbarous and inhumane dealings of the northerne Irish rebels* (London)

Hardiman, J. (ed.) (1846) *A Chorographical Description of West or h-Iar Connaught written AD 1684* (Dublin)

Harris, W. (ed.) (1747) 'Pynnar's Survey of Ulster' in *Hibernica or Some Antient Pieces relating to Ireland* (1st edn) (Dublin)

Haukes, E. (1661) *Hecatonstichon, or, An Elegy upon the much deplored death and solemn funeral of the Right Honourable Charles Earl of Mountrath* (London)

Hempton, J. (ed.) (1861) *A True Account of the Siege of Londonderry by the Rev Mr. George Walker* (Derry)

HLJ vol. 13 (6 November 1680)

Hickson, M. (ed.) (1884) *Ireland in the Seventeenth Century* (2 vols, London)

Hinton, E. (1935) *Ireland through Tudor Eyes* (Philadelphia)

HMC (1874) *Fourth Report of the Royal Commission* on *Historical Manuscripts* (London)

HMC (1899) *Report on the Leyborne-Poham Ms* (London)

HMC (1905) *Egmont Ms* i (2 vols, London)

HMC (1903) *Calendar of Ms of the Marquess of Ormond at Kilkenny* New Series ii (London)

HMC (1906) *Calendar of Ms of the Marquess of Ormond at Kilkenny* New Series iv (London)

Hogan, E. (ed.) (1873) *The History of the Warr of Ireland from 1641 to 1653 by a British Officer of the Regiment of Sir John Clotworthy* (Dublin)

—— (ed.) (1881) H. Fitzsimon, *Words of Comfort to Persecuted Catholics written in exile, anno 1607* (Dublin)

—— and Plunkett, G. (eds) (1894) *The Jacobite War in Ireland 1688–1691* (Dublin)

Hogan, J. (ed.) (1934) *Négociations de M. le Comte D'Avaux en Irlande* (Dublin)

—— (1936) *Letters and Papers relating to the Irish Rebellion between 1642–46* (Dublin)

Howell, J. (1644) *Mercurius Hibernicus* (Bristol)

Hutton, A. (ed.) (1873) *The Embassy in Ireland of Rinuccini* (Dublin)

Japikse, N. (1937) *Correspondentie van Willem III en van Hans Willem Bentinck* ('S-Gravenhage)

Jennings, B. (ed.) (1964) *Wild Geese in Spanish Flanders 1582–1700. Documents relating to Irish regiments from the Archives Generales du Royaume and other Sources* (Dublin)

Jones, H. (1642) *A Remonstrance of Divers Remarkable Passages concerning the Church and Kingdom of Ireland* (London)

Jullien, A. (ed.) (1915) *Soldats Suisses au Service Etranger* (Geneva)

Kavanagh, S. (ed.) (1932–49) in O'Ferrall and O'Connell *Commentarius Rinuccinianus* (6 vols, Dublin)

Kazner, J.F.A. (1789) *Lebən Friedrichs von Schonburg* (2 vols, Mannheim)

Keaveney, A. and Madden, J.A. (eds) (1992) Sir William Herbert *Croftus sive de Hibernia liber* (Dublin)

Kelly, M. (ed.) (1848) *Cambrensis Eversus* (3 vols, Dublin)

King, W. (1692) *State of the Protestants of Ireland* (London)

Kinsella, T. and Ó Tuama, S. (1981) *An Duanaire: Poems of the Dispossessed* (Mountrath)

Knowler, W. (ed.) (1799) *Earl of Strafford's Letters and Dispatches* (2 vols, London)

La Gouz, F. (1653) *Les Voyages et Observations de Monsieur de la Boullay la Gouz* (Paris)

Langford, P. (ed.) (1997) *The writings and speeches of Edmund Burke* vol. i (Oxford)

Latimer, W.T. (ed.) (1896) *A Farther Impartial Account of the Actions of the Inniskilling-Men* (Belfast)

Lawrence, R. (1649) *The Taking of Wexford* (London)

—— (1655) *The Interest of England in the Irish Transplantation* (London)

—— (1656) *England's Great Interest in the Well Planting of Ireland with English people Discussed* (Dublin)

—— (1682) *The Interest of Ireland in its Trade and Wealth Stated* (London)

Legg, Marie-Louise (ed.) (2005) *The Census of Elphin* (Dublin)

Leyburn, G. (1722) *Memoirs of George Leyburn being a journal of his agency for Prince Charles in Ireland in 1647* (London)

Lombard, P. (1632) *De Regno Hiberniae, sanctorum insula, Commentarius* (Louvain)

Ludlow, E. (1698) *Memoirs* (2 vols, Vivay)

Lynch, J. (1660) *Alithinologia* (St Omer)

—— (1662) *Cambrensis Eversus* (St Omer)

—— (1667) *Supplementium Alithinologia . . .* (St Omer?)

Lynch, P. (ed.) (1815) *The Earl of Castlehaven's Memoirs . . .* (Dublin)

Lytton Sells, A. (ed.) (1962) *The Memoirs of James II His Campaigns as Duke of York 1652–1660* (London)

MacCurtin, H. (1728) *The Elements of the Irish Language, Gramatically Explained in English* (Louvain)

Mac Erelean, Rev. J.C. (1917) *Duanaire Dháibhidh Uí Bhruadair* (London)

MacGeoghegan, J. Abbé (1758) *Histoire de l'Irlande* (Paris)

MacLysaght, E. (ed.) (1951) 'The Arthur Manuscript' in *N. Munster Antiq. Jn.* vi

—— (ed.) (1967) 'Seventeenth-century Hearth Money Rolls with full transcripts relating to County Sligo' in *Anal. Hib.* no. 24

—— (ed.) (1982a) *Letters From Ireland 1698* (Dublin)

—— (ed.) (1982b) John Dunton *Teague Land or A Merry Ramble to the Wild Irish* (Dublin)

Mc Manus, M.J. (1939) *Irish Cavalcade 1500–1850* (London)

McNeill, C. (ed.) (1943) *The Tanner Letters* (Dublin)

McNeill, C. and Otway-Ruthven, A.J. (eds) (1960) *Dowdall Deeds* (Dublin)

Maxwell, C. (ed.) (1923) *Irish History from Contemporary Sources 1509–1610* (London)

Millet, B. (ed.) (1966) 'Nunziatura di Fiandra' *Collect. Hib.* no. 9

—— (1969a) 'Nunziatura di Fiandra' *Collect. Hib.* no. 12

—— (1969b) 'Some Eighteenth-Century Broadsides' in *Collect. Hib.* no. 12

—— (1970) 'Nunziatura di Fiandra' in *Collect. Hib.* no. 13

Molesworth, Robert Viscount (1723) *Some Considerations for the promoting of Agriculture and Employing the Poor* (Dublin)

Molyneux, W. (1698) *The Case of Ireland Stated* (Dublin)

Moran, P.F. (ed.) (1874) *Spicilegium Ossoriensie Being a Collection of Original Letters and Papers Illustrative of the history of the Irish Church* (Dublin)

—— (ed.) (1884) *The Analecta of David Rothe Bishop of Ossory* (Dublin)

Morton, G. (ed.) (1971) *Elizabethan Ireland* (London)

Mulloy, S. (ed.) (1983) Franco-Irish Correspondence December 1688–February 1692 (3 vols, Dublin)

Murray, Rev. R. (ed.) (1912) *The Journal of John Stevens Containing a Brief Account of the War in Ireland 1689–1691* (Oxford)

Myers, J.P. (ed.) (1969) Sir John Davies, *A discovery of the true causes why Ireland was never entirely subdued [and] brought under obedience of the crown of England until the beginning of his Majesty's happy reign* (Washington)

Nicholls, K. (ed.) (1990) *Annals of the Kingdom of Ireland*, vi (7 vols, Dublin, 1990)

NLI Ms No. 345 'An Account of the War in Ireland since 1641'

O'Byrne, E. (ed.) (1981) *The Convert Rolls* (Dublin)

Ó Ciardha, É. and Ohlmeyer, J. (eds) (1998) *The Irish Statute Staple Books 1596–1687* (Dublin)

Ó Donnchadha, T. (ed.) (1916) *Saothar Filidheadhachta an Athar Pádraigín Haicéad* (Dublin)

—— (ed.) (1931) 'Cín Lae Ó Mealláin' *Anal Hib* no. 3 (Dublin) pp. 1–61

O'Donovan, J. (ed.) (1856) *Annals of the Kingdom of Ireland*, v (Dublin)

O'Hara, C. 'Description of County Sligo', MS20.397

Oldmixon, J. (1716) *Memoirs of Ireland* (London)

O'Rahilly, C. (1952) (ed.) *Five Seventeenth Century Political Poems* (Dublin)

Orrery, Roger Boyle, Earl of (1662) *The Irish colours displayed in a reply of an English Protestant to a late letter of an Irish Roman Catholique* (London)

—— (1662) *An Answer to A Scandalous Letter lately written and subscribed by Peter Walsh* (Dublin)

Ó Tuama, S. and Kinsella, T. (1994) *An Duanaire 1600–1900 Poems of the Dispossessed* (Dublin)

Parker, R. (1757) *Memoirs of the Most Remarkable Military Transactions* (London)

Pender, S. (1939) *Census of Ireland 1659* (Dublin)

Petty, W. (1691) *The Political Anatomy of Ireland* (London)

Philips, A. (ed.) (1770) *Letters written by his Excellency Hugh Boulter* (2 vols, Dublin)

Piers, H. (1682) *A Description of the County of Westmeath* (London)

Pringle, J. (1764) *Observations on the Diseases of the Army* (London)

Public Record Office State Papers 63/208

Reilly, Hugh (1742) *The Impartial History of Ireland* (2nd edn) (London)

Renwick, W.L. (ed.) (1970) Edmund Spenser, *A View of the present state of Ireland* (Oxford)

Rhodes, N. et al. (eds) (2003) *King James VI and I: Selected Writings* (Ashgate)

Richard, M. (ed.) (1968) Issac Dumont de Bostaquet *Mémoires D'Issac Dumont de Bostaquet* (Paris)

Richardson, J. (1712) *A Short History of the Attempts that have been made to convert the Popish Natives of Ireland to the Established Religion* (Dublin)

Rolleston, T.W. (ed.) (n.d.) *Thomas Davis Selections from his Prose and Poetry* (Dublin)

'R.S' (1662) *A Collection of Some of the Murthers and Massacres committed on the Irish in Ireland* (London)

Rushworth, J. (ed.) (1708) *Historical Collections* (6 vols, London)

Samson, T. (1680) *A Narrative of the Late Popish Plot in Ireland* (London)

Scott, T. (1925) (ed.) *The Prose works of Jonathan Swift D.D.*, vii (London)

Shirley, E.P. (ed.) (1856–57) 'Extracts from the Journal of Thomas Dineley' in *Royal Society of Antiquaries of Ireland Journal*, iv

Simington, R.C. (1936) *Civil Survey 1654–1656* vol. 9, Co. Wexford (Dublin)

—— (1938) *Civil Survey 1654–56* vol. 4, Co. Limerick (Dublin)

—— (1970) *The Transplantation to Connacht, 1654–58* (Dublin)

Stackhouse, T. (ed.) (1906) *An Abridgement of Bishop Burnet's History of His Own Times* (London)

Story, G. (1691) *A True and Impartial History of the Most Material Occurrences* (London)

—— (1693) *A Continuation of the Impartial History of the Wars of Ireland* (London)

Sutton, D.F. (ed.) (2000) William Camden, *Annales Rerum Gestarum Angliae et Hibernia Regnante Elizabetha* (1615 and 1625)

Swift, J. (ed.) (1701) 'An Essay upon the present State and Settlement of Ireland' in *Select Letters . . . All Written by Sir William Temple*, iii (3 vols, London)

Taaffe, Nicholas Viscount (1761) *Observations on Affairs in Ireland* (London)

TCD Ms 747 f. 164 v. (1609) 'A Projecte for the devision and plantacon of the Escheated Landes'

TCD Ms 811 (Depositions, Co. Wicklow)

TCD Ms 812 (Depositions, Co. Carlow)

TCD Ms 813 (Depositions, Co. Kildare)

TCD Ms 814 (Depositions, King's County)

TCD Ms 815 (Depositions, Queen's County)

TCD Ms 816 (Depositions, Co. Meath)

TCD Ms 817 (Depositions, Co. Westmeath & Co. Longford)

TCD Ms 825 (Depositions, Co. Cork)

TCD Ms 826 (Depositions, Co. Cork)

TCD Ms 829 (Depositions, Co. Limerick)

TCD Ms 830 (Depositions, Co. Roscommon)

TCD Ms 831 (Depositions, Co. Mayo & Co. Leitrim)

TCD Ms 832 (Depositions, Co. Cavan)

TCD Ms 833 (Depositions, Co. Cavan)

TCD Ms 834 (Depositions, Co. Louth & Co. Monaghan)

TCD Ms 836 (Depositions, Co. Armagh)

TCD Ms 837 (Depositions, Co. Down)

TCD Ms 838 (Depositions, Co. Antrim)

TCD Ms 839 (Depositions, Co. Tyrone, Londonderry & Donegal)

Temple, Sir John (1646) *The Irish Rebellion* (Dublin)

Temple, Sir William (1680) *Miscellanea* (London)

Tindal, N. (1751) *Continuation of the History of England by M. Rapin de Thoyras*, ii (4 vols, London)

Turner, J. (1683) *Pallas Armata Military Essayes on the Art of War* (London)

Ua Duinnín, P. (ed.) (1934) *Dánta Phiarais Feiritéir* (Dublin)

Vallancey, C. (1770) *Collectanea de rebus Hibernicis*, i (Dublin)

Walsh, P. (1674) *The History and Vindication of the Loyal Formulary or Irish Remonstrance* (London)

—— (ed.) (1916) *The Flight of the Earls by Tadhg Ó Cianáin* (Dublin)

Ware, J. (ed.) (1633) Edmund Spenser *A View of the State of Ireland* (Dublin)

Waring, T. (1650) *A Brief Narration of the Plotting, Beginning and Carrying on of that Execrable Rebellion and Butchery in Ireland* (London)

Secondary sources

Aalen, F.H.A. (1997) 'The Irish Rural Landscape: synthesis of habitat and history'; 'Fields'; 'Houses and agricultural buildings' in F.H.A. Aalen, K. Whelan and M. Stout (eds) *Atlas of the Irish Rural Landscape* (Cork)

Adamson, J. (1995) 'Strafford's Ghost: The British Context of Viscount Lisle's Lieutenancy of Ireland' in J. Ohlmeyer (ed.) *Ireland from Independence to Occupation 1641–1660* (Cambridge)

—— (1997) (ed.) 'England without Cromwell' in N. Ferguson, *Virtual History* (London)

Andrews, J.H. (1976) 'Land and People c. 1685' in T.W. Moody, F.X. Martin and F.J. Byrne (eds) *A New History of Ireland III Early Modern Ireland 1534–1691* (Oxford)

—— (1997) *Shapes of Ireland Maps and their Makers 1564–1839* (Dublin)

—— (2000) 'Plantation Ireland: A Review of Settlement History' in T. Barry (ed.) *A History of Settlement in Ireland* (London)

—— (2001) 'The Mapping of Ireland's Cultural Landscape, 1550–1630' in P. Duffy, D. Edwards and E. Fitzpatrick (eds) *Gaelic Ireland: Land Lordship and Settlement c. 1250–c. 1650* (Dublin)

Anon (1741) *The Life of Oliver Cromwell* (4th edn, London)

Aringhi, P. (1774) *Memorie Istoriche della vita del venerabile servo di Dio, Piero Francesco Scarampi* (Rome)

Armitage, D. et al. (2000) *The Ideological Origins of the British Empire* (Cambridge)

Armstrong, R. (2001) 'Ormond, the Confederate peace talks and Protestant royalism' in Micheál Ó Siochrú (ed.) *Kingdoms in Crisis Ireland in the 1640s* (Dublin)

—— (2005) *Protestant War: The British of Ireland and the Wars of the Three Kingdoms* (Manchester)

Arnold, L.J. (1993) *The Restoration Land Settlement in County Dublin 1660–1688* (Dublin)

Aylmer, G.E. (2000) 'The First Duke of Ormond as Patron and Administrator' in T. Barnard and J. Fenlon (eds) *The Dukes of Ormonde, 1610–1745* (Woodbridge)

Bacci, L. (2000) *The Population of Europe* (Oxford: Blackwell)

Bagwell, R. (1916) *Ireland under the Stuarts and during the Interregnum,* iii (London)

Barber, S. (2001) 'The Formation of Cultural Attitudes: the example of the three kingdoms in the 1650s' in A. Macinnes and J. Ohlmeyer (eds.) *The Stuart Kingdoms in the Seventeenth-Century* (Dublin)

Bardon, J. (1996) *A Shorter Illustrated History of Ulster* (Belfast)

Barnard, T.C. (1973) 'Planters and Policies in Cromwellian Ireland' in *Past and Present* no. 61

—— (1975) *Cromwellian Ireland: English government and reform in Ireland 1649–1660* (Oxford)

—— (1990) 'Crisis of Identity among Irish Protestants, 1641–1685' in *Past and Present*, vol. 127

—— (1991) 'The Uses of 23 October 1641 and Irish Protestant celebrations' *English Historical Review*

—— (1995) 'The Protestant Interest, 1641–1660' and 'Conclusion. Settling and Unsettling Ireland: The Cromwellian and Williamite Revolutions' in J. Ohlmeyer (ed.) *From Independence to Occupation* (Cambridge)

—— (1997) '1641: A Bibliographical Essay' in B. MacCuarta (ed.) *Ulster 1641 Aspects of the Rising* (Belfast)

—— (1999) 'British History and Irish History' in G. Burgess (ed.) *The New British History Founding a Modern State 1603–1715* (London and New York)

—— (2004a) *The Kingdom of Ireland, 1641–1760* (Basingstoke)

—— (2004b) *Irish Protestant ascents and descents 1641–1770* (Dublin)

—— (2004c) *Making the Grand Figure: Lives and Possessions in Ireland 1641–1770* (Yale)

Bartlett, T. (1982) 'The O'Haras of Annaghmore c. 1600–c. 1800: Survival and Revival' in *Ir. Econ. & Soc. Hist.*, ix

—— (1992) *The Fall and Rise of the Irish Nation* (Dublin)

—— (2003) *'The Academy of Warre' Military Affairs in Ireland 1600 to 1800* (Dublin)

—— (2004) 'Ireland, Empire and Union, 1690–1801' in Kevin Kenny (ed.) *Ireland and the British Empire* (Oxford)

Baxter, S.B. (1966) *William III* (London)

Béaslaí, P. (n.d) *Éigse Nua-Ghaedhilge* (Dublin)

Beckett, J.C. (1959) 'The Confederation of Kilkenny Reviewed' *Historical Studies* no. 2

—— (1969) *The Making of Modern Ireland 1603–1923* (London)

—— (1985) *Swift and Ireland* (Belfast)

—— (1990) *The Cavalier Duke: a life of James Butler, 1st Duke of Ormond* (Belfast)

Begley, J. (1927) *The Diocese of Limerick in the 16th and 17th Centuries* (Limerick)

Beirne, F. (2000) *The Diocese of Elphin People, Places and Pilgrimage* (Dublin)

Benedictow, O.J. (1987) 'Morbidity in Historical Plague Epidemics' *Population Studies* vol. 41 no. 3

Bennett, M. (1997) *The Civil Wars in Britain and Ireland 1638–51* (Cambridge, Mass.)

—— (2000) *The Civil Wars Experienced Britain and Ireland, 1638–1661* (London & New York)

Berleth, R. (1978) *The Twilight Lords: An Irish Chronicle* (New York)

Berresford-Ellis, P. (1975) *Hell or Connaught! The Cromwellian Colonisation of Ireland 1652–1660* (London)

—— (1976) *The Boyne Water: The Battle of the Boyne, 1690* (Belfast)

Blaney, R. (1996) *Presbyterians and the Irish Language* (Belfast)

Bliss, A. (1976) 'The English Language in early Modern Ireland' *A New History of Ireland III Early Modern Ireland 1534–1691* (Oxford)

Bossy, J. (1971) 'The Counter-Reformation and the People of Catholic Ireland 1596–1641' in T.D. Williams (ed.) *Historical Studies* VI

Bottigheimer, K.S. (1971) *English Money and Irish land: The 'Adventurers' in the Cromwellian Settlement of Ireland* (Oxford)

—— (1976) 'Kingdom and Colony: Ireland in the Westward Enterprise 1536–1660' in K.R Andrews, N.P. Canny and P. Hair (eds) *The Westward Enterprise English Activities in Ireland, The Atlantic and America, 1480–1650* (Liverpool)

—— (1985) 'The failure of the reformation in Ireland: *une question bien posée*' in *Jn Ecc. Hist.*, xxxvi

Bradshaw, B. (1975) 'Fr. Wolfe's Description of Limerick City, 1574' *N. Munster Antiq. Jn.* xvii.

—— (1978a) 'Sword, word, and strategy in the Reformation in Ireland' in *Historical Journal*, xxi

—— (1978b) 'Native reaction to the westward enterprise: a case study in Gaelic ideology' in K. Andrews et al. (eds) *The Westward enterprise* (Liverpool)

—— (1994) 'Nationalism and Historical Scholarship in Modern Ireland' in C. Brady (ed.) *Interpreting Irish History: The Debate on Historical Revisionism* (Dublin)

Brady, C. (1994) *The Chief Governors: the rise and fall of reform government in Tudor Ireland 1536–1588* (Cambridge)

—— (1995) 'Comparable histories?: Tudor reform in Wales and Ireland' in S. Ellis and S. Barber (eds) *Conquest & Union Fashioning a British State 1485–1725* (London)

—— (1996) *Life and Times of Shane O'Neill* (Dundalk)

—— and Ohlmeyer, J. (2005) 'Making Good, New Perspectives on the English in Early Modern Ireland' in ibid (eds) *British Interventions in Early Modern Ireland* (Cambridge)

Brady, D. (ed.) (2003) Eustace Budgell *Memoirs of the lives and characters of the Illustrious family of the Boyles* (Waterford)

Brady, J. and Corish, P.J. (1971) *The Church Under the Penal Code* (Dublin)

Brennan, M. (2003) 'Conformity in Early Modern Kilkenny' in V. Carey and U. Lotz-Heumann (eds) *Taking Sides? Colonial and Confessional Mentalités in Early Modern Ireland* (Dublin)

Briggs, R. (1998) *Early Modern France 1560–1715* (Oxford)

Brunicardi, N. (2000) 'The Battle of Manning Ford, 4 June 1643' *Irish Sword* no. 87

Burghclere, Winifred, Baroness (1912) *The Life of James First Duke of Ormonde 1610–1688* (2 vols, London)

Burke, J. (1990) 'The New Model Army and the Problems of Siege Warfare, 1648–51' in *I.H.S.* no. 105, pp. 1–29

—— (2001) 'Siege Warfare in Seventeenth-Century Ireland' in P. Lenihan (ed.) *Conquest and Resistance War in Seventeenth-Century Ireland* (Brill)

Burke, P. (2004) *Languages and Communities in Early Modern Europe* (Cambridge)

Burke, W. (1907) *History of Clonmel* (Waterford)

—— (1914) *The Irish Priests in the Penal Times 1660–1760* (Waterford)

Burne, A. and Young, P. (1959) *The Great Civil War* (London)

Burns, R.E. (1989) *Irish parliamentary Politics in the Eighteenth-Century* i (2 vols, Washington)

Butler, W.T.F. (1918) *Confiscation in Irish History* (Dublin)

Butlin, R.A. (1976) 'Land and People, c. 1600' in *A New History of Ireland III Early Modern Ireland 1534–1691* (Oxford)

Byrne, M.J. (ed.) Philip O'Sullivan Bear *Compendium of the History of Catholic Ireland* (Dublin)

Caball, M. (1998a) 'Faith, culture and sovereignty: Irish nationality and its development, 1558–1625' in B. Bradshaw and P. Roberts (eds) *British Consciousness and Identity: The Making of Britain 1533–1707* (Cambridge)

—— (1998b) *Poetry and Politics Reaction and Continuity in Irish Poetry, 1558–1625* (Cork)

—— (1999) 'Innovation and Tradition: Irish Gaelic Responses to Early Modern Conquest and Colonization', in H. Morgan (ed.) *Political Ideology in Ireland* (Dublin)

Canny, N.P. (1970) 'The Treaty of Mellifont and the Re-Organisation of Ulster, 1603' *Irish Sword* vol. IX no. 37

—— (1971) 'The Flight of the Earls 1607' *I.H.S.* xvii

—— (1976) *The Elizabethan Conquest of Ireland: a pattern established, 1564–76* (Hassocks)

—— (1977) 'Early Modern Ireland: an Appraisal Appraised' in *Ir. Econ. & Soc. Hist.* iv

—— (1979) 'Why the Reformation Failed in Ireland: Une Question Mal Posée' *Journal of Ecclesiastical History* vol. 30 no. 4

—— (1982a) 'The formation of the Irish mind: religion, politics and Gaelic Irish literature 1580–1750 *Past & Present* no. 95

—— (1982b) *The upstart earl, a study of the social and mental world of Richard Boyle, first earl of Cork, 1566–1643* (Cambridge)

—— (1985) 'Migration and Opportunity: Britain, Ireland and the New World' *Ir. Econ. & Soc. Hist.* xii

—— (1987) *From Reformation to Restoration: Ireland 1534–1660* (Dublin)

—— (1988) *Kingdom and Colony: Ireland in the Atlantic World 1560–1800* (Johns Hopkins)

—— (1994) 'English Migration into and across the Atlantic during the Seventeenth and Eighteenth Century' in ibid. (ed.) *Europeans on the move: Studies on European Migration 1500–1800* (Oxford)

—— (1995) 'What Really Happened in Ireland in 1641?' in J. Ohlmeyer (ed.) *Ireland: From Independence to Occupation, 1641–1660* (Cambridge)

—— (1996) 'The Attempted Anglicisation of Ireland in the Seventeenth-Century: An Exemplar of British History' in J.F. Merritt (ed.) *The Political World of Thomas Wentworth Earl of Strafford 1621–1641* (Cambridge)

—— (1997) 'Religion, Politics and the Irish Rising of 1641' in J. Devlin and R. Fanning (eds) *Religion and Rebellion: Historical Studies XX* (Dublin)

—— (2001) *Making Ireland British, 1580–1650* (Oxford)

Carey, V. (1999a) 'John Derricke's Image of Irelande, Sir Henry Sidney, and the massacre at Mullaghmast, 1578' *I.H.S.* no. 123

—— (1999b) 'Neither Good English nor Good Irish: bi-lingualism and identity formation in sixteenth-century Ireland' in H. Morgan (ed.) *Political Ideology in Ireland 1541–1641*

—— (2002) *Surviving the Tudors: The 'Wizard' Earl of Kildare and English Rule in Ireland* (Dublin)

—— (2004) 'What pen can paint or tears atone?: Mountjoy's scorched earth campaign' in H. Morgan (ed.) *The Battle of Kinsale* (Bray)

Carlin, N. (1993) 'Extreme or Mainstream? The English Independents and the Cromwellian Reconquest of Ireland 1649–1651 in B. Bradshaw, A. Hadfield and W. Maley (eds) *Representing Ireland: literature and the origins of conflict 1634–1660* (Cambridge)

Carlton, C. (1990) 'The Face of Battle in the English Civil War' in M.C. Fissel *War and Government in Britain, 1598–1650* (Manchester)

—— (1991) 'The Impact of the Fighting' in J. Morrill (ed.) *The Impact of the English Civil War* (London)

—— (1992) *Going to the Wars: The experience of the British Civil Wars, 1638–1651* (London)

Carpenter, A. (1998) *Verse in English from Eighteenth-Century Ireland* (Cork)

—— (2003) *Verse in English from Tudor and Stuart Ireland* (Cork)

Carte, T. (1736) *Life of James Duke of Ormond* (3 vols, London)

—— (1851) *The Life Of James Duke Of Ormonde* (6 vols, Oxford)

Casway, J. (1984) *Owen Roe O'Neill and the Struggle for Catholic Ireland* (Philadelphia)

—— (2001) 'The Decline and Fate of Dónal Ballagh O'Cahan and his family' in Micheál Ó Siochrú (ed.) *Kingdoms in Crisis Ireland in the 1640s* (Dublin)

Chandler, D. (1976) *The Art of Warfare in the Age of Marlborough* (London)

Childs, J. (1996) 'The Williamite War, 1689–91' in T. Bartlett and K. Jeffrey (eds) *A Military History of Ireland* (Cambridge)

Cipolla, C.M. (1973) *Cristofano and the Plague A Study in Public Health in the Age of Galileo* (London)

—— (1981) Before the Industrial Revolution: European Society and Economy 1000–1700 (London)

Clarendon, Edward, Earl of (1807) *The History of the Rebellion*, ii (Oxford)

Clarke, A. (1965) 'The Policies of the "Old English" in Parliament, 1640–41', *Historical Studies*, v (London)

—— (1966) *The Old English in Ireland, 1625–42* (London)

—— (1970) 'Ireland and the General Crisis' *Past and Present* no. 48

—— (1976) 'The Government of Wentworth 1632–4'; 'The Irish economy, 1600–60'; and R. Dudley Edwards 'Pacification, plantation and the catholic question, 1603–23' *NHI*, iii (Oxford)

—— (1981) 'The Genesis of the Ulster Rising of 1641' in P. Roebuck (ed.) *Plantation to Partition: Essays in Ulster History* (Belfast)

—— (1988) 'Sir Piers Crosby, 1590–1646: Wentworth's "tawney ribbon"', *I.H.S.* xxvi no. 102

—— (1989a) 'Bishop William Bedell' in C. Brady (ed.) *Worsted in the Game Losers in Irish History* (Belfast)

—— (1989b) 'Varieties of Uniformity: the first century of the Church of Ireland' in W.J. Shiels and Diana Wood (eds) *The Churches, Ireland, and the Irish* (Oxford)

—— (1995) '1659 and the Road to Restoration' in J. Ohlmeyer (ed.) *From Independence to Occupation* (Oxford)

—— (1997) 'The 1641 Rebellion and Anti-Popery in Ireland' in B. MacCuarta (ed.) *Ulster 1641: Aspects of the Rising* (Belfast)

—— (1999) *Prelude to Restoration in Ireland: The End of the Commonwealth 1659–1660* (Cambridge)

—— (2003) 'A Woeful Sinner: John Atherton' in V. Carey and U. Lotz-Heumann (eds) *Taking Sides? Colonial and Confessional Mentalités in Early Modern Ireland* (Dublin)

Clarkson, L.A. (1975) *Death, Disease and Famine in Pre-Industrial England* (Dublin)

—— (1981) 'Irish Population Revisited 1687–1821' in J.M. Goldstrom and L. Clarkson (eds) *Irish Population, Economy and Society: Essays in honour of the late K.H. Connell* (Oxford)

—— (1999) 'The Modernisation of the Irish Diet, 1740–1920' in J. Davis (ed.) *Rural Change in Ireland* (Dublin)

—— and M. Crawford (eds) (2002) *Feast and Famine: A History of Food and Nutrition in Ireland 1500–1920* (Oxford)

Coffey, J. (1997) 'Political Thought of the Scottish Covenanters' in
J. Young (ed.) *Celtic Dimensions of the British Civil Wars* (Edinburgh)

Colley, L. (1992) *Britons: forging the nation 1707–1837* (London)

Connell, K.H. (1950) *The Population of Ireland, 1750–1845* (Oxford)

Connolly, S.J. (1990) 'The Penal Laws' in W.A. Maguire (ed.) *Kings in
Conflict: The Revolutionary War in Ireland and its Aftermath
1689–1750* (Belfast)

—— (1992) *Religion, Law and Power The Making of Protestant Ireland
1660–1760* (Oxford)

—— (1996) 'Eighteenth-century Ireland: Colony or *ancien regime*? in
D.G. Boyce and A. O'Day (eds) *The Making of Modern Irish
History. Revisionism and the Revisionist Controversy* (London)

—— (1998) 'Swift and Protestant Ireland: Images in Reality' in
A. Douglas, P.H. Kelly and I.C. Ross (eds) *Locating Swift* (Cornell)

—— (2000) 'The Glorious Revolution in Irish Protestant political
thinking' in ibid (ed.) *Political Ideas in Eighteenth Century Ireland*
(Dublin)

—— (2004) 'The Moving Statue and the Turtle Dove' in *Ir. Econ. & Soc.
Hist.* xxxi

Coonan, T.L. (1954) *The Irish Catholic Confederacy and the Puritan
Revolution* (Dublin)

Corish, P. (1976) 'The Rising of 1641 and the Confederacy, 1641–5':
'The Cromwellian conquest, 1649–53' and 'The Cromwellian
regime, 1650–60' in T.W. Moody, F.X. Martin and F.J. Byrne (eds)
A New History of Ireland III Early Modern Ireland 1534–1691
(Oxford)

—— (1981) *The Catholic Community in the Seventeenth and Eighteenth
Centuries* (Dublin)

Corkery, D. (1979) *The Hidden Ireland* (London)

Cosgrove, A. (1987) 'Two Centuries of Catholicism in County Wexford'
in K. Whelan (ed.) *Wexford: History and Society* (Dublin)

Cosgrove, A. and McCartney, D. (eds) (1979) *Studies in Irish History
Presented to R. Dudley Edwards* (Dublin)

Coughlan, P. (ed.) (1989) *Spenser and Ireland* (Cork)

Cox, R. (1692) *Hibernia anglicana, or The history of Ireland from the
conquest thereof by the English to this present time . . .* (Dublin)

Crawford, J.G. (1993) *Anglicizing the Government of Ireland. The Irish Privy Council and the expansion of Tudor rule, 1556–1578* (Dublin)

Crawford, W.H. (1968) 'The Rise of the Linen Industry' in L.M. Cullen (ed.) *The Formation of the Irish Economy* (Cork)

―――― (1975) 'Landlord-Tenant Relations in Ulster 1609–1820' in *Economic and Social History of Ireland Journal*, ii

Cregan, D. (1979) 'The Social and Cultural Background of a Counter Reformation Episcopate, 1618–60' in A. Cosgrove and D. McCartney (eds) *Studies in Irish History presented to R. Dudby Edwards* (Dublin)

Creighton, A. (2004) 'The Remonstrance of December 1661 and Catholic Politics in Restoration Ireland' in *I.H.S.* xxxiv no. 133

Croft, P. (2003) *King James* (Basingstoke and New York)

Cronin, M. (1996) *Translating Ireland, Translation, Languages, Cultures* (Cork)

Cullen, L.M. (1969) 'The Hidden Ireland: Reassessment of a Concept', *Studia Hibernica* (Dublin)

―――― (1972) *An Economic History of Ireland since 1660* (London)

―――― (1974–75) 'Population Trends in Seventeenth Century Ireland' in *Economic and Social Review* no. 6

―――― (1976) 'Economic Trends 1660–9' in T.W. Moody, F.X. Martin and F.J. Byrne (eds) *A New History of Ireland III Early Modern Ireland 1534–1691* (Oxford)

―――― (1981a) *The Emergence of Modern Ireland 1600–1900* (London)

―――― (1981b) 'Population Growth and Diet, 1600–1850' in J.M. Goldstrom and L.A. Clarkson (eds) *Irish Population, Economy and Society* (Oxford)

―――― (1986a) 'Economic Developments 1691–1750' in T.W. Moody and W.E. Vaughan *A New History of Ireland* iv; *Eighteenth Century Ireland, 1691–1800* (Oxford)

―――― (1986b) 'Catholics under the Penal Laws' in *Eighteenth-Century Ireland* i

―――― (1990) 'Catholic Social Classes under the Penal Laws' in T.P. Power and Kevin Whelan (eds) *Endurance and Emergence Catholics in Ireland in the Eighteenth Century* (Dublin)

—— (1993) 'Caoineadh Airt Uí Laoghaire: The Contemporary Political Context' *History Ireland*

—— (1995) 'A Story of Growth and Change: Dublin 1560–1800' in Howard B. Clarke (ed.) *Irish Cities* (Cork)

—— (2003) 'Eighteenth-Century Flour Milling in Ireland' in Andy Bielenberg (ed.) *Irish Flour Milling: A History 600–2000* (Dublin)

Curl, J.S. (1986) *The Londonderry Plantation 1609–1914* (Southampton)

Curry, J. (1773) *An Historical and Critical Review of the Civil Wars in Ireland* (Dublin)

Cunnane, D.W. (1999) 'Catastrophic Dimensions: The Rupture of English and Irish Identities in Early Modern Ireland, 1534–1615', *Essays in History* vol. 41

Cunningham, B. (1984) 'The Composition of Connacht in the lordships of Clanricard and Thomond, 1577–1641', *I.H.S.* vol. 24

—— (1986) 'Native culture and political change in Ireland, 1580–1640', in C. Brady and R. Gillespie, *Natives and Newcomers the Making of Irish Colonial Society* (Dublin)

—— (ed.) (1996) 'Clanricard Letters' *Galway Arch. Soc. Jn.* no. 48

—— (2000) 'Representations of king, parliament and the Irish people in Geoffrey Keating's *Foras Fease an Éirinn* and John Lynch's *Cambrensis Eversus* (1662)' in J. Ohlmeyer (ed.) *Political thought in seventeenth-century Ireland* (Cambridge)

—— (2001) *The World of Geoffrey Keating History, myth and religion in seventeenth-century Ireland* (Dublin)

—— and Gillespie, R. (1995) 'The most adaptable of saints: the cult of St Patrick in the seventeenth century' *Archiv. Hib.* xlix

Curl, J.S. (1986) *The Londonderry Plantation 1609–1914* (Southampton)

Currie, E.A. (1979) 'Landscape Development in South Derry in the Eighteenth Century' *Studia Hibernica* no. 19

Dalrymple, Sir John (4th edn 1773) *Memoirs of Great Britain and Ireland* (Dublin)

D'Alton, J. (1863) *The History of Drogheda with its environs* (Dublin)

Davis, T. (1893) *The Patriot parliament of 1689* (Dublin)

Dawson, J. (1995) 'Anglo–Scottish protestant culture and integration in sixteenth-century Britain' in S.G. Ellis and S. Barber (eds) *Conquest & Union Fashioning: A British State 1485–1725* (London)

De Blácam, A. (1929) *Gaelic Literature Surveyed* (Dublin)

De Fréine, S. (1965) *The Great Silence* (Westport)

Derry, K. (1970) *A History of Scandinavia* (London)

De Vries, Jan (1976) *The Economy of Europe in an Age of Crisis 1600–1750* (Cambridge)

Dickens, A.G. (1967) *The English Reformation* (London)

—— (1974) *The German Nation and Martin Luther* (London)

Dickson, D. (1979) 'Middlemen' in T. Bartlett and D. Hayton (eds) *Penal Era and Golden Age* (Belfast)

—— (1987) *New Foundations: Ireland, 1660–1800* (Dublin)

—— (1989) 'The Gap in Famines: A Useful Myth?' in M. Crawford (ed.) *Famine: The Irish Experience* (Oxford)

—— (1991) 'No Scythians here: women and marriage in seventeenth-century Ireland' in M. MacCurtain and M. O'Dowd (eds) *Women and Society in Early Modern Ireland* (Edinburgh)

—— (1997) *Arctic Ireland The Extraordinary story of the Great Frost and Forgotten Famine of 1740–41* (Belfast)

—— (2000) *New Foundations* (Dublin)

—— (2005) *Old World Colony Cork and South Munster 1630–1830* (Cork)

—— C. Ó Gráda and S. Daultrey (1982) *Hearth Tax, Household Size and Irish Population Change 1672–1821* (Dublin)

Dineen, P. (ed.) (1911) *Dánta Aodhagáin Uí Rathaille* (London)

—— (1927) *Irish-English Dictionary* (Dublin)

Doherty, R. (1998) *The Williamite War in Ireland* (Dublin)

Donlan, S. (2003) 'Little better than cannibals': Sir John Davies and Edmund Burke on property and progress', *Northern Ireland Legal Quarterly* 54

Dowd, J. (1890) *Limerick and its sieges* (Limerick)

Doyle, T. (1989) 'Jacobitism, Catholicism and the Irish protestant Elite, 1700–1710' in *Eighteenth Century Ireland* IV

Doyle, W. (1991) *The Old European Order 1660–1800* (Oxford)

Dudley Edwards, R. (1952) 'The Cromwellian Persecution and the Catholic Church in Ireland', *Blessed Oliver Plunket Historical Studies* (Dublin)

Duffy, C. (1977) *The Army of Maria Theresa: The Armed Forces of Imperial Austria 1740–1780* (London)

Duffy, E. (1992) *The Stripping of the Altars: Traditional Religion in England 1400–1580* (Yale)

Duffy, P.J. (1983) 'Farney in 1634: An examination of John Raven's Survey of the Essex Estate' *Clogher Record* XI

—— (1998) 'The Evolution of Estate properties in South Ulster 1600–1900' in W. Smyth and K. Whelan (eds) *Common Ground Essays on the Historical Geography of Ireland* (Cork)

Dunne, T. (1980) The Gaelic response to conquest and colonisation: the evidence of the poetry' in *Studia Hibernica*, xx

Durkacz, V.E. (1983) *The Decline of the Celtic Languages* (Edinburgh)

Eccleshall, R. (2001) 'The Political Ideas of Anglican Ireland in the 1690s' in D.G. Boyce, R. Eccleshall and V. Geoghegan (eds) *Political Discourse in Seventeenth and Eighteenth Century Ireland* (Basingstoke)

Edwards, D. (ed.) (1999) 'Ideology and Experience: Spenser's *View* and Martial law in Ireland' in H. Morgan (ed.) *Political Ideology in Ireland 1541–1641* (Dublin)

—— (2003) *The Ormond Lordship in County Kilkenny, 1515–1642* (Dublin)

—— (2004) 'Legacy of Defeat: the reduction of Gaelic Ireland after Kinsale' in H. Morgan (ed.) *The Battle of Kinsale* (Dublin)

Edwards, F. (2005) *The Succession, Bye and Main Plots of 1601–1603* (Dublin)

Ehrenpreis, I. (1968) 'Swift on Liberty' in A.N. Jeffares (ed.) *Swift: Modern Judgements* (London)

Eisenstein, E.L. (1983) *The Printing Revolution in Early Modern Europe* (New York)

Elliott, M. (2001) *The Catholics of Ulster: A History* (New York)

Ellis, P.B. (1975) *Hell or Connaught!: The Cromwellian colonisation of Ireland, 1652–1660* (London)

Ellis, S.G. (1995) 'Tudor state formation and the shaping of the British Isles' in S.G. Ellis and S. Barber (eds) *Conquest and Union, Fashioning a British State 1485–1725* (London)

—— (1998) *Ireland in the Age of the Tudors 1447–1603 English Expansion and the End of Gaelic Rule* (London)

—— (1999) 'The Collapse of the Gaelic World 1450–1650', *I.H.S.* no. 124

Estyn Evans, E. (1957) *Irish Folkways* (London)

—— (1979) *The Making of the Habsburg Monarchy 1550–1700* (Oxford)

—— (1992) *The Personality of Ireland Habitat, Heritage and History* (Dublin)

—— (1996) *Ireland and the Atlantic Heritage* (Dublin)

Fabricant, C. (2003) 'Swift the Irishman' in C. Fox (ed.) *The Cambridge Companion to Jonathan Swift* (Cambridge)

Fagan, P. (1989) 'The Dublin Catholic mob (1700–1750)' in *Eighteenth-Century Ireland* iv

—— (1997) *Divided Loyalties: The Question of an Oath for Irish Catholics in the Eighteenth Century* (Dublin)

—— (1998) *Catholics in a Protestant Country: The Papist Constituency in Eighteenth-Century Dublin* (Dublin)

—— (2001) *The Diocese of Meath in the Eighteenth Century* (Dublin)

Falkiner, L.C. (1904) *Essays Relating to Ireland* (London)

Falls, C. (1936) *The Birth of Ulster* (London)

—— (1950) *Elizabeth's Irish Wars* (London)

Falvey, J. (1989) 'The Church of Ireland Episcopate in the Eighteenth-Century: An Overview' in *Eighteenth-Century Ireland* iv

Fenning, H. (1990) *The Irish Dominican Province 1698–1797* (Dublin)

Ferguson, K. (1990) 'The Organization of King William's Army in Ireland' in *The Irish Sword* no. 70 pp. 67, 77–9

Firth, C.H. (1900) *Oliver Cromwell* (London)

Fitzgerald, G. (1984) 'Estimates for baronies of minimum level of Irish speaking amongst successive decennial cohorts', *Proceedings of the Royal Irish Academy* 84 (Dublin)

—— (1990) 'The Decline of the Irish Language, 1771–1781' in M. Daly and D. Dickson (eds) *The Origins of Popular Literacy in Ireland: Language Change and Educational Development 1700–1920* (Dublin)

Fitzpatrick, B. (1988) *Seventeenth-Century Ireland. The War of Religions* (Dublin)

Fitzpatrick, T. (1903) *The Bloody Bridge* (New York)

Flanagan, E. (1999) 'The anatomy of Jacobean Ireland: Captain Barnaby Rich, Sir John Davies and the failure of reform, 1609–22' in H. Morgan (ed.) *Political Ideology in Ireland 1541–1641* (Dublin)

Flynn, T.S. (1993) *The Irish Dominicans 1536–1641* (Dublin)

Ford, A. (1986) 'The Protestant Reformation in Ireland' in C. Brady and R. Gillespie (eds) *Natives and Newcomers: The Making of Irish Colonial Society* (Dublin)

—— (1995) 'The Reformation in Kilmore', *Cavan Essays on the History of an Irish County* (Dublin)

—— (1997) *Protestant Reformation in Ireland, 1590–1641* (Dublin)

—— (1998) 'James Ussher and the creation of an Irish protestant identity' in B. Bradshaw and P. Roberts (eds) *British Consciousness and Identity: The Making of Britain 1533–1707*

—— (2001) ' "Firm Catholics" or "Loyal Subjects"? Religious and Political Allegiance in early Seventeenth-Century Ireland' in D.G. Boyce, R. Eccleshall and V. Geoghegan (eds) (2001) *Political Discourse in Seventeenth and Eighteenth Century Ireland* (Basingstoke)

—— (2003) 'Criticising the Godly Prince: Malcolm Hamilton's Pasages and consulations' in V. Carey and U. Lotz Heumann (eds) *Taking Sides Colonial and Confessional Mentalites in Early Modern Ireland* (Dublin)

—— (2006) ' "Force and Punishment": protestants and religious coercion in Ireland 1603–33' in E. Boran and C. Gribben (eds) *Enforcing Reformation in Ireland and Scotland, 1550–1700* (Ashgate)

Forde Johnstone, J. (1977) *Castles & Fortifications of Britain and Ireland* (London)

Forrestal, A. (1998) *Catholic Synods in Ireland, 1600–1690* (Dublin)

Forristal, D. (1975) *Oliver Plunkett in his own words* (Dublin)

Forster, J. (1664) *England's Happiness Increased* (London)

Foster, R.F. (1988) *Modern Ireland 1600–1972* (London)

Fraser, A. (2001) *Cromwell* (London)

Fraser, T.G. (2001) 'Introduction: the siege: myth and reality' in W. Kelly (ed.) *The Sieges of Derry* (Dublin)

Gacquin, W. (1996) *Roscommon before the Famine: The Parishes of Kiltoom and Cam 1749–1845*

Gahan, D. (1987) *The Estate System of Co. Wexford, 1641–1876*, in K. Whelan (ed.) *Wexford, History and Society* (Dublin)

—— (1990) 'Religion and Tenure in 18th century Ireland' in R.V. Comerford, M. Cullen, J.R. Hill and C. Lennon (eds) *Religion, Conflict and Coexistence in Ireland* (Dublin)

Gale, P. (1834) *An Inquiry into the Ancient Corporate state of Ireland* (London)

Galloway, B. (1986) *The Union of England and Scotland 1603–1608* (Edinburgh)

Galloway, P.R. (1988) 'Basic Patterns in Annual Variations in Fertility, Nuptiality, Mortality, and Prices in Pre-industrial Europe' *Population Studies*, vol. 42 no. 2

Garcia Hernán, E. (2004) 'Philip II's Forgotten Armada' in H. Morgan (ed.) *The Battle of Kinsale* (Bray)

Gardiner, S.R. (1903) *History of the Commonwealth and Protectorate*, i (4 vols, London)

Garnham, N. (1999) 'The Trials of James Cotter and Henry, Baron Barry of Santry' *I.H.S.* no. 123

Gebler, C. (2005) *The Siege of Derry* (London)

Gentles, I. (1992) *The New Model Army in England, Ireland and Scotland, 1645–1653* (Oxford)

Gibbs, G.C. (1990) 'The European Origins of the Glorious Revolution' in W.A. Maguire (ed.) *Kings in Conflict The Revolutionary War in Ireland and its Aftermath 1689–1750* (Belfast)

Gibney, J. (2004) 'Edmund Murphy, Oliver Plunkett and the Popish Plot' *History Ireland* vol. 12 no. 4

Gibson, O. (1989) *The Western Protestant Army; Ireland 1688–90* (Omagh)

Gillespie, R. (1985) *Colonial Ulster The Settlement of East Ulster 1600–1641* (Cork)

—— (1986) 'The End of an Era: Ulster and the outbreak of the 1641 rising' in R. Gillespie and C. Brady (eds) *Natives and Newcomers The Making of Irish Colonial Society* (Dublin)

—— (1991) *The Transformation of the Irish Economy 1550–1700* (Dundalk)

—— (1993) 'The Murder of Arthur Champion and the 1641 Rising in Fermanagh', *Clogher Record* xiv. no. 3

—— (1994) 'Irish Funeral Monuments and Social Change 1500–1700' in ibid and B. Kennedy (eds) *Ireland: Art into History* (Dublin)

—— (1995a) 'The Irish Economy, 1641–1660' in J.H. Ohlmeyer (ed.) *Ireland from Independence to Occupation 1641–1660* (Cambridge)

—— (1995b) 'Dissenters and Nonconformists 1661–1700' in K. Herlihy (ed.) *The Irish Dissenting Tradition 1650–1750*

—— (1997) *Devoted People. Belief and Religion in Early Modern Ireland* (Manchester)

—— (2006) *Seventeenth Century Ireland* (Dublin)

Gleeson, D.F. (1938) *The Last Lords of Ormond* (London)

Glendenning, V. (1999) *Jonathan Swift* (London)

Glozier, M. (2005) *Marshal Schomberg 1615–1690* (Brighton)

Goff, H. (1990) *Land Settlements in County Wexford, 1640–1710* (PhD, Maynooth)

Graham, J. (1970) 'Rural Society in Connacht 1600–1640' in N. Stephens and R. Glasscock (eds) *Irish Geographical Studies in honour of E. Estyn Evans* (Belfast)

Greaves, R.L. (1997) *God's Other Children: Protestant Nonconformists and the Emergence of the Denominational Churches in Ireland* (Stanford)

Haddick-Flynn, K. (2003) *Sarsfield and the Jacobites* (Cork)

Hadfield, A. (ed.) (2001) *The Cambridge Companion to Spenser* (Cambridge)

Hale, J.R. (1985) *War and Society in Renaissance Europe 1450–1620* (London)

Hamilton, E. (1920) *The Irish Rebellion of 1641, with a history of the events which led up to and succeeded to it* (London)

Hammer, P. (2003) *Elizabeth's Wars: War and Government in Tudor England 1544–1604* (Basingstoke: Macmillan)

Hanrahan, D. (2003) *Colonel Blood the man who stole the Crown Jewels* (Stroud)

Hardiman, J. (1820) *History of Galway* (Dublin)

Harris, T. (2005) *Restoration: Charles II and his Kingdoms 1660–1685* (London)

—— (2006) *Revolution. The Great Crisis of the British Monarchy 1685–1720* (London)

Harris, W. (1770) *The History of the Life and Reign of William-Henry* (Dublin)

Hartmann, C.H. (1951) *The King's Friend A Life of Charles Berkeley, Viscount Fitzhardinge Earl of Falmouth* (London)

Hayes-McCoy, G.A. (1937) Scots Mercenary Forces in Ireland 1656–1603 (London)

—— (1941) 'Strategy and Tactics in Irish Warfare 1593–1601' *I.H.S.* no. 7

—— (1969) *Irish Battles A Military History of Ireland* (London)

—— (1976) 'The Completion of the Tudor Conquest and the Advance of the Counter-Reformation 1571–1603' *NHI* iii

Hayton, D.W. (1975) *Ireland and the English Ministers, 1707–1716* (DPhil, Oxford)

—— (1979) 'The Beginnings of the Undertaker System' in T. Bartlett and D.W. Hayton (eds) *Penal Era and Golden Age. Essays in Irish History 1690–1800* (Belfast)

—— (2004) *Ruling Ireland 1685–1742 Politics, Politicians and Parties* (Woodbridge)

Hazlett, H. (1938) *A history of the military forces operating in Ireland 1641–49* (PhD thesis, Queens University Belfast)

Hazlett, I. (2003) *The Reformation in Britain and Ireland: An Introduction* (London)

Healy, T.M. (1917) *The Great Fraud of Ulster* (Kerry)

Henry, G. (1993) *The Irish Military Community in Spanish Flanders 1586–1621* (Dublin)

Hill, C. (1961) *The Century of Revolution 1603–1714* (London)

—— (1970) *God's Englishman Oliver Cromwell and The English Revolution* (London)

Hill, G. (1873) *An Historical Account of the MacDonnells of Antrim* (Belfast)

—— (1877) *An Historical Account of the Plantation of Ulster 1608–1622* (Belfast)

Hindley, R. (1990) *The Death of the Irish Language* (London)

Hore, P.H. (1904) *History of the Town and County of Wexford* i, iv, v, vi (London)

Hore, H. (ed.) (1858–59) 'A chorographic description of the southern part of the county of Wexford, written anno. 1684 by Robert Leigh' in *Journal of the Kilkenny and South-East of Ireland Archaeological Society Journal* ii 1858–59

Horning, A.J. (2001) 'Dwelling Houses in the old Irish barbarous manner. Archaeological Evidence for Gaelic Architecture in an Ulster Plantation Village' in P. Duffy, D. Edwards and E. Fitzpatrick (eds) *Gaelic Ireland Land Lordship and Settlement c. 1250–c. 1650* (Dublin)

Houston, R.A. (1992) *The Population History of Britain and Ireland 1500–1750* (London)

Hunter, R.J. (1981) 'Ulster Plantation Towns 1609–41' in D.W. Harkness and M. O'Dowd (eds) *The Town in Ireland* (Belfast)

—— (1995) 'Plantation in Donegal' in William Nolan (ed.) *Donegal History and Society* (Dublin)

Hutton, R. (1982) *The Royalist War Effort 1642–46* (London)

—— (1989) The *Restoration: A Political and Religious History of England and Wales 1658–1667* (Oxford)

—— (1997) 'The Triple Crowned Islands' in Lionel K.J. Glassey *The Reigns of Charles II and James VII & II* (London)

—— and W. Reeves (1998) 'Sieges and Fortifications' in J. Kenyon and J. Ohlmeyer (eds) *The Civil Wars: A Military History of England, Scotland and Ireland 1638–1660* (Oxford)

Irwin, L. (1980) 'Politics, Religion and Economy: Cork in the Seventeenth-Century' in *Cork Hist. Soc. Jn.* no. 85

—— (1995) 'Sarsfield: The Man and Myth' in Bernadette Whelan (ed.) *The Last of the Great Wars* (Limerick)

Israel, J. (1995) *The Dutch Republic – Its Rise, Greatness and Fall 1477–1806* (Oxford)

—— (1996) 'England, the Dutch, and Mastery of World Trade' in D. Hoak and M. Feingold (eds) *The World of William and Mary: Anglo-Dutch Perspectives on the Revolution of 1688–89* (Stanford)

James, G.F. (1973) *Ireland in the Empire 1688–1770* (Harvard)

Jennings, B. (1937) 'The Religious Orders in Ireland in the Seventeenth Century' in *Blessed Oliver Plunkett Historical Studies* (Dublin)

Johnson, J.H. (1970) 'The Two Irelands at the Beginning of the Nineteenth Century' in N. Stephens and R. Glasscock (eds) *Irish Geographical Studies in honour of E. Estyn Evans* (Belfast)

Johnston, E.M. (1974) *Ireland in the Eighteenth-Century* (Dublin)

Johnston, J. (ed.) (1970) *Bishop Berkley's Querist in Historical Perspective* (Dundalk)

Johnston, J. (1988) 'Settlement Patterns in County Fermanagh 1610–1660' *Clogher Record* vol x no. 2

Jones, W.R. (1974) 'Giraldus Redivivivus: English historians, apologists, and the works of Gerald of Wales' ix *Éire-Ireland*

Jones, J.R. (1978) *Country and Court England 1658–1714* (London)

—— (1987) *Charles II, Royal Politician* (London)

Kamen, H. (1971) *The Iron Century: Social Change in Europe 1550–1660* (London)

—— (1984) *European Society 1500–1700* (London)

Kearney, H.F. (1961) *Strafford in Ireland 1633–41* (Manchester)

Keeble, N.H. (2002) *The Restoration: England in the 1660s* (Oxford)

Kelly, P. (1987) 'Lord Galway and the Penal Laws' in C.E.J. Caldicott et al. (eds) *The Huguenots and Ireland Anatomy of an Emigration* (Dublin)

—— (1991) 'Ireland and the Revolution' in R. Beddard (ed.) *The Revolutions of 1688* (Oxford)

Kelly, M. (ed.) (1848–52) Lucius Gratianus Hibernus [John Lynch] *Cambrensis Eversus* (3 vols, Dublin)

Kelly, W. (1993) 'Most Illustrious Cavalier' or 'Unkinde Deserter' James Butler, first Duke of Ormonde 1610–1688' in *History Ireland*, 2 pp. 18–22

—— (1997) 'James Butler, twelfth Earl of Ormond, the Irish Government, and the Bishop's Wars, 1638–40' in J. Young (ed.) *Celtic Dimensions of the British Civil Wars* (Edinburgh)

—— (2003) (ed.). *Dowcra's Derry A Narration of events in North-West Ulster 1600–1604* (Belfast)

Kemmy, J. and Walsh, L. (1990) *The Old Limerick Journal 1690 Siege Edition* (Limerick)

Kenyon, J. (1972) *The Popish Plot* (New York)

Kenyon, J. (1978) *Stuart England* (London)

—— and Ohlmeyer, J. (1998) 'The Background to the Civil Wars in the Stuart Kingdoms' in ibid (eds) *The Civil Wars A Military History of England, Scotland and Ireland 1638–1660* (Oxford)

Kerney Walsh, M. (1986) *'Destruction by Peace' Hugh O Neill after Kinsale: Glanconcadhain 1602–Rome 1616* (Armagh)

—— (1996) *An Exile of Ireland; Hugh O'Neill Prince of Ulster* (Dublin)

Kerrigan, P. (1980) 'Seventeenth-century forts and fortifications; a preliminary list' in *Irish Sword* xiv

—— (1995) *Castles and Fortifications in Ireland 1485–1945* (Cork)

—— (2001) 'Ireland in Naval Strategy 1641–1691' in P. Lenihan (ed.) *Conquest and Resistance War in Seventeenth-Century Ireland* (Leiden)

Kew, G. (1998) 'The Irish Sections of Fynes Moryson's Unpublished Itinerary' *Anal. Hib.* no. 37 (Dublin)

Kilroy, P. (1994) *Protestant Dissent and Controversy in Ireland 1660–1714* (Cork)

Kishlansky, M. (1996) *A Monarchy Transformed Britain 1603–1714* (London)

Lacy, B. (1990) *Siege City: the story of Derry and Londonderry* (Belfast)

Lecky, W. (1892) *A History of Ireland in the Eighteenth Century* (London)

Lee, C. (2003) *The Death of Elizabeth I and the Birth of the Stuart Era* (London)

Leerssen, J. (1996a) *Mere Irish & Fior Ghael* (Cork)

—— (1996b) *The Contention of the Bards (Iomarbhágh na bhFileadh) and its Place in Irish Political and Literary History* (Dublin)

Leighton, C.D.A. (1994) *Catholicism in a Protestant Kingdom A Study of the Irish Ancien Régime* (Dublin)

Lenihan, P. (1997) 'War and Population 1649–52' *Ir. Econ. & Soc. Hist.* vol. 24

—— (2001a) *Confederate Catholics At War, 1641–49* (Cork)

—— (2001b) 'Strategic Geography 1641–1691' in ibid (ed.) *Conquest and Resistance War in Seventeenth-Century Ireland* (Brill)

—— (2003) *1690 Battle of the Boyne* (Stroud)

Lenman, B. (1984) *The Jacobite Risings in Britain 1689–1746* (London)

—— (2001) *England's Colonial Wars 1550–1688 Conflicts, Empire and National Identity* (London)

Lennon, C. (1994) *Sixteenth Century Ireland: The Incomplete Conquest* (Dublin)

—— (2003) 'Taking Sides: The Emergence of Irish Catholic ideology' in V. Carey and U. Lotz-Heumann (eds) *Taking Sides? Colonial and Confessional Mentalités in Early Modern Ireland* (Dublin)

—— (2005) *Sixteenth Century Ireland* (Dublin)

Le Roy Ladurie, E. (2000) *L'Ancien Régime 1610–1715* (Paris)

Lietchley, J. (1987) 'Testing the Depth of Catholic/Protestant conflict: the case of Thomas Leland's History of Ireland *Archiv. Hib.* xlii

Lindley, K. (1972) 'The impact of the 1641 rebellion on England and Wales, 1641–5', *I.H.S.* no. 18

Little, P. (2001a) 'Providence and Prosperity: A Letter from Lord Mountnorris to his Daughter' *I.H.S.* xxxii no. 128

—— (2001b) 'The Irish "Independents" and Viscount Lisle's lieutenancy of Ireland', *Historical Journal* 44

—— (2001c) 'The English Parliament and the English Constitution, 1641–9' in Micheál Ó Siochrú (ed.) *Kingdoms in Crisis: Ireland in the 1640s* (Dublin)

—— (2004) *Lord Broghill and the Cromwellian Union with Ireland and Scotland* (Woodbridge : Boydell)

Litton Falkiner, C. (1909) *Essays Relating to Ireland* (Dublin)

Livingstone, P. (1980) *The Monaghan Story: A Documented History of the County from the Earliest Times to 1976* (Enniskillen)

Lockyer, R. (1985) *Tudor and Stuart Britain* (London)

Loeber, R. (1991) *The Geography and Practice of English Colonisation in Ireland from 1534 to 1609* (Athlone)

Logan, P. (1959) 'Medical services in the armies of the Confederate Wars (1641–52)' *Irish Sword* no. 14

Lotz-Heumann, U. (2005) 'Confessionalism in Ireland: Periodisation and Character 1534–1649' in J. McCafferty and A. Ford (eds) *The Origins of Sectarianism in Early Modern Ireland* (Dublin)

Lowe, J. (1959–60) 'The Glamorgan Mission to Ireland 1645–46' *Studia Hibernica* 4

—— (1964) 'Charles I and the Confederation of Kilkenny' in *I.H.S.* no. 53

—— (ed.) (1983) *Clanricarde letter book 1643–47* (Dublin)

Lydon, J.F. (1998) *The Making of Ireland From Ancient Times to the Present* (London)

Macafee, W. (2000) 'The population of County Tyrone 1600–1991' in C. Dillon and H. Jefferies (eds) *Tyrone History and Society* (Dublin)

Mac an Ghallóglaigh, D. (1971) 'Leitrim 1600–1641' in *Breifne* no. 14

Macaulay, T.B. (1858) *History of England* iii (London)

MacCaffrey, W.T. (1992) *Elizabeth I War and Politics 1588–1603* (Princeton)

MacCarthy-Morrogh, M. (1986) *The Munster Plantation: English migration to Southern Ireland 1583–1641* (Oxford)

MacCraith, M. (1996) 'Litríocht an 17ú hAois: Tonnbhriseadh an tSeanghnáthaimh nó Tonnchruthú an Nuaghnáthaimh' in R. Ó hUiginn (ed.) *Léachtaí Cholm Cille* XXVI (Maynooth)

—— (1998) 'Foinś an radachais in Éireann' in G. Ó Tuathaiqh (ed.) *Éirí Amach 1798 in Éirinn*

Mac Cuarta, B. (2001) 'The Plantation of Leitrim, 1629–41' in *I.H.S.* xxxii no. 127

MacCurtain, M. (1972) *Tudor and Stuart Ireland* (Dublin)

MacInnes, A. (2003) 'The Multiple Kingdoms of Britain and Ireland: The British Problem' in B. Coward (ed.) *A Companion to Stuart Britain* Oxford)

—— (2005) *The British Revolution 1629–1660* (Basingstoke)

MacLysaght, E. (1973) *The Surnames of Ireland* (Dublin)

—— (1979) *Irish Life in the Seventeenth-Century* (Dublin)

Maginn, C. (2003) 'The Baltinglass Rebellion 1580: English dissent or a Gaelic uprising?' *The Historical Journal* vol. 47 no. 2

Maguire, W.A. (1990) 'The Land Settlement' in ibid (ed.) *Kings in Conflict: the Revolutionary War in Ireland and its Aftermath 1689–1750* (Belfast)

Malcolm, J.L. (1979) 'All the King's Men: the impact of the crown's Irish soldiers on the English Civil War' in *I.H.S.* no. 83 (Dublin)

Malcolmson, A.P.W. (1974) 'Absenteeism in Eighteenth-Century Ireland', *Ir. Econ. & Soc. Hist.* i

—— (1978) *John Foster: The Politics of the Anglo-Irish Ascendancy* (Oxford)

Maley, W. (1997) *Salvaging Spenser: Colonialism, Culture and Identity* (Oxford)

—— (1998) 'The British problem in three tracts on Ireland by Spenser, Bacon and Milton' in B. Bradshaw and P. Roberts (eds) *British Consciousness and Identity The Making of Britain 1533–1707* (Cambridge)

Manseragh, M. (2003) *The Legacy of History* (Cork)

Mant, R. (1840) *History of the Church of Ireland* (London)

Marshall, A. (1999) *The Age of Faction: Court Politics, 1660–1702* (Manchester)

McBride, I. (1997) *The Siege of Derry in Ulster Protestant Mythology* (Dublin)

Mc Cabe, R.A. (2002) *Spenser's Monstrous Regiment Elizabethan Ireland and the Politics of Difference* (Oxford)

McCafferty, J. (2002) 'When Reformations Collide' in A. Macinnes and J. Ohlmeyer (eds) *The Stuart Kingdoms in the Seventeenth-Century* (Dublin)

McCavitt, J. (1994) 'The Flight of the Earls, 1607', *I.H.S.* no. 29

—— (1998) *Sir Arthur Chichester Lord Deputy of Ireland* (Belfast)

—— (2002) *The Flight of the Earls* (Dublin)

McCormack, A.M. (2005) *The Earldom of Desmond 1463–1583* (Dublin)

McCourt, D. (1981) 'The Decline of Rundale, 1750–1850' in P. Roebuck (ed.) *Plantation to Partition: Essays in Ulster History* (Belfast)

McCracken, J.L. (1971) *The Irish Parliament in the Eighteenth Century* (Dundalk)

—— (1986) 'The Political Structure, 1714–60' in T.W. Moody and W.E. Vaughan (eds) *A New History of Ireland: iv, Eighteenth-Century Ireland* (Oxford)

Mc Donnell, H. (2004) 'Surviving Kinsale Scottish Style – The McDonnells of Antrim' in H. Morgan (ed.) *The Battle of Kinsale* (Bray)

McGowan-Doyle, V. (2004) ' "Spent blood": Christopher St Lawrence and Pale loyalism' in H. Morgan (ed.) *The Battle of Kinsale* (Bray)

McGrath, C.I. (2000) *The Making of the Eighteenth-Century Irish Constitution: Government, Parliament and the Revenue, 1692–1714* (Dublin)

McGuire, J. (1973) 'Why Was Ormond Dismissed in 1669?' *I.H.S.* vol. xviii no. 71

—— (1979) 'The Irish Parliament of 1692' in T. Bartlett and D.W. Hayton (eds) *Penal Era and Golden Age: Essays in Irish History, 1690–1800* (Antrim)

—— (1989) 'Richard Talbot earl of Tyrconnell (1630–91) and the Catholic Counter-Revolution' in C. Brady (ed.) *Worsted in the Game* (Belfast)

—— (1990) 'James II and Ireland' in W.A. Maguire (ed.) *Kings in Conflict. The Revolutionary War in Ireland and its Aftermath 1689–1750* (Belfast)

McGurk, John (1997) *The Elizabethan Conquest of Ireland: The 1590s' Crisis* (Manchester)

—— (2001) 'Terrain and Conquest 1600–1603' in P. Lenihan (ed.) *Conquest and Resistance War in Seventeenth-Century Ireland* (Brill)

—— (2004) 'English Naval Operations at Kinsale' in H. Morgan (ed.) *The Battle of Kinsale* (Bray)

McKenny, K. (1995) 'The Seventeenth Century Land Settlement in Ireland' in J. Ohlmeyer (ed.) *Ireland: From Independence to Occupation 1641–1660* (Cambridge)

—— (2005) *The Laggan Army in Ireland 1640–1685* (Dublin)

McNally, P. (1997) *Parties, Patriots and Undertakers: Parliamentary Politics in Early Hanoverian Ireland* (Dublin)

—— (2004) 'William King, patriotism and the "national question" ' in C. Fauske (ed.) *Archbishop William King and the Anglican Irish Context* (Dublin)

Meehan, C.P. (1882) *The Confederation of Kilkenny* (Dublin)

—— (1872) *The Rise and Fall of the Irish Franciscan Monasteries and Memoirs of the Irish hierarchy in the Seventeenth-Century* (Dublin)

—— (1886) *The fate and fortunes of Hugh O'Neill, earl of Tyrone, and Rory O'Donnell, earl of Tyrconnell, their flight from Ireland and death in exile* (Dublin)

Meigs, S.A. (1997) *The Reformations in Ireland* (Dublin)

Merritt, J.F. (1996) 'Introduction: The historical reputation of Thomas Wentworth' in ibid (ed.) *The Political World of Thomas Wentworth Earl of Strafford 1621–1641* (Cambridge)

Miller, A.C. (1971) 'The Battle of Ross: a controversial military event' *Irish Sword* no. 39

Miller, J. (1973) *Popery and Politics in England 1660–1688* (Cambridge)

—— (1977) 'Tyrconnel and James II' *The Historical Journal* 20, 4

—— (1990) 'The Glorious Revolution' in W.A. Maguire *Kings in Conflict: the Revolutionary War in Ireland and its Aftermath 1689–1750* (Belfast)

—— (2004) *The Stuarts* (London)

Miller, K.A. (1985) *Emigrants and Exiles: Ireland and the Irish Exodus to North America* (Oxford)

Mitchison, R. (1983) *Lordship to Patronage Scotland 1603–1745* (Edinburgh)

Moody, T.W. (1939) *The Londonderry Plantation* (Belfast)

—— (1967) *The Course of Irish History* (Cork)

Moran, P.F. (1884a) *Persecution of Irish Catholics* (Dublin)

Morgan, H. (1993) *Tyrone's Rebellion: The Outbreak of the Nine Years War in Tudor Ireland* (Dublin)

—— (1999) 'Giraldus Cambrensis and the Tudor conquest of Ireland' in Hiram Morgan (ed.) *Political Ideology in Ireland 1541–1641* (Dublin)

—— (2004) 'Missions comparable? The Lough Foyle and Kinsale landings of 1600 and 1601' in ibid (ed.) *The Battle of Kinsale* (Bray)

Morrill, J. (1993a) *The Nature of the English Revolution* (London)

—— (1993b) 'The Britishness of the English Revolution' in R. Asch (ed.) *Three Nations – A Common History? England, Scotland, Ireland and British History c. 1600–1920* (Bochum)

—— (1996) 'Three Stuart Kingdoms 1603–1689' and 'Politics in an Age of Revolution 1630–1690' in J. Morrill (ed.) *Oxford Illustrated History of Tudor and Stuart Britain* (Oxford)

—— (1999) 'The War(s) of the Three Kingdoms' in G. Burgess (ed.) *The New British History: Founding a Modern State 1603–1715* (London and New York)

Mullett, M.A. (1998) *Catholics in Britain and Ireland 1558–1829* (London)

Mulloy, S. (1983) 'French Engineers with the Jacobite Army' in *Irish Sword* no. 61

—— (1990) 'The French Navy and the Jacobite War in Ireland, 1689–91' in *Irish Sword* no. 70

Murphy, C. (1990) 'The Wexford Catholic Community in the later Seventeenth-Century' in *Religion, Conflict and Coexistence in Ireland Essays Presented to Monsignor Patrick J. Corish* (Dublin)

Murphy, D. (1885) *Cromwell in Ireland* (Dublin)

Murphy, I. (1991) *The diocese of Killaloe in the eighteenth century* (Dublin)

Murphy, R. (1968) *The Battle of Aughrim* (New York)

Murtagh, H. (1990a) 'Irish Jacobite Army, 1689–91' in *Irish Sword* no. 70

—— (1990b) 'The War in Ireland 1689–91' in W.A. Maguire (ed.) *Kings in Conflict: the Revolutionary War in Ireland and its Aftermath, 1689–1750* (Belfast)

—— and O'Dwyer M. (eds) (1991) *Athlone Besieged: Eyewitness and other Contemporary Accounts of the Sieges of Athlone 1690 and 1691*

Nicholls, K. (1972) *Gaelic and Gaelicised Ireland in the Middle Ages* (Dublin)

—— (ed.) (1990) *Annals of the Kingdom of Ireland*, vi (7 vols, Dublin)

—— (2004) 'Richard Tyrrell, soldier extraordinary' in Hiram Morgan (ed.) *The Battle of Kinsale* (Dublin)

Nicholls, M. (1999) *A History of the British Isles 1529–1603: The Two Kingdoms* (Oxford)

Ní Cheallacháin, M. (ed.) (1962) *Filíocht Phádraigín Haicéad* (Dublin)

Noonan, K. (1998) ' "The Cruell Pressure of an enraged, barbarous people": Irish and English Identity in seventeenth-century policy and propaganda', *The Historical Journal* 41, 1

Ó Beolan, A. (1979) *Merriman agus filí eile* (Dublin)

O'Brien, I. (1991) *Murrough the Burner* (Whitegate)

O'Brien, G. (1989) 'The Strange Death of the Irish language 1780–1800' in ibid (ed.) *Parliament, Politics and People: Essays in eighteenth-Century Irish History* (Dublin)

Ó Buachalla, B. (1982–83) 'Annála Ríoghachta Éireann is Foras Feasa Feasa ar Éirinn: An Comhthéacs Comhaimseartha' *Studia Hibernica* XXII–XXIII

—— (1992a) 'Poetry and Politics in Early Modern Ireland' in *Eighteenth-Century Ireland* vol. 7

—— (1992b) 'Irish Jacobite poetry' *Irish Review* vol. 12

—— (1996) *Aisling Ghéar Na Stiobhartaigh agus an tAos Léinn* (Dublin)

O'Byrne, Emmett (2003) 'The Walshes and the Massacre at Carrickmines' *Archaeology Ireland* Autumn vol. 17, no. 65

O'Callaghan, J.C. (1869) *History of the Irish Brigades in the Service of France* (Dublin)

O'Callaghan, S. (2001) *To Hell or Barbados* (Brandon)

Ó Ciardha, É. (1998) 'The Stuarts and Deliverance in Irish and Scots-Gaelic Poetry' in S. Connolly (ed.) *Kingdoms United? Great Britain and Ireland since 1500* (Dublin)

—— (2000) 'The Unkinde Deserter and The Bright Duke: contrasting views of the Dukes of Ormonde in the Irish royalist tradition' in T. Barnard and J. Fenlon (eds) *The Dukes of Ormonde, 1610–1745* (Woodbridge)

—— (2002) *Ireland and the Jacobite Cause, 1685–1766 A Fatal Attachment* (Dublin)

Ó Ciosáin, N. (2005) 'Gaelic Culture and Language Shift' in ibid (ed.) *Explaining Change in Cultural History* (Dublin)

Ó Clabaigh, C. (2002) *The Franciscans in Ireland, 1400–1534 From reform to Reformation* (Dublin)

O'Connor, P.J. (1982) 'The Munster Plantation Era: Rebellion, Survey and Land Transfer in North County Kerry' in *Journal of the Kerry Historical and Archaeological Society*

—— (1987) *Exploring Limerick's Past: An Historical Geography of Development in Country and Town* (Newcastlewest)

—— (2003) *Fairs and Markets of Ireland A Cultural Geography* (Newcastlewest)

O'Connor, T. (2004) 'Hugh O'Neill: free spirit, religious chameleon or ardent Catholic?' in H. Morgan (ed.) *The Battle of Kinsale* (Bray)

Ó Cuív, B. (1976) 'The Irish Language in the Early Modern period' in T.W. Moody, F.X. Martin and F.J. Byrne (eds) *A New History of Ireland* iii; *Early Modern Ireland 1534–1691* (Oxford)

—— (1986) 'Irish Language and Literature, 1691–1845' in T.W. Moody and W.E. Vaughan (eds) *A New History of Ireland* iv; *Eighteenth Century Ireland, 1691–1800* (Oxford)

O'Dowd, M. (1988) 'Land and Lordship in sixteenth and early seventeenth-century Ireland' in R. Mitchison and P. Roebuck (eds) *Economy and Society in Scotland and Ireland, 1500–1939* (Edinburgh) pp. 17–26

—— (1991a) *Power, Politics and Land: Early Modern Sligo 1568–1688* (Belfast)

—— (1991b) 'Women and War in Ireland in the 1640s' in ibid and M. MacCurtain (eds) *Women in Early Modern Ireland* (Edinburgh)

O'Faolain, S. (1942) *The Great O'Neill A Biography of Hugh O'Neill Earl of Tyrone* (London)

—— (1947) *The Irish* (London)

Ó Fiach, T. (1957) 'Edmund O'Reilly, Archbishop of Armagh, 1657–1669' in Franciscan Fathers (eds) *Father Luke Wadding* (Dublin)

—— (1969) 'The Language and Political Identity' in B. Ó Cuív (ed.) *A View of the Irish Language* (Dublin)

O'Grady, H. (1923) *Strafford and Ireland* (2 vols, Dublin)

Ó hAnnracháin, E. (2001) 'Some early Wild Geese at the Invalides' in *Irish Sword* xxii no. 89 pp. 249–56

Ó hAnnracháin, T. (1997) 'Rebels and Confederates: The Stance of the Irish Clergy in the 1640s' in J. Young (ed.) *Celtic Dimensions of the British Civil Wars* (Edinburgh)

—— (2001) 'The Strategic Involvement of Continental Powers in Ireland 1596–1691' in P. Lenihan (ed.) *Conquest and Resistance War in Seventeenth-Century Ireland* (Leiden)

—— (2002) *Catholic Reformation in Ireland The Mission of Rinuccini 1645–1649* (Oxford)

O'Hara, D. (2006) *English Newsbooks and Irish rebellion 1641–1649* (Dublin)

O'Hart, J. (1884) *The Irish and Anglo-Irish Landed Gentry* (Dublin)

O'Hearn, D. (2005) 'Ireland in the Atlantic Economy' in T. McDonough (ed.) *Was Ireland a Colony?* (Dublin)

Ó hUallacháin, C. (1991) *The Irish Language in Society* (Ulster)

Ohlmeyer, J. (1989) 'The Dunkirk of Ireland, Wexford Privateers during the 1640s', *Journal of the Wexford Historical Society* no. 12

—— (1992) 'The "Antrim Plot" of 1641 – a myth?' in *Historical Journal* no. 35

—— (1993) *Civil War and Restoration in the three Stuart Kingdoms; the career of Randal Mac Donnell Marquis of Antrim, 1609–1683* (Cambridge)

—— (1995) 'Ireland independent: Confederate foreign policy and international relations during the mid-seventeenth century' in ibid (ed.) *Ireland from Independence to Occupation* (Cambridge)

—— (1998a) 'The Civil Wars in Ireland' in J. Kenyon and J. Ohlmeyer (eds) *The Civil Wars: A Military History of England, Scotland and Ireland 1638–1660* (Oxford)

—— (1998b) ' "Civilizinge of those Rude Partes": Colonization within Britain and Ireland, 1580s–1640s' in N. Canny (ed.) *The Origins of Empire* (Oxford)

—— (1999) 'Seventeenth-Century Ireland and the New British and Atlantic Histories' in *American History Review* vol. 104 no. 2

—— (2000) 'Introduction: for God, King or country? Political thought and culture in seventeenth-century Ireland' in ibid *Political Thought in Seventeenth-Century Ireland* (Cambridge)

—— (2004) 'A Laboratory for Empire?: Early Modern Ireland and English Imperialism' in K. Kenny (ed.) *Ireland and the British Empire* (Oxford)

O'Regan, P. (2000) *Archbishop William King of Dublin (1650–1729) and the Constitution in Church and State* (Dublin)

O'Riordan, M. (1990) *The Gaelic Mind and the Collapse of the Gaelic World* (Cork)

—— (1997) 'The Native Ulster *Mentalité* as Revealed in Gaelic Sources 1600–1650' in B. MacCuarta (ed.) *Ulster 1641 Aspects of the Rising* (Belfast)

Osborough, W.N. (1990) 'Catholics, Land and the Popery Acts of Anne' Laws' in T.P. Power and K. Whelan (eds) *Endurance and Emergence Catholics in Ireland in the Eighteenth Century* (Dublin)

Ó Siochrú, Micheál (1999) *Confederate Ireland 1642–1649: A Constitutional and Political Analysis* (Dublin)

—— (2005a) 'Confederate Catholics and the Constitutional Relationship between England and Ireland 1641–49' in C. Brady and J. Ohlmeyer (eds) *British Interventions in Early Modern Ireland* (Cambridge)

—— (2005b) 'The Duke of Lorraine and the International Struggle for Ireland, 1649–1653', *Historical Journal* vol. 48 no. 4

O'Sullivan, H. (1997) 'The Magennis Lordship of Iveagh in the early Modern period, 1534 to 1691' in L. Proudfoot (ed.) *Down History and Society* (Dublin)

—— (2003) 'Land Confiscations and Plantations in County Armagh' in A.J. Hughes and W. Nolan (eds) *Armagh History and Society* (Dublin)

—— (2005) 'Dynamics of regional development: processes of acculturation and division in the marchland of south-east Ulster in late medieval and early modern Ireland' in C. Brady and J. Ohlmeyer (eds) *British Interventions in Early Modern Ireland* (Cambridge)

Ó Tuama, S. (1965) *Dónal Ó Corcora agus filíocht na Gaeilge* (Dublin)

Outram, Q. (2001) 'The Socio-Economic relations of Warfare and the Military Mortality Crises of the Thirty Year's War' *Medical History*, 45

Palmer, P. (2001) *Language and Conquest in Early Modern Ireland* (Cambridge)

Palmer, W. (1994) *The Problem of Ireland in Tudor Foreign Policy* (Woodbridge)

Parker, G. (2002) *Empire, War and Faith in Early Modern Europe* (London)

Patterson, W.B. (1997) *King James VI and I and the reunion of Christendom* (Cambridge)

Pawlisch, H. (1985) *Sir John Davies and the Conquest of Ireland: A Study in Legal Imperialism* (Cambridge)

Perceval-Maxwell, M. (1973) *The Scottish Migration to Ulster in the reign of James I* (London)

—— (1978) 'The Ulster Rising of 1641 and the Depositions' in *I.H.S.* xxi no. 82

—— (1990) 'Ireland and Scotland 1638–1648' in John Morrill (ed.) *The Scottish National Covenant in its British Context, 1638–51* (Edinburgh)

—— (1994a) *The Outbreak of the Irish Rebellion of 1641* (Dublin)

—— (1994b) 'The Antrim Plot of 1641 – A Myth? A Response', *The Historical Journal* 37, 2

Petráň, J. and Petráňová, L. (1998) 'The White Mountain as a Symbol in Czech History' in M. Teich (ed.) *Bohemia in History* (Cambridge)

Petrie, C. (1953) *The Marshal Duke of Berwick; Portrait of an Age* (London)

—— (1972) *The Great Tyrconnel A Chapter in Anglo–Irish Relations* (Cork)

Pettegree, A. and Hall, M. (2004) 'The Reformation and the Book: A Reconsideration' *The Historical Journal* 47, 4

Pillorget, R. (1995) 'Louis XIV and Ireland' in B. Whelan (ed.) *The Last of the great Wars: Essays on the Wars of the Three Kings in Ireland 1688–91* (Limerick)

Pittock, M. (1998) *Jacobitism* (London)

Pochin Mould, D.C. (1957) *The Irish Dominicans* (Dublin)

Post, J.D. (1985) *Food Shortage, Climatic Variability, and Epidemic Disease in Pre-industrial Europe* (Cornell)

Power, B. (2000) *White Knights, Dark Earls The Rise and Fall of an Anglo–Irish Dynasty* (Cork)

Power, T.P. (1990) 'Converts' in T.P. Power and K. Whelan (eds) *Endurance and Emergence Catholics in Ireland in the Eighteenth Century* (Dublin)

Prendergast, J. (1875) *The Cromwellian Settlement of Ireland* (Dublin)

Prunty, J. (2004) *Maps and Map-Making in Local History* (Dublin)

Quinn, D.B. (1966a) *The Elizabethans and the Irish* (New York)

—— (1966b) 'The Munster Plantation: Problems and Opportunities' *Cork Hist. Soc. Jn* no. 71 (Cork)

Rafferty, O.P. (1994) *Catholicism in Ulster 1603–1983: An Interpretative History* (Dublin)

Ramsey, R. (1933) *Henry Cromwell* (London)

—— (1949) *Henry Ireton* (London)

Ranger, T. (1967) 'Strafford in Ireland: A Revaluation' in T. Aston (ed.) *Crisis in Europe 1560–1660* (New York)

Ranke, L. Von (1875) *A History of England principally in the Seventeenth Century*, vi (6 vols, Oxford)

Recio Morales, O. (2004) 'Spanish Army Attitudes to the Irish at Kinsale' in H. Morgan (ed.) *The Battle of Kinsale* (Bray)

Redworth, G. (2004) 'Irish Catholics and the Spanish Match' in H. Morgan (ed.) *The Battle of Kinsale* (Bray)

Reid, S. (1998) *All the King's Armies: A Military History of the English Civil War 1642–1651* (Kent)

Reilly, T. (1999) *Cromwell An Honourable Enemy* (Dingle)

Rice, G. (1997) 'The Five Martyrs of Drogheda' in *Ríocht na Midhe* ix no. 3

Robbins, J. (1995) *The Miasma: Epidemic and Plague in Nineteenth-Century Ireland* (Dublin)

Robinson, P. (1978) 'British Settlement in County Tyrone 1610–66' in *Ir. Econ. & Soc. Hist.* vi

—— (1984) *The Plantation of Ulster* (Dublin)

—— (2000) *The Plantation of Ulster* (Belfast)

Ross, A. and Woolley, D. (eds) (1984) *Jonathan Swift* (Oxford)

Rousset, C. (1891) *Histoire de Louvois* iv (Paris)

Roy, I. (1998) 'George Digby, Royalist intrigue and the collapse of the cause' in I. Gentles et al. (eds) *Soldiers, writers and statesmen of the English revolution* (Cambridge)

Royle, T. (2004) *The British Civil War: The Wars of the Three Kingdoms 1638–1660* (New York)

Ruff, J.R. (2001) *Violence in Early Modern Europe 1500–1800* (Cambridge)

Russell, C. (1990) *The Causes of the English Civil War* (Oxford)

—— (1991) *The Fall of the British Monarchies 1637–42* (Oxford)

—— (1996) 'The Reformation and the Creation of the Church of England 1500–1640' in J. Morrill (ed.) *The Oxford Illustrated History of Tudor and Stuart Britain* (Oxford)

Rutledge, V.M. (1989) 'Court-Castle Faction and the Irish viceroyalty: the appointment of Oliver St. John as lord Deputy in 1616' in *I.H.S.* xxvi no. 103

Ryan, J.M. (1833) *The History and Antiquities of County Carlow* (Dublin)

Salaman, R. (1949) *History and Social Influence of the Potato* (Cambridge)

Samuel, R. (1998) *Island Stories, Unravelling Britain: Theatres of Memory* (London)

Sarti, R. (2002) *Europe At Home Family and Material Culture 1500–1800* (Yale)

Schama, S. (2001) *A History of Britain: The British wars 1603–1776* (London)

Scott, D. (2004) *Politics and War in the Three Kingdoms, 1637–49* (Basingstoke)

Sergeant, P.W. (1913) *Little Jennings and Fighting Dick Talbot: A Life of the Duke and Duchess of Tyrconnel* (London)

Shagan, E. (1997) 'Constructing discord: ideology, propaganda, and English responses to the Irish rebellion of 1641', *Journal of British Studies* 36

Shaw, D. (2006) 'Thomas Wentworth and monarchical ritual in early modern Ireland' *The History Journal* vol. 49 no. 2

Sheehan, A.J. (1982a) 'Official reaction to native land claims in the plantation of Munster' in *I.H.S.* xxiii no. 92

—— (1982b) 'The Population of the Plantation of Munster: Quinn Reconsidered' in Cork Hist. Soc. Jn.

—— (1983) The Recusancy Revolt of 1603: a re-interpretation' Archiv. Hib. xxxviii

—— (1986) 'Irish Towns in a Period of Change, 1625' C. Brady and R. Gillespie (eds) Natives and Newcomers The Making of Irish Colonial Society 1534–1641 (Dublin)

Silke, John J. (1970) Kinsale: The Spanish Intervention at the End of the Elizabethan Wars (Liverpool)

Simms, H. (1997) 'Violence in County Armagh, 1641' in B. Mac Cuarta (ed.) Ulster 1641 Aspects of the Rising (Belfast)

—— (1997) 'Violence in County Armagh, 1641' in B. Mac Cuarta (ed.) Ulster 1641 Aspects of the Rising (Belfast)

Simms, J.G. (1956) The Williamite Confiscation in Ireland 1690–1703 (London)

—— (1969) Jacobite Ireland (London)

—— (1973–74) 'Cromwell at Drogheda 1649' in Irish Sword no. 45

—— (1974) The Jacobite parliament of 1689 (Dundalk)

—— (1976) 'The Restoration 1660–85' in T.W. Moody et al. (eds) A New History of Ireland iii (Oxford)

—— (1986) 'Jacobite Peace Tactics', 'The Jacobite Parliament of 1689', 'County Sligo in the Eighteenth Century', 'The Siege of Limerick 1651', 'Schomberg at Dundalk' and 'The Making of A Penal Law (2 Anne, c. 6) 1703–4' in D. Hayton and G. O'Brien (eds) War and Politics in Ireland 1649–1730 (London)

—— (1991) 'Schomberg at Dundalk, 1689' in Irish Sword no. 38

Simms, K. (1989) 'Bards and Barons: The Anglo–Irish Aristocracy and the Native Culture' in R. Bartlett and A. MacKay (eds) Medieval Frontier Societies (Oxford)

Slack, P. (1985) The Impact of the Plague in Tudor and Stuart England (Oxford)

Smith, D.L. (1998) A History of the Modern British Isles 1603–1707: The Double Crown (Blackwell)

Smith, M. (1996) 'Flight of the Earls?' Changing Views on O'Neill's departure from Ireland' in History Ireland

Smith, W.J. (ed.) (1963) *Herbert Correspondence* (Cardiff and Dublin)

Smyth, J. (2001) 'Siege, myth and history: Derry 1688–1998' in W. Kelly (ed.) *The Sieges of Derry* (Dublin)

Smyth, W.J. (1988) 'Society and Settlement in Seventeenth Century Ireland; the evidence of the 1659 census' in W. Smyth and K. Whelan (eds) *Common Ground* (Cork)

—— (1997) 'The Making of Ireland: Agendas and Perspectives in Cultural Geography' in B.J. Graham and L.J. Proudfoot *An Historical Geography of Ireland* (London)

—— (2006) *Map-Making, Landscapes and Memory A Geography of Colonial and Early Modern Ireland c. 1530–1750* (Cork)

Somerset, E. (1997) *Elizabeth I* (London)

Speck, W.A. (1988) Reluctant Revolutionaries, Englishmen and the Revolution of 1688 (Oxford)

Spurr, J. (2000) *England in the 1670s* (Oxford)

Stevenson, D. (1981) *Scottish Covenanters and Irish Confederates: Scottish-Irish relations in the mid-seventeenth century* (Belfast)

—— (1990) 'Cromwell, Scotland, and Ireland' in J. Morrill (ed.) *Oliver Cromwell and the English Revolution* (London)

Stevenson, J. (1920) *Two Centuries of Life in Down 1600–1800* (Belfast)

Stewart, A.T.Q. (2001) *The Shape of Irish History* (Belfast)

Stewart, R.W. (1991) 'The Irish Road: Military Supply and Arms for Elizabeth's army during the O'Neill Rebellion in Ireland 1598–1601' in M.C. Fissel (ed.) *War and Government in Britain 1598–1650* (Manchester)

Stradling, R.A. (1994) *The Spanish Monarchy and Irish Mercenaries 1618–68* (Dublin)

Sturdy, D. (2002) *Fractured Europe 1600–1721* (Blackwell)

Taaffe, D. (1810) *An Impartial History of Ireland* vol. I (Dublin)

Tait, C. (2002) *Death, Burial and Commemoration in Ireland 1550–1650* (London)

—— (2006) 'Namesakes and Nicknames: naming practices in early modern Ireland, 1540–1700' in *Continuity and Change* 21 (2)

Tallett, F. (1992) *War and Society in Early Modern Europe 1495–1715* (London)

Tawney, R.H. (1922) *Religion and the Rise of Capitalism* (London)

Thomas, A. (1992) *The Walled Towns of Ireland* (Dublin)

Tilly, C. (1990) *Coercion, Capital and European States* (Cambridge, Mass.)

Treadwell, V. (1998) *Buckingham and Ireland 1616–1628 A Study in Anglo–Irish Politics* (Dublin)

Trench Chenevix, C. (1997) *Grace's Card: Irish Catholic Landlords 1690–1800* (Dublin and Cork)

Trevor Roper, H. (1987) *Catholics, Anglicans & Puritans* (London)

Troost, W. (1983) *William III and the Treaty of Limerick (1691–97)* (PhD, Leiden)

Turner, B.S. (1975) 'An Observation on Settler Names in Fermanagh', *Clogher Record* vol. viii no. 3

Wall, M. (1961) *The Penal Laws 1691–1760. Church and State from the Treaty of Limerick to the accession of George III* (Dundalk)

—— (1969) 'The Decline of the Irish language' in B. Ó Cúiv (ed.) *A View of the Irish Language* (Dublin)

Walshe, H.C. (1989) 'Embracing the Elizabethan Settlement: the vicissitudes of Hugh Brady, bishop of Meath 1563–84' *I.H.S.* xxvi no. 104

Walter, J. (1989) 'Famine, Disease and Crisis Mortality in Early Modern Society' in J. Walter and R.S. Schofield (eds) *Famine, Disease and the Social Order in Early Modern Society* (Cambridge)

Wanklyn, M. and Jones, F. (2006) *A Military History of the English Civil War* (Harlow)

Wauchope, P. (1992) *Patrick Sarsfield and the Williamite War* (Dublin)

Webb, J.J. (1918) *Municipal Government in Ireland: Medieval and Modern* (Dublin)

Wedgewood, C.V. (1973) *Oliver Cromwell* (London)

—— (1958) *The King's War 1641–47* (London)

Wheeler, J.S. (1990) 'Logistics and supply in Cromwell's conquest of Ireland' in Mark Charles Fissel (ed.) *War and Government in Britain 1598–1650* (Manchester)

—— (1993) 'Four Armies in Ireland' in J. Ohlmeyer (ed.) *Independence to Occupation: Ireland 1641–1660* (Cambridge)

—— (1999) *Cromwell in Ireland* (Dublin)

—— (2001) 'Sense of Identity in the army of the English republic, 1645–51' in A. Maci nes and J. Ohlmeyer (eds) *The Stuart Kingdoms in the Seventeenth-Century* (Dublin)

—— (2002) *The Irish and British Wars 1637–1654* (London)

Whelan, K. (1988) 'The Regional Impact of Irish Catholicism 1700–1850' in W. Smyth and K. Whelan (eds) *Common Ground Essays on the Historical Geography of Ireland* (Cork)

—— (1997) 'The Modern Landscape: From Plantation to Present' and 'Towns and Villages' in F.H.A. Aalen, K. Whelan and M. Stout (eds) *Atlas of the Irish Rural Landscape* (Cork)

—— (1998) 'An Underground Gentry? Catholic Middlemen in Eighteenth-Century Ireland' in J. Donnelly jr and K. Miller (eds) *Irish popular Culture 1650–1850* (Dublin)

—— (2000) 'Settlement and Society in Eighteenth-Century Ireland' in T. Barry (ed.) *A History of Settlement in Ireland* (London and New York)

Wiggins, K. (2000) *Anatomy of a Siege: King John's Castle, Limerick, 1642* (Bray)

Williams, G. (1999) *Wales and the Reformation* (Cardiff)

Williams, N. (1994) 'Na Canúintí a Theacht chun Solais' in K. Mc Cone et al. (eds) *Stair na Gaeilge* (Maynooth)

—— (1998) 'The Irish Language in County Offaly' in W. Nolan and T.P. O'Neill (eds) *Offaly History and Society* (Dublin)

Wilson, D. (2003) *All the King's Women Love, Sex and Politics in the Life of Charles II* (London)

Withers, C.W.J. (1988) *Gaelic Scotland: The Transformation of a Cultural Region* (London)

Woolrych, A. (2003) *Britain in Revolution 1625–1660* (Oxford)

Wormwald, J. (1981) *Court, Kirk and Community Scotland 1470–1625* (London)

Wrigley, E.A. (1987) *People, Cities and Wealth The Transformation of Traditional Society* (Oxford)

Wrigley, E.A. and Schofield, R.S. (1989) *The Population History of England 1541–1871* Cambridge)

Anal. Hib. Analecta Hibernica, including the reports of the Irish Manuscripts Commission (Dublin, 1930–)

Archiv. Hib. Archivium Hibernicum: or Irish historical records (Maynooth 1912–)

B.L. British Library

Collect. Hib. Collectanea Hibernica: sources for Irish history (Dublin 1958–)

Galway Arch. Soc. Jn. Journal of the Galway Archaeological and Historical Society (Galway, 1900–)

HLJ House of Lords Journal

I.H.S. Irish Historical Studies: the joint journal of the Irish Historical Society and the Ulster Society for Irish Historical Studies (Dublin, 1938–)

Ir. Econ. & Soc. Hist. Journal of Irish Economic and Social History

Jn Ecc. Hist. Journal of Ecclesiastical History (London 1950–)

Cork Hist. Soc. Jn. Journal of the Cork Historical and Archaeological Society (Cork 1892–)

NLI National Library of Ireland

N. Munster Antiq. Jn. North Munster Antiquarian Journal (Limerick 1936–)

TCD Trinity College, Dublin

Index